BETWEEI
AND INT

Between Authority and Interpretation

*On the Theory of Law and
Practical Reason*

JOSEPH RAZ

OXFORD
UNIVERSITY PRESS

Great Clarendon Street, Oxford OX2 6DP

Oxford University Press is a department of the University of Oxford.
It furthers the University's objective of excellence in research, scholarship,
and education by publishing worldwide in

Oxford New York

Auckland   Cape Town Dar es Salaam   Hong Kong   Karachi
Kuala Lumpur Madrid Melbourne Mexico City   Nairobi
New Delhi Shanghai Taipei Toronto
With offices in
Argentina Austria Brazil Chile Czech Republic France Greece
Guatemala Hungary Italy Japan South Korea Poland Portugal
Singapore Switzerland Thailand Turkey Ukraine Vietnam

Oxford is a registered trade mark of Oxford University Press
in the UK and in certain other countries

Published in the United States
by Oxford University Press Inc., New York

ISBN 978-0-19-959637-9

Printed and bound by CPI Group (UK) Ltd, Croydon, CR0 4YY

Acknowledgements

The following chapters were originally published as indicated:

'Can There be a Theory of Law?', *The Blackwell Guide to the Philosophy of Law and Legal Theory* (ed M Golding and W Edmundson, Oxford: Blackwell, 2004).

'Two Views of the Nature of the Theory of Law: A Partial Comparison' (1998) 4 Legal Theory 249–282.

'On the Nature of Law' (The Kobe Lectures of 1994) (1996) 82 Archiv für Rechts- und Sozialphilosophie 1–25.

'The Problem of Authority: Revisiting the Service Conception' (2006) 90 Minnesota Law Review 1003–1044.

'About Morality and the Nature of Law' (2003) 48 The American Journal of Jurisprudence 1–15.

'Incorporation by Law' (2004) 10 Legal Theory 1–17.

'Reasoning with Rules' (2001) 54 Current Legal Problems 1–18.

'Why Interpret?' (1996) 9 Ratio Juris 349–363.

'Interpretation without Retrieval', *Law and Interpretation* (ed A Marmor, Oxford: OUP, 1995) 155–176.

'Intention in Interpretation', *The Autonomy of Law* (ed RP George, Oxford: OUP, 1996) 249–286.

'On the Authority and Interpretation of Constitutions: Some Preliminaries', *Constitutionalism: Philosophical Foundations* (ed L Alexander, Cambridge: CUP, 1998) 152–193.

'Postema on Law's Autonomy and Public Practical Reasons' (1998) 4 Legal Theory 1–20.

Table of Contents

1

Introduction

General theories of law struggle to do justice to the multiple dualities of the law. The law combines power and morality, stability and change, systemic or doctrinal coherence and equitable sensitivity to individual cases, among others. The dualities pose a double explanatory challenge. First, are the concepts commonly used in legal theory adequate to the task of explaining these dualities and the attendant conflicts or tensions in our understanding of the law? Second, to the extent that legal activities are conscious of their own nature, how do these dualities affect the activities and the law? A special aspect of this second question results from the fact that some of these apparent conflicts (especially the relation of power and morality within the law) are a matter of moral importance. Theories of law tend to divide into those which think that, by its very nature, the law successfully reconciles the duality of morality and power, and those which think that its success in doing so is contingent, depending on the political realities of the societies whose law is in question. Belonging with the second tendency, I have suggested that it is essential to the law that it recognizes that its use of power is answerable to moral standards and claims to have reconciled power and morality. It may not live up to its own aspirations.

Hopefully, the chapters which follow, containing almost all I have published in legal philosophy since 1994, and one previously unpublished essay, will explain the preceding paragraph. They contain several of the elements of an account of the general nature of law. In that, they develop and supplement what I have written on the subject before. But they do not replace those writings. Parts of the account are not dealt with here at all, and others are discussed elsewhere in greater detail. In the introduction I will briefly explain why the issues here discussed are central to a theory of law, starting with the controversial point made above that taking itself as answerable to certain standards is part of the nature of the law.

One feature of theories of law (common to philosophical accounts of action, morality and normative politics, among others) is that they deal with activities, attitudes, institutions and related phenomena which are themselves informed by some self-understanding, however imperfect. Simply put, this means that judges are not merely people some of whose decisions have the force of legally binding judgements. They are people whose decisions are legally binding partly because they render them intending that they be binding. Legislators are not merely people whose pronouncements make law. They make law only when they act with the intention to set binding rules. The same is true of a host of other legal officials: their acts have legal effect only if they are intended to be binding. Indeed many ordinary transactions have legal effect only if the people involved intend them to have the relevant normative effects: marriages are not legally valid unless the married contracted the marriage intending to do so; wills are not legally valid unless the testators intended them to determine the disposition of their property after their death; and so on. A theory of law identifies and explains the concepts involved in legal actions, and explains the nature of law given that legal actions have that character. In that way the theory of law is in part about the way those legal actors understand themselves and their actions.

And that is why we can say that the law makes certain claims for itself. Given that it is institutionalized, in that its norms can be changed and applied by institutions, and given that the institutions make certain statements and perform other speech acts in the course of their official actions, we can identify the presuppositions of those statements and actions. So that if a legal institution or official says: I hereby grant you a right to this and that (thus purporting to confer those rights on those people), this reveals that it presupposes that it has the normative power to grant such rights. If it turns out—as it does—that it is in the nature of law to have institutions which can purport to grant rights to people, it follows that it is in the nature of law to claim entitlement to confer rights on people. That would mean that the law holds itself subject to certain normative standards. Though whether and to what degree it succeeds in living up to them is another matter.

The preceding observations give rise to three difficult problems. First, if the law aspires to meet, that is holds itself subject to, certain standards, can it be that it completely fails to live up to them? Second, if it can fail to live up to them, at least to a degree, do we need a different language to refer to it and describe its products when it so fails? Finally, if the law lives through the activities of its own institutions, which aim to make, apply and follow its standards, and if it is self-conscious of its own activities in the sense that its institutions know some of their own institutional features and aim to conform to standards by which they hold such institutions to be bound, does it not follow that the law is aware of itself in parochial terms, ie using concepts which exist, or are available to people, in some cultures but not in others? And if so can there be a universal theory of law, that is one which applies to law regardless of the concepts through which its institutions are aware of their own existence?

The last question is central to the first couple of essays in the book, which reflect on methodological issues: what kind of theory is the theory of law, and what kind of explanations can it hope for? They argue for the possibility of a general theory of law, regardless of the way particular legal systems conceive of themselves. At the same time they allow that as the concepts used by legal institutions change, and as the cultural background of their activities changes, the theory of law faces new questions, new challenges. Thus this view of the nature of the theory of law explains why the task legal theories face is never-ending, why theoretical explanations will change and develop for as long as our interest in the law persists. The emergence of new explanations is not necessarily a result of the failure of old ones. It may well be the consequence of the emergence of new questions with the changing concepts and assumptions on which we rely in understanding social and legal phenomena.

The first question (if the law aspires to meet, that is holds itself subject to, certain standards, can it be that it completely fails to live up to them?) hovers over the second part of the book (and the Appendix). It is a way of approaching the question of the normativity of law. There is an unfortunate tendency to deal with the question of the nature of the normativity of the law as if it were the question of what, if any, necessary relations exist between law and morality. As moral reasons are only one kind of (normative) reasons, and the question of normativity is whether, and when, laws constitute or provide reasons (and of what kind) to those subject to them, the question of the normativity of law is the wider and more fundamental one.[1]

---

[1] The law deals with rights, duties, liabilities, responsibilities, with shares and bonds, with copyright and trade marks, with corporations and other legal persons and much more besides. Like many other writers since Bentham I believe that all these concepts and institutions are so many conditions for, and consequences of, normative reasons which people have or could have. That is why the introduction focuses on the normative reasons the law provides or constitutes.

The book presupposes the view I have argued for in earlier publications, namely that the content of the law can be established without resort to moral considerations bearing on the desirability or otherwise of any human conduct, or of having any particular legal standards.[2] Moreover, the law consists of standards which are the product of human activity, largely of actions intended to impose duties, confer rights, and more generally to set binding standards. This suggests two conclusions. First, legal standards can fail to be morally sound, indeed they can be evil, just as other human activities and their products can fail to be morally sound, and can be evil. (It does not follow, of course, that it is possible for a legal system to be entirely without moral merit, any more than it is possible for a person to spend a lifetime without performing any morally worthy actions.) Second, given that legal institutions purport to impose and enforce duties on people, given that they take it upon themselves to deprive those who disregard their legally imposed standards of property and liberty (and sometimes of their life), it follows that those institutions take themselves to be legitimate, that is to have the moral right to act as they do (and that individuals who occupy positions of power and responsibility within legal institutions believe, or make it appear that they believe, that they have such rights). Legal institutions can, and sometimes do, allow that legal rules are imperfect, or worse, and in need of revision. But, so long as they continue to exist, they necessarily claim that their own existence and powers are (morally) justified. Moreover, some exceptions apart, they regard legal standards which were legitimately created as binding even if imperfect, until properly amended and revised.

A result of this second point is that legal discourse is moral discourse. Legal institutions take their activities to impose and enforce real, morally binding, rights and duties, and they refer to them in the

---

[2] This formulation conforms to the view I have explained before, but diverges, hopefully in a clarifying way, from the formal statement of the view previously given. It may be worth pointing out that the view does not require that *every* person should be able to identify the law without recourse to moral considerations. The existence of people with cognitive disabilities is irrelevant to this view. Nor does it deny that it may be possible to identify the law using moral reasoning. Indeed, it follows from my doctrine of authority, that if one knows that the legislature did enact the morally required law it should be possible to identify the law by establishing which law was morally required. However, the thesis that it is possible to identify the law without recourse to moral argument is not satisfied if to identify the law one has either to rely on moral considerations or to rely on the word of an expert who relies on moral considerations. This second method also relies on moral considerations (contrast the discussion of these and related points in Jules Coleman, *The Practice of Principle* (Oxford: OUP, 2001) especially lecture 9).

usual normative language familiar from moral discourse. It does not follow that they are right to do so, that the legal standards they establish and enforce are morally binding. But it is not surprising that even those who believe that they are not morally binding use moral terminology in discussing the law. After all, they are dealing with powerful institutions which hold the standards to be legally binding. If they are to deal with them they have no choice (exceptional cases apart) but to address them on the supposition that their standards are really binding (ie morally binding). I have described elsewhere some of the features of what I called 'detached' discourse, and I do not return to the issue here.[3]

Part II of the book offers explanations of the way the law purports to be integrated within morality, and the way its standards can be, when the law is legitimate, both an application of pre-existing moral standards, and yet new, imposing duties and rights which do not exist without the law. The root problem is sometimes referred to as the bootstrapping problem: how can duties and rights spring into existence by the say-so of a person, or an institution? This problem also arises in the case of promises and other forms of commitments. In the case of legal and other authorities there is another difficulty: how is it that one person can, by his say-so, impose a duty on another? In discussing these and related problems I paid only scant attention to complications arising out of the systemic nature of the law. What are those complications?

In fact rules made by people (I will refer to all such rules, whether customary, legislated, or others, as social rules) hardly ever stand alone. Typically they emerge within an institutional structure, and form part of a system of social rules. It simplifies matters to ignore this background and discuss rules as if they stood on their own. But confusion may ensue. We rightly have a three-way distinction between rule-making activities (legislation, rendering judgements which set binding precedents, etc), legal rules, and the law (taken as a whole). The law is the product of many acts of law-making usually over long stretches of time, through processes which, far from displaying coherent design, are contributed to by many bodies, only partially aware of each other, often pursuing divergent, even conflicting, ends.

There is no one-to-one correlation, or any other regular correlation between law-making activities and rules of law. References to rules are references to units of content. Given the size and complexity of a legal system it is not surprising that we have ways of referring to aspects or

---

[3] See *Practical Reason and Norms* (2nd ed, Oxford: OUP, 1999) 170–177.

parts of it. We do so at a variety of levels of complexity, with rules being a basic unit (though obviously one can also refer to an aspect or a part of a rule). When referring to doctrines, for example, we take in view a body of rules united by some fundamental features (eg governed by one set of rules of responsibility or of remedies) or dealing with some degree of coherence with a certain subject matter.

Rules, especially long-standing rules, are often the product of a variety of law-creating acts, some legislative some judicial, fashioning the current rule, changing and developing it, over time. Similarly, single acts of legislation, like the passing of one Act by the legislature, typically create or modify more than one rule.

A crucial issue concerns the relations between particular rules of law and the law to which they belong. The following is a summary of the view taken here: We start outside the law. Generally what we ought, all told, to do depends on the way a variety of (normative) reasons bear on the matter. The reasons for and against an action are various good and bad features of it. They determine if and in what ways it serves valuable ends which we have, or should have. So we distinguish between all-things-considered propositions, specifying that one has an undefeated reason for or against an action, and propositions about particular reasons which specify good or bad, desirable and undesirable, aspects of actions. What we have undefeated reason to do is determined by the different reasons for and against the relevant actions.[4]

How does the law come into the picture? It matters whether it is morally legitimate or not. The question is more complicated than it appears. For example, a government may have legitimate authority over some but not over others, or regarding some matters but not others. I will disregard such complications in this brief sketch. If the law is not morally legitimate then its existence in itself is not a reason for any action, though of course the fact that other people, employers, friends, courts, police, are influenced by it may well provide such reasons. These exist also if the law is legitimate, but in that case its very existence constitutes a reason.

Many writers on law and philosophy describe the way different reasons determine what one has undefeated reason to do as a matter of balancing. If the term is understood to convey no meaning other

---

[4] Undefeated reasons are to be distinguished from conclusive reasons. There may be an undefeated reason to perform an action, as well as an undefeated reason to perform a conflicting action. If the reasons for an action are conclusive then they defeat all reasons for conflicting actions.

than that what one ought to do all things considered (what one has undefeated reason to do) is determined by the reasons for and against the action, there may be no harm in using the 'balancing' terminology. Typically, however, the use of the term misleads, not least in suggesting that there is one kind of relationship between conflicting reasons, namely determining which one weighs more or is more important than the other. Worse still is the suggestion that reasons come with weights attached. There are no such reasons. A better metaphor compares propositions about reasons to premises in arguments which establish what action is supported by the better reasons.

Those accustomed to 'balancing' talk may think that the existence of a (morally) legitimate law establishing a duty to perform a certain action is a reason for it, to be added to other reasons for that action and balanced against whatever reasons there are against it. That is a very misleading and wrong-headed view.

A simplified picture captures the gist of the matter: laws are normally made to settle actual or possible disagreements about which standards those subject to them should follow, as well as actual or possible disagreement about whether it is important that they should follow any (uniform standard). The need to have legal rules settling such matters is due to the fact that while there are reasons why those subject to the law should behave as the law requires, but for the law they may not, whereas the law makes them more likely to do so. They may not realize that that is what they should do, or they may take advantage of others doing their duty by not doing so themselves, and so on and so forth. So the law sets things straight: telling people 'this is what you should do and whether you agree that this is so or not, now that it is the law that you should you have the law as a new, special kind of reason to do so'. The law is a special kind of reason for it displaces the reasons which it is meant to reflect. It functions as court decisions do: the litigants disagree about what they have reason to do. The court determines matters. Of course they may still disagree, and the one in whose favour the court decides may not deserve to win. Possibly the other side should have won. It does not matter. The court's decision settles matters. It displaces the original reasons (the cause of action) and now the parties are bound by the decision instead. Similarly, a law, when it is binding, pre-empts the reasons which it should have reflected, and whether it successfully reflects them or not it displaces them, and is now a new source of duties.

This is a simplified introductory explanation of the way legitimate law relates to moral and other reasons which exist independently of it.

The book, and my previous writings, offer more detailed discussions of some aspects of this relationship. The point to bear in mind here is that it is the law, the legal system as a whole, which pre-empts those background considerations, not any of the legal rules taken singly. What the law requires, what rights it grants, what its conditions of responsibility etc are, depend on the combined effect of all its rules, though in each case only some of them are relevant.[5] Each legal rule is a reason and what the law requires is what one has, given the way all relevant legal rules bear on the issue, undefeated legal reason to do. A legal reason is a reason, like any other, though one constituted or provided by a legal rule.

One conclusion emerging from this view of the normative character of legitimate law is that its pre-emptive force, being addressed, as it were, to the law's subjects, does not affect legal institutions when they exercise power to modify the law. This helps towards a more nuanced understanding of the way a legitimate legal system is, on the one hand, an autonomous, that is independent, normative system, and the way it is also, on the other hand, just part of morality. In as much as legal rules and doctrines have an internal structure they form a system of inter-related reasons, yielding conclusions as to what rights, duties, liabilities, and so, on exist by law (all legal things considered).[6] In this way the law confronts its subjects as a system of reasons which is, due to its pre-emptive force, isolated from other considerations, from the considerations which it pre-empts.[7]

---

[5] Some have suggested that all legal rules bear on the outcome of each case. This exaggeration is made plausible when confused with two other, sensible, claims. First, while given that the law is as it is only some of its rules bear on any individual case, it could have included other rules which could have had a bearing on the case. Second, when deliberating whether to change the law law-makers, including courts, may draw analogies and disanalogies from any branch or part of the law, as part of arguments designed to show the advantages of different ways of changing the law or leaving it as it is'.

[6] Cf. my discussion of the topic in 'The Inner Logic of the Law', *Ethics in the Public Domain* (Oxford: Clarendon Press, 1995) ch 11. As is made clear there, the law also provides guidelines for its own development. It provides reasons for law-makers to make laws, or develop existing law in ways which meet certain constraints, or follow certain moral principles.

[7] The pre-emption is not complete. The law itself indicates, often implicitly, that when certain other considerations apply they may justify disregarding legal requirements. I am assuming, however, that law-makers are (morally) required to consider all relevant considerations, and in making law to design it in a way which reflects the way they bear on the law's subjects. Therefore, unless the law limits its own pre-emptive force, the general rule, that it pre-empts those considerations on which law-makers should have based the rules they make, pre-empts everything.

As mentioned above, when the law is not (morally) legitimate its existence does not constitute valid reasons. However, if it is in fact the legal system by which a country is governed then inevitably some people, eg legal officers, hold it to be legitimate and to provide valid reasons. The rest of the population may well have an interest in thinking of it as if it provides valid reasons in order to facilitate interactions with the legal institutions. If however, the law is legitimate then its rules do constitute reasons for action. In that case, a more comprehensive understanding of the law would emphasize the limits on its autonomy. It would point to the fact that it provides reasons because it instantiates certain background moral reasons, that it is an applied moral system, always to be developed along moral lines.

As always things are more complex than these brief remarks suggest. The doctrine of *res judicata* endows many judicial decisions (and not only the legal system as a whole) with pre-emptive force, pre-empting the reasons (including the legal reasons) which the court should have recognized in its decision. There is another way in which the preceding pages are misleadingly simple. They ignore the special way in which the law is continuously in flux. In countries with which I have some familiarity the law appears to many lay people either as an awesome alien monolith or a complicated device manipulated at will by unprincipled lawyers. By way of contrast many participants and close observers perceive the law as a complex web held together by subtle logic. Many of them have little time for philosophical theories of law by either contemporaries or any of the philosophers from Plato on who offered theories of law. We cannot dismiss this as the usual contempt of practitioners for theoreticians presuming to explain their practice. There are aspects of legal practice in many countries which have often been neglected by philosophers, and whose discussion, when it happens, is not altogether successful. Prominent among those is the way the law is interpreted by the courts.

The difficulty is due to the fact that in interpretive reasoning the distinction between law application and law creation is obscured. This tends to make any theory about the nature of law appear inadequate. For in claiming that the possession of certain properties is essential to the law one is marking a boundary between what is law, and possesses those properties, and what is not because it does not possess them. It is sometimes thought that the problem arises for only some theories of law. In recent times some so-called 'legal positivist' theories were sometimes accused (even by some self-identified 'legal positivist' writers) of inability to deal with interpretation because of the way they draw the boundaries of the law. This, I believe, misidentifies the difficulty. It afflicts any theory of law.

Early in his work Ronald Dworkin, making this problem the pivot for the development of his own ideas, showed that HLA Hart was mistaken in thinking that the problem requires no more than recognition that the ordinary meaning of terms such as 'law' admits of vagueness and a penumbra of indeterminacy. Instead he suggested that legal decisions do not change the content of the law. Therefore in analysing legal interpretation we need not distinguish between innovative and conserving interpretations, nor need we analyse the conditions under which precedent-setting decisions have law-making effect. The attraction of this suggestion is that it transcends the dualities (law/extra-legal, law-applying/law-creating) whose explanation is a challenge for other theories. The drawback is the difficulty of reconciling the theory with the existence of the common-law, simple observations that certain norms are not legally binding while others are, that the law has developed over (say) the last ten years in ways which cannot be accounted for by legislation alone, and much else—all being facts whose recognition presupposes those troublesome distinctions.[8]

The approach I have taken with these problems dominates the discussion of interpretation in Part III of the book, but is not unique to this issue. We need well-honed analytic tools to explain legal phenomena, including the nature of the law. This means that while the explanations employ concepts which are also employed in 'the life of the law', they are given sharper focus and definition in the theories, designed to illuminate whatever it is which makes these phenomena interesting theoretically or important practically, so that they are only roughly the same as the concepts employed in the course of legal activities. There may be more than one way of sharpening those concepts. Nothing in my approach implies that there is one best theory of the nature of law. On the contrary, it strongly suggests the possibility that while many theories are badly defective, there may well be more than one possible (ie ones which have not necessarily been developed and advanced by anyone) adequate theory. How does this affect the concept of law itself? It does figure in legal practice, for the law may refer to the legal system as a whole. Sometimes this happens in contexts which require demarcation

---

[8] As I understand it, later on Dworkin did not repeat the denial that those distinctions apply, but refrained from explicitly dealing with their explanations.

between what belongs within and what lies outside the legal system concerned. At other times there are good reasons for legal institutions to shy away from doing so.

Various reasons propel courts to develop a distinction between what is part of their legal system and what is not. For example, in some countries Conflict of Law rules allow courts certain grounds for refusing to apply foreign law which would not justify refusing to apply domestic law. Different rules regarding what the courts know and what has to be established before them (and how) apply depending (among other things) on whether the rule to be established is part of the law, or is recognized and enforced by the court because it is a rule of some other kind (a rule of a corporation, a commercial custom, etc). These are but two examples. Different legal systems generate different questions to do with the boundary between what is part of them and what is not. Each of these questions, each of the boundaries which they demarcate, bears on a variety of practical concerns, and there is no reason to expect that they all align to suggest one uniform boundary. We can expect various legal systems to conclude that insofar as this is the issue, the boundary between what belongs to the system and what does not is this, but insofar as the issue is that other one a different boundary prevails. In some legal systems such a pragmatic approach may be rejected as unprincipled, but in others it would be entirely acceptable. In short we cannot expect the law of any one country to have a uniform way of demarcating the boundary between what belongs to it and what lies outside it, let alone expect to find that all legal systems demarcate the boundary in the same way.

Some are inclined to conclude that legal theory should not include a doctrine about the nature of law, for that will lead to a discrepancy between it and the view taken by various legal systems. That seems to me a mistaken conclusion, misconceiving the relations between the theory of the nature of law and the law. It ignores the fact that the law is important to people other than lawyers, and I do not mean important in establishing their legal liabilities. It is an important social institution and there is an interest in understanding its nature as a distinctive social institution. That it is an institution of a certain character is not contradicted by the fact that in this or that country it has accrued certain extensions, or has shied away from some areas. If you like, the theory of law proceeds in two stages, or alternatively has a limited ambition. The first and most important stage establishes the kind of social institution the law is, the second explains why the law in this or that country has extended itself beyond some boundaries or shied away from possessing its full territory. These deviations need not negate the claim that its character as a distinctive institution is as the theory describes. So the theory implies boundaries, and allows for deviations from those boundaries in individual cases. We are familiar with this structure in all human products. A watch is an instrument marking the time, but a plasticine watch does not. A bed is an item of furniture made for people to lie on, but this sculpture is a bed, but not made for this purpose, and so on. In all these cases, the deviations do not undermine the core characterizations because they depend on them; their explanation is that of deviation from the core or standard case, thus they presuppose the standard case (as determined by the nature of the type), and have no meaning without it.

Aside from the special issues which force legal systems to have a view about their limits, there is a general case for the law not to adopt a general test regarding its own boundary. As background to this case we should be reminded that any changes to the law should, other things being equal, be continuous with existing law. Typically we would expect any changes to fit well with existing legal defences, remedies, procedures, doctrines of legal competence and much else, besides having to cohere with existing law on the matter they deal with (landlord and tenant, the powers and liabilities of company directors, or whatever) or else they are likely not to achieve their aims, and are likely to undermine the working of other parts of the law. This is true of primary legislation and is doubly true of regulation and of judicial decisions, if only because regulators and courts do not have the power to introduce comprehensive reforms, and have to make sure that their measures fit well within existing legal frameworks.

In making law it is often impractical to worry too much whether a particular provision is already implied by existing law. When it is needed it may be safer to enact it without worrying whether this changes existing law or not. I have argued that this is particularly true, and inevitably so, when it comes to judicial precedent-setting through reasoning by analogy.[9] The same is true of judicial interpretive reasoning.

The account of interpretation in Part III relies heavily on the dependence of the standards by which interpretations are evaluated on the purposes that they are meant to, or should, serve. The distinction between conserving interpretations, designed to display or explain the meaning the original has independently of them, and innovative interpretations,

---

[9] 'Law and Value in Adjudication', *The Authority of Law* (Oxford: OUP, 1979) ch 10.

which explain or display meaning the original has in part because of the interpretation, is crucial to the understanding of what interpretations are, for they are ways of understanding meaning which assume the possibility of a plurality of incompatible and of changing meanings. The distinction is also important in trying to find out an interpretation. Different considerations may militate in favour of an interpretation, depending on whether it is to be a conserving or an innovative one.

It does not follow, however, that it is always advisable or even possible to classify any single interpretation as being either wholly conserving or wholly innovative. Legal interpretations offered by courts as part of their reasoning are a case in point. Whether or not courts merely apply existing law, or do so while moulding it and adapting it to the purpose at hand, their reasoning has, for good reasons, to maintain its attachment to existing law. The innovations are, most of the time, interstitial interventions in the law. The book considers interpretation in general, interpretation as it figures in our relations to the arts, history, literature, and religion as well as to the law. This broader perspective helps to make the functioning of interpretation in the law less baffling, while never losing sight of its distinctive characteristics. It argues that innovative legal interpretation is always conserving in part, and that while sometimes it is possible, often it is not possible to distinguish between its conserving and its innovative elements. And yet, it is the relationship between these two strands which makes legal interpretation what it is. The fusion of the elements in the practice of the law is compatible with the need to understand them as separate components of interpretation, in its various spheres, for in their combination lies the key to its distinctive character.

PART I
METHODOLOGICAL ISSUES

2

Can There be a Theory of Law?[1]

'Why not?' you may ask. And indeed few challenge the possibility of theorizing about the law, if that is taken to mean 'engaging in theoretical debates' about the law. Yet the thought that there can be a theory of law, that is a set of systematically related true propositions about the nature of law, has been challenged, and from several directions. None of the challenges is entirely successful. But through examining some of them we gain a better understanding of what a theory of law can be, and how its success can be established.

I will be using 'a theory of law' in a narrow sense, as referring to an explanation of the nature of law. It is a sense central to philosophical reflection about the law throughout its history. But in choosing this narrow understanding of 'theory of law' I do not mean to dispute the appropriateness of other theoretical investigations about the law, some of which I dabbled in myself on other occasions, nor to deny them the title of theories of law.[2] My choice to use the term in the narrow sense explained here is purely a matter of terminological convenience.

Therefore, as here understood, a theory of law provides an account of the nature of law. The thesis I will be defending is that a theory of law is successful if it meets two criteria: First, it consists of propositions about the law which are *necessarily* true, and, second, they *explain* what the law is.

All theories aim to be successful, or at least to be more successful than their rivals. To understand what theories are we need to understand what it would be for them to be successful, that is what it would be for them to be what they aim to be. When discussing what a legal theory

---

[1] This chapter uses material and ideas included in chapter 3, 'Two Views of the Nature of the Theory of Law: A Partial Comparison', and chapter 4, 'On the Nature of Law'.

[2] Notable among them are theories about the appropriate form or content that legal institutions should have, theories about the concepts and principles which govern various legal areas (property, commercial law, torts, contract, etc).

is I will assume that we are concerned with understanding the character of wholly successful theories, that is of theories which meet the two conditions. Sections II and III of this chapter will discuss the two conditions. The first section aims to clarify the relationship between the thesis as stated above and the traditional way of understanding the task of legal theory as explaining the concept of law. The remaining sections (IV to VI) examine several difficulties with the idea that there can be a theory of law in general, a theory which since true is necessarily true of the law wherever and whenever it is to be found. The problems there examined arise out of the changing nature of concepts, out of the dependence of law on concepts, and out of the alleged impossibility of understanding alien cultures, using alien concepts.

I. Essence and Concept

A. What is the relation between the concept of a thing and its nature?

Concepts, as objects of philosophical study, as the target of conceptual analysis or elucidation, are a philosophical creation.[3] Here is an example of one non-philosophical use (quoted from the Oxford English Dictionary):

Techniques of testing product concepts in advertising could conceivably become as important as new physical research techniques have been to the chemical and metals industries.

(C Ramond in R Barton *Handbook of Advertising Management* (1970) xxii. 19)

Here 'product concepts' means something like ideas about possible products. There is, however, a common core to the philosophical and non-philosophical uses. They relate to how people conceive certain objects, or phenomena.

Metaphorically speaking, concepts (and from now one I will confine myself to the philosophical use of the term, and will feel free to suggest emendations of it) are placed between the world, aspects of which they are concepts of, and words or phrases, which express them (the concepts) and are used to talk about those aspects of the world. Some writers exaggerate their proximity to words and phrases and identify

---

[3] See chapter 3.

them with word or phrase meaning. Others associate them closely with the nature of their objects, the nature of what they are concepts of. When Ryle wrote about the concept of mind, or Hart the concept of law they meant, in advancing explanations of the concepts of mind and of law, to offer explanations of the nature of mind and of the law. Ryle opens his book saying:

This book offers what may with reservations be described as a theory of the mind.[4]

Hart opens saying

My aim in this book has been to further the understanding of law, coercion, and morality as different but related social phenomena.[5]

For them as for many other philosophers there was no difference between an explanation of concepts and of the nature of things of which they are concepts. Some may even claim that there is no conflict between these two ways of understanding concepts, a view which dates back at least to the beginning of the twentieth century and the growth of 'conceptual analysis' as a prime method of philosophical inquiry, which was often equated with analysis of the meanings of words and phrases.

The view I will advance allows that there is some truth in both approaches. But both are mistaken and misleading. Concepts are how we conceive aspects of the world, and lie between words and their meanings, in which they are expressed, on the one side, and the nature of things to which they apply, on the other.

The law offers an easy illustration of the non-identity of concepts and (word) meanings. Hart's *The Concept of Law* does not explain, nor does it aim to explain the meaning of the word 'law'. It has nothing to say about divine law, mathematical or logical laws, laws of nature, nor many others. Nor do I think that it is a partial explanation of the meaning of the word. 'Law' is not ambiguous, and *The Concept of Law* does not explain one of its meanings. When used in legal contexts 'law' bears the same meaning as in other contexts. Nor is it plausible to think that its univocal meaning is explained by a list of alternatives, as if saying that 'law' means what it means in legal contexts, *or* what it means in religious contexts, *or* what it means in mathematical contexts, etc. The word is used

---

[4] *The Concept of Mind* (London: Hutchinson, 1949) 9.
[5] *The Concept of Law* (Oxford: OUP, 1961) v.

in all these contexts to refer to rules of some permanence and generality, giving rise to one kind of necessity or another.

Those who offer explanations of the concept of law usually do mean, as Hart did, to explain the nature of a familiar social institution. It would have been possible for a language to contain a word which refers to this social institution and to nothing else. It may be mere accident that we do not have such a word, though there are good historical-intellectual explanations why 'law' has the meaning it has. But things being as they are the meaning of the expression 'the law' is not (identical with) the concept of law which Hart, and other philosophers of law, sought to explain.

Of course we express the concept, use it and refer to it by using words. But we need not use the word 'law' or 'the law' to refer to it. We could talk of the law by talking of the system of courts and legislature and the rules they endorse in a state, for example. And we could do so in a large number of other ways. Most importantly, we rely on context, linguistic and non-linguistic, to determine whether we are talking of the right sort of law when talking of law, or whether we are talking of scientific or other laws. The availability of context to determine reference establishes that there is no need for concepts to be identified by the use of specific words or phrases.

I will make two assumptions about concepts: First, I will assume that we can explain what they are by explaining what it is to have and understand them. That is, we explain a particular concept by setting out the conditions under which it is true of people that they have and understand that concept. Second, I will assume that concepts differ from each other by the information required to have and understand them, and by the skills and abilities involved in their possession. I call these assumptions, for in making them I am deviating from the ordinary meaning of 'concepts', narrowing it down, and fashioning it in accordance with the way it is normally used in philosophical writings. Normally, rather than always, for the philosophical use is not uniform, and because in any case we should keep the freedom to deviate from philosophical usage where it would make sense to do so.

Those who, like Hart and Ryle, emphasize the close connection between concepts and the nature of things can be said to be implicitly committed to the view that a complete understanding of a concept consists in knowing and understanding all the necessary features of its object, that is of that of which it is a concept. I will follow them in equating complete mastery of a concept with knowledge and understanding of all the necessary features of the objects to which it applies. Thus, complete mastery of the concept of a table consists in knowledge and understanding of all the essential properties of tables, and so on.

Is it an objection to this view that complete mastery of one concept can be identical with complete mastery of another without the two concepts being identical? Not necessarily. It is an objection only if we individuate concepts by the conditions for their complete mastery. Let me explain.

The concepts of an equilateral triangle and of an equiangular triangle are not the same concepts, but the necessary features of equilateral triangles are the same as those of equiangular ones. The necessary features of the one kind of triangle are the same as the necessary features of the other. We can accept that complete mastery of these concepts involves knowing that they apply to the same triangles, knowledge that the conditions for their complete mastery are the same. But they apply to the same triangles in different ways, for different reasons, the one because they are equilateral, while the other because they are equiangular.

How does this difference manifest itself? Primarily by the fact that concepts are individuated not merely by the conditions for their complete mastery, but also by the minimal conditions for having them. One may have the concept of an equilateral triangle without realizing that it is part of the nature of such triangles to be equiangular. Admittedly, one's understanding of the concept will then be incomplete. But then the notion of complete understanding, as explained above, is very demanding. Most of the concepts we have and understand we master and understand incompletely. What one cannot fail to know, if one has the concept of equilateral triangles, is that the concept applies to and only to triangles with equal sides. This is where the two concepts (of equilateral and equiangular triangles, in the example) differ. They differ in the minimal conditions for their possession. For, of course, someone who does not know that the concept of equiangular triangles applies only to triangles with equal sides may still have (an incomplete mastery of) that concept. But if he does not know that it applies to all and only triangles of equal angles then he does not have the concept at all.

Following this line of thought I will maintain that an explanation of a concept has four parts:

(1) Setting the condition for the knowledge involved in complete mastery of the concept, which is the knowledge of all the essential features of the thing it is a concept of.

(2) Explaining the understanding involved in complete mastery of the concept.

(3) Explaining the conditions for minimal possession of the concept, that is those, essential or non-essential, properties of what the concept is a concept of, knowledge of which is necessary for the person to have the concept at all, however incomplete his or her mastery of it may be.

(4) Explaining the abilities required for minimal possession of the concept.[6]

The first condition determines what the concept is a concept of. But all of them together determine the identity of the concept.

As with other aspects of this inquiry my use of 'minimal conditions for the possession of a concept' is partly responsive to our normal notions, and partly a stipulative regimentation of these notions. It allows that people may know things about concepts, while not having these concepts. One may know that N is an animal without having the concept of N. One may know that mauve is a colour without having the concept, or that snakes lay eggs without having the concept of a snake. As this last example shows, knowledge that is inadequate for even minimal possession of a concept may be knowledge those who have mastered the concept (incompletely) may not have.

The mention of knowledge of non-essential properties as among the possible conditions for minimal possession of the concept is meant to allow that people may have knowledge which is sufficient to enable them to use the concept correctly in the circumstances of their life, but which is not true of it in all conditions. They may rely on the fact that swans that they have come across are white as crucial to their ability to identify swans. That may be part of what would justify judging them as having the concept.[7]

---

[6] In the present chapter I will not dwell on the role of understanding ability in concept possession. My assumption is that understanding consists in knowing important relations among the essential properties of the things the concepts apply to, and among them and some other properties. I mention skill and abilities to indicate that for possession of a concept the verbal or conceptual abilities which manifest themselves in giving explanations of the concept or its use are not sufficient. It requires some non-verbal skills or abilities as well, abilities which manifest themselves in its correct use, rather than in any explanation of it.

[7] Note that not all essential properties are used in identifying instances or occurrences of the things they are essential properties of. Some essential properties are useless for identificatory purposes. It may be an essential property of real tennis that it is the ball game first developed in France in the fourteenth century, but normally you cannot identify a

These considerations allow that people can refer to concepts which they do not possess. But this seems obvious for independent reasons as well. Reference to a concept need not employ any of its necessary features. For example, given that yesterday my friends discussed the concept of cruelty I can refer to it as the concept my friends discussed yesterday. I need know nothing more about it successfully to refer to it. They also allow that people may possess a concept and yet fail to recognize that it is identical with another, or think that there is only one, where there are two (the minimal conditions for the possession of the concepts of WATER and of TWATER are the same, though the concepts are not identical since the conditions for their complete mastery differ).

It is possible for any person to invent or develop a new concept. Some concepts which emerge in that way make their way into the general culture, usually more or less modified along the way. But for the most part concepts exist independently of any one of their users. For the most part, we learn concepts, rather than invent or develop them. It must be so. Given the richness of our concepts and the limits of our abilities it is not possible for anyone to invent or modify more than a fractional margin of them. Given their role in communication it would be self-defeating to do so. The fact that for the most part concepts are there independently of any one of us does not mean of course that they are independent of us collectively. The conditions fixing the identity of particular concepts are idealizations constructed out of our conceptual practices, ie out of the use of those concepts in general. They need not reflect any individual's practice. While it is impossible for a concept that no one knows anything about to exist, it is possible that no one has a completely correct understanding or knowledge of a concept, or indeed of any concept, including the concept of a concept.

Furthermore, while the conditions for concept possession are what they are because of our conceptual practices, it does not follow that we can identify the concept an individual uses, or intends to use, except by reference to our knowledge of what concepts there are. In part this is

---

game of real tennis as being that by reference to that property. Furthermore, properties which can be used for identification often are not essential properties. Possibly the only essential property of water is that it is H_2O. But few people use that to identify water. Finally, often we rely on non-essential properties to identify instances of concepts. They may be reliable marks of instances of the concept in all normal circumstances. Note also that there is no reason to suppose the same property is used to identify items falling under the concept by everyone who has the concept. Some essential properties may be used in this way by some people, and not be used, indeed not be even known to others who nevertheless have mastered the concept some other way.

due to the fact that, with rare exceptions, when people use a concept, or try to, they intend to use a concept that is there (the one normally expressed by the word they use, etc). Identification of intentions generally depends on (defeasible) presumptions of normality invoked by their manifestations (if you walk to the door then you intend to do so, unless some circumstances defeating the presumption obtain; if you say 'I will open the door' then you mean what is normally meant when the sentence is uttered in like circumstances, unless some circumstances defeating the presumption obtain). Similarly, when you utter words to express a concept you express the concept that would normally be used when those words are uttered in those circumstances, unless defeating conditions obtain. Knowledge of the concept is presupposed in identifying the use of a concept. The speaker's intention to use the concept is identified by reference to presumptions of normality which presuppose such knowledge.

The preceding remarks show (1) how people can have incomplete understanding of concepts they possess, (2) how they can make mistakes about such concepts, including (3) mistakes about the identity of the concepts they possess and use.

These sketchy and rather dogmatically stated remarks were meant to explain why explaining a concept is close to explaining the nature of what it is a concept of (see the first condition of concept identity above), and yet why the two tasks differ (see the other conditions). They also explain why I regard the explanation of the nature of law as the primary task of the theory of law. That the explanation of the concept of law is one of its secondary tasks is a result of the fact that part of the task of explaining the nature of law is to explain how people perceive the law, and therefore, where the law exists in a country whose population has the concept of law, it becomes relevant to know whether the law is affected by its concept.

II. Can the Law Change Its Nature?

A theory consists of necessary truths, for only necessary truths about the law reveal the nature of the law. We talk of 'the nature of law', or the nature of anything else, to refer to those of the law's characteristics which are of the essence of law, which make law into what it is. That is those properties without which the law would not be law. As the *Oxford English Dictionary* explains, the nature of a thing consists of the essential qualities or properties of a thing; the inherent and inseparable combination of properties essentially pertaining to anything and giving it its fundamental character.

Naturally, the essential properties of the law are universal characteristics of law. They are to be found in law wherever and whenever it exists. Moreover, these properties are universal properties of the law not accidentally, and not because of any prevailing economic or social circumstances, but because there is no law without them. This does not mean that there are no social institutions, or normative systems, which share many of the law's characteristics, but do not have the essential properties of the law. When surveying the different forms of social organization in different societies throughout the ages we will find many which resemble the law in various ways. Yet if they lack the essential features of the law, they are not legal systems.

This way of looking at the question may give rise to the suspicion that something has gone wrong right at the beginning of the inquiry. It seems to presuppose something which is plainly false. It presupposes that law has—indeed that it must have—an unchanging nature. But is not that a mistake? Surely—the objection runs—the nature of the law changes. Think of the law and the legal cultures of the Roman Empire, of European countries during feudalism, or in the age of absolutism. 'Law' had different meanings during these different periods, and the modern Western notion of law differs from all of them. What was essential to the law of one period was absent in the law of another period. A theory of law which overlooks these facts cannot be a good theory.

But can the law change its nature? No doubt the law of any country can change, and does change. Moreover the institutions and practices of a country which constitute its law may lose the properties which are essential to the law. If that happens the result is not that the law changes its nature, but that the country no longer has a legal system (though it may have an institution which is not unlike the law in some or even many respects).

How do I know that the nature of law cannot change? That is a misconceived question. Following a well-established philosophical practice, I am using the term 'the nature of law' and related terms such as 'essential properties' to designate those properties which any (system of) law must possess to be law. This practice deviates from the way 'the nature of' is sometimes used in non-philosophical English. But it is important not to get hung up on terminological questions.

The question is whether the law has essential properties, thus understood. And if it does, does understanding them enjoy a special role in understanding what the law is?

This reply to the objection that the inquiry is based on a false presupposition is not the end of the matter. It leads directly to a new criticism. It leads to a charge of arbitrariness, a charge of arbitrary verbal legislation which obscures important points. The use of 'essential properties' and of 'nature' which I propose to follow obscures the fact that in reality the nature of law changes with time, and therefore it obstructs rather than helps the development of a theoretical or philosophical account of law.

There is something right, as well as something wrong, in this objection. As has already been admitted, the use of 'essential properties' and of 'the nature of...' which I briefly delineated is not the only use these terms have. It is perfectly in order, indeed true, to say that with the rise of capitalism the nature of the State has undergone a profound change. Or to say that the absolute protection of property and contract has become an essential function of the State. 'The nature of X', in other words, is often used to refer to properties of X which are taken to be of great importance, even though they are not definitive of the identity of X, ie even though X will not cease being what it is without them. It will merely undergo radical change.

When Jeremiah asks 'Can the Ethiopian change his skin or the leopard his spots?' (Jeremiah 13:23) is he assuming that the change is metaphysically impossible or conceptually inconceivable (for he thinks that a spotless leopard is no leopard, etc) or just that it is impossible as a matter of fact? There is no answer to the question. In most communication and thought the distinction is rarely drawn, nor is there any reason to draw it. It is not surprising, however, that the distinction is of philosophical importance. Therefore it is not surprising that philosophers have established a technical meaning for the terms, and I will follow it. Doing so does not prejudge the questions: does the law have a nature, in that sense of the word? And if so, is it illuminating to investigate it? It is true, of course, that there is no point in using this philosophical terminology unless the answer to these questions is affirmative. The only point I have been arguing for so far is that the fact that the notions of essential properties, and of the nature of something, are philosophical notions does not in itself disqualify them, nor does it in itself impugn the enquiry into the nature of law.

III. Does the Law Have Essential Properties?

It is time to return to the argument: Defining the object of a theory of law as a search for an explanation of the nature of law threatens to lead to its immediate abandonment, for it raises an obvious objection to the enterprise. I have conceded that it is part of our common understanding of the law that its nature (when that word is understood as it usually is) changes over time, both with changes in social and political practices, and with changes in culture, in philosophy, or more generally, in ways of understanding ourselves and our societies. Does not that show not only that the philosophical notion of the nature of a thing or of its essential properties is absent from our common discourse, but also that it has no application, or at least that it does not apply to the law? If this is so then by setting itself the goal of accounting for the nature of law legal theory condemns itself to inevitable failure. The argument that this is indeed the fate of legal theory so understood is simple: Over time we have been happy to operate without the philosophical distinction between essential and non-essential properties, so that whenever changes in the character of the law or in our ideas or ways of understanding it so required we changed our concept of law. And this was true of any changes, however great. Does this not show that the thought that the law has a fixed nature is an illusion?

As it happens this argument is not a good one. It is not generally the case that belief that something has essential properties is a precondition of it having such properties. If being made of H_2O is of the nature of water then this is so whether or not people believe that it is so, and whether or not they believe that water has essential properties. More specifically, what counts is not the common understanding of expressions like 'the nature of law', nor even the fact that the concept of law changes over time. What counts is the nature of the institution which the concept of law (ie the one we currently have and use) designates. To make its case the objection has to show that our concept of law (as it is at the moment) does not allow for the application of the (philosophical) notion of essential properties to the law, that is that the law has no essential properties.

Prima facie the evidence points against the objection. It is part of our understanding of the law that certain social institutions are instances of law whereas others are non-legal.[8] The distinction between the legal and the non-legal is part and parcel of those of our practices which determine the concept of law. We know that the regulations of a golf club are not a legal system, and that independent states have legal systems. I know that an Act of the British Parliament is legally binding, but a resolution of my neighbours to deny any non-resident access to our street has no legal validity. And so on. Moreover, while the distinction is not marked by the presence of the same linguistic cues, it is fairly stable, used by lawyers, politicians, bureaucrats, and lay people, in a whole variety of contexts, always in the same way, always referring to the same set of practices and institutions. Indeed some may add that the very talk of 'changes occurring in the concept of law' shows that once such changes occur it is no longer the same concept. It is a case of a new concept replacing the old one though they happen to share the same term.[9] Rather than challenging the thought that the law is marked by essential properties talk of a change in the concept seems to confirm the thought, it seems to presuppose it.

This can be seen, of course, as a trivial point. The understanding of a concept includes an understanding of what determines what falls under the concept and what does not. In itself this does not show that the law has essential properties, that is properties without which there can be no law. As we are often reminded the concept of law may be a family

---

[8] Here and in the sequel I will use 'law', as it is often used, to refer sometimes to a legal system, and sometimes to a rule of law, or a statement of how the law is on a particular point. Sometimes I will use the word ambiguously to refer to one or the other of these, as it does not matter for the purposes of the discussion of this chapter which way it is understood.

[9] Compare a different case: the way the meaning of 'knight' changed in the Middle Ages. 'Knight', the *Oxford English Dictionary* explains, means (among other things):

3. …A military servant or follower (of a king or some other specified superior); later, one devoted to the service of a lady as her attendant, or her champion in war or the tournament;… This is logically the direct predecessor of sense 4, the 'king's knight' having become the 'knight' *par excellence*, and a lady's knight being usually one of knightly rank.
4. Name of an order or rank. a. In the Middle Ages: Originally (as in 3), A military servant of the king or other person of rank; a feudal tenant holding land from a superior on condition of serving in the field as a mounted and well-armed man. In the fully-developed feudal system: One raised to honourable military rank by the king or other qualified person, the distinction being usually conferred only upon one of noble birth who had served a regular apprenticeship (as page and squire) to the profession of arms, and thus being a regular step in this even for those of the highest rank.

No one would deny that changes of meaning of this kind occur, but while there is no harm in referring to them as changes in the concept of a knight there is no reason to regard them as anything other than a case in which one concept has replaced another.

resemblance concept.[10] Not all the items designated by a family resemblance concept share a common property, and *ipso facto* they do not have essential properties.

I believe that the news of family resemblance concepts has been much exaggerated. A family resemblance concept is meant to be an unstructured concept. It applies to some instances in virtue of their possession of a set of features, say A, B, C, to other instances it applies in virtue of a different, partly overlapping, set of features, say B, C, D, to others still in virtue of a set of features still further removed from the instances we started with, say C, D, E, and so on. I doubt that many concepts are of this kind. Elsewhere I have argued that the concept of a game, a paradigm of a family resemblance concept, is not a family resemblance concept after all.[11] While the meaning of many terms in natural languages cannot be given by a set of properties essential to their application, they usually have a core meaning with a structured set of extensions. This is why 'root' can be used to refer to the root of the question, or 'school' to a school of thought.

Up to a point this debate is beside the point, beside our point. The notion of a family resemblance was developed by Wittgenstein in an argument against too regimented a way of accounting for the meanings of words and expressions. But the essential properties of law of which legal theory is trying to give an account are not invoked to account for the meaning of any term or class of terms. We are inquiring into the typology of social institutions, not into the semantics of terms. We build a typology of institutions by reference to properties we regard, or come to regard, as essential to the type of institution in question.

The distinction between inquiring into the meaning of terms and into the nature of institutions is often lost on legal theorists, perhaps in part because social institutions depend on the existence of complex practices including practices which can be broadly called linguistic, ie practices of discussing certain matters by reference to aspects of these institutions. By coincidence it could happen that there is a term or more than one which derive their meanings exclusively from their employment to designate a central aspect of a particular social institution. In such a case the tasks of explaining the nature of the institution and explaining the meaning of the terms will be closely allied. Fortunately

---

[10] Some regard the fact that law is a vague concept as another reason for denying that it makes sense to talk of the essential properties of law. We will discuss vagueness later in the book.

[11] *Practical Reason and Norms* (2nd edn, Oxford: OUP, 1999) ch 4.

this is not the case with 'law'. While legal scholars sometimes write as if they think that the term is exclusively used to refer to the law of states, and courts, etc the truth is otherwise. 'Law' is employed in relation to sciences, grammar, logic, language, and many other areas. Moreover, while the law, ie the law as we are interested in it, is replete with technical terms ('fee simple', 'intestate', etc) and other ordinary terms are used within the law with a technical meaning ('shares', 'bonds', 'equity') these are terms specific to one legal system or to a type of legal system. The general terminology of the law is no more specific to it than the word 'law' itself. It consists of terms like 'person', 'status', 'property', 'rights', 'duties', which are part of the common terminology of practical discourse in general.[12]

Not only is the general terminology used to talk about the law common to practical discourse generally, but there is no single way in which we always mark that it is the lawyer's law that we have in mind when we talk of people's rights and duties, about what they are entitled to do or required to do, of benefits they enjoy or liabilities or risks they are subject to. Sentences of these kinds and many others can be used to assert how things are according to law, or how they are morally, or by the customs of the place, and so on. It is always possible to clarify which statement is made by prefacing one's words with 'according to law' or by other devices. But most commonly we leave it to the context to clarify what exactly is being stated (and, of course, often we prefer not to disambiguate our meaning). It follows from these observations that while in the course of giving an account of the nature of law one may well engage in explaining the meaning of certain terms, the explanation of the nature of law cannot be equated with an analysis of the meaning of any term.

---

[12] It is not clear whether any philosopher of any stature ever supposed otherwise. Bentham's account is accompanied by a penetrating analysis of the semantic explanation of normative terms (see *Of Laws in General* (ed HLA Hart, London: Athlone Press, 1970) and Hart, *Essays on Bentham* (Oxford: Clarendon Press, 1982)). But its purpose is to show that his account of the law is semantically legitimate. It does not establish that he thought of it as an explanation of the meaning of the word 'law' in English. Clearly Hart never meant to offer a semantic analysis of the word 'law' (*The Concept of Law*, ch 1). It is strange that RM Dworkin, who did not make the mistake himself, thought that Hart and many others were guilty of it. For my own previous repudiations of this view see 'The Problem about the Nature of Law', ch 9 in *Ethics in the Public Domain* (rev edn, Oxford: Clarendon Press, 1995), among other places. Many other philosophers of law were less sensitive to the issue and did not discuss it directly. Yet the general character of their work would suggest that they did not think of themselves as providing a semantic analysis of the word 'law'. It would be strange to attribute such a view to Hobbes, or to Locke, or Kant or Hegel, for example.

What then is an account of the nature of law, of its essential properties? We are trying, I have suggested, to explain the nature of a certain
kind of social institution. This suggests that the explanation is part of
the social sciences, and that it is guided or motivated by the considerations which guide theory construction in the social sciences. In a way
this is true, but this way of making the point may encourage a misguided
understanding of the enterprise. It makes it sound as if some abstract
theoretical considerations determine the classification of social institutions, considerations like theoretical fruitfulness, simplicity of presentation, deductive or computational simplicity, or elegance.

Considerations like these may indeed be relevant when a classification, a typology, or a concept is introduced by academics for the purpose of facilitating their research or the presentation of its results. The
notion of law as designating a type of social institution is not, however, part of the scholarly apparatus of any learned discipline. It is
not a concept introduced by academics to help with explaining some
social phenomena. Rather it is a concept entrenched in our society's
self-understanding. It is a common concept in our society and one
which is not the preserve of any specialized discipline. It is used by each
and all of us to mark a social institution with which we are all, in various ways, and to various degrees, familiar. It occupies a central role in
our understanding of society, our own as well as other societies.

In large measure what we study when we study the nature of law is
the nature of our own self-understanding. The identification of a certain social institution as law is not introduced by sociologists, political
scientists, or some other academics as part of their study of society. It is
part of the self-consciousness of our society to see certain institutions as
legal. And that consciousness is part of what we study when we inquire
into the nature of law.

But why should we? Is it not our aim to study the nature of law, rather
than our culture and its concept of law? Yes and no. We aim to improve
our understanding of the nature of law. The law is a type of social institution, the type that is picked up—designated—by the concept of law.
Hence in improving our understanding of the nature of law we assume
an understanding of the concept of law, and improve it.

IV. Parochial or Universal?

At this point a new objection may be raised. Does not the fact that we
study the nature of an institution which is picked out by *our* concept of

law make the inquiry parochial rather than universal? Talk of *the* concept of law really means *our* concept of law. As has already been mentioned, the concept of law changes over time. Different cultures have different concepts of law. There is no one concept of law, and when we refer to the concept of law we just mean our concept. Therefore, to the extent that the inquiry is limited to the nature of law as understood in accordance with our concept of it it is a parochial study of an aspect of our culture rather than a universal study of the nature of law as such. Far from coming together, as has been suggested above, the study of the nature of law as such and of our self-understanding (in as much as it is encapsulated in our concept of law) are inimical to each other. Some people may develop the point further to the conclusion that there is no such thing as 'the nature of law as such'. To claim otherwise is to commit the mistake of essentialism, or of objectification. Others would merely conclude that the study of the nature of the thing (the law) and of our concept of it are not as closely related as has been suggested above, and that one must choose which one to pursue.

Common though this line of thought is, it is misguided. Think of it: we and other cultures have different concepts; not only different concepts of law. What makes some of them alternative concepts of law, whereas others are concepts of government, religion, tribes, or whatever but not of law? What accounts for the difference? What makes a concept 'the so and so concept of law' (eg 'the medieval concept of law')? Ignoring the occasions on which 'the concept of...' is used to refer to the common opinions which people held about the law (the medieval concept of law being the views about the law, its role and function, common in medieval Europe) different *concepts* of law are concepts of *law* in virtue of their relations to our concept of law. Most commonly these are relations of similarity (X's concept of law is a concept of a social institution very much like, though not quite the same as, what we understand by law), or of a common origin (our concept of law developed out of the medieval concept, etc). The point to note is that it is our concept which calls the shots: other concepts are concepts of law if and only if they are related in appropriate ways to our concept.

Let us accept that what we are really studying is the nature of institutions of the type designated by the concept of law. These institutions are to be found not only in our society, but in others as well. While *the concept* of law is parochial, ie not all societies have it, our inquiry is universal in that it explores *the nature* of law, wherever it is to be found. Even so the charge of parochialism is liable to reappear in a new form.

Is it not the case that the institution of law is to be found only in societies which have the concept of law (ie our concept of law)? Since it has been allowed earlier that the concept of law as we know it has developed in the West in modern times, and is certainly far from a universal feature of human civilization, a theory of law which concentrates on the nature of law, in the sense explained above, is relevant to modern Western societies only. It may be universal in a formal sense. In the philosophically stipulated sense of 'the nature of law' the inquiry applies to all the legal systems which ever existed or that could exist. But this way—my imagined objector goes on to say—of rebutting the charge of parochialism is a pyrrhic rebuttal. The inquiry, when successful, is universally valid for a narrow concept of law, the modern Western concept of law. It is relevant not to all legal systems, as the term is usually—and non-philosophically—understood, which include the law of the Aztecs, of the countries of medieval Europe, of the Roman Empire, or of China in the fifth century BC and so on. The philosophical inquiry would have to exclude those, as they do not conform to the modern, capitalist, or post-industrial, concept of law.

Put in this form the objection is based on a mistaken understanding of our concept of law. One way in which it has been changing over the last two to three centuries is to make it more inclusive and less parochial. As our knowledge of history and of the world has expanded, and as our interest in history and our interaction with other parts of the world have become more extensive, the concept of law has developed to be more inclusive. Admittedly, it responds not only to our interest in other societies, but also to our understanding of ourselves and our society, and the two may conflict. Features which seem to us central in ourselves and in our society may be lacking in other societies. Their importance to us in our societies tends to encourage forging more parochial concepts. To some this factor appears to be the only or the dominant factor influencing our concepts. This leads to further (or reformulated) objections to the universalist ambition of philosophical theories.

Some theorists take parochialism in their stride and allow it to fashion their theories. The outstanding example of a legal theory of this kind is RM Dworkin's. From the beginning he saw his theory as a theory of the law of the USA and of the UK. Of course it may be true of other legal systems as well. But it is not its declared ambition to be universal.[13]

---

[13] These comments are offered as an interpretation of a point on which Dworkin's views are not altogether clear.

One reason elaborated by Dworkin in justification of this modest ambition is the fact that the concept of law is part of the practice of law.[14] Dworkin has pointed out that courts of law are sometimes confronted with issues which force them to reflect about the nature and boundaries of the law. They may refer to philosophical theories in answering these questions, and their answers and arguments buttressing them are on a par with philosophical discussions of these issues. This is not to say that their answers and discussions are as good as philosophical theories. They may be better or worse. The point is that they are engaged in the same enterprise as philosophers. Their conclusions rival philosophical conclusions: if they disagree then one is wrong and the other may be right.

It is tempting to reinforce the point just made by adding that while often courts will not attend to theoretical disputes about the nature of law since nothing in contention between the parties turns (or was claimed to turn) on disagreements about the nature of law, nevertheless any court's decision presupposes some view or other about the nature of law. This seems to me to go beyond what the evidence warrants. The fact that if challenged to defend an action of mine I will have to advance theoretical arguments does not establish that I already have a theoretical view of one kind or another. I may have none, not even implicitly, and I may not be committed to any.[15] One cannot infer that a person has certain beliefs, or beliefs of a certain description, just because he should have them. And while the courts may be committed to the view that there is some way of justifying their decisions, they are not committed to any view about which way justification lies.

It is wiser, therefore, not to reinforce the observation that the courts sometimes engage in a theoretical argument about the nature of law with the further point that all their decisions presuppose a view about the nature of law. The observation itself, however, is correct and beyond dispute.[16] What lessons should we learn from them? Dworkin suggests that this establishes that law and legal philosophy are part of the same, self-reflective, practice. This implies that American legal philosophy is part of American law, that legal philosophy when studied in an American

[14] RM Dworkin, *Law's Empire* (Cambridge, Mass: Harvard University Press, 1986), ch 1.
[15] This matter turns in part on the pragmatic character of explanation (including justificatory explanations) which is discussed in the next chapter.
[16] During the 1960s countries of the British Commonwealth saw a series of decisions regarding the validity of coup d'état, secession and the like which took the courts deep into theoretical disputes, leading in turn to a spate of theoretical discussions in the journals.

university is related to legal philosophy as studied in Italy in the same way that property law studied in an American university relates to property law studied in Italy. They are studies of analogous parts of the law, but are basically very different enterprises: an account of property law or an aspect of it may be true of Italy and false of the USA. Similarly a theory about the nature of law may be true of the USA but false of Italy. If it is true of both countries this is a contingent result of some historical developments which could have been otherwise. Theories of law, in other words, are necessarily parochial.

Whether or not they are parochial, this argument does not prove that they are. Perhaps it is no exaggeration to say that any issue, from astrophysics to economics to biblical exegesis, can be relevant to some legal decision or another. This would not show that any of those studies are part of American law in America and of Chinese law in China. The fact that a certain theoretical issue is material to a court's decision would only show that the court should aim to get the matter right, to learn from the discipline concerned how things stand in the matter at issue. It does not show that by engaging in economic, sociological or biblical arguments courts can change the conclusions of those disciplines, that the fact that they come to some conclusion in these areas makes those conclusions true in economics or sociology, etc. Nor will this conclusion change if in some country or another once a court has taken a decision based on such grounds it would not be open to challenge on the ground that it got its economics, etc wrong.

All this is plain enough, but is it not different with legal theory? While the courts have no special authority in economics or political science, do they not have special authority regarding the concept of law? The answer is that it depends. Consider, by way of analogy, the same question raised about the notion of an undertaking. A case may turn on whether or not one person undertook to perform a service for another. Has the law authority to decide what counts as undertaking to do something? Yes and no. The courts have authority to decide when the law of their country would view an action as a binding undertaking. But the notion of an undertaking has life outside the law. And the court has no authority to decide what is an undertaking in that sense. I do not mean to say that it is precluded from forming a view on the matter, or from relying on that view. It may be required by law to form such a view since the plaintiff in a case may be entitled to relief only if the defendant has undertaken (in the ordinary sense of the word) to perform a service for him. The point I am urging is that if the court gets this wrong its decision would not change the nature of undertakings, any more than if it gets an economic argument wrong its decision can change economic theory.

If things look differently in the case of an undertaking than in economics this is because a mistaken decision of the court may be the first step towards the emergence of a special technical sense of undertaking in the legal system concerned. That may be so even if the court did not mean it that way, even if it meant simply to find out what is an undertaking in the ordinary sense of the word. It is the same with the concept of law as it is with the concept of an undertaking. Of course, unlike the concept of an undertaking the concept of law applies only to the law. But like the concept of an undertaking it is a common concept in our culture which applies not only to our law but to the law of other countries, now as well as in the past or the future. It also applies to law in fiction, and in hypothetical cases. In short it is not a concept regarding which the courts have special authority. When a decision turns on a correct elucidation of the concept the courts try to get it right, as they do when it is about an undertaking, or about an economic argument. If they fail this may lead to the emergence of a technical sense for the term in that legal system. But it will not lead to a change in the notion of law. The claim that a theory of law is parochial, since legal theory is part of legal practice, is misguided. Legal theory is not part of legal practice, at least not in the sense required to establish its parochial nature.

V. Can there be Law without the Concept of Law?

Another argument for the parochial nature of legal theory turns on the claim that there is no law in a society which does not have the concept of law. Since I have admitted that the concept of law (that is our concept of law) is parochial and that not all societies which had law also had our concept of law, it follows that not all of them had institutions recognized as law by our concept. A theory of law which aims to explain the nature of the institutions and practices which our concept of law recognizes as law is therefore only nominally universal. It applies to all that our concept recognizes as law, but our concept fails to recognize as law many legal systems for the reason that they did not have our concept of law, and there is no law without the concept of law.

We have to distinguish two versions of the argument. One claims that there cannot be law in a society which does not have a concept of law.

According to it societies which do have some concept of law can have institutions and practices which are clear instances of the concept of law (as we have it). The other, more radical version claims that only societies which have our concept of law can have institutions and practices which are instances of the concept of law that we have. To make its conclusion good the radical version of the objection has to show that no society which does not have our concept of law can have a legal system, as that institution is understood by our concept. That is an unlikely claim, which can be easily refuted by example, by simply pointing to some far-away society, say that of Egypt in the fourth Century BC, which did not have our concept of law, but had the institutions which that concept recognizes as legal.

Even the weaker claim—that there cannot be law in a society which does not have some concept of law—is probably mistaken. The rest of this section is devoted to an examination of this weaker claim. Remember the following three theses:

- First, that the concept of law (our concept) is local in the sense that while some societies have it, others do not.
- Second, that there is no law in a society which does not have a concept of law (though it need not have our concept).
- Third, that a successful theory of law, being a correct account of a type of institution designated by a concept of law, applies only to institutions which prevail in cultures which possess the concept of law which designates the type of institution the theory explains.

Together they lead to the conclusion that there are many valid theories of law, each applicable to a different type of social institution, picked out by a different concept of law. A theory of the institutions picked out by our concept of law applies only to the law in societies which have (or had) our concept of law.

I have already endorsed the first of these propositions. We undermine the strong version of the argument by rejecting the third premise. To refute the weak version one has to show that there is no reason to accept the second premise. Undermining the second premise also undermines the third, which presupposes it. So let us examine the second premise, and with it the conclusion that legal theory understood as the study of the nature of the institutions identified as law by the (ie our) concept of law is valid only of legal systems equipped with some concept of law. I will argue that it is not the case that only a society with a concept of law can be governed by law.

What would it be like for law to exist in a society which does not have a concept of law? It would mean that they would not think of its law as law. It is true that we have law and that we think of it as law. But is it not possible for a society which has a legal system not to be aware of it as a legal system? I will argue that it is.

This means that in legal theory there is a tension between the parochial and the universal. It is both parochial and universal. On the one hand it is parochial, for it aims to explain an institution designated by a concept that is a local concept, a product of modern Western civilization. On the other hand it is universal theory for it applies to law whenever and wherever it can conceivably be, and its existence does not presuppose the existence of its concept; indeed it does not presuppose the existence of any legal concept.

HLA Hart in *The Concept of Law* argued that it is necessary for a satisfactory account of law to explain how the law is perceived and understood by the people who live under it. To use his terminology—which in general I will avoid as it is open to diverse and confusing interpretations—he argued that a legal system cannot exist in a country unless at least part of its population has an internal attitude to the law, regards the law from the internal point of view, or accepts the law as a guide to its behaviour—these being alternative descriptions of the same attitude. This claim of Hart, perhaps the central claim of his theory of law, has since been widely accepted. But its meaning is much in dispute. I think that Hart was right to insist that it is in the nature of law that in general its existence is known to those subject to it, and that normally it plays a role in their lives.

I say 'normally' for it is of course possible for people to disregard the law, to be mindless of its existence. But that condition is abnormal not only, if at all, in being rare. It is abnormal because it is of the essence of law that it expects people to be aware of its existence and, when appropriate, to be guided by it. They may not be. But that marks a failure in the law. It shows that it is not functioning as it aspires to function.

I find nothing amiss in personalizing the law, as I just did in the previous paragraph. We do refer to the law as imposing requirements and duties, conferring rights and privileges, and so on. Such expressions are unexceptional. The law's actions, expectations, and intentions are its in virtue of the actions, expectations, and intentions of the people who hold legal office according to law, that is we know when and how the actions, intentions, and attitudes of judges, legislators, and other legal officials, when acting as legal officials, are to be seen as the actions, intentions, and expectations of the law. They, acting as officials, express the demand and the expectation that people be aware of the law and that they be guided by it.

Hart in describing the internal attitude which legal officials necessarily have, and which others are expected to have, strove to identify only those aspects of their attitude to the law which are essential to its existence. He saw no conflict between the fact that officials and others in every society with law adopt the internal point of view towards the law and the universal character of the law. And in a way he was right. There is no contradiction between the two. But I think that while his views are compatible with my emphasis on the parochial nature of the concept of law he was unaware of these implications.

The question is: does people's awareness of rules of law mean an awareness of them as rules or an awareness of them as rules of law? Need they, in other words, possess the concept of law in order to be members of a political community governed by law? Hart assumed, and surely he was right, that in our cultures the concept of law is available to all, that most people have a fairly good general grasp of it. He has identified certain features as the uncontroversial core of the common understanding of the concept of law. His own account of the concept merely deepens our understanding by drawing out some of the implications of the concept as it is commonly understood, the concept of law as we have it.

But our possession of the concept is logically independent of the fact that we live in a political community governed by law. We could have had the same concept had we lived in a state of nature. We might then have used the concept to understand the difference between the law-free society we inhabit and the condition of other countries which do live under legal systems, and the difference between the current state of our society and what it might have been or may become. Contrariwise it would seem that Hart is not committed to the view that to live in a society governed by law we need be aware of the concept of law, beyond an awareness of the rules which in fact constitute the law of our society.

By way of contrast Dworkin's theory of law assumes that an awareness of the concept of law is necessary for the existence of law in any society. For him the law is an interpretive practice which exists only in societies which are aware of the nature of that practice and of its interpretive character, and thus possess the concept of law.[17] In this, however,

---

[17] Though it is possible that all his theory requires is that those living in a society subject to law regard the law as instantiating some interpretive concept or another rather than the concept of law specifically.

Hart's position is the correct one. Our concept of law does not make an awareness of it in a society a precondition of that society being governed by law. I will illustrate this point with one example only.

Jewish religious rules and practices are rich and diverse. They did, at an earlier stage of their development, govern the life of independent Jewish communities, and, in more recent times, they governed many aspects of life in Jewish communities in many parts of the world. Whenever theocratic autonomous Jewish communities existed or may exist they would be subject to law, ie Jewish religious law. But the concept of law is not part of the Jewish religion, and where such communities existed in the past they often existed in societies whose members did not possess the concept of law. Jewish religious thought and doctrine encompass much more than law. They encompass what we regard as comprehensive systems of law, ethics, and religion, areas which though overlapping are also, in our eyes, distinct. To the Orthodox Jew of old there is no division within Judaic doctrines which captures the divisions indicated by 'our' concepts of law, religion, and ethics. Yet beyond doubt theocratic Jewish communities did have a legal system even though they lacked the concept of law, or at any rate some of them (those which had not learnt it from other cultures) lacked it.

I believe that much the same is true of some other religious systems. 'Our' concept of law is probably alien to the culture of Islamic theocracies, but it would be absurd to think that Iran, for example, does not have a legal system, or that its having a legal system depends on Iranians having acquired the concept of law before their Islamic revolution, or through their acquaintance with the law of other countries. Rather, the correct conclusion is that while the concept of law is itself a product of a specific culture, a concept which was not available to members of earlier cultures, this does not show that those cultures did not have law. The existence of law requires awareness by (at least some) members of the society of being guided by rules, awareness of disputes regarding the meaning of the rules, and regarding claims that they have been breached, being subject to adjudication by human institutions, and—in many, though not necessarily all cases—awareness that the rules, or some of them, are the product of deliberate rule-creation by some people or institutions. But none of these features is unique to the law. They are shared by it and many other social structures, such as religions, trade unions, and a variety of associations of many kinds. Therefore, awareness of these features does not presuppose awareness of them as aspects of a legal system. And there is nothing else in the concept of law which requires that people be aware of their institutional structure as a legal system in order for their institutions to constitute a legal system. Notice, however, that there is a discrepancy between my use of the example of Jewish religious law and the more abstract argument I provided. The argument rejected the second premise mentioned on p 37, that is the premise that law can exist only in a society which has some concept of law, on the ground that (1) the correct proposition that law can exist only in a society in which at least part of the population accepts its rules and is guided by it does not yield the second premise as a conclusion; and (2) that the example of Jewish law shows that our concept of law does apply to legal systems which do not have our concept of law. The example is not sufficient by itself to show that our concept of law identifies as legal systems practices existing in societies which had no concept of law whatsoever. That would be more difficult to show by example. The case rests on the absence of a reason to think otherwise, given the rest of the argument.

We can therefore conclude that the charge, or the ready admission, that a theory of law must be parochial, for it can apply only to countries which possess our concept of law, or to countries which possess some concept of law, is mistaken. The law can and does exist in cultures which do not think of their legal institutions as legal, and a theory of law aims to give an account of the law wherever it is found, including in societies which do not possess the concept of law.

VI. On the Alleged Impossibility of Understanding Alien Cultures

I have argued that while the concept of law is parochial, legal theory is not. Legal theory can only grow in cultures which have the concept of law. But its conclusions, if valid at all, apply to all legal systems, including those, and there are such, which obtain in societies which do not have the concept of law.

This conclusion has been criticized from a slightly different direction. The fact that concepts emerge within a culture at a particular juncture is often seen as a vindication of some radical philosophical thesis such as relativism, or post-modernism, or ethnocentrism. In particular it is taken to show our principled inability to understand, or at any rate to understand completely, alien cultures. In fact it shows little, certainly not that concepts can only apply to phenomena which exist in cultures which have those concepts. Consider, for example, the notion of 'the standard of living'. It may well not have been available to people in medieval Europe. But there is nothing in this fact to invalidate discussions of the effect of the Wars of the Roses on the standard of living in Lancashire. People would enjoy the same standard of living whether or not they were aware of the notion, or of the measurement of their own standard of living. The same is true of many other economic notions.

Some concepts are different. Arguably since gifts are gifts only if intentionally given *as such* there cannot be gifts among people who do not possess the concept of a gift. As we saw, something like this is true of rules. People are not guided by rules unless they are aware of them as rules. But, and that is the crucial point, they need not be aware of rules as legal rules in order to be guided by rules which are in fact legal.

On reflection there is nothing surprising in this. Of crucial importance is the fact that concepts like that of the law are essential not only to our understanding of the practices and institutions of our own societies, but also to our understanding of other societies. In our attempts to understand societies with cultures radically different from ours we encounter a conflict. On the one hand, to understand other societies we must master their concepts, for we will not understand them unless we understand how they perceive themselves. But, on the other hand, we cannot understand other cultures unless we can relate their practices and customs to our own. Their concepts will not be understood by us unless we can relate them to our own concepts. How can this conflict be resolved? It seems to land us in an impasse which forces us to admit the impossibility of truly or completely understanding alien cultures.

This pessimism is, however, unjustified. We can meet both conditions for understanding alien cultures. While there may be a tension between the need to understand them in terms of some of our concepts, even though they do not have those concepts, and the need to understand how they understand themselves, ie in terms of concepts which we do not have, there is no contradiction here. Both conditions can be fully met. Far from being irreconcilable they are interdependent. That is, the understanding of alien cultures requires possession of concepts which apply across the divide between us and them, concepts which can be applied to the practices of other cultures as well as to our own. Reliance on such concepts is necessary to make the alien cultures intelligible to us. They are required to enable us better to understand their concepts which we do not share.

Let us examine the argument to the contrary, the pessimistic argument. The fact that some cultures do not possess all of our concepts, and that they possess concepts which we do not have, makes them alien. If we need to rely on concepts which they do not possess in our attempt to understand them, as we commonly do, then our attempts are doomed to failure. They fail, the argument goes, to satisfy the other condition of understanding a culture, that is that one must understand how its members understood themselves. This condition requires, so the argument continues, understanding the alien culture from inside, that is using only concepts which were available to its members, only concepts that they used in understanding themselves.

Where does the pessimistic argument go wrong? It overlooks the ways in which we acquire many of the concepts that we muster. Concept acquisition often results from a combination of establishing, through explicit explanation or by observing how they are used by others, relations between them and other familiar concepts on the one hand, and learning their use by osmosis, by using them or observing their use, being set right by others when one makes a mistake, or, more commonly, observing through the reactions of others that one's use of the concept was not altogether happy. Let us call those two ways, often inter-related and not clearly distinguished in practice, learning by definition and learning through imitation. It is sometimes thought that some concepts are learnt one way and some another. Colour concepts are thought to be examples of concepts acquired by imitation, by ostension. Mathematical concepts, and generally abstract concepts are thought to be learnt through definitions. In fact it is reasonable to suppose that all our concepts which have use outside narrowly delimited groups of users and purposes of use[18] are learnt through a combination of both methods. To acquire the concept of red one needs to know that it is a colour concept, that it is a perceptual concept, that nothing can be both red and green all over, and other matters one is likely to learn partly through definitions. To acquire the number concept 'two' one needs to know that when two drops of water merge there is only one drop of water there, and to have other knowledge likely to be acquired partly by imitation.

I am not arguing that any single stage in the process of acquiring the concept, like the ones I mentioned, depends only on one or the other of the two methods. Most, perhaps all, of them can succeed through either

---

[18] Such as the names of widgets in the building trade, or some theoretical terms in science.

method. I am saying, however, that it is humanly impossible to acquire concepts generally except through a combination of both methods.

Some people who share these views about concept acquisition may find in them further argument for the pessimistic conclusion about our alleged inability to understand alien cultures. But this seems to me to overlook the role of imagination and thought experiments in the process of learning and understanding. In principle we can understand alien cultures because we can acquire their concepts, provided we have a substantial enough body of data to allow learning by imitation, either real imitation of one who visits or joins the alien culture, or through imaginative and sympathetic engagement with and reflection on reports of the nature of the culture and its habits, and other historical data. Naturally the material available about that culture may be insufficient. It may leave gaps in our mastery of its concepts and our understanding of its ways. But these are practical, not principled, limitations.

Our understanding of alien cultures will, however, remain incomplete until we can relate their concepts to ours. Why is this a necessary condition of understanding? After all, it may well be that none of the members of the alien culture understands our culture. If they can understand their own culture, as surely they can, without relating it to ours why cannot we do the same? The short answer is: because we, unlike them, know and understand our culture. Given our situation we cannot understand the alien culture without relating it to ours. Here is an analogy: Native French speakers have complete mastery of French, even if they have no knowledge of English. But native English speakers who study French as a foreign language cannot understand it if they do not know what 'un homme', 'une maison', 'plaisir', and so on, mean in English.[19]

There is an asymmetry here between one's knowledge of French and one's knowledge of English. Only when the English speakers' command of French and its relations to English reaches a very high level of subtlety and expertise, or when it is reflective knowledge leading them to reflect about the similarities and the differences between the languages does it becomes appropriate to say that their understanding of English is improved by their deep knowledge of French. For ordinary English speakers who study French for practical purposes and are not inclined

---

[19] These are examples, which do not imply that our native English speakers must have a perfect ability to translate French into English to qualify as French speakers—only that they need to have some such ability.

to reflect on its nature, no such benefit occurs: That is, their knowledge of French is improved by their growing ability to translate French into English. But their knowledge of English is not affected. This asymmetry is the main manifestation of what I will call 'the route dependence' of understanding in general. We understand new things by relating them to what we already understand, even though had we started somewhere else we could have gained an understanding of those things without understanding how they relate to what we in fact know. Moreover, while in some ways, and under some conditions our newly acquired understanding can deepen or improve what we understood already, it need not do so.

The route-dependence of understanding is sometimes stated by saying that we understand whatever we understand from our personal 'point of view'. While there is nothing wrong in applying this overused expression in this context, it can have unfortunate connotations. For some people it carries associations of blinkers, of limitations and distortions. If we can understand alien cultures *only* from our point of view it shows—or so it is alleged—that we do not understand them as they really are, that our understanding is imperfect, and distorted. After all, we understand the alien cultures through *our* modern Western perspective, relying on *our* notions and on *our* knowledge of history and of many cultures not known to members of the cultures which we are studying. So our understanding of their cultures differs from their own understanding of their own cultures, and cannot be altogether objective, or perfect, or something like that.

The example of a native English speaker acquiring French was meant to disprove that thought. To be sure, it is difficult to acquire perfect command of a second language, which is learnt after one has acquired one's first language. But it is possible in principle, and in practice as the example of people like Conrad and Nabokov shows. To master a second language one has to relate it to one's first language, whereas a native speaker of that second language need know no other. Nevertheless, in principle both can have perfect command of that language. I have explained the fact that while they arrive at the same destination only one of them must, to get there, know how what is to him the second language relates to his first by saying that understanding (and explanation) are route-dependent. But until we understand why this is so we cannot be confident that route-dependence does not affect the possibility of perfect knowledge, or its objectivity. This is a topic for another occasion. Let us take stock of the conclusions tentatively arrived at so far.

We have already travelled some way from the goal of establishing the possibility of legal theory. That was made necessary because the challenge to the possibility of theory depends on assumptions with much wider ramifications. Now we have to travel even further afield. To establish the possibility of a theory of law, a theory which explains the nature of law, we need to examine some issues concerning the function of explanation. The aim of the examination would be to vindicate the conclusion tentatively arrived at in this chapter (at the end of the previous section). Namely, that legal theory has universal application, that it—when successful—provides an account of the nature of law, wherever and whenever it is to be found. The objectivity and universality of the theory of law is not affected by the fact that the concept of law (which is our concept of law) is parochial and not shared by all the people nor by all the cultures, which live or lived under the law.

That conclusion was based on the claim that to understand an alien culture and its institutions we need to understand both how its members understand themselves, and how their concepts, practices, and institutions relate to ours. This means that to understand alien cultures we must have concepts whose application is not limited by the boundaries of our culture, which apply to alien cultures as well to our own. I neither have argued nor will argue that our culture has the intellectual resources which make it possible, with good will and sympathetic imagination, to understand alien cultures. I take it for granted that that is so. I have argued that if we have these resources, and if such understanding is possible then the concept of law is one such concept. I have argued for that by the use of the example of theocratic societies, and the fact that we apply the concept of law to their institutional arrangements. The concept of law is among the culture-transcending concepts. It is a concept which picks out an institution which exists even in societies which do not have such a concept.

That does not establish that a theory of law is in principle possible, or that if it is possible it can achieve objective knowledge, rather than provide a blinkered way of understanding those alien cultures, albeit the best understanding which can be achieved from our subjective point of view. To establish positively the possibility of a theory of law we need to examine the nature of explanation and of objectivity. The reflections here offered do, however, remove some misunderstandings which sometimes lead people to doubt the possibility of such a theory.

3

Two Views of the Nature of the Theory of Law: A Partial Comparison[1]

In *Law's Empire*, Ronald Dworkin advanced a new theory of law, complex and intriguing. He calls it law as integrity. But in some ways the more radical and surprising claim he makes is that not only were previous legal philosophers mistaken about the nature of law, they were also mistaken about the nature of the philosophy of law or jurisprudence. Perhaps it is possible to summarize his main contentions on the nature of jurisprudence in three theses. First, jurisprudence is interpretive: 'General theories of law...aim to interpret the main point and structure of legal practice' (*LE*, 90).[2] Second, legal philosophy cannot be a semantic account of the word 'law'. Legal philosophers 'cannot produce useful semantic theories of law' (ibid). Third, legal philosophy or jurisprudence 'is the general part of adjudication, silent prologue to any decision at law' (ibid).

Of these, the only surprising aspect of the first thesis is that it should be thought new and different from what many contemporary legal philosophers took themselves to be doing. An interpretation of something is an explanation[3] of its meaning. Many if not all legal philosophers think of themselves as explaining the essential features of legal practices, and explaining the relations between them and related phenomena such as other forms of social organization, other social practices, and morality. HLA Hart explained in the Postscript to *The Concept of Law* that his aim was 'to give an explanatory and clarifying account of law as a complex social and political institution with a

[1] I am grateful to Andrei Marmor, Grant Lamond, Penelope Bulloch, and Timothy Endicott for very helpful comments on a draft of this chapter.
[2] *LE* refers to Ronald Dworkin, *Law's Empire* (Cambridge, Mass: Belknap Press, 1986). Page numbers in parentheses are from this 1986 edition.
[3] Except that interpretations through performance (of music, a play, etc) display rather than explain the meaning of what they interpret.

rule-governed (and in that sense "normative") aspect'.[4] In other words, he was seeking to interpret the complex social institution the law is. If Hart and others did not make as extensive a use of 'interpretation' as Dworkin does, this is in part because fashions dictate the use of terms, and because they may well have wished to avoid being associated with theories that, in their eyes, misconstrued the nature of interpretation.[5]

Dworkin's conception of legal philosophy surprises not in regarding its task as interpretive, but in the arguments he deploys to support it, in particular the argument he dubbed the 'semantic sting'.[6] The argument purports to establish the second thesis, that is, a theory of law cannot be an explanation of the meaning of the word 'law'. Until Dworkin published his semantic sting argument, many, including myself, took this second thesis to be as firm and as uncontroversial as anything in legal philosophy at the time. It was, therefore, surprising that Dworkin saw a need to argue for it, and even more surprising that he thought that in doing so he was rebutting the conceptions of legal philosophy endorsed by many philosophers who did not think of themselves as in the business of explaining the meaning of the word 'law'.[7]

It seemed that no one need pay much attention to the semantic sting. It may be a sting, but an idle one. It stings no one. Thus, Hart starts his reply by simply denying that the argument applies to his theory:

Though in the first chapter *of Law's Empire* I am classed with Austin as a seman-tic theorist and so as deriving a plain-fact positivist theory of law from the meaning of the word 'law', and suffering from the semantic sting, in fact noth-ing in my book or in anything else I have written supports such an account of my theory. Thus, my doctrine that developed municipal legal systems contain a rule of recognition specifying the criteria for the identification of the laws

---

[4] HLA Hart, Postcript, *The Concept of Law* (Oxford: Clarendon Press, 1994) 239.

[5] In one of the best studies of Hart's work, DN MacCormick has described Hart's internal point of view, reliance on which was central to his methodological innovation, as 'hermeneutic'. See *H.L.A. Hart* (London: Arnold, 1981) 37–40. I remember a conversa-tion with Hart in which it was clear that he saw nothing wrong with the description. He was more ambiguous about the attractiveness of the word.

[6] His other argument, consisting in a new and challenging account of the nature of interpretation, shows not that other theorists did not see their accounts as explanations of the meaning of—ie as interpretations of—social practices, but that they did not share his understanding of interpretation. I will not discuss Dworkin's own account of interpret-ation in the present chapter.

[7] By the time the book was published, Dworkin was aware of the fact that Hart and others did not think of themselves as explaining the meaning of 'law'. Nevertheless, he persisted in thinking that that was exactly what Hart was doing. Cf. Dworkin, *Law's Empire*, above n 2, at 418 n 29.

which courts have to apply may be mistaken, but I nowhere base this doctrine on the mistaken idea that it is part of the meaning of the word 'law' that there should be such a rule of recognition in all legal systems.[8]

But one must wonder why Dworkin did not take this answer, of which, as I pointed out, he was aware, as sufficient. Hart himself must have puzzled over this, and, as the rest of his reply in the Postscript shows, he realized that the matter is not that straightforward.

In this chapter my aim is to explain (1) why Dworkin was wrong to think that Hart and others were concerned with the meaning of the word 'law'; (2) why nevertheless if the semantic sting is a good argument against explanations of the meaning of the word 'law' it is also a good argument against any explanation of the concept of law, including that which Hart provides; and (3) why it is a bad argument. My reason for this last conclusion will be different from Hart's. Hart's response is to deflect the argument: it may sting, but I (Hart) am not its target. I agree with Dworkin (though not entirely for his reasons) that if the argument is good then Hart's explanation of law is stung by it. I do not think, however, that the argument is valid. I will then (4) explain some mistakes that may have led Dworkin to endorse his third thesis about the nature of legal philosophy, namely the thesis that jurisprudence is a silent prologue to any legal decision.

I. Philosophy of Language in the Service of Legal Philosophy

At its most fundamental, legal philosophy is an inquiry into the nature of law, and the fundamental features of legal institutions and practices. Yet some writers think that it is, at least in part, an inquiry into the semantic meaning of words, or of some words, such as 'law' or 'rights'. Why do they think so and to what extent are they right?

The first point to emphasize is that our question is about the relevance and role of questions about the meaning of words in legal philosophy, not about the relevance of all questions of meaning. 'Meaning' is sometimes used to mean point or value. 'What is the meaning of law?' can mean 'What is the point or value of law?' This is what 'meaning' means in 'the meaning of life'. Alternatively, meaning is often used to refer

---

[8] Hart, *The Concept of Law*, above n 4, at 246.

to content. 'What did he mean?' means something like: 'What did he say?', 'What was the content of his utterance?' 'What is the meaning of this law?' can mean 'What is the content of this law? Or what is its significance, its aims or likely consequences?'[9] When referring to semantics I will use the term narrowly to refer to the study of the meaning of words, phrases, sentences, and other linguistic elements.[10]

How, then, did Hart see the relevance of semantics, and philosophy of language generally, to legal philosophy? He thought of it as central to his investigation. His philosophical outlook was formed at the time when many regarded Russell's theory of descriptions as a paradigm of philosophical explanation. The theory of descriptions 'solved' the problem of the reference of definite descriptions while avoiding the need to postulate fictional or other non-existing objects. The statement 'The present king of France is bald' is not *about* a non-existing king (and how can we tell whether the non-existing king is or is not bald?). It is simply the false statement that there is one and only one person who is both king of France and bald.

Eventually, Russell's account was challenged by Strawson, and later by others. The truth of Russell's account does not matter. What matters is that it showed how logical analysis can solve an ontological mystery. Moreover, the mystery was deemed highly relevant to the philosophy of law, for law is overpopulated by mysterious objects such as rights and duties, corporations and states, and many more. This was the point at which, for Hart, Russell's theory touched base with Bentham's account of fictions, and of rights, etc. In short, the motivation was an endorsement of naturalism (though not under that name) according to which the only things there are (or the only things whose existence has duration) are things located in space, knowledge about which is gained from the natural sciences, or at any rate is subject to correction by them. Naturalism created the problem of how to understand legal notions such as rights, duties, and corporations. Logic provided the answer, or more precisely it provided the programme—that is, the faith—that the answers will be found in that way. The same motivation and the same

---

[9] When I remarked that interpretation is the explanation of the meaning of its object, I used 'meaning' broadly to include non-semantic meaning. Explaining the meaning of words ('bachelor' means an unmarried male, etc) is never an interpretation, and explaining the literal meaning of sentences only given some special circumstances.

[10] In that narrow sense of 'semantics', one needs more than semantics to answer questions of content. That when he said 'I wish I were dead' he meant that he is very unhappy, and cannot see a way out, is not something we can learn from the meaning of the words or the sentence uttered (by itself) nor from rules for its use (alone).

hope dominated the work of many legal philosophers in the middle of the twentieth century.

But logic is not semantics, nor is it the philosophy of language, you may say. However, soon after Russell's important work the emphasis shifted from logic to language and to the philosophy of language. The notorious linguistic turn in twentieth-century philosophy led to a reinterpretation of logic, which to a degree came to be absorbed in either mathematics or the theories of language. We can see how the theory of descriptions is part of the theory of language; in Chomskyan terminology it shows that the surface structure of sentences including definite descriptions is not their deep structure.

In the early years of his career, Hart sought to find help particularly in the then brand-new theory of speech acts, developed by JL Austin.[11] Hart believed that various problems with explaining responsibility would be dissolved once we allowed for non-assertoric use of language.[12] He also believed that the problems about the ontological standing of legal 'things' such as law, rights, and corporations, which troubled Bentham and many others, can be dissolved with the judicious application of speech-act theory.[13] By the time Hart published *The Concept of Law* many of these hopes had receded. But his faith in the benefits for legal analysis of learning the lessons of speech-act theory is manifested in his way of understanding legal statements as statements from what he called the internal point of view.

His view on this point derives as much from the attempts by Stevenson, and later RM Hare, to apply linguistic analysis to moral utterances as from the persisting influence of JL Austin. Both Stevenson and Hare made their respectively emotivist and prescriptivist accounts of moral utterances more plausible by allowing that, apart from pure assertions and pure expressions of emotions (in Stevenson's case), or prescriptions (in Hare's case), there are utterances that combine both. Hart's legal statements from an internal point of view are one such case of a hybrid statement: stating how things are under the law, while endorsing or expressing an endorsement of the law at the same time. The problem Hart sought to solve in this way was the problem of the relations

---

[11] In part the same approach was supported by Wittgenstein's reflections on the variety of language games. For Hart's comment on those years, see *Essays in Jurisprudence and Philosophy* (Oxford: OUP, 1983) 2–3.

[12] 'The Ascription of Responsibility and Rights' (1948/9) 49 *Proc. Aristotelian Soc.* 171 later disavowed by him.

[13] 'Definition and Theory in Jurisprudence', repr. in *Essays*, above n 11.

between law and morality in the face of two philosophical beliefs: first, his doubts about the objectivity of ethics and of all evaluative judgements, and second, his belief in the objectivity of law. The objectivity of the law is accounted for by his social-practice-based explanation of the existence of the law and its content. The non-objectivity of morality and of all evaluative judgements is compatible with the fact that the evaluative component of legal judgments (which according to Hart need not be a moral evaluation) is their (as it were 'subjective') expression of an endorsement of (rather than assertion of the value of) the law.[14] This enables Hart to remain true to a naturalist view of the world, and to an empiricist epistemology, and yet to reject the reductive accounts of legal statements advocated by Bentham and his followers, including both American and Scandinavian realists, who regarded statements of law as factual statements about commands, or sanctions, and so on.

There are probably no general lessons to learn from the story I have told, but it strikes me as a sad one. Very little seems to have been gained in all of Hart's forays into philosophy of language. The problems with the explanation of responsibility, legal agents such as corporations, the nature of rights and duties, the relations between law and morality—none of them was solved nor their solution significantly advanced by the ideas borrowed from philosophy of language. Moreover, the reason for that was not that Hart borrowed bad ideas from the philosophy of language, nor that he did not understand properly the ideas he borrowed. Essentially the fault was in the philosophical analysis of the problems which speech-act theory and other ideas from the philosophy of language were meant to solve. Hart's failure on all the points I mentioned resulted from his adherence to naturalism and to empiricist epistemology, and his rejection of evaluative objectivity.

You may feel that I have been disingenuous in overlooking, or disregarding, the most obvious source of the dependence of jurisprudence on philosophy of language, namely the web of issues to do with interpretation. Interpretation, however, is a bigger subject, belonging to the theory of understanding of action, of cultures, and of their products. It is not a topic that philosophy of language by itself can explain. Still,

---

[14] My claim is not that Hart's analysis of legal statements and utterances is incompatible with belief in the objectivity of value and of morality. It is that the plausibility of the analysis depends on the rejection of the objectivity of value and morality. Once their objectivity is admitted there is no reason for accepting Hart's analysis rather than the view that legal statements and utterances are just like all other statements.

interpretation gives rise to problems with which philosophy of language can help, notably the problems arising out of vagueness.

None of this means that legal philosophers can avoid philosophy of language, or that they cannot be led into error by supporting misguided views in semantics. But possibly philosophy of language and semantics can help primarily by providing clarifications where misunderstanding of language or its use may lead to an error. By and large, as long as in one's deliberation about the nature of law and its central institutions one uses language without mistake, there is little that philosophy of language can do to advance one's understanding.

II. Is the Question of the Nature of Law a Question of the Meaning of 'Law'?

It is time to turn to our first topic: does the question about the nature of law itself—that is, when taken in its most general form—call for significant help from semantics? As mentioned, until recently many writers, myself included, assumed that it does not. Hart and Dworkin were among the clearest in repudiating the idea that it does. However, recently Stavropoulous[15] has offered a revisionist interpretation of Dworkin, arguing that his theory can be understood as an explanation of the meaning of 'law', and Dworkin may have come to accept the same or a similar view.[16] That view is not without initial plausibility. After all, a theory about the nature of law attempts to elucidate a concept, the concept of law, and what is the elucidation of a concept if not an explanation of its meaning? And what could that be if not the explanation of the meaning of the concept-word?[17]

But what is the word the meaning of which is explained by the explanation of the concept of law? It is not an explanation of the meaning of the word 'law', which applies to many things, scientific laws, mathematical laws, divine laws, and others to which the concept of law, the one the explanation of which legal philosophy is after, does not apply. But, it may be claimed, the explanation of that concept of law

---

[15] See N Stavropoulos, *Objectivity in Law* (Oxford: Clarendon Press, 1996), 129–36. For a conflicting view, see K Kress, 'The Interpretive Turn' (1987) 97 *Ethics* 834, 855 ff.

[16] To judge from conversations with him, and from a draft of an unpublished reply to Hart's Postscript.

[17] I should make it clear that this is not Dworkin's reason for regarding the question as a semantic one. I will come to his reason later.

is *part* of the explanation of the meaning of the word 'law' or 'the law'. Perhaps the explanation of the meaning of the word 'law' consists in a list of all the different kinds of law to which the word applies, the laws studied by jurisprudence being among them, and jurisprudence studies that part of the meaning of the word. Alternatively, perhaps the word has different, albeit cognate, meanings, and jurisprudence explains one of them. Perhaps. Though it is interesting to note that it may be otherwise. It may be that the word is univocal, and is susceptible of a general explanation: 'laws', let us say, being general rules of some permanence, or general rules giving rise to a degree of necessity ('given the law, it must be thus and thus'). 'The law' may refer to the situation obtaining under some system of laws. If so, then the law studied by jurisprudence is just one instance of law, a species of law, and does not merit special mention in the explanation of the meaning of the word 'law'. In the definition of a genus we do not refer to its species.

Perhaps concepts need not be associated that closely with words after all. The following is a 1985 example of the use of the word 'concept' I found in the *Oxford English Dictionary*: 'We aim to sell a total furnishing concept based on the "one pair of eyes" principle.' This illustrates a contemporary use of the word to mean something like 'a general notion or idea, esp. in the context of marketing and design; a "theme", a set of matching or coordinated items, of e.g. furniture, designed to be sold together. Chiefly advertisers' jargon.' Plainly, we are not interested in this use of the notion. But the chief meaning of 'concept' is not unrelated. It is, in its logical and philosophical use, 'an idea of a class of objects, a general notion or idea'—or so the *OED* tells us. There is nothing here about necessarily having a distinctive word, which in at least one of its meanings expresses that concept and nothing else. The context, rather than the use of a word, may be part of what indicates that the concept of law being talked about is the one we are interested in. The context, rather than any special linguistic device may—or may not—indicate whether the law talked about is that of a state rather than a moral law, etc. While we can do little with language without words, we can express in words concepts and ideas for which we have no specific words or phrases.[18]

We may suspend the question whether the explanation of the concept of law explains the meaning of any word. Possibly in explaining concepts we encounter many of the problems we face in explaining

---

[18] Even when we count words with several meanings as several words, one for each meaning.

semantic meanings. What, then, counts as an explanation of a concept? It consists in setting out some of its necessary features, and some of the essential features of whatever it is a concept of. In our case, it sets out some of the necessary or essential features of the law.

Broadly speaking, the explanation of a concept is the explanation of that which it is a concept of. But this statement has to be qualified, and clarified. Different concepts can apply to the same object or to the same property: equilateral triangles are also equiangular triangles, and the property of being an equilateral triangle is necessarily such that whatever possesses it also has the property of being an equiangular triangle. Each concept picks out its object or property via a different aspect of it. An explanation of a concept involves explaining the feature through which it applies to its object or property, but also explaining more broadly the nature of the object or property that it is a concept of. This does not mean providing a comprehensive explanation of the nature of that of which it is a concept—explanations are context-sensitive. An explanation is a good one if it consists of true propositions that meet the concerns and the puzzles that led to it, and that are within the grasp of the people to whom it is (implicitly or explicitly) addressed.

You may say that, taken in that sense, explanations of concepts, inasmuch as they include explanations of (the puzzling aspects of) what the concept is a concept of, are more than just explanations of the concepts involved, narrowly conceived. However, Hart and others, when they offered explanations of the concept of law, or the concept of mind, or others, understood conceptual explanations in that wider sense; and therefore, to understand and evaluate their methodology I will use the notion as they did.

It is essential to remember, however, that *having a concept* can fall well short of a thorough knowledge of the nature of the thing it is a concept of. People have a concept if they can use it correctly in normal circumstances.[19] Having a concept in that sense is compatible with a shallow and defective understanding of its essential features, and of the nature of what it is a concept of. Hence, while some ordinary explanations of a concept may aim at making people competent users of it, a philosophical explanation has different aims. It assumes that they are

---

[19] Perfect command of a concept implies being able to use it correctly in all possible circumstances. But not only is that a condition which in fact few achieve, it gives rise to theoretical difficulties. One who has perfect command of a concept can make mistakes in its application or use. But the boundary between a mistake about the concept and a mistake about its application is vague, as is its theoretical nature.

competent users, and it aims at improving their understanding of the concept in one respect or another.[20]

Should explanations of concepts set out necessary and sufficient conditions for their application? Sometimes this stronger condition is objected to on the ground that one can rarely state necessary and sufficient conditions for the application of interesting concepts. This objection seems to me to spring from exaggerated expectations of what necessary and sufficient conditions can provide, leading to unjustified pessimism about their availability. They can, for example, be very vague. Possibly it is a necessary and sufficient condition of being a good person that one is like Jesus. But this explanation of the concept, even if true, is not necessarily instructive and helpful. Possibly, in order to know in what ways Jesus was a good person, one needs an understanding of the concept in the first place. Explanations can more often than is sometimes supposed provide necessary and sufficient conditions for the application of the concept. Nevertheless, it is a mistake to believe that all good explanations must do so.

First, some essential characteristics of some concepts are neither necessary nor sufficient conditions for their application. They may be defeasible conditions for their application. Second, to insist that conceptual explanations provide necessary and sufficient conditions is to concentrate excessively on the distinctive features of concepts, overlooking the importance of other features. An explanation of 'a human being' as 'a rational animal (ie one belonging to a species of rational animals)' may well provide necessary and sufficient conditions for the application of the concept. But it is false to conclude that human beings' rational nature is 'more important' or more crucial to their understanding than the fact that they are sexual animals, for example, even though they are not unique in their sexuality as they are in their rationality.

A third doubt about the suitability of the necessary-and-sufficient-condition requirement for good explanations is that it misses out on an important part of the explanatory task. Conceptual explanations not only explain the conditions for correct application of a concept ('an act of torture is an infliction of pain or suffering for its own sake or to obtain some benefit or advantage') but also its connections with others ('torture is worse than murder'). We explain concepts in part by locating them in

---

[20] These remarks about the difference between philosophical explanations of concepts and the conditions for having concepts are consistent with and parallel C Peacocke's distinction between possession and attribution conditions for concepts: *A Study of Concepts* (Cambridge, Mass: MIT Press, 1992) 27–33.

a conceptual web. These aspects of conceptual explanations can be said to be statements of conditions for the application of the concept only by stretching the idea of a condition for application.

Finally, the fourth objection to the necessary-and-sufficient-condition view of conceptual explanation is that it results from a false picture of what explanations seek to achieve. In particular, it is associated with the view that, while one can partially explain a concept through necessary or through sufficient conditions for its application, only a list of necessary and sufficient conditions will provide a complete explanation. But concepts can have more than one set of necessary and sufficient conditions for their application, and they may have many other conditions that do not readily fall into place as part of sets of necessary and sufficient conditions. If there were a complete explanation it would consist of the minimal finite list of essential features of the concept, possession of which entails possession of all its essential features. There need not be such explanations regarding all concepts. There is certainly no reason to aspire to provide them. They may resemble telephone directories in being long lists devoid of interest. Explanations are of puzzling or troubling aspects of concepts, and they are therefore almost always 'incomplete'.

One important point reinforces the previous one. There is no uniquely correct explanation of a concept, nothing which could qualify as *the* explanation of the concept of law. There can be a large number of correct alternative explanations of a concept. Not all of them will be equally appropriate for all occasions. Appropriateness is a matter of relevance to the interests of the expected or intended public, appropriateness to the questions which trouble it, to the puzzles which confuse it. These vary, and with them the appropriateness of various explanations. The appropriateness, aptness, or success of explanations presupposes their truth. But the truth of an explanation is not enough to make it a good explanation. To be good it has also to be appropriate, that is (1) responding to the interests of its public and (2) capable of being understood for what it is by its public (should they be minded to understand it).

The relativity of good explanations to the interests and the capacities of their public makes them ephemeral and explains why philosophy has a never-ending task. It also helps explain away the impression that philosophy is forever engaged in a fruitless debate on unsolvable questions. The shifting kaleidoscope of explanations, which is the history of philosophy, has that character, at least in part, because of the shifting interests of its public. It is important to emphasize that there is nothing in the relativity of good explanations to their public to threaten the non-relativity of truth.

John Austin thought that, necessarily, the legal institutions of every legal system are not subject to—that is, do not recognize—the jurisdiction of legal institutions outside their system over them. (I am somewhat reinterpreting his claim here.[21]) Kelsen believed that necessarily constitutional continuity[22] is both necessary and sufficient for the identity of a legal system. We know that both claims are false. The countries of the European Union recognize, and for a time the independent countries of the British Empire recognized, the jurisdiction of outside legal institutions over them, thus refuting Austin's theory. And the law of most countries provides counter-examples to Kelsen's claim.[23] I mention these examples not to illustrate that legal philosophers can make mistakes, but to point to the susceptibility of philosophy to the winds of time. So far as I know, Austin's and Kelsen's failures were not made good. That is, no successful alternative explanations were offered. In spite of this there is no great flurry of philosophical activity to plug the gap. Rather, the problem that their mistaken doctrines were meant to explain, namely the problem of the identity and continuity of legal systems, lost its appeal to legal philosophers, who do not mind leaving it unsolved. Interest has shifted elsewhere.

III. The Semantic Sting

Dworkin's semantic sting argument is meant to show that certain concepts cannot be given a semantic account.[24] In particular, Dworkin

---

[21] To be precise, his claim was that they do not habitually obey the commands, ie laws, of such institutions. That condition, strictly understood, would mean that they are not disposed to obey, do not have a habit of obeying.

[22] Two laws are constitutionally continuous if either they derive their validity from the same authorizing norm (directly or indirectly) or one of them is a basic norm and the other derives from it.

[23] Most of the countries that gained their independence from Britain and France after the Second World War became independent without a break in constitutional continuity. On the other hand, most countries absorb breaches in constitutional continuity without much effect on their identity. In Britain the loss of the Great Seal in 1688 and the House of Lords' Practice Statement of 1966 are sometimes mentioned as examples.

[24] Strictly speaking, this sentence is false. Dworkin says (*LE*, 45) 'I shall call the semantic sting the argument I have just described', and that is 'the argument that unless lawyers and judges share factual criteria about the grounds of law there can be no significant thought or debate about what the law is' (*LE*, 44). I believe that I follow most readers

concludes that legal theory cannot provide a semantic account of 'law' (*LE*, 45–46). I argued before that the conclusion is right, for an account of the concept of law is not an account of the meaning of the word 'law'. However, this is not Dworkin's reason for the conclusion, and as expressed his conclusion seems to rest on a verbal misunderstanding. To say of an account that it is a semantic account or explanation does not characterize the type of explanation it gives, except by identifying its object: it is an explanation of the meaning of a word, or some other linguistic component. There is no reason to think that Dworkin believes that the meaning of the word 'law' cannot be explained. If so, then the conclusion of his argument should be not that there is no semantic explanation of 'law', but that a particular type of semantic explanation is misguided. As I mentioned, Dworkin may have come to the view that his conclusion should be rephrased. He seems willing to regard his own theory as a semantic account of the word 'law': it is an interpretive explanation of the meaning of the word. As revised, the semantic sting argument claims that certain words, including the word 'law', cannot be explained by criterial semantics.

What is criterial semantics? It claims that 'we follow shared rules...in using any word: these rules set out criteria that supply the word's meaning' (*LE*, 31). Later we learn by implication that the criteria set conditions for the correct application of the words the meaning of which they define.[25] As I argued, an explanation of the concept of law is not a semantic account of anything, but that does not show that the semantic sting argument does not apply to it. Arguably, it applies to explanations of many concepts, whether or not they are associated with concept-words. To make the argument apply to the law we need to reformulate it to apply beyond the explanation of the meanings of words.

---

of Dworkin in taking the sting to refer not to the argument which he finds mistaken, but to his own argument, which is meant to refute the mistaken argument, and exhibit its absurdity. In any case, the quotation above cannot refer to the issue of how to explain the meanings of words or of concepts, since it incorporates the claim that the law is identified by factual criteria, which is not part of that dispute.

[25] Eg 'Semantic theories suppose that lawyers and judges use mainly the same criteria...in deciding when propositions of law are true or false; they suppose that lawyers actually agree about the grounds of law' (*LE*, 33). Dworkin nowhere limits the rules to conditions of application in the narrow sense, ie conditions under which statements of the form 'it is the law that...' are true. Even though his discussion gravitates in that direction, we should remember that it is meant to apply to an explanation by reference to shared rules that provide criteria for the meaning of the word. Like all explanations, criterial explanations are successful to the degree that they respond to the interests that prompted them.

'A criterial explanation' of a concept, let us say, (1) states a rule setting out conditions for the (correct) use of a concept; and (2) is a true explanation by virtue of the fact that it is a correct statement of the conditions for the correct use of the concept actually used by those who use it.[26]

Dworkin's conclusion that certain concepts, the concept of law among them, cannot be given a criterial explanation rests on the claim that the application of criterially explained concepts cannot be subject to dispute regarding what he calls 'pivotal cases'. Therefore, where, as in the case of the law, the application of a concept can be disputed in pivotal cases, the concept is not susceptible to criterial explanation.

What are pivotal cases? We have to distinguish, Dworkin explains,

two kinds of disagreements, the distinction between borderline cases and test-ing or pivotal cases. People sometimes do speak at cross-purposes in the way the borderline defense describes. They agree about the correct tests for applying some word in what they consider normal cases but use the word somewhat dif-ferently in what they all recognize to be marginal cases.... Sometimes, however, they argue about the appropriateness of some word or description because they disagree about the correct tests for using the word or phrase on any occasion. We can see the difference by imagining two arguments among art critics about whether photography should be considered a form or branch of art. They might agree about exactly the ways in which photography is like and unlike activities they all recognize as 'standard' uncontroversial examples of art like painting and sculpture. They might agree that photography is not fully or centrally an art form in the way these other activities are; they might agree, that is, that pho-tography is at most a borderline case of an art. Then they would probably also agree that the decision whether to place photography within or outside that cat-egory is finally arbitrary, that it should be taken one way or another for con-venience or ease of exposition, but that there is otherwise no genuine issue to debate whether photography is 'really' an art. Now consider an entirely different kind of debate. One group argues that (whatever others think) photography is a central example of an art form, that any other view would show a deep mis-understanding of the essential nature of art. The other takes the contrary pos-ition that any sound understanding of the character of art shows photography to fall wholly outside it, that photographic techniques are deeply alien to the aims of art. It would be quite wrong in these circumstances to describe the argu-ment as one over where some borderline should be drawn. The argument would be about what art, properly understood, really is; it would reveal that the two

---

[26] The circularity in this characterization can be easily eliminated by making clear that the identity of the concept is determined by the existence of a population that uses a con-cept with criteria for correct use that are correctly described by the explanation.

groups had very different ideas about why even standard art forms they both recognize—painting and sculpture—can claim that title.

(LE, 41–42)

I had to provide this long quotation, for Dworkin does not offer an abstract characterization of pivotal cases, and their difference from borderline cases. The metaphorical analogy with spatial location—at the border or in the middle of an area—is useful in dramatizing the contrast, but it provides little guidance in trying to classify cases. The text provides one crucial guide: disputes regarding pivotal cases involve, as disputes about borderline cases do not (never? one wonders), a disagreement about the criteria for the correct use of the concept, and not merely (as in borderline cases (always?)) about their application to the instant case. As this is far from a clear criterion, it is important to bear the example in mind when evaluating Dworkin's argument.

Criterial explanations cannot explain concepts regarding which pivotal disputes are possible. Why so? Nothing in the definition of criterial explanations makes the conclusion obvious. Dworkin may be assuming that all competent users of a concept, which can be explained criterially, agree on its explanation, ie on the criteria for its correct application. Were this the case then they could not disagree on pivotal cases. On this assumption, when two people converse using a concept that can be criterially explained, then each of them uses the concept according to a set of criteria for its correct use, and each knows or can easily find out the criteria used by the other; and if they match, they are using the same concept and cannot disagree regarding the criteria for its correct use, whereas if they do not match then they are using two different concepts and there is no disagreement between them. If they do not realize that, then they are talking at cross-purposes. Is that Dworkin's argument? It seems to be. The following is as explicit a statement of the argument as I can find:

Notice the following argument. If two lawyers are actually following *different* rules in using the word 'law', using different factual criteria to decide when a proposition of law is true or false, then each must mean something different than the other when he says what the law is. . . . [here I omit Dworkin's example] So the two judges are not really disagreeing about anything when one denies and the other asserts this proposition. They are only talking past one another.

(LE, 43–44)

There is nothing wrong with this passage. But why should Dworkin think that it describes the situation which must obtain when people disagree about a criterion for the use of a concept that can be criterially explained? Dworkin never explains why he believes that concepts capable of being explained criterially land one in this situation. I will explain how once one avoids three possible mistakes it becomes plain that the argument fails. First, it is not the case that believing of a concept that it is susceptible to a criterial explanation commits one to an individualistic explanation of it. Second, one needs to be aware of the diversity of criteria for the correct use of concepts and of their possible opacity. And finally, one needs to remember that criterial philosophical explanations of concepts differ somewhat from other criterial explanations.

IV. Criterial Explanations and the Rejection of Individualism

The argument of the semantic sting inhabits a territory much discussed over the last fifty years, namely the question of the relation between agreement and understanding. Disagreement, we are often told, presupposes a degree of agreement. Why? Because disagreement means endorsement of inconsistent propositions. It therefore presupposes the common use of the same concepts, the concepts that feature in the inconsistent propositions. This is not democratic, you say. Oh yes it is, say I. We disagree. A precondition of our disagreement is that we both use the same concept of democracy. Agreement in concepts, however, implies agreement in judgement. Where concepts can be explained by criterial explanations, it means agreement over the criteria for application of the concept.

The argument I have just rehearsed trades on an ambiguity in the notion of disagreement. In one sense it means, as I said, the endorsement of inconsistent propositions. In another sense it means a conversation, discussion, or some other encounter in which people communicate but disagree (in the first sense). Disagreement in the first sense does not presuppose sharing concepts because it does not presuppose communication. Jesus and Genghis Khan disagreed on many issues, and this is so even if there are few concepts which they shared. To bring out their disagreement it may be necessary to deploy concepts that neither of them possessed or understood. This does not mean that there are no limits to possible disagreement, no sharing in judgements which is presupposed by it. Possibly the very possession of a faculty of judgement, of a power to have opinions, presupposes certain beliefs, which will therefore be shared by all believers. But the argument we are interested in is not of that kind. It is about the limits on disagreement imposed by the sharing of the same concepts. What are they? They are in the knowledge one must have to possess the concepts. If, for example, one cannot understand the concept of a cheque without knowing that banks are financial institutions in which people can deposit their own money, then anyone who possesses the concept of a cheque shares the knowledge that banks are financial institutions.

Criterial explanations presuppose that the possession of concepts consists in knowing how to use them in normal circumstances, namely in the possession of rules setting criteria for their correct use. It would seem to follow that those who share a concept share the criteria for its correct use and cannot disagree about them. The question is: what are these criteria and what does sharing them consist *in*? We can approach the matter through the second issue.

The individualistic picture regards each person as holding to a set of criteria that he or she follows when applying the concept. In principle each person may be the only person using that concept, ie the only one using these criteria. Those who have the concept may make mistakes in application (due to misperception, miscalculation, etc) but cannot make mistakes about the criteria. Each person's criteria define the concept for that person. If others follow different criteria, that cannot show that either of them made a mistake. It only shows that they are following different concepts. You will recognize that Dworkin's articulation of the semantic sting contains echoes of this view.

A series of arguments, deriving from the work of Wittgenstein, Putnam, and Burge,[27] shows that the individualistic picture is mistaken, but its rejection does not require rejecting criterial explanations of concepts. Here is one way to approach the matter. By the criterial approach to explanation, according to both the individualistic and the non-individualistic versions of it, when one speaks, one is uttering

---

[27] Wittgenstein's rule-following argument in *Philosophical Investigations* (trans GEM Anscombe, 2nd edn, Oxford: Blackwell, 1958), Putnam's twin-earth arguments in 'The Meaning of Meaning' and 'Is Semantics Possible?', in H Putnam, *Mind, Language and Reality* (Cambridge: CUP, 1975) 215, 139. See also S Kripke, *Naming and Necessity* (Cambridge, Mass: Harvard University Press, 1980). T Burge, 'Individualism and the Mental' (1979) 4 *Midwest Studies in Philosophy* 73, and 'Other Bodies', in *Thought and Object* (ed A Woodfield, Oxford: Clarendon Press, 1982) 97. My remarks in the sequel are not meant to relate to all aspects of their arguments. In particular, they do not relate to Putnam's conclusions regarding the 'world-involving' aspects of natural kind words. Nor is there reason to expect my comments to be entirely in line with the arguments of these philosophers.

sentences and using terms, relying on a rule that sets the criteria for their correct use. This does not mean that speakers always consider the rule for the use of the terms before using them. It means that they take themselves to be using the terms according to the rule and the criteria it embodies. They hold themselves responsible to the criteria set by their rule. For example, they are committed to admitting (at least to themselves) that their statements are mistaken if, when understood by these criteria, they are mistaken. If other people make the same utterance, holding themselves responsible to a different rule, ie one that sets different criteria, then they are using the words with different meanings, and there is no disagreement between them.

So far so good. Where the individualistic approach goes wrong is in thinking that the criteria set by each person's personal rule for the correct use of terms and concepts are fully specified. In fact, their personal rules are not specified. Each person takes his use of terms and concepts to be governed by the common criteria for their use. That is all their personal rule says. The criteria that govern people's use of language are simply the criteria generally relied on in their language community for the use of those terms. People who think that they understand a term or a concept think that they have at least some knowledge of what the common criteria are. They may be wrong. They may be partially or completely mistaken about the common criteria. It is part of each person's rule for the use of the term or concept that mistakes can occur, for the rule refers to the criteria as they are, rather than to what that person thinks they are. What they are, however, does depend on what people think they are. The correct criteria are those that people who think they understand the concept or term generally share, ie those that are generally believed to be the correct criteria are the correct criteria.[28] An example will bring out the point.

When I say 'This is a table' I am taking myself to have used 'table' according to the criteria governing its use in English,[29] which I believe to include the condition that any item of furniture up to four feet high with a flat top normally used to place things on is a table. Suppose that I am wrong. I call an item a table and am told that I made a mistake. It

---

[28] Note that there is no implication here that a linguistic community can share criteria only if there is someone who knows them completely. The criteria may be shared by the linguistic community even if no single person knows all aspects of them.

[29] Or in British English, or in some dialect, depending on the language I am using at the time. It may be undetermined.

is a drawing-board. On the individualistic account I should say: 'Do not correct me. I made no mistake. You simply misunderstood what I said. You took me to be using "table" in the meaning you are using it. But I did not. I used it according to a meaning rule by which this object is a table.' As we know that is not how people react on these occasions. They acknowledge that they made a mistake. They meant to use 'table' in its so-called ordinary meaning. They had a view on what this meaning is, and they made a mistake. Note that the same is true not only of what I say, but of what I think. Overhearing a conversation between others, I may realize that whereas I always thought that this object is a table in fact it is not, and my understanding of the rule for the use of 'table', the very same rule which I was using, was mistaken.

I am making this as a point about an important feature of speech, communication, and thought. The example, and others like it, cannot establish that things must be so, only that they are so. Our practices may change, and individualism may be right regarding such changed practices.[30] I share with others the belief that not all concepts and words can be explained in a way consistent with individualism, that fundamentally language and thought are not susceptible to individualistic explanations. But we need not argue that point here. Be that as it may, given how things are, most of our concepts and terms cannot be explained individualistically, and this shows that what we think and what we mean is 'not in the head'. Individualism is mistaken.[31] Two people thinking about the same object 'This is a table' will have different thoughts in mind depending on whether their linguistic community has one or another rule for the correct use of 'table'.

The rejection of individualism does not amount to a rejection of criterial explanations. Criterial explanations are explanations in terms of rules setting criteria for the correct use of concepts, or words—and there is nothing individualistic in that—which are the correct rules if they are shared by the linguistic community. That sharing is precisely what

---

[30] Burge has tried to show how radical and unappealing such a change will have to be. See eg his 'Individualism and Psychology' (1986) 95 *Phil. Rev.* 3.

[31] Burge defines individualism as 'the view that if one fixes those non-intentional physical and functional states and processes of a person's body whose nature is specifiable without reference to conditions beyond the person's bodily surfaces, one has thereby fixed the person's intentional mental states and processes in the sense that they could not be different intentional states and processes from the ones that they are'. See T Burge, 'Cartesian Error and the Objectivity of Perception', in *Subject, Thought, and Context* (ed P Pettit and J McDowell, Oxford: Clarendon Press, 1986) 117.

non-individualism insists on. The sharing is established by the fact that all language users hold themselves responsible to the common criteria, whatever they are.

Does Dworkin tacitly assume that supporters of criterial explanations are guilty of individualism? It is a moot point. When he introduces the subject of semantic explanations of 'law', he is careful to add:

> It does not follow that all lawyers are aware of these rules [the shared rules for correct use of 'law'] in the sense of being able to state them in some crisp and comprehensive form. For we all follow rules given by our common language of which we are not fully aware.
>
> (*LE*, 31)

The penultimate sentence is irrelevant to the issue. One can have perfect knowledge of rules without 'being able to state them in some crisp and comprehensive form'. The question is whether Dworkin is aware that one can use words and concepts in accord with rules with only partial knowledge of their content. Does his reference to not being 'fully aware' of the rules refer to not knowing them all that well, or does it repeat the idea of the previous sentence, referring merely to one's ability to articulate the content of the rules? The context of the passage, and the rest of Dworkin's discussion, suggest the second. On several occasions he repeats that supporters of criterial explanations allow for the fact—indeed, build on the fact—that people may be unable to articulate the rules they know. Nowhere does he seem to allow that supporters of criterial explanations build on the fact that people may not know well the rules governing the use of their words.

The point is of some importance in assessing the force of the semantic sting argument. It stings those whose account denies that one can have disputes about the criteria set by the rules for the correct use of terms. If criterial explanations are committed to the view that people who use concepts that can be explained by them cannot be mistaken about the criteria for their application, then they cannot explain the existence of disputes about these criteria.

As we saw, this argument fails. Criterial explanations of concepts are consistent with the fact that people who use the rules setting out these criteria may make mistakes about which criteria are set by the rules.[32]

---

[32] Naturally, they cannot make just any mistake. To be people who use the rule, they must have some notion of what the criteria are.

This means that there could be disagreements about the criteria for the use of concepts, even if the concepts are susceptible to criterial explanations. But in and of itself this does not explain the possibility of theoretically interesting disputes about such criteria. To do that we have to add other elements to the rejection of individualism.

V. The Complexity and Non-transparency of Criterial Explanations

A. The general case from complexity and non-transparency

Agreement on the actual use of concepts is, of course, neither necessary nor sufficient for agreement on the criteria for their application. It is not necessary, for people may and do make mistakes in applying concepts even when they have a very clear and correct understanding of the criteria for their application. It is not sufficient, because people who agree about the use of a concept in all the cases that they have examined so far, or will examine in the future, may still disagree about the criteria. Their disagreement may reveal itself in disagreement about some hypothetical cases, had such cases come to their attention.

The criteria used in explaining a concept are typically statements about its relation to other concepts, or applications of it to criterial examples. But which other concepts? And which examples? Talk of criteria may suggest some official definitions, like the mathematical or scientific definitions one learned at school: 'A triangle is an area of the plane enclosed by three straight lines,' or 'Water is H_2O.' In such cases there are fixed paradigmatic ways of explaining concepts. They display the criteria by which a concept is to be explained. Explanations in other terms are derivative, and secondary. But such cases are the exception rather than the rule. For the most part there are no canonical explanations for concepts. They can be explained in many ways, using or avoiding various other concepts, or examples. The pragmatic considerations that distinguish a good explanation from a bad one, considerations of what puzzles the addressees of the explanation, what they are or are not interested in, and of their capacities to understand, are among the considerations guiding the choice of concepts to be used, and examples to refer to in good explanations. You may say that there are no criteria for the use of most concepts, only concepts and examples which are used as criteria—that is, used to explain the rules governing the correct use of the concepts on one occasion or another. Moreover, it is virtually always the case that explanations are not exhaustive. They point to one or another essential feature of the concept explained, and leave many others unmentioned (and unentailed).

As we saw, even explanations in terms of necessary and sufficient conditions are not exhaustive.

All this points to endless possibilities of disagreement. Imagine that you are used to explaining a concept one way. I am used to explaining it another way. Do we agree? And if we do not, who is right? These questions are as complex as any questions comparing different concepts or analysing different examples. The suggestion that, because the correctness of the explanations of concepts is judged by their faithfulness to the shared rules governing their use, such explanations are so transparent that they leave little room for doubt about their correctness or accuracy lacks plausibility.

Another result of these considerations is that dispute and disagreement may come apart. People may dispute each other's explanations even when there is no disagreement between them. Their dispute may result from a failure to realize that both offer compatible explanations.

B. Concepts explained by example

Let me illustrate these points with reference to explanations using examples. A common, correct, and effective way to explain what is a table is to say, 'It is an item of furniture like this one' (pointing to a table as one speaks). For most purposes such an explanation would do perfectly. If the rule one learned from needs correcting or supplementing, this could be done when the need arises. But suppose that you have just learned the word by such an explanation, and that I want to find out how good your understanding of the notion is now. It could be a somewhat lengthy process, involving other examples, and various descriptions. Now suppose that instead of this rather simple notion we are discussing the notion 'a good person' and we both agree that a good person is someone who is like Jesus. Not surprisingly, while in a pub conversation we may leave it at that; if we really want to establish whether we understand the notion in the same way, we could spend a productive evening comparing the ways in which being like Jesus shows one to be a good person. The very act of establishing agreement will be prolonged, as may be the process of establishing the location and scope of any disagreement.

Some concepts, including some evaluative concepts, cannot be explained except with the help of examples, with the inevitable elaborate exploration of their reach and direction that any attempt to study systematically such concepts involves. The notion of good looks is such a concept. It is futile to explain what it is to have good looks, to be good-looking, except by pointing to examples.

Focusing on evaluative concepts, an objecter may grant all I wrote so far and reply that it still fails to explain the sort of disagreement which marks disputes about, for example, whether justice requires redistribution to the poor, or whether abortion is murder. We should admit that that is so, and it is hardly surprising. It would be a mistake to think that all evaluative disagreements are of a kind. The fact that the disagreements I gestured towards are not like those about distribution and justice, or about abortion and murder, does not mean that they are not typical examples of common evaluative disagreements.

C. The ethical significance of disputes about criterial explanations

It may seem that disputes that concentrate on identifying what are the criteria for the correct use of concepts cannot be significant evaluative disputes, for they are merely disputes about the content of shared rules, and one can always dissent from them. The first point to note here is that even if this contention is correct it does not vindicate the semantic sting. If the remarks above are correct, then the semantic sting argument does not have a sting. Its conclusion was that there cannot be disputes about the criteria for the application of criterially explainable concepts. That conclusion is mistaken. So far as Hart's own understanding of his own theory goes, this is the end of the matter, for he denied that the explanation of the nature of law is evaluative. For him it was a 'descriptive' enterprise. For reasons explained by John Finnis[33] and others,[34] I believe that Hart is mistaken here, and Dworkin is right in holding that the explanation of the nature of law involves evaluative considerations. In any case, it is of interest to see the place that conceptual disputes about criterially definable concepts can occupy within normative disputes.

---

[33] *Natural Law and Natural Rights* (Oxford: Clarendon Press, 1980), ch 1.
[34] For my own explanation, see eg *Ethics in the Public Domain* (rev edn, Oxford: Clarendon Press, 1995), chs 9 and 10.

Where criterially explainable concepts are concerned, evaluative disputes begin (the objection is) only after conceptual disputes are settled, and at the point at which one raises the question of whether or not the concept under discussion should find its place in the articulation of a correct evaluative theory. It is true, we can say in reply, that the very moral or evaluative legitimacy of concepts can be called into question. I can doubt whether one should use the notion of honour in today's circumstances, on the ground that the value it refers to has its place in a society with an aristocracy, and a valuing of ceremony and of formal standing that has no room, should have no room, in our society. That being said, it remains the case that the clarification of evaluative concepts has an important role in evaluative disputes. Most of the time we neither wish nor are able to jettison the concepts we have. The point is very well known. We need concepts to be able to criticize or jettison other concepts. It does not follow that some specific concepts are immune from change. But change can only be gradual. At any given time we are inescapably committed to most of the concepts we have.

The same goes for our beliefs: we assess some of them while relying on others. We cannot do otherwise. We are committed to our beliefs, and when wondering about issues about which we are not clear, much of the time our process is not so much a process of belief revision as of finding out what are the implications of the beliefs we have for the matters we are undecided about. An important part of such deliberation is a process of clarifying to oneself the contours of one's own concepts. One is committed to them, in the way one is committed to one's beliefs, but one may not understand them all that well, as one is not always clear about the implications of one's beliefs. Trying to make up one's mind on an issue, or trying to sort out whether a view incompatible with one's own has some merit, is primarily a process of examining the implications of one's beliefs, and the contours of one's concepts, an exploration proceeding through a debate about the adequacy of various criterial explanations of them.

One reason the significance of conceptual clarification may be misunderstood is the mistaken belief that if the truth of a statement of criteria for the use of a concept depends on the fact that they pick out the common rule for the use of the concept, then the only possible argument supporting such a statement is that this is how everyone uses the concept. Such statistical claims, this mistaken argument proceeds, are not the stuff that normative disagreements are made of. The argument confuses the presupposition for the sharing of concepts with the reasons used in debates about the contours of concepts. To be sure, on occasion argument becomes pointless. If someone claims to be my blood relation because I donated blood to him before an operation, or if someone says that entrenched constitutions are consistent with democracy because trenches are dug by working people, there is little one can do but point out that the other is talking about a different concept from the one commonly referred to by these words. But such cases are the exception rather than the rule. If you deny that a certain feature is a necessary feature of a concept and I assert that it is, we will proceed by appealing to clear examples, to analogies, or to agreed conceptual connections, and will pursue their implications. When one defines 'a table' as an item of furniture made to put things on, the typical response is not: 'This is not how the term is used' (though this response is true), but: 'By your definition a drawing-board is a table, therefore the definition is mistaken.' The sharing of the rule is assumed. It is not part of the argument.

D. Refuting the sting through the relative independence of interlinked concepts

I remarked earlier that different concepts have different shapes, and therefore their explanations relate them to other concepts in a variety of ways. Let me illustrate the relevance of the point to the possibility of disagreement and dispute, using the examples of the notions of justice and of just war. Let us assume that a condition of a war being a just war is that the measures used in its pursuit are proportionate to the harm avoidance of which makes it necessary to use them. Judgement of proportionality involves comparing the severity of various harms. Does it follow that a comprehensive understanding of how to compare the severity of different harms is part of understanding the concept of a just war? Not according to the notion of a concept as we have it. We understand the concept if, among other things, we understand that it includes a condition of proportionality. We can understand that even if we are at a loss as to how to compare the severity of various harms. Such ignorance means that sometimes we will not know whether this war or that is just. But it does not mean that we will have a defective or incomplete understanding of the concept of a just war. The criteria by which we judge the relative severity of harms are not part of the rules governing the correct use of the concept of a just war.

The reasons for that are deep-rooted. Given that in explaining concepts we inevitably use other concepts, but for the fact that the criteria for one are not necessarily the criteria for any other that it is necessarily connected with, we would have ended up with a vast array of concepts sharing the same criteria for understanding such that we either understood all of them or none of them; and if we understand one of them to a certain degree only, then we understand all of them to a degree not higher than that. That is not how concepts are, and they are not like that because of the relative independence of inter-related concepts.

The relative independence of inter-related concepts is consistent with the thesis that concepts like just war can be explained criterially. Does Dworkin ignore the point when he charges supporters of criterial explanations with not being able to account for disagreement about the criteria for the application of concepts? It seems to me that he does. He charges supporters of criterial explanations with inability to explain the existence of what he calls 'theoretical disputes', which he identifies with disagreements about what he terms 'the ground of law' (*LE*, 4–5). As far as I can tell, these are disagreements about the truth conditions of legal propositions, or of some class of them. Dworkin does not distinguish here between levels of abstraction in the description of the truth conditions. Both disagreement about whether proportionality is a condition of just war and disagreement over whether cost of repair is the exclusive test of proportionality are disagreements about the truth conditions of propositions of the form 'so and so is [was, will be] a just war'. Therefore, in Dworkin's terms they are both disputes about the criteria for the application of the concept of a just war. This amounts to overlooking the relative independence of inter-related concepts. The relative independence of concepts establishes that Dworkin is mistaken in his criticism of criterial explanations.

Assume, for the sake of the argument, that the concept of a just war can be criterially explained, but that the notion of proportionality of harm must be explained by Dworkin's interpretive method. It follows that even according to Dworkin there can be a theoretical dispute over the criteria for application of the proportionality of harm. As we saw, this would constitute a disagreement regarding the truth conditions of statements about just war, which is, by assumption, criterially explainable. Because Dworkin regards all disagreements about the truth conditions of a concept as theoretical, it follows that once the relative independence of concepts is allowed it must be recognized that there can be so-called theoretical disagreements regarding concepts which can be criterially explained.

.

This refutation of the semantic sting presupposes that some concepts are not capable of being criterially explained. Those who believe that many concepts, including the concept of law, can be criterially explained need not deny this. It is Dworkin who used the semantic sting to deny that concepts like the concept of law or that of justice can be criterially explained. This refutation shows that it fails to do so. Notice that considerations like those which apply to just war apply to justice as well.

Suppose, for example, that a just state is a state the basic institutions of which make it highly likely that, given the conditions of life at the place and time, all its inhabitants will have a good life, should they conduct themselves rationally. It follows that to know whether this state or that is just one has to know what a good life is. But one's understanding of the notion of a just state is not defective just because one has mistaken views on that issue. Such mistakes will, most likely, lead to mistakes in judging which states are just, but not to a failure properly to understand the notion of a just state. As before, it follows that, for all that Dworkin's argument shows, the notion of a just state can be explained criterially, whereas those who use it engage in so-called theoretical disputes about the truth conditions of judging states to be just.[35]

The argument from the relative independence of interlinked concepts refutes the semantic sting argument, and that refutation is independent of its refutation (in the previous section) by the argument from the opacity and complexity of criterial explanations. Two distinctions, between the refutation of the sting which is based on the non-transparency of criterial explanations and that based on the relative independence of interlinked concepts, bring out their differences. The refutation from non-transparency establishes the possibility of disagreements about the rule for the use of a concept, which show that at least one of those who disagree has an incomplete grasp of the concept.[36] The refutation from relative independence does not assume such lack of mastery. It shows that even those who have complete understanding of the concept may

---

[35] In the Postscript, above n 4, at 246, Hart writes that one mistake which led Dworkin to belief in his semantic sting argument is his conflation of meaning with criteria of application. (See also *The Concept of Law*, 160.) I do not know how Hart understood that distinction. Possibly my remarks regarding the relative independence of interlinked concepts is relevant to an elucidation of such a distinction. However, in the absence of an explanation of his distinction it is impossible to evaluate this reply by Hart.

[36] The same is true of Dworkin's interpretive disputes about the meaning of a concept. They too presuppose that at least one of the parties has an incomplete understanding of the concept.

disagree about the truth conditions of propositions applying it to concrete cases. The second difference between the refutations is that the one from relative independence shows that the semantic sting does not apply to criterially explainable concepts, which are interlinked to other concepts regarding which there could be so-called theoretical disagreements. The lack of transparency argument shows that there could be such disagreements regarding criterially explainable concepts that are sufficiently complex to lack transparency.

E. Theoretical and other criterial explanations

There is a difference of some importance between 'ordinary' and theoretical criterial explanations. It cannot be adequately discussed here; a few observations will have to do. As has already been noted, ordinary criterial explanations are offered in reply to specific questions reflecting a puzzle or a difficulty which is indicated in the question, or understood from its context. This is true of explanations one gives to oneself as well. If you ask what is a state because you wonder whether Lichtenstein is a state, the answer is likely to be other than if you ask what is a state wishing to know whether the European Union is a state. Theoretical explanations, philosophical explanations among them, are somewhat different. They too relate to a purpose, or purposes, and they too vary with the interests of their public. But their interest is different. They seek a more systematic understanding of the concepts (and we are discussing only explanations of concepts, and not stipulations of new concepts in the process of theory construction). This means that they are looking for a more comprehensive explanation, and one that will not only guide correct use but will also improve understanding.

It is common for this interest in comprehensiveness and improved understanding to lead to a freer attitude to existing practice. Theorists usually feel free to make their explanations less vague than the concept they explain. Explanations that aim at accuracy should be vague where the concept is vague. 'Ordinary' explanations are vague, partly because they explain vague concepts and partly because they are incomplete. Theoretical explanations also are incomplete, but they aim to be relatively (ie relative to the concerns of the theory in question at the time) complete. They tend to be more precise than the contours of the vague concept would allow, were one to be true to them. Their interest in improved understanding facilitates this. Being built around ideas deemed important for our self-understanding, they can and do use these ideas to reduce the vagueness in the concept as we find it in the more chaotic, more fluctuating social life of the linguistic community. In some cases theorists may not only reduce vagueness but also introduce distinctions between different uses or senses of the terms or phrases used to express the concept, distinctions not normally noticed by ordinary speakers, and which redraw somewhat the boundaries of the concept.[37]

Theoretical explanations, while dependent for their success on achieving their theoretical goals, are also criterial. Their truth or adequacy is tested also by their conformity to the rules governing the use of the concept. Had they not been so tested they would fail in their aim to explain the concept as it is, the concept that people use to understand features in their own life and in the world around them. To succeed in explaining our own self-understanding through the explanation of some of our concepts requires explaining them as they are. Therefore, if ordinary explanations of them are criterial, so must their theoretical explanations be, subject to the minor latitude in deviating from common practice that I explained.

This means that the reduction in vagueness can only be limited, or the explanation will not be true to the concept explained. A correct account of the nature of law will be more or less vague in the same way as the concept of law is vague. As a result, there sometimes is no answer to questions of the form: is this a legal system?

In *Law's Empire*, Dworkin deploys what is in effect a second argument against criterial explanations of the concept of law, an argument altogether independent of the semantic sting. He thinks that the nature of adjudication shows that courts always presuppose a correct answer to the question 'How should this case be decided?' and that this question is the same as the question 'What is the law which applies to this case?' As the rules by which people judge correctness of use of the concept of law do not always yield such an answer, they cannot provide the explanation of the concept of law. This shows that the concept cannot be criterially explained.

The major flaw in this second argument is its identification of the two questions. It reflects Dworkin's view that the only norms by which

---

[37] Do we use one concept of 'promise' or two when saying 'I promise to get you the book by tomorrow', and when saying 'I'll break your bones if you do it again, and that's a promise'? Most philosophers who have written on promises take it for granted that two concepts are involved. I believe that that position is not based on an analysis of the common understanding of the concept(s) of a promise, but on theoretical reasons they have for drawing the boundaries between promises and threats.

courts are allowed, according to law, to decide cases are the law of that legal system. Or perhaps the right way to express Dworkin's view is that what makes norms into the law of a system is that, by law, the courts are allowed to rely on them in deciding cases. The argument about this claim of Dworkin's has continued since his first major essay.[38] But important as that issue is, it is irrelevant to the debate about the possibility of criterial explanation of the concept of law, for a determination of the content of the law of this legal system or that and the explanation of the concept of law are very different enterprises. This is denied by Dworkin's third thesis about jurisprudence, the thesis that it is a silent prologue to any legal decision. It is time to examine this thesis.

VI. Law and Its Theory

The semantic sting argument stands on its own and falls on its own. Its demise does not in itself undermine Dworkin's wider view of the nature and role of legal philosophy. Hart disagrees with him about that too, but in the Postscript his disagreement is muted. Having decided to restrict the Postscript to deflecting or refuting Dworkin's criticism of his own views, he is content to point out that Dworkin's theoretical aims are different from his, as if that makes them compatible. To be sure, Hart is right that their understandings of the character of legal philosophy differ. Hart regards his own enterprise as describing those features of the law which are general, ie shared by all legal systems.[39] Dworkin takes the task of legal philosophy to be the construction of a theory of adjudication, a theory which if correctly followed yields a uniquely correct answer to any question of American law. But it does not follow that that makes the theories compatible. Dworkin is right to maintain that if his theory is correct then Hart's is flawed at its foundations. In this section I want to show (1) how Dworkin's conception of the role of legal philosophy is not affected by the fault in the semantic sting argument and (2) why that view of jurisprudence is not merely different from but incompatible with Hart's conception of descriptive jurisprudence.

---

[38] Reprinted as 'The Model of Rules: I', in *Taking Rights Seriously* (Cambridge, Mass: Harvard University Press, 1977).

[39] Note that that task is wider than the explanation of the nature of law, which is confined to essential features of the law, ie features without which it would not be law.

We can start again with the semantic sting. At a conference in Jerusalem Ruth Gavison pointed out to Dworkin that neither Hart nor many others take Hart to be affected by the semantic sting because Hart was not offering an account of the meaning of 'law'. In reply, Dworkin added a note to *Law's Empire*:

It is sometimes said that the goal of the theories I call semantic is not, as that name suggests, to develop theories about what the word 'law' means, but rather to lay bare the characteristic and distinctive features of law as a social phenomenon. See, e.g., Ruth Gavison, 'Comments on Dworkin', in Papers of the Jerusalem Conference (forthcoming).[40] But this contrast is itself a misunderstanding. The philosophers I have in mind... recognize that the most distinctive aspect of law as a 'social Phenomenon' is that participants in institutions of law deploy and debate propositions of law and think it matters, usually decisively, whether these are accepted or rejected. The classical theories try to explain this central and pervasive aspect of legal practice by describing the sense of propositions of law—what these mean to those who use them—and this explanation takes the form either of definitions of 'law' in the older style or accounts of the 'truth conditions' of propositions of law—the circumstances in which lawyers accept or reject them—in the more modern style.

(*LE*, 418–419)

Hart replies to this with some puzzlement:

[E]ven if the meaning of... propositions of law was determined by... their truth conditions this does not lead to the conclusion that the very meaning of the word 'law' makes law depend on certain specific criteria. This would only be the case if the criteria provided by a system's rule of recognition and the need for such a rule were derived from the meaning of the word 'law'. But there is no trace of such a doctrine in my work.[41]

Granted that Hart was right in what he wrote, is it not the case that truth conditions of all propositions of law follow from an explanation of the concept of law, including Hart's own? According to Hart the law is a normative system combining primary and secondary rules, one of which, the rule of recognition, exists as a social practice, and its content sets conditions for the validity of the other rules in that system. Does it not follow that a proposition of law is true, according to Hart, if there is a social practice, a rule of recognition, setting out criteria for the validity of rules of law, and that the proposition states the content of a rule or

---

[40] Since published as R Gavison, *Issues in Jurisprudence: The Influence of H.L.A. Hart* (Oxford: OUP, 1987).
[41] Postcript, above n 4, at 247.

rules meeting these criteria (or of the rule of recognition itself), or follows from them? This formulation has to be refined, and hedged, but is essentially correct.

There is, however, one important caveat. Many of the conditions that propositions must meet to be true legal propositions, and all the fundamental conditions of this kind, are that they were made law by content-independent processes or activities. Content-independent conditions are those that can endorse different propositions regardless of their content. Typically, they can endorse both a proposition and its contradictory, though this is not always the case, and there can be degrees of content-independence (make any law, make any law that does not violate human rights, make any law—regulation—necessary to the implementation of a fair rent act, etc). If a condition of the truth of a legal proposition is that it conforms with the demands of justice, for example, the condition is content-dependent: it depends (not exclusively, but among other things) on the content of the proposition. If the condition of the truth of a legal proposition is that it was endorsed by the legislature, then the condition is content-independent, since while the legislature's endorsement was probably motivated by the content of the proposition, it is itself an act that can give validity to propositions of varying contents.[42] It is the act of endorsing the content of a bill, whatever it may be.

Content-independence is, as I pointed out, a matter of degree. A central feature of Hart's explanation of the nature of law is that it is just about absolutely content-independent at bottom. That is, the fundamental criteria for validity, those whose existence does not presuppose others, are almost entirely content-independent. Jurisprudence stipulates that legal systems are systems with a certain structure (including law-making and law-applying authorities). But beyond that, all is contingent. The content of the law and the specific identity and powers of its institutions are entirely dependent on the relevant practices in the country, ie on its rule of recognition. It is an equally central feature of Dworkin's account of the law that it is not entirely content-independent. No general theory of law can hope to succeed unless it is content-independent to some extent. To deny that

---

[42] Legal rules are typically expressed by normative propositions (assigning rights, liabilities, responsibilities, etc) or propositions setting conditions for the application of normative propositions. While often legislative measures are not formulated in such terms, their meaning is expressed by them, and we can say that the legislation endorses the propositions or makes them into law.

the criteria which determine the content of the law of this country or that have a content-independent component is to deny that there can be law-making authorities. Dworkin's theory no less than Hart's leaves room for content-independent criteria among those determining what he calls 'the grounds of legal propositions'. In his most abstract formulations, this expresses itself in the role of the history of the legal system as an element contributing to the determination of its content. But his account of law emphasizes the importance of content-dependent determinants of its content. It is part of Dworkin's account that the theory of law makes the truth of legal propositions depend on values such as justice, and an alleged value which he calls integrity.

This difference may explain why Hart is surprised at the suggestion that his theory provides an account of the truth conditions of legal propositions. An account of the nature of law that regards it as determined largely by content-dependent factors is much more readily thought of as providing truth conditions for legal propositions than is one that regards the law as determined by content-independent processes like legislation. It has much more of substance to say about the content of the law. Nevertheless, Dworkin is right in arguing that both stake claims as to what determines the content of the law, and therefore the truth of propositions about the law.

It does not belong to this chapter to evaluate the relative claims of Hart's and Dworkin's theories. Our subject is their different conceptions of legal philosophy, its tasks and methods, not the relative merits of their different theories. As far as I can see, the fact that the concept of law can be criterially explained is consistent both with the view that the explanation is largely content-dependent and with the view that it is largely content-independent. It appears, however, that Dworkin thinks otherwise. He explains:

Legal philosophers are in the same situation as philosophers of justice and the philosopher of courtesy we imagined. They cannot produce useful semantic theories of law. They cannot expose the common criteria or ground rules lawyers follow for pinning legal labels onto facts, for there are no such rules.... [T]hey are constructive interpretations: they try to show legal practice as a whole in its best light, to achieve equilibrium between legal practice as they find it and the best justification of that practice. *So no firm line divides jurisprudence from adjudication or any other aspect of legal practice. Legal philosophers debate about the general part, the interpretive foundation any legal argument must have. We may turn that coin over. Any practical legal argument, no matter how detailed and limited, assumes the kind of abstract foundation jurisprudence offers. . . . So any judge's opinion is itself a piece of legal philosophy.*

(*LE*, 90, emphasis added)

To repeat, we can agree with Dworkin that legal philosophers do not produce semantic explanations of the word 'law'. But they do produce explanations of the law, and therefore also of the concept of law, the concept which singles out legal systems from other normative and social institutions and practices. Dworkin's theory of law, in being an account of the nature of law, is also an explanation of the concept of law; that is, if true, it improves our understanding of the concept, mastery of which enables us to identify legal systems and to distinguish them from other phenomena, and understanding of which yields understanding of the nature of law. I should make it clear that I am using 'concept' in its normal meaning. Dworkin provides a sketchy discussion of 'concepts' (*LE*, 92–93) from which it appears that his understanding of the term is idiosyncratic. My statement that his theory provides an account of the concept of law is therefore consistent with the claim that he, using his own special notion of concept, does not view it as including an account of the concept of law.

In providing an explanation of the concept of law, legal philosophers aim to improve our understanding of the law-that-is: theirs are interpretive explanations.[43] Interpretive explanations can be criterial explanations. The rejection of the semantic sting argument does not force us to revise our understanding of legal philosophy as an exploration of the meaning of certain social practices and institutions. This is not to say, of course, that all interpretations are criterial explanations of concepts. An interpretation of *Hamlet* (the play) is not an interpretation of the concept of Hamlet, if there is such a concept. Similarly, an interpretation of the French Revolution is not an explanation of the concept of the French Revolution, nor is an interpretation of the Rent Act 1984 an interpretation of any concept.[44]

When in the course of rendering judgment a court interprets the law, it does not interpret the concept of law. It interprets the law as it

---

[43] You may say that not every explanation that improves understanding is an interpretation. But every explanation that improves the understanding of a phenomenon with a meaning, or a content, is an interpretation, for interpretation is an explanation, or display, of the meaning of what is explained. Here what is explained are social practices and institutions that constitute the backbone of legal systems. Their meaning is illuminated by jurisprudential explanations.

[44] Though in all these instances an interpretation of this concept or that may be part of the case for the interpretation of the play, historical events, or law.

bears on the issue before it. Is Dworkin denying that? The answer is far from clear. The boundaries of jurisprudence or legal philosophy are not clear. Some who write about the economic principles that, in their view, should govern town planning regulations, or about the proper definition of the offence of rape in English law, regard themselves as writing legal philosophy. Courts certainly engage in reasoning about such issues. It is a little hyperbolic to think that every one of their decisions is a 'piece of legal philosophy' on that account. But that does not matter much. What does is that Dworkin does not seem to have such considerations, or not only them, in mind when he declares all judicial opinions to be 'pieces of legal philosophy'. The crucial question is whether the passage I quoted from Dworkin applies, in his view, to the account of the nature of law—that is, whether he believes that every judicial opinion is a piece of legal philosophy because it includes such an account. The textual evidence suggests that he does. The relevant distinctions are not drawn by Dworkin, but that is part of the evidence, for the drift of the passage and of his general argument is to deny the importance, sometimes the possibility, of such distinctions. In what follows I consider the truth of the quotation regarding the account-of-the-nature-of-law part of legal philosophy, the part exemplified by *Law's Empire*.

The quotation drifts from the moderate to the extreme. It starts with a denial of a sharp line between jurisprudence and any part of legal practice. It proceeds to say that any legal argument assumes a basic part which legal philosophy provides, and it concludes by saying that all judicial decisions are 'pieces of legal philosophy'. The three claims are very different from each other. The first, for example, entails that conveyancing is part of a continuum at one end of which is jurisprudence, with no sharp boundary anywhere. I tend to believe that no boundaries worth bothering with are sharp. That does not mean that they lack theoretical or practical importance. It merely means that they are vague, and some questions of their location yield only indeterminate answers. It is best to put Dworkin's first point on one side. It is too vague to have any theoretical bearing in itself. We could also put on one side the third hyperbolic claim that '*any judge's opinion is itself a piece of legal philosophy*'. A 'piece' of legal philosophy they may be, but discussions, arguments, or whatever regarding the nature of law they are not.

There is no denying that questions about the nature of law can arise in courts, and can feature in judicial decisions. But so can just about any other issue, from astrophysics to biology, sociology, and the rest. That does not make judicial decisions into dissertations in any of these areas. In some areas it is easy to overlook this fact. This is because some courts' decisions set precedents. They create law that may be difficult to overturn. As always, where courts' decisions set precedents they do so even when they are mistaken or misguided (though certain mistakes can deny them precedent status or weaken it—it depends on the detailed regulations of the specific country in question). Therefore, if a court makes a mistake in its disquisition on the nature of law, its mistake may nonetheless set the law for that country. There were some intriguing examples of this during the 1960s and 1970s, as various constitutional regimes of the then new states of the British Commonwealth were swept aside by coups d'état.[45] Kelsen's theory found favour with various courts. On some occasions the courts' misunderstandings of Kelsen's misguided theory became the law of their countries.

Such judicial use of jurisprudential ideas may sometimes be in place, but it is analogous to the judicial use of ideas from biology. Dworkin's claim, as I understand it, does not rely on the fact that jurisprudence is occasionally invoked by the courts. It relies on a claim that jurisprudential theses are among the presuppositions of any decision by the courts, such that if the jurisprudential presuppositions of this or that court's opinion are false the decision is flawed. The chain of reasoning leading to this conclusion seems to be as follows. The court relies on some or other propositions of law. In relying on them it relies on some criteria for their truth according to which, in its opinion, they are true propositions. But the assumption, explicit or implicit in the decision, that these are criteria for the truth of the propositions is a jurisprudential assumption. It is part of, or a consequence of, an account of the nature of law. Hence—as in Dworkin's middle proposition in the quotation earlier (somewhat recast in light of the discussion above)—every judicial decision presupposes the truth of a theory about the nature of law, even when it does not discuss such a theory explicitly.

Persuasive as this argument appears, it is not valid as it stands. The thought that in order to know their own law the courts need to know that it falls under a general concept of law, or, indeed, that they require legal theory in order to have the concept of law, is surprising. But before I explore these concerns I will clarify one crucial point. My discussion is of the argument I spelled out, and not of its conclusion, which may be

---

[45] Similar litigation occurred in Rhodesia after it unilaterally declared independence. See discussions of these in J Eekelaar, 'Principles of Evolutionary Legality' and J Finnis, 'Revolutions and Continuity of Law', in *Oxford Essays in Jurisprudence* (2nd series, ed AWB Simpson, Oxford: Clarendon Press, 1973).

established by some other arguments. It will become clear that if I am right in the observations that follow, then this is unlikely. Nevertheless, this limitation of my inquiry is of some importance. Assume, as Dworkin claims, that some theory of the nature of law is presupposed by every judicial decision. It may then be possible to establish that that is so by considering the nature of a theory of law (plus some basic knowledge of the nature of judicial opinions). On the other hand, it may be impossible to establish the conclusion without actually establishing the correct theory of law, and showing that it entails that conclusion. Arguably, Dworkin is pursuing both methods towards the same conclusion. Arguably, his theory of law, if true, is presupposed by anyone who reasons cogently about the law. As this chapter is about conceptions of legal philosophy I will not explore such avenues here. My interest is in the argument set out in the previous paragraph, which purports not to assume the truth of Dworkin's own theory of law (at that stage of the book we do not know yet what it is).[46] It is meant to tell us something about the nature of legal philosophy in general, and it is interesting to see why it does not.

The argument (and while it is based on Dworkin's ideas, it is not one advanced in these terms by him) claims that to know the law governing each case one must be making, explicitly or implicitly, assumptions about the nature of law. Why so? American courts are required to decide in accordance with American law, just as Chinese courts are required to decide in accordance with Chinese law. It would follow that in rendering decisions American judges, acting in good faith, as we can assume that they do, presuppose that their decisions are in accordance with American law. They presuppose, perhaps, something about American law. This need not be much. It could be that it contains a particular rule, and that nothing else in it modifies the application of the rule to the facts of this case. Courts usually rely on a much richer set of beliefs, but these are commonly only about a tiny fragment of the law. They invariably rely on the assumption that there is nothing else in the law to upset the conclusion reached on the basis of the rules they relied on.[47] To make such an assumption, even to be justified in making it, one need have little idea of what the rest of the law is, let alone an idea of how

---

[46] Though, importantly, we do know that it has to accommodate the existence of 'theoretical disputes' about the law.

[47] In these comments I wish neither to endorse nor to deny the view that courts' decisions always represent the state of the law at a time just prior to their decision, as the courts believe it to be.

exactly it is to be established. An analogy may illustrate the point. To believe that if I move my legs I will walk forward, I need to assume that no natural force will stop me, but I need have no specific ideas about what natural forces there are, and hardly any idea at all how to find out what they are. I am not suggesting, of course, that judges have very little knowledge of the law outside that which is relevant to the case before them. How much knowledge they actually have is a contingent matter that is neither here nor there. The point is that they need not make any specific assumptions about the content of the rest of the law or of the way to establish it when they believe that it makes no difference to the case before them.

These remarks would refute Dworkin's thesis if it is understood to be about what judges presuppose when rendering judgment. But the thesis can be readily adjusted to be about what has to be true if their decisions are to be correct, or justified according to law. It can be read to say that any judicial decision or any legal argument is sound only if the correct theory of the nature of law would bear them up, or at any rate would not contradict their conclusions. I believe that even this modest claim is mistaken. By American law, let me repeat, American judges have to decide cases according to American law (including its conflict of law doctrines). It is a mistake to believe that that duty is discharged in, or in some sense presupposes, two stages, the first establishing what the law is (the answer being provided by legal philosophy) and the second applying these conclusions to establish the content of American law. Judicial decisions in American courts are vulnerable to the charge that they are wrong as a matter of American law. But it is irrelevant to their justification that they conform, if we can make sense of the notion, with the correct theory of the nature of law. Of course, we know well that if some theory of law yields the result that American law is not law, it is a misguided theory of law.

But suppose we are discussing some marginal case. Suppose we are discussing the putative law established by some government in exile over a country which it does not control, or where its control is minimal, and suppose that its judges discover that by the correct legal theory their system is not a legal system, for it lacks the necessary characteristics of control. This may make them decide to resign, or rebel, though I can see little reason why it should.[48] The point is that their duty (under

---

[48] I can see plenty of reasons why they should not penalize people for violation of laws which were not in effect in the country, and so on. Such facts have a moral bearing on the

the system in whose courts they sit) is to judge in accordance with the rules of that system, and it matters not at all whether these rules are legal ones.[49] I have argued elsewhere[50] that there could be legal systems in cultures that do not have the concept of law. The concept of law is a historical product, changing over the years, and the concept as we have it is more recent than the institution it is used to single out. If one accepts the point, it helps to illustrate my argument here. A court in a country with law but which does not think of it as such will be concerned to decide cases in accordance with the rules of its system, which are in fact rules of law, but that fact is not one the court is aware of, and *a fortiori* it makes no difference to the court.

There is another reason why the reconstructed argument fails, or is at best misleading. It assumes that legal philosophy creates the concept of law, whereas in fact it merely explains the concept that exists independently of it. To see the point, we must suspend for the sake of argument the previous objection. The argument was that the soundness of legal arguments establishing conclusions according to the law of the United States, let us say, depends on their conformity with the correct theory of law (or even on the correct theory having them among its consequences). But that confuses the theory of law and the concept of law. If we waive the previous objection, we accept that legal arguments are sound only if they and their conclusions involve, or are consistent with, correct use of the concept of law. But the concept of law is not a product of the theory of law. It is a concept that evolved historically, under the influences of legal practice, and other cultural influences, including the influence of the legal theory of the day. Legal philosophy seeks to understand the nature of law, and that involves improving our understanding of the concept of law. If they acquire such understanding, judges will gain in the same way that they will gain if their understanding of history, economics, and politics is improved. But the soundness of their arguments, even if it depends on correct application of the concept of law, does not depend on their having the understanding which legal philosophy aspires to provide.

---

issue of the justice of these courts. The theoretical conclusion that the system they operate is or is not a legal system seems to have little bearing.

[49] Unless, of course, that system refers them to the writings of jurisprudence as setting a test of validity in it.

[50] See chapter 4, 'On the Nature of Law'.

VII. Conclusion

It will be obvious that the arguments of the preceding section rely on an understanding of the task of explaining the nature of law, which is alien to Dworkin. For example, he writes:

> In the heyday of semantic theories, legal philosophers were more troubled by the suggestion that wicked places really had no law. Semantic rules were meant to capture the use of 'law' generally and therefore to cover people's statements not only about their own law but about very different historical and foreign legal systems as well. It was a common argument against strong 'natural law' theories, which claim that a scheme of political organisation must satisfy certain minimal standards of justice in order to count as a legal system at all, that our linguistic practice does not deny the title of law to obviously immoral political systems.... if useful theories of law are not semantic theories..., however, but are instead interpretive of a particular stage of a historically developing practice, then the problem of immoral legal systems has a different character. Interpretive theories are by their nature addressed to a particular legal culture, generally the culture to which their authors belong. The more abstract conceptions of law that philosophers build are not.... But there is no reason to expect even a very abstract conception to fit foreign legal systems developed in and reflecting political ideologies of sharply different character.

> *(LE, 102–103)*

It is passages like this that prompt Hart to deny that Dworkin's theory competes with his own. Read literally, it seems to say that Dworkin is interested more in some of the law's provinces than in its empire. I suggested that this reconciliation of the two enterprises cannot be sustained because if Dworkin is right even only about the law of the USA then Hart's explanation of law is mistaken. But beyond that is the fact that the book belies the modesty of passages like the above. Time and again, from its beginning to its very last section, it declares itself to be offering an account of law, unqualified, in all its imperial domains.

Hart's claim that 'it is not obvious why there should be or indeed could be any significant conflict between enterprises so different as my own and Dworkin's conceptions of legal theory'[51] denies, by implication, that Dworkin's is a theory of the nature of law, not even of American law. To maintain that his is a theory of law, Dworkin has to show that it is wrong to think that there can be a general theory of the

---

[51] Hart, Postscript, above n 4, at 241.

nature of law, even legal systems 'developed in and reflecting political ideologies of sharply different character'. He has to establish that the concept of law does not single out a form of political organization with central features that make it a major factor in understanding all societies in which it is to be found, however much they differ in their political ideology. After all, the fact that some countries differ in one important respect (their political ideologies) does not mean that they differ in all major respects, and therefore that there is no possibility of regarding their different institutions of government and conflict resolution as exemplifying the same type that we have, the law, whose essential features are of great importance to an understanding of forms of social organization.

That is why the semantic sting is so crucial to Dworkin's case for his conception of jurisprudence. It is his main argument to deny that there is a possible alternative to his way of conceiving the tasks of legal philosophy. Without that argument he has little to rely on, and his 'concession' that his theory does not apply to various legal systems is tantamount to conceding that his is not a theory about the nature of law. But if Hart's implied claim that Dworkin does not offer an explanation of the nature of law at all is correct, then the considerations which showed that if he has a correct account of American law then Hart is wrong in his explanation of the nature of law are reversed. It would now seem that Hart may come closer to a correct understanding of the tasks and methods of a central element in legal philosophy: the inquiry into the nature of law. For if Dworkin does not have a method to explain the nature of law in general he cannot explain the nature of American law either (it is the same). His book is not so much an explanation of the law as a sustained argument about how courts, especially American and British courts, should decide cases. It contains a theory of adjudication rather than a theory of (the nature of) law. Dworkin's failure to allow that the two are not the same is one reason for the failure of his conception of the tasks and method of jurisprudence.

PART II

LAW, AUTHORITY, AND MORALITY

4

On the Nature of Law

I. Authority and Community

When I travel long distances to far-away countries to deliver lectures to audiences whose culture is very different from my own, I often find the occasions daunting. This is not only because of the honour and responsibility of the invitation, and the prestige of the inviting institution. True, I normally have a safe and pleasant journey. I always travel well. But do my ideas also travel well? Will they survive the distance?*

This may strike some of you as a strange worry. How can philosophy be a matter of geography? Is not philosophy universal? It is—I want to reply—but it is also parochial. The explanation of this thought will take up the first part of this chapter.

A. The universal and the parochial in legal philosophy

It is easy to explain in what sense legal philosophy is universal. Its theses, if true, apply universally, that is they speak of all law, of all legal systems; of those that exist, or that will exist, and even of those that can exist though they never will. Moreover, its theses are advanced as necessarily universal. In this chapter I will try to say something about the nature of law, that is I will be advancing views which belong to the general theory of law. So let me confine my remarks here to that aspect of the philosophy of law. The general theory of law is universal for it consists of claims about the nature of all law, and of all legal systems, and about the nature of adjudication, legislation, and legal reasoning, wherever they may be, and whatever they might be. Moreover, its claims, if true, are necessarily true. I will leave the question of the kind of necessity involved unexplored. Suffice it to say that the truth of the

---

* These concerns weighed on my mind at the original presentation of this chapter, for the Kobe Lectures of 1994.

theses of the general theory of law is not contingent on existing political, social, economic, or cultural conditions, institutions, or practices. To be sure such social facts determine whether legal institutions of one kind or another exist in this country or that. But they do not determine the nature of law, they only affect its instantiation. But its instantiation, the determination whether one or another legal institution or practice exists in one country or another is not itself a philosophical question.

The universality of the theses of the general theory of law is a result of the fact that they claim to be necessary truths, and there is nothing less that they can claim. In as much as the general theory of law is about the nature of law it strives to elucidate law's essential features, ie those features which are possessed by every legal system just in virtue of its being legal, by every legislative institution in virtue of its being legislative, by every practice of legal reasoning in virtue of its being a practice of legal reasoning, and so on. A claim to necessity is in the nature of the enterprise.

While the general theory of law is universal it is also parochial. And I do not mean that it is parochial when it fails to be universal. To be sure most, if not all, the theories of law which have been advanced over the centuries were flawed. One way in which many of them were flawed is that they failed to capture adequately universal and necessary features of the law. They mistook the local for the universal. They were parochial in their failure, in unconsciously elevating the parochial to the status of the universal, of mistaking the contingencies of their own societies for the necessary features of law.

My claim, however, is that all successful legal theories are parochial as well; that success can be obtained only through being parochial. I will approach this point indirectly, by reminding you of HLA Hart's contribution to contemporary legal philosophy. Hart, who revived legal philosophy in English, which was moribund when he was young, by reuniting it with mainstream philosophical thought, is better known for his emphasis on the universal aspect of philosophy than for any interest in its parochial aspect. But, influenced by Wittgenstein, he emphasized the importance of the internal point of view to our understanding of law. That is one aspect of his theory which won universal acceptance, and remains virtually unchallenged.[1] Not so its meaning and implications.

---

[1] These remarks about the boundary of the philosophical should not be taken to indicate that their application to the classification of specific questions as philosophical or not is clear and uncontroversial. There are many borderline cases, for the determination of the boundary of the philosophical is itself determined by the theory of law, and various theories place the boundary at different places.

They are as much in contention now as they were immediately following the publication of Hart's *Concept of Law*.

There are, according to Hart, two ways of describing or analysing the law. One can provide an account of the law either from an external or from an internal point of view. Accounts of both types can be true, but only an account from the internal point of view can be adequate to its task. The difference between the two approaches is that an account from an internal point of view is focused on the way the law is understood by the people whose law it is. Or, to be more precise, an account of the law from an internal point of view is focused on the way the law is understood by people whose law it is and who accept it as binding. External accounts are not concerned with elucidating the way those subject to the law view it.

I want to emphasize two lessons we should learn from Hart here. First, that truth is not enough. A good theory of law is, of course, true. But it is not a good theory just because it is true. Even inadequate accounts— such as those proceeding from an external point of view—can be true. What makes them inadequate is that they miss the purpose of a theory of law, they miss its point.

Second, it is of the nature of law that its existence is known to those subject to it, and that normally it plays a role in their life. I say 'normally' for it is of course possible for people to disregard the law, to be mindless of its existence. But that condition is abnormal not only, perhaps not at all, in being rare. It is abnormal because it is of the essence of law that it expects people to be aware of its existence and, when appropriate, to be guided by it. They may not be. But that marks a failure in the law. It shows that it is not functioning as it aspires to function.

I find nothing amiss in personalizing the law. We do refer to the law as imposing requirements and duties, conferring rights and privileges, and so on. Such expressions are unexceptional. The law's actions, expectations, and intentions are its in virtue of the actions, expectations, and intentions of the people who hold legal office according to law, that is we know when and how the actions, intentions, and attitudes of judges, legislators, and other legal officials, when acting as legal officials, are to be seen as the actions, intentions, and expectations of the law. They, acting as officials, express the demand and the expectation that people be aware of the law and that they be guided by it.

Hart in describing the internal attitude which legal officials necessarily have, and which others are expected to have, strove to identify only those aspects of their attitude to the law which are essential to its existence. He saw no conflict between the internal point of view and the universal character of the law. And in a way he was right. There is no contradiction between the two. But I think that while his views are compatible with my emphasis on the parochial nature of the concept of law he was unaware of these implications.

The question is: does people's awareness of rules of law mean an awareness of them as rules or an awareness of them as rules of law? Need they, in other words, possess the concept of law in order to be members of a political community governed by law? Hart assumed, and surely he was right, that in our cultures the concept of law is available to all, that most people have a fairly good general grasp of it. He has identified six features as the uncontroversial core of the common understanding of the concept of law. His own account of the concept merely deepens our understanding by drawing out some of the implications of the concept as it is commonly understood, the concept of law as we have it.

But our possession of the concept is logically independent of the fact that we live in a political community governed by law. We could have had the same concept had we lived in a state of nature. We might then have used the concept to understand the difference between the law-free society we inhabit and the condition of other countries which do live under legal systems, and the difference between the current state of our society and what it might have been or may become. Contrariwise it would seem that Hart is not committed to the view that to live in a society governed by law we need be aware of the concept of law, beyond an awareness of the rules which in fact constitute the law of our society.

By way of contrast let me mention that it seems that Dworkin's theory of law assumes that an awareness of the concept of law is necessary for the existence of law in any society. For him the law is an interpretive practice which exists only in societies which are aware of the nature of that practice and of its interpretive character, and thus possess the concept of law.[2] In this, however, Hart's position is the correct one. Our concept of law does not make an awareness of it in a society a precondition of that society being governed by law. I will illustrate this point with one example only.

Jewish religious rules and practices are rich and diverse. They did, at an earlier stage of their development, govern the life of independent

---

[2] Though it is possible that all his theory requires is that those living in a society subject to law regard the law as instantiating some interpretive concept or another rather than the concept of law specifically.

Jewish communities, and, in more recent times, they governed many aspects of life in Jewish communities in many parts of the world. Whenever theocratic autonomous Jewish communities existed or may exist they would be subject to law, ie Jewish religious law. But the concept of law is not part of the Jewish religion, and where such communities existed in the past they often existed in societies whose members did not possess the concept of law. Jewish religious thought and doctrine encompasses much more than law. It encompasses what we regard as comprehensive systems of law, ethics, and religion, areas which though overlapping are also—in our eyes—distinct. To the Orthodox Jew of old there is no division within Judaic doctrines which captures the divisions indicated by 'our' concepts of law and ethics. Yet beyond doubt theocratic Jewish communities did have a legal system even though they lacked the concept of law, or at any rate some of them (those which had not learnt it from other cultures) lacked it.

I believe that much the same is true of some other religious systems. 'Our' concept of law is probably alien to the culture of Islamic theocracies, but it would be absurd to think that Iran, for example, does not have a legal system, or that its having a legal system depends on Iranians having acquired the concept of law before their Islamic revolution. Rather, the correct conclusion is that the concept of law is itself a product of a specific culture, a concept which was not available to members of earlier cultures which in fact lived under a legal system.

The fact that concepts emerge within a culture at a particular juncture is often seen as a vindication of some radical philosophical thesis such as relativism, or post-modernism or ethnocentrism. In fact it shows little, certainly not that concepts can only apply to phenomena which exist in cultures which have those concepts. Consider, for example, the notion of 'the standard of living'. It may well not have been available to people in medieval Europe. But there is nothing in this fact to invalidate discussions of the effect of the Wars of the Roses on the standard of living in Lancashire. People would enjoy the same standard of living whether or not they were aware of the notion, or of the measurement of their own standard of living. The same is true of many other economic notions.

Some concepts are different. Arguably since gifts are gifts only if intentionally given as such there cannot be gifts among people who do not possess the concept of a gift. As we saw, something like this is true of rules. People are not guided by them unless they are aware of them as rules. But, and that is the crucial point, they need not be aware of rules as legal rules in order to be guided by rules which are in fact legal.

On reflection there is nothing surprising in this. Of crucial importance is the fact that concepts like that of the law are essential not only
to our understanding of the practices and institutions of our own societies, but also to our understanding of other societies. To understand
other societies we must master their concepts, for we will not understand them unless we understand how they perceive themselves. But
we cannot understand other cultures unless we can relate their practices and customs to our own. Their concepts will not be understood
by us unless we can relate them to our own concepts, so the understanding of alien cultures requires possession of concepts which apply
across the divide between us and them, concepts which can be applied
to the practices of other cultures as well as to our own. Only with the
help of concepts which apply to our own as well as to alien cultures can
we understand the concepts used by alien cultures in their own understanding of their own practices and institutions and not shared by us.
The centrality of the law in social life makes it natural that the concept
of law would be one of these bridge-building concepts, ie one which
we could apply to societies which themselves do not use it in their own
self-understanding.

B. Consequences of parochialism

So far it may seem to you that while conceding the fact that the concept of law like all concepts is parochial in being the product of a
specific culture I am denying that this fact has any interesting jurisprudential consequences. But this is not at all my view. Many lessons are
to be learnt from the parochiality of our concepts. I will only mention
three here.

First, it is important to remember that while the concept of law is
'our' concept of law, the fact that other cultures had different ways of
analysing the nature of their political organization does not cast any
doubt on the validity of the concept of law, ie of 'our' concept of law.
It is true that if we rely exclusively on our concepts we will not fully
understand, we may distort and misrepresent, alien political structures,
for we will be unaware of the way they conceived their own practices
and institutions. The crucial point here is that the way a culture understands its own practices and institutions is not separate from what they
are. Social practices and human institutions are a product of intentional,
purpose-oriented conduct of many people interacting with one another.
While normally no individual, nor any small number of individuals can

shape such practices to their design, it remains the case that they—the practices and the institutions—are in part shaped by the way they are understood by the people whose practices and institutions they are. They are manifestations of the self-understanding of their culture. Just as we cannot understand an alien culture without the use of 'our' concepts, so we cannot understand it without the use of the concepts with which that culture understood itself, even if they have no currency and no use in our society.

The second lesson follows from the first. For it follows from it that the concept of law plays a different role in cultures which possess it than in those which do not. Our society not only is ruled by law. It also conceives of itself as being ruled by law. Some other societies are governed by law, but their own self-understanding makes no use of the concept of law. They may regard themselves as subject to a religious system or something else. It follows that in working out a theory of law we are explicating our own self-understanding of the nature of society and politics, but even when, as we hope, our theory of law is true of all societies subject to law, it does not necessarily capture the way those societies understood their own organization and practices.

Third, and finally, a degree of impermanence in the theory of law is indicated by these reflections. Let me start indirectly by recalling a point which we found in Hart: Truth is not enough. The general theory of law is the study of essential properties of law. It would be, however, wrong to think of it as striving for an exhaustive statement of law's essential properties. Hart was right to claim that a combination of what he called primary and secondary rules is essential to law. But he was wrong to intimate that therein lay the key to the study of jurisprudence. There are other essential properties to the law. I have argued, for example, that it is essential to the law that it claims to have legitimate, moral, authority, and that it is source-based, and that it claims to have peremptory force, etc. These claims do not conflict with Hart's view that necessarily the law combines primary and secondary rules, that it includes a rule of recognition, and that it is accepted by the legal officials, and normally also by many others in the population it applies to.[3]

While the law has many essential features we are not aware of all of them. They come to light as we find reason to highlight them, in response to some puzzle, to some bad theory, or to some intellectual

---

[3] As it happens Hart and I disagree on some of the features here enumerated. My point is merely that there is no contradiction between them, that one can endorse all of them.

preoccupation of the time. The study of jurisprudence is never-ending, for the list of the essential properties of law is indefinite. There is neither point in nor possibility of listening to them all. We explore them not just because they are true but because they answer to a current concern. This makes for cycles of novelty, and explains one reason for theories going out of fashion, without having been refuted. But the previous remarks point to another source of impermanence in legal theory. Because legal theory attempts to capture the essential features of law, as encapsulated in the self-understanding of a culture, it has a built-in obsolescence, since the self-understanding of cultures is forever changing. A clear example of such a change occurred over the last half century in the English-speaking cultures regarding rights. The notion of a right changed from designating concrete enforceable entitlements to designating any normally sufficient ground for a judgement of what ought to happen; even when there is no one who ought to bring it about, provided it is based on the interest of an individual human being or another animal or a group. Such conceptual changes accompany changes, which we cannot trace here, in people's views about the political responsibilities of states to their subjects, and of individuals to each other. Similar transformations have overtaken various legal theories which came to have mere historical significance as a result of changes in the basic concepts about the nature of political communities, ie the concepts of the state and of the law.

All this puts a gloss on the meaning of the claim that legal theory aims to provide an account of the essential features of the law. There are, I said, essential features of the law, though possession of the concept of law is not itself necessary in all cultures which have legal systems. Moreover, other concepts, similar to the concept of law, do govern the self-understanding of the basic structures and practices of political communities in those other cultures. Where they are sufficiently similar to the concept of law, or just historically continuous with it, we naturally talk of differing concepts of law. Legal theory is merely the study of the necessary features of law, given 'our' concept of law.

Finally, since our own concept is liable to be forever in flux, since legal theory is itself part of the culture to which 'our' concept of law belongs, it is inevitable that legal theory is no mere passive mirror of the concepts of that culture. To the extent that legal theorists acquire influence their views tend to be self-verifying. This led some post-modernists to identify theory with advocacy. This is a misleading view. Theory aims at understanding. By and large, only bad theory can lead to change. If its wrong conclusions are accepted their acceptance may lead to a change in the self-understanding of the culture which will make the bad theory true. But such bad theories succeed only by not trying, ie by claiming—however erroneously—that they state how things are, and not that they advocate change. Once they avow that they advocate change they lose the claim they have on our attention, they join reformers in an activity to be judged by different standards altogether.

In resisting the confusion of theory and advocacy I am not motivated by a love of clear demarcation lines. None such exist in my view, and theory does indeed involve advocacy. It shades into advocacy in those areas where the self-understanding of our culture includes diverse and inconsistent elements. My aim is to point to two important lessons: First, that the attempt to establish the essential and universal features of the law should not be confused with a craving for permanence or with the denial of the parochial nature of the concept of law. Second, that the concept of law is not reflexive, ie that it applies to social practices in societies where the concept itself is neither used nor known. That, I claimed, is an instance of the general fact that social concepts, at their most general, are not and cannot be reflexive for we need general non-reflexive concepts to be able to understand alien cultures and institutions.

C. Law as the authoritative voice of a political community

One change in the modern conceptions of the law, not a recent change but one which grew over more than three hundred years, is the growing emphasis on law's instrumental role. The accelerated rate of change in socio-economic conditions, as a result of ever faster technological changes, and of the vast increase in movements of populations, has led to a growth in the importance of legislation and a decline in the role of custom. The law has come to be seen as subject to change in response to changing circumstances, and to changing moral beliefs. It has become the way 'we', 'society' discharge our obligations to each other in an environment of relatively rapid change. Thus grew an instrumental view of the law, which regards it as a means of social regulation by deliberate design with the purpose of securing certain desired goals (be they justice, efficiency, etc or more concrete and detailed goals).

These changes in social reality and in its perception have led to a growing emphasis on the role of institutions in accounts of the law. The emphasis on legislation is—in this context—self-explanatory. But the courts as well gained added importance in the theoretical accounts. In some quarters this was a result of rule-scepticism which, especially in the USA, with its constitution entrusted to the stewardship of the courts, presented the courts as the real power behind the law.[4] But the functioning of the courts was also seen as providing the means by which the instrumentalist conception of the law can be reconciled with the continued validity of customary law, of legal doctrine and of the common law. Viewed as legally binding in as much as they are endorsed and followed by the courts they too can be absorbed within the instrumental approach to the law.

In previous writings I tried to do justice to the instrumental approach, without overlooking the non-instrumental aspect of the law.[5] The key to this synthesis, as well as to much else, is in the question: What special claim or meaning is conveyed by saying not that 'this is what one ought to do (or what one is entitled to, etc)', but that 'legally, this is what one ought to do'? Legal statements say both more and less than the corresponding non-legal statements.[6] Legal statements say less for they do not always convey the view of the speaker of what one ought to do. In many contexts legal statements are detached. They are statements of what the speaker believes the law requires, without commitment on his part as to whether there is any reason to act as the law requires.[7] For the rest of this chapter I will disregard that fact. I will discuss only committed legal statements, ie those which convey the normative judgement of the speaker. Committed legal statements convey something more than is conveyed by the corresponding non-legal judgement. They convey that the requirement which the statement specifies enjoys a certain standing. In being the law of that society it is authoritative within it.

---

[4] Gray, now nearly forgotten, was the path-blazer in adopting the terminology of the legislation-dominated Austinian theory and applying it to the courts. Holmes gave these ideas a local American stamp, a pungent expression and the authority of his name which American theory is still labouring to shake off. He also manifests the second motivation for focusing on the courts: their stewardship of the common law.

[5] See *The Authority of Law* (Oxford: OUP, 1979), essays ('Respect for Law'), and *The Morality of Freedom* (Oxford: OUP, 1986) pt 1.

[6] I am aware that one may make legal statements, statements about how the law stands, without the use of qualifiers such as 'legally'. And one can make the combined statement that this is what one ought to do, and that that is what the law requires of one (or at least imply both) by the utterance of one sentence only. My comments are about the statements one makes not about the sentences one utters.

[7] See my *Practical Reason and Norms* (2nd edn, Oxford: OUP 1999).

What is it to be the law of a political community? And what is it to be authoritative? These questions will occupy the rest of this section.

I may have views about how certain matters should be arranged in this country (no litter should be dropped in the street, no unleaded petrol be used in vehicles, etc). These may be good sound views but they are not authoritatively binding on anyone, not even on me. Their lack of authority is not due to the fact that they are minority views. Even if almost everyone shares the same views they still lack the stamp of authority. Moreover, even if almost everyone behaves according to these views they may still lack that authority. Some social practices, for example that when driving one stops at a red light, are legally binding, while others, for example that one baptizes one's new-born children, are not. Wherein lies the difference? It is not in the importance of the rule, nor in its content. Trivial as well as important matters are often regulated by law, trivial as well as important matters are left unregulated by it. And while possibly rules with a certain content cannot exist outside the law, most rules can either be part of the law or be left out of it.

Legal rules are as such authoritative, and that quality belongs to them in virtue of their standing in the political community to which they belong and which they, partly, constitute. Their authoritativeness is intertwined with their being the law of a political community. Each of the two features of the law partly explains the other. The point I am making is a familiar one. Some carried it to excess, as did Kelsen when he asserted that the legal order and the state are one and the same. Put more moderately: The law and the state are mutually dependent; they partly constitute each other.[8] I prefer to talk of a 'political community' rather than 'The State', for other forms of political community are also partly constituted by legal orders of the kind familiar from contemporary states. What is common to all of them is a view of the community as an agent which is capable of decision and action.

In particular, political communities are societies which decide how their own members should conduct themselves. This means that regarding political communities we recognize a distinction between standards of conduct which express the decisions of the community regarding the way people should behave, the entitlements they have, etc, and views about these matters, however sound and however popular, which do not

---

[8] I will not explore here the numerous ramifications of this point. For my own contribution to the exploration of this theme see *The Authority of Law* (Oxford: OUP, 1979); as well as *The Concept of a Legal System* (2nd edn, Oxford: OUP, 1980).

have the imprimatur of the community. By and large the law represents those standards which are considered in that community to be binding as expressing the decisions of the community.[9] Perhaps the point I am making is clearer if put slightly differently: The generic concept of a political community, and the more specific concepts of types of political communities, for example the state, apply only to societies within which one can discern the distinction between standards which express the decisions of these societies and those which do not. If no such distinction is to be found in any particular society then it is not a political community, and *a fortiori* not a state. Where the distinction is to be found the law represents the voice of the community, those of its standards which express its decisions as to the conduct of people.

D. The instrumental and the non-instrumental views of law

There are three ways in which standards can be said to be the standards of a society or a group. First, they can be its standards simply in being enshrined in the practices of the community. Second, where the community is personalized by its members and treated as a separate entity and as an object for identification (identification which is expressed by one's ability to say 'I am Japanese', 'I am from the University of Oxford', etc) then some of its practices may be regarded as expressing the spirit of the community, its essential ethos or long-standing traditions, and thus they may be considered by its members to represent the community, to be its standards, in a special way. Neither of these senses of the idea of standards of a community assumes that the community is an organized political community, and neither assumes that the community is capable of independent action.

In being the standards of political communities legal standards exemplify a third way in which standards belong to communities. Political communities are conceived by their members as agents, a conception which corresponds to the fact that they have organs, leaders, and political institutions which can in appropriate circumstances act for the community. In the context of a political community standards are the

---

[9] In recent years Dworkin has emphasized the fact that the concept of law is intertwined with viewing political communities governed by law as persons. He did, however, proceed to claim, that political communities have interests with moral weight independently of the interests of individuals. That view, which does not follow from the personification of political communities, is not one which I espouse. See *Law's Empire* (Cambridge, Mass: Harvard University Press, 1986) 178ff.

standards of the community because they stand in certain relations to the political organs of the community, for example by being the standards which constitute such organs or in being standards which are recognized and followed by them, or even standards which are made by them.

The distinction between those standards which partly constitute a community in the second and third ways I identified, on the one hand, and those which are standards of a society in the first sense, or which, however wise and morally sound, are not standards 'of any society' at all, captures a divide of some importance. In large measure its importance derives from the fact that our perception of ourselves, of who we are, depends among other things on our ability to identify with communities we live in, on our ability to belong to these communities in the full sense of the word. In as much as the law belongs to a kind of standard which is a standard of a community in one of these ways it can have intrinsic value.[10]

At the same time, the distinction between the second and third way in which standards are standards of communities marks the way in which norms deriving from authority can be the standards of a community. In as much as the law belongs to the standards of political communities, it exists because it is made or endorsed by authority and as such it can have instrumental value. So herein lies the explanation of how the law can combine both instrumental and intrinsic value. But these cryptic remarks require some amplification.

First, I am discussing, here and throughout, not the value the law has but the value it can have. Whether the law of any political community has value depends on its content, and the circumstances of the community. I am neither asserting nor denying that just because they are law all legal systems have some value. That question cannot be addressed here. What is clear is that any legal system can fail to live up to the ideal, and in as much as it falls short of the ideal it lacks value which it should have. To understand the nature of law is to understand, among other things, the ideal which the law should live up to, and also to understand that it can fail to live up to that ideal. In that the explanation of the concept of law is no different from the explanation of other normative concepts. To understand the concept of a promise—to give but one example—is to understand under what circumstances promises are binding, but also to understand that they can fail to be binding.[11]

---

[10] I am not implying that the law or elements of it cannot have intrinsic value for other reasons.

[11] This point is, or should be, common ground to supporters and opponents of the traditional natural law approach to legal theory. For a notable example of the point

Second, in as much as the law consists of the standards of political communities it claims to have authority over its subjects. Put in a different way: It is part of the ideal of law that it should have such authority, though it often fails to live up to that ideal. This point requires little additional explanation here. It follows from the fact that the law consists of those standards which become the standards of a political community by being enacted, endorsed, or enforced by the organs of that community, as it is plain that those organs claim legitimate moral authority, and in claiming that they are authoritative they claim that the standards that they lay down or endorse are so as well.[12]

Third, the basic way in which claims to authority are to be judged, the basic way in which legitimate authority is shown to exist, is through the instrumental approach.

Think of it this way: only an authority which on the whole acts wisely and morally is a legitimate authority. In as much as its role is, as in the case of legal authorities, to issue and enforce directives, it is legitimate only if its directives are on the whole wise and morally sound. They are wise and morally sound if the way they order social relations, commercial activities, and individual conduct is such that in following the directives their subjects would be acting in a reasonable way, that is will be conforming to right reason, and moreover, they would be able to conform to right reason to a greater degree by following the authority than by disregarding it and trying to follow right reason independently of it.

In practice the most reliable way in which authorities can meet this test of legitimacy is by attempting to follow right reason in laying down or endorsing directives. This vindicates the instrumentalist approach which emphasizes the fact that the law is a means for deliberately moulding and fashioning individual conduct and social relations.

The instrumentalist conception is liable to attract a number of misguided criticisms. Here are two. It is sometimes supposed that those who adopt the instrumental approach are committed to an optimistic view about the degree to which political authorities can effect social and economic changes through legal reform. But no such optimism is built into

forcibly made by a supporter see J Finnis, *Natural Law and Natural Rights* (Oxford: OUP, 1980) ch 1.

[12] If this point requires argument then it is to be found in several of my writings, as well as in those of many others. Eg, *Ethics in the Public Domain* (Oxford: OUP, 1994), *The Authority of Law* (Oxford: OUP, 1979) ch 1. This view is at the heart of Kelsen's analysis of the normativity of law. See *The Pure Theory of Law* (2nd edn). It is also central to Finnis's theory of the nature of law (ibid.), and is endorsed by many other writers.

the instrumental approach. All it is committed to is: (1) Legal doctrines and institutions have social and economic consequences (not necessarily those intended by the powers which maintain and enforce them as law). (2) Legal authorities should be guided by the foreseeable consequences of the law in deciding whether to maintain it as it is or to change it, for these consequences are the most important consideration bearing on the justifiability of the law, and legal authorities will achieve better results if they follow their best efforts to form informed judgements on the likely consequences of the law than if they decide on the way the law should develop disregarding their best judgement of its consequences.

One realizes how modest these claims are when remembering that one judgement legal institutions may come to is that certain areas of social or economic relations should be left unregulated by law, as people and corporations may act more sensibly or develop more successful practices if the law leaves them to act as they judge best without intervening. The instrumentalist approach asserts that decisions about the limitations of legal regulation should also be based on the best judgement available to legal authorities.

Another unjustified criticism of the instrumental approach is that it unjustifiably politicizes all aspects of the law, whereas in fact large tracts of the law such as classical criminal law, contract law, and tort law are a matter of professional lawyers' judgement and have evolved through the collective wisdom of the common law (or equivalent institutions in other types of legal systems) through the centuries. The response to this criticism is slightly more complex. The instrumentalist approach is consistent with the plain fact that much of the law evolved gradually through the practices of the courts and of other legal authorities. It reminds us, however, that even that part of the law is endorsed, maintained, and enforced continuously by legal authorities, who can change it, and therefore bear the responsibility to do so if such change is wise or morally required. Supporters of the instrumental approach are also more, and better, aware than their opponents that even legal doctrines which seemed far removed from politics or from currently debatable moral concerns often have controversial moral and political consequences which simply escape public attention for the time being.[13]

---

[13] The changes, accepted or still controversial, over the law regarding marital rape, and regarding provocation in homicide in the English common law, illustrate how aspects of the law which at one time seem to be far removed from current public or political concern really do have far-reaching political and social significance. The transformation of the nineteenth-century doctrine of freedom of contract, through statutory interventions

Fourth, so far I have been defending the instrumental approach. But as I have already intimated it has its limitations. One crucial non-instrumental aspect of the law derives from the fact that full membership of political communities, ie membership which enables the member to identify with the community is—assuming the communities themselves are morally decent—intrinsically good.

This is too large a theme to discuss adequately here. Luckily it is also one which in its general contours is not controversial. To prosper in life people need a secure sense of self-respect and of their own worth and security in their ability to find their bearing in their world. By an ability to find one's bearing I mean an understanding of the nature of options and opportunities, and of what is involved in pursuing them. People's sense of self-respect and self-worth, and their ability to have a secure sense of orientation in their environment, depend to an extent on their being full members of various communities they are part of, on feeling identification with these communities, and believing that the communities are, and are accepted as being, worthwhile, as being respected and respectable communities. Identification with a community depends on our ability and willingness to accept the standards which these communities endorse as our own. This ability itself is partly fostered by the culture, and achieved through successful socialization. But it also depends on one's moral judgement giving basic approval to those standards.

Given the importance of political communities in the life of their members, an ability to identify with one's political community is, within the framework of the considerations I mentioned, intrinsically valuable. Any account of the law which disregards that aspect of it is incomplete. Therefore any account which adopts exclusively the instrumental approach is incomplete. To understand the nature of the law we have to understand its role as partly constitutive of a political community and therefore as an object for identification, as playing an important role in people's sense of who they are.

II. Authority and Interpretation

Earlier in this chapter I emphasized one aspect of the fact that the law is a structure of authority, as well as—thought of as a system of norms,

(eg Unfair Contract Terms Act, 1977) and through the evolution of common law doctrines of implied terms and of unconscienability, is another example of the growing realization that what was thought to be lawyers' law lying well outside politics was not so.

of standards and doctrines—the product of that structure of authority, which it itself constitutes. I have emphasized that as a structure of and a product of authority it is also a product of, an expression of, a political community as well as being, in part, constitutive of that community. Here I will further explore some of the consequences of the connection between law and authority. This time I will focus on the connection between authority and interpretation.

First, I will discuss the way in which the connection between law and authority leads to a dual interest in the study of law: an interest in the process leading to the authoritative laying down or endorsement of a standard, and an interest in how the fact that a standard has authoritatively been laid down affects its standing. Second, I will consider the main way in which the fact that law is authoritative affects its interpretation. Finally, I will consider the way in which the authoritative nature of law makes interpretation central to legal reasoning.

To simplify the discussion I will assume throughout that the law enjoys legitimate moral authority over its subjects. I will be making this assumption not because it is true, but because it is in the nature of law that it claims authority over its subjects, and it is treated as law by and large only by people who accept that claim. To understand it we have to understand what it claims to be and what it is taken to be by those who accept its claims. We need to do that in order to understand even legal systems which do not enjoy legitimate moral authority over their subjects.

A. The decisive moment

I have suggested that law exists within political communities, that is societies which have political organizations, with institutions claiming to act in the name of the community as a whole. It is both a community and an institution. It is a community in as much as its subjects are—ideally—also its members, that is people who identify with the community, and regard their membership as important to their own sense of who they are. It is an institution in having a formal structure of rules constituting organs for the making, implementation, and enforcement of standards for the conduct of affairs among those subject to the community. My focus in this chapter is on the institutional rather than on the communal side of the law.

Political sociologists, and some legal scholars, naturally emphasize the continuity of the legal process: To take one type of case: from the formation of circumstances which give rise to an alleged social, or a commercial need, to the perception of the alleged need, to the mobilization of political will and influence to do something about it, to the formation of a political coalition to meet the need in a certain way, to the embedding of that resolve in legal standards, to the publicity given to that step, and the adjustment made by people and organizations in light of the change in the law, to the policing and enforcing of the standards, and to people's adjustments and responses in the face of these policing and enforcement measures—it is a complex continuous process.

These scholars are right to point out that at no point in the process is the result of actions taken at that stage likely to be the result intended. They are likely to point out that explicit or implicit bargaining takes place at each stage of the process; that the process leading to forming a coalition of political powers strong enough to secure the formulation and adoption of a legislative measure does no more than set the stage for the bargaining between companies, or between regulatory bodies and the regulated agents, or between the public and the police, which while being affected by the law, only takes it as one factor in the equation ultimately leading to one result or another.

We need deny none of this in order to insist that the adoption of a legal standard, its endorsement by the competent legal authority—legislative, administrative, or judicial—is a decisive moment, effecting a basic transformation of the situation. That endorsement turns a standard which hitherto was probably no more than an idea favoured by some and resisted by others into the law of the land. That the law of the land can be used, and is often used as a bargaining chip does not explain what it is to be the law of the land. And without explaining that we do not understand how it can be a bargaining chip.

To say that the law provides economic incentives is not so much to be wrong (for of course sometimes what the law does has nothing to do with economic incentives) as to miss the fact that the answer misses the question, which is how it is that my saying 'do not exceed 55 miles an hour' does not provide such incentives, whereas the law's saying so does. It is only through doing something else that the law can provide economic incentives. That something else is that the law provides a reason for action for its subjects through being a decree laid down or endorsed by a legitimate authority. Its authoritative nature is itself sufficient to establish that the law is a reason for compliance for its subjects, and that independently of and in addition to any sanctions or incentives it may provide. Because commonly people who are subject to the law, and in particular legal officials, take it to be authoritative and therefore as establishing reasons for compliance, the law can and does provide incentives for people to behave in one way or another.

The continuities I mentioned notwithstanding, there is then a decisive moment in the legal process: the moment in which legal standards come into existence, and provide new reasons for action. Prior to that moment the legal process, at whatever level, legislative, administrative, or judicial, is a process aiming to influence the content of the law. Wielding arguments of principle, jockeying for position, mobilizing power, manipulating, and applying pressure—all aim either at promoting the chances of certain standards being adopted by the relevant authorities, or at preventing their adoption. From the moment of adoption of a standard and its transformation into law things change. The arguments of principle remain valid, if they ever were. The influence and the pressure are still there. But now they aim either at the preservation and implementation of the standard or at its repeal or frustration.

The authoritative laying down of standards is the decisive moment in the legal process not merely because in it new reasons are created. It is the decisive moment because those new standards, those new reasons, are there to put an end to the argument and struggle about what is to be done, to resolve the argument and the struggle by replacing them for the time being. This point should not be misunderstood. The argument and the struggle can and often do continue. But now they are about whether and how to change the new law, and no longer about whether to adopt it.

The pivotal place of the law in the organization of society is precisely in its authoritative nature. That is why I can say that for the time being, that is while it is in force, the law resolves the argument and the struggle about how things should be in society. Take a simple example: Suppose some people disagree over whether it is reasonable to drive at 60 miles an hour on a certain road, or whether it is reasonable to pick apples from the overhanging branches which enable one to reach the apples without trespassing on their owner's land. Some people maintain that there is no reason not to drive at that speed, no reason not to pick the apples. Now further suppose that things have changed and that a 50 mph speed limit has been decreed by law, and that a law clarifying that fruit on a plant belongs to the owner of the plant has been passed.[14] The discussion

---

[14] I am assuming an asymmetry between legal permission and legal prohibitions. That the law permits one to behave in a certain manner does not pre-empt discussion about the reasonableness of the conduct in the way that a legal prohibition does. Lack of clarity in the law also leave the matter open to discussion as will be explained below.

about the reasonableness of the conduct can continue. After all none of the arguments have lost their force. But now it is no longer a discussion about whether or not there is reason not to drive at 60 mph or not to pick your neighbour's apples. Now if we know the law we know that we may not pick the apples nor drive at 60 mph. Now the discussion is about the reasonableness of having these laws.

I am not denying of course that some people will say 'to hell with the law. I think that there is nothing wrong with driving at 60 mph or with picking the apples, and I'll just do it'. Or they may say 'anyone can do it'. My point is not that such attitudes are not to be found. It is merely that they are inconsistent with acknowledging the authority of the law. People who display these attitudes deny that the law has authority. One cannot both accept that the law is binding since it has been passed by a (morally) legitimate authority and that there is no reason to do that which it makes obligatory.

This then is the nature of the decisive moment in the legal process. This is the sense in which the laying down of the law resolves the dispute about what people have reason to do or to avoid. The dispute is not resolved if that means reaching an agreement on the issue originally debated, namely about what is (the law apart) best or reasonable to do. The law resolves the dispute by pre-empting it. It changes the situation in such a way that whether or not there is a law-independent reason to avoid picking the apples there is now a reason to avoid it in the law itself.[15]

I hope that at least the main drift of my remarks so far does not raise any controversy. I hope that you wonder why I bother to state the obvious. The reason is that these obvious points have implications for two central concerns in legal philosophy: the relations between fact and morality in the law, and the nature of legal interpretations. These implications are the subject of this chapter.

---

[15] To avoid lengthy cumbersome formulations I am simplifying the situation, and as a result what I said is only approximately true. I am assuming a disagreement about what is best, reasonable, or right to do. This may have been part of a disagreement about what the law should be, since the law should require only what is right or best. The statement has to be finessed, however, to allow for the fact that it may be right or best to pass a law prohibiting or requiring certain conduct even if it is not prohibited or not required in the absence of a law stipulating so. In that case, and it is not at all rare, the argument about whether it is best to have a law prohibiting or requiring a mode of conduct does not depend on judgement of what is prohibited or required, right or wrong, in the absence of law.

B. Fact and value in the law

The argument about the relative roles of social facts and moral values in the explanation of the law is one of the perennial arguments in the philosophy of law. The very persistence of the debate suggests that its solution is not to be found in simple answers. My own view derives from the considerations I have just explained and in those covered in the first part of this chapter. Let me pull some of them together:

First, legal philosophy is not value-free. In the previous part I tried to explain how the sort of philosophical enterprise of which the explanation of the nature of law as an instance is an attempt to explain our own self-understanding; it is an explanation of the law from the internal point of view, to use Hart's way of putting a related idea. Our self-understanding includes a conception of the nature of the practices and institutions around us. Moreover, our self-understanding is practical, that is it is part of our attempt to fix our own orientation in the world, to find our bearing by identifying who we are and what is right and wrong, good or bad, important or trivial in our surroundings. As a result our self-understanding also is shot with value through and through, and inevitably so is its philosophical study.

Second, the law claims to have legitimate moral authority. This explains why the law is presented in moral terms. The fact that legal and moral terminology overlap and that terms such as authority, duty, obligation, right, and liberty are common to both has been a source of much confusion and contributed to various mistakes. On the one hand it leads many to assume that as the law can be described as a system of rights and duties it must be merely one part of morality. At the other extreme the common terminology of law and morality may have encouraged Bentham in his view that statements of rights and duties are not normative statements at all. He attempted to analyse their meaning in relation to command, or to sanction. Many others have followed in his steps.[16]

The significance of the shared terminology is different. It does not attest to what the law is but to what it aspires to be. It is an expression of

---

[16] See Hart, *Essays on Bentham* (Oxford: Clarendon Press, 1982), Hacker, 'Sanction Theories of Duty', in: Simpson (ed), *Oxford Essays in Jurisprudence* (3rd series, Oxford: OUP, 1973). All the 'predictive' accounts of rights and duties belong here. Kelsen was the first seriously to attempt a normative explanation of legal language which is not committed to a traditional natural law account of law. See *The General Theory of Law and State* and *The Pure Theory of Law*. In this he was followed by Hart in *The Concept of Law* (Oxford: Clarendon Press, 1982).

the fact that the law necessarily claims legitimate authority. It follows, of course, that where a legal system is in force many, most notably its officials, believe that claim to be justified. What does not follow is that it is justified. Still the fact is crucial to the understanding of the sort of institution the law is, and—from the moral point of view—it sets the standards by which the law is to be judged. The law, as a complex social institution, is to be judged good only if its claim to authority is morally warranted, and only if its institutions conduct themselves as legitimate authorities should conduct themselves. The moral doctrine of legitimate authority is crucial to our understanding and assessment of the law.

Third, the law and its institutions are among the central constituents of a community: a political community. Not all authorities essentially belong to communities. Legal authorities are part of what makes a state, or more broadly a political community. Moreover, while people belong to many groups they identify only with some of them. Only some of them contribute to people's sense of who they are. Political communities are commonly objects of such identification. I mean not that most people identify with the political community they belong to, but—and more importantly—that in modern states failure so to identify, a failure which may be morally justified or even required, is a sign of alienation, and is in some respects undesirable from the point of view of the individual concerned.

This point shows the law to have a dual aspect. On the one hand the role of authority is to enable people better to conform to reason, that is to make it more likely that they will, given good will, conduct themselves as reason requires. To that extent the law is to be treated essentially instrumentally. On the other hand, in being partly constitutive of a community which is normally a focus of identification, the law can be intrinsically valuable.

Fourth, as I already mentioned the law can fail morally. It may not justify the moral claims it is making. If it were not so then the very idea of criticizing the law, or at least of criticizing it on moral grounds would be incoherent. This is another fact which, while incontrovertible in itself, has bred many confusions. In particular it has led many to claim that any connection between law and morality must be contingent.[17] This is not the place to explore what necessary connections between

---

[17] Or even more implausibly, that a legal system may exist which implements no moral values.

law and morality may exist. Instead I want to turn to a different, and a diametrically opposed view.

Several writers[18] think that the law can only modestly fail in its claims. They think that while it may fail to the extent that it contains some bad, even some unjust and immoral laws, it cannot fail to have the moral legitimacy that it claims to have. They think that there is therefore a strong necessary connection between law and morality: the law inevitably enjoys moral legitimacy, and therefore there is a *prima facie* obligation to obey any legal system.

It will be clear that the disagreement about this point is complex. It is not primarily that the writers who take this line have a rosier view of human institutions than I have. Primarily the disagreement involves both a dispute about what would count as a good argument for the legitimacy of an authority, and a dispute about the nature of law. I believe, for example, that there have been, maybe there are, viciously racist legal systems, which lacked all legitimate authority: that is, legal systems whose lack of legitimacy casts no doubt on their character as legal systems (and of course they did claim legitimate authority, and were thought to have such authority by many whose racism blinded them to the wickedness of their law). Those who maintain that the law inevitably enjoys legitimate authority will doubt not the existence of such political societies, but the status of their system of rules and institutions as legal. They will deny that such societies have law, or they will insist that while we can call it law it is not really law in the full sense of the word.

In some ways the disagreement here is not great. Those who hold that all law enjoys legitimate authority and therefore that there is a *prima facie* obligation to obey any legal system allow that the rules and government in power in some political societies lack moral legitimacy. So they are really distinguishing between two types of statement about the law: moral statements which entail legitimacy and obligation to obey, and non-moral statements which lack this entailment. The second type of statement is then regarded by them as secondary. It is a degenerate case or an exceptional extension of the first.

For my part I have suggested a view very close to this. Typical legal statements can be either committed or detached. Committed statements, I suggested, entail the legitimacy of the law. Detached statements do not include this implication. I too regard committed statements as primary. The difference between my view and its rival is that I believe

[18] Finnis and Dworkin among them.

that far from non-committed statements being relatively rare, and an extension of the discourse of law to describe political systems which are not legal *strictu senso*, detached statements are prevalent in legal discourse about our own or any other legal system. This makes it possible for me to say that there are legal systems in the world even if we are mistaken about which ones, if any, enjoy moral legitimacy. On the alternative view, if all legal systems lack legitimacy then all the statements to the effect that there are legal systems are simply false. I will not try to resolve the dispute here. My point in raising the issue was to point to the complexity of the debate about the relations between law and morality, and to express my feeling that all too often the issues in question are not completely understood by protagonists on either side.

My *fifth* and final point derives directly from my comments at the beginning of this section. Since the moral force of the law, its moral claim to our attention derives from the moral authority, if any, of the authorities which made it into law, it follows that the content of the law can be identified without resort to moral argument. As usual this bold statement has to be qualified to make it accurate. But rather than worrying about its details let me explain its rationale.

Imagine first that it is generally known which institutions have authority to do what. We ought to follow the law they make or endorse because they have authority over us. The laws they make are based on their best judgement regarding the way people should conduct themselves. But in the matters over which they have authority their subjects will be more likely to conform to reason if they follow the law rather than disregard it and attempt to follow right reason directly (ie irrespective of the law). But for this condition to be met it is necessary that the subjects of the authority are able to establish the content of the law. How can they do this? By establishing which rules were made or endorsed by the authorities. This can involve establishing the acts of the authority and their meaning. But it cannot consist of establishing which law the authority should have passed. Authorities are legitimate only if they are better able to establish that than their subjects. In fact they exist precisely to avoid the need for their subjects to base their actions on their own estimation of what is best to do. That is their main rationale, and it will be defeated if to establish the content of the law they would have to deliberate the very considerations the law exists to pre-empt.

This argument allows for the possibility that the identity of the authority, and the scope of its power, are determined by moral considerations: after all they are matters which depend on moral considerations.

When we are dealing with a single authority this is indeed so. The law, however, is a complex structure of authority, a structure with many authorities established by rules laid down by other authorities. Its value in society largely depends on its complexity, and on the fact that the identity of legal authorities is public knowledge, and their legitimacy is generally acknowledged. The legitimacy of the law depends in part on its efficacy. As I have argued elsewhere,[19] the law is a second-order co-ordinating structure. It provides not only the solution to problems of social co-ordination, but also the solution to the question when is a question a co-ordination question, and who has the public authority to solve it.[20]

So for the law to be able to fulfil its function, and therefore to be capable of enjoying moral authority, it must be capable of being identified without reference to the moral questions which it pre-empts, ie the moral questions on which it is meant to adjudicate. This is the ethical rationale for the fact that the law is a social institution. This rationale has obvious and far-reaching consequences to our understanding of the nature of the law.

C. Legal continuities: the problem of interpretation

I talked of the authoritative endorsement of a standard as the decisive moment because it is the moment in which—to speak metaphorically—value is transformed into fact. Normally to find out what is permitted and what not, what is within our rights and what not, we have to engage in evaluative reasoning. But in legal matters to establish the law we engage in factual reasoning. This is the lesson we learn from the fact that the law revolves around that decisive moment. It is time to turn to the second lesson of the decisive moment: its implications for the nature of legal interpretation. The first point to note is that the authoritative nature of law, the fact that its standards are to be identified without recourse to evaluative reasoning, explains the centrality of interpretation to legal reasoning.

We are so used to the fact that so much legal reasoning is interpretive that we do not often ask why is it so? Moral reasoning, and other

---

[19] See a more detailed discussion of these considerations: *The Morality of Freedom*, ch 3, and 'Facing Up', (1989) 62 Southern California Law Review 1153.

[20] The law does more than help with the solution of co-ordination problems. For brevity's sake I omit reference to its other functions here. But see *The Morality of Freedom*, chs 3 and 4.

types of evaluative reasoning are not interpretive.[21] Why should legal reasoning, which in many ways deals with similar problems and which should be governed by morality, be so radically different? Why should it be predominantly interpretive? The explanation lies in the authoritative nature of law: when engaging in legal reasoning, when trying to establish the legal status of an action, we need to ascertain whether any of the authoritatively binding rules and doctrines of the law bear on it and if so how. That means establishing what has been done by the authorities, what decisions they have taken and what they mean.

This answer leads directly into what some see as the main difficulty with the line of thinking I have been developing so far. If I am right, the question will arise, would we not expect two clearly separate stages in legal reasoning: an interpretive-factual stage and a (purely) moral? First one would establish what authoritatively laid-down law says on the issue at hand, and then either if it does not provide a determinate disposition of the issue, or if one wants to determine whether the way it disposes of the issue is morally acceptable, one would move to the second purely moral stage in the argument. In fact we do not find that legal reasoning divides in that way. Legal reasoning displays a continuity through all its stages.

I believe that this point is overstated, and that legal reasoning is not all of a kind. However, there is no denying that it is predominantly interpretive. That, however, far from being a difficulty for the line of thought I have been pursuing, is not only consistent with it, but reinforces it. The difficulty we are examining can be stated in more abstract terms: how to reconcile the two aspects of legal reasoning. On the one hand, legal reasoning aims to establish the content of authoritative standards; on the other hand, it aims to supplement them, and often to modify them, in the light of moral considerations. The difficulty is often noted only to be dismissed with a vague formula. Hart, for example, noted how law constrains discretion. He did not have a general account of how limited discretion is to be understood.

Later on I will show that in a way I believe he was right and that there is no theory of how such discretion is constrained. But he never explained why this is so. Without such an explanation we are continuously facing the two opposed mistakes. The nihilist tendency claims

---

[21] A contrary view is taken by M Walzer in *Interpretation and Social Criticism* (Cambridge, Mass: Harvard University Press, 1987). And—I would predict—it is going to become one of the popular mistakes of the next few years.

that the idea of a constrained discretion is an illusion, masking the fact that courts and other legal authorities can do, and do do, what they like. The opposing sanguine tendency assumes that there is a general theory, familiar to judges, which guides them in creating a rationally compelled coherent whole of the disparate elements in the law, the elements of authoritative standards and moral reasons.[22] What we can expect of a general account of legal reasoning is not a theory of how to reconcile its two aspects, but rather an explanation of how they merge into a seeming continuity, and why no general theory is either possible or necessary. The key to both is in the interpretive character of much legal reasoning.

Think of interpretation generally. Think for example of musical interpretation. A pianist playing a piano sonata has to be faithful to the score, but his own musicality shows in the way he plays it. As we know different performances may differ enormously while being equally faithful to the original. The same is true of interpretations of plays or of other literary works. A work can be understood and (in the case of a play) performed as a celebration of the natural world, or as a utopian reflection on social ideals. Or it can be seen as an exploration of the rift between generations or alternatively as a crisis of adolescence and immaturity. Here again, different, even contrasting interpretations can be consistent with the original. Interpretation is the activity which combines reproduction and creativity. Hence its importance in the law.

Second, while some interpretations are better than others, and some are plainly wrong, there are no recipes for creating good interpretations. More importantly there are no general theories about what makes an interpretation good. Ever since Aristotle's *Poetics* there has been no dearth of theories proposed for the role, theories which attempted to tell us how to tell a good interpretation from a bad or an indifferent one. They all failed. They were all doomed to failure for no such theory can exist. At best theories which aspire to explain the nature of tragedy, or the novel or the opera, etc, are mere descriptions of the taste of a period, or of an artistic movement within a period. A theory of what counts as a good interpretation in the arts is impossible because interpretation of works of art is but one expression of the human desire to combine innovation with tradition. Staying within a tradition is necessary for people to enjoy a secure sense of belonging and of an ability to understand their

---

[22] Or, to use the terminology of the most imaginative exponent of this tendency, Dworkin, the elements of fit and value.

world, an ability to find their bearing in it. At the same time innovation is needed to satisfy not only the sense of adventure and a taste for danger, but also to establish the individuality of each one of us. Our individuality resides in our difference from others, whereas tradition represents what is common to all of us. Interpretation enables the interpreter, and to an extent his public, to combine faithfulness to a tradition with a display of originality and a distinctness of character, taste or attitude.

Now, while tradition, always backward looking, possibly can be captured within a general description,[23] innovation defies generalization. A theory of originality, in the sense we are considering, is self-defeating. The moment a general statement of how to be successfully original comes to the attention of any person originality for him (unless he is the author of the statement) must consist in flouting the statement, in showing how to be different from what it predicts.

You may think that these considerations are special to interpretation of works of art and irrelevant to legal interpretation. Here we deal with matters of moral importance which are subject to the universality of reason. And there is no denying that legal interpretation differs in important respects from the interpretation of works of art. Yet the combination of faithfulness to a past and looking towards an unpredictable future exists here too. To an extent there are fashions in morals, that is there are fashions in the ways societies find it acceptable to regulate their own affairs. There are patterns of behaviour which are regarded as unacceptable in one society, whereas their prohibition is regarded as unacceptable in another, where the truth is that both are right as both are wrong for what makes them acceptable or unacceptable is no more than that they are so regarded by the people whose behaviour is in question. There is, in other words, a conventional component to morality. Therefore both societies are right in treating that conduct as they do in their own societies, and both are wrong in condemning the way it is treated in the other society.

To the extent that morality is conventional it is subject to unpredictable changes which while affecting what is a good interpretation of the law cannot be captured by a general theory which enables people to tell in advance (i.e. before the fashion has come to pass) what is a good or bad interpretation. The main reason why there cannot be a general

---

[23] Though I would want to dissent from that too. Historical interpretations are as subject to the polarity of faithfulness to an original and innovation as interpretations of works of art.

theory of legal interpretation is, however, different. It results from the fact that there cannot be a moral theory capable of stating in specific terms which do not depend on a very developed moral judgement for their correct application what is to be done in all the situations possible in a particular society. That is even if we exclude the problem of predicting how morality will apply in radically changed social conditions[24] it is still impossible to articulate 'useful' moral theories, that is theories which would enable a person whose moral understanding and judgement are suspect to come to the right moral conclusions regarding situations he may face by consulting the theory.

I am not trying to do moralists or moral philosophers out of a job. I do not deny that there is a lot we can learn from writings about morality and about moral philosophy. I am simply endorsing the claim made by many[25] that 'operational' moral theories of the kind that Kant and the Utilitarians hoped for, and that Rawls attempted to provide for the political morality of contemporary liberal democracies, are unobtainable. Most importantly, this view should not be taken as lending any support at all to moral subjectivism, that is to the view that there are no 'objective' moral truths, and that morality is in the eye of the beholder. On the contrary, the mistaken belief that everything pertaining to matters on which opinions can be either true or false can be captured in theories of the kind I am discussing, what I called 'operational' theories, this mistaken belief has encouraged many to embrace moral subjectivism: once they realized that regarding any area of concern there are no 'operational' theories which apply to it, they have concluded that it is not susceptible of truth or falsity. Realizing that the belief is without foundation is an important step in refuting moral subjectivism. While I cannot here show that it is generally wrong, nor that morality cannot be stated in a general theory of this kind, it is worth pointing out that the requirement is not one we generally observe. For example, there is no general theory of the weather of this kind, and for all we know none can be had. In general regarding many matters of fact of the kind we encounter in everyday life no general

[24] And thus also excluding the effect of conventional variations in morality as it bears on any society.
[25] For example, B Williams, *Ethics and the Limits of Philosophy* (London: Fontana 1985); J Dancy, *Moral Reasons* (Oxford: Blackwell, 1993). For reasons of space I am unable to develop the case for this conclusion as I see it here. See my 'Moral Relativism and Social Change' in *Multiculturalism and Moral Pluralism*, edited by Ellen Paul (Cambridge: CUP, 1994).

theory of the kind moralists like Kant and the Utilitarians have looked for can be found. We do not regard this as undermining the objectivity of that area of discourse.[26]

D. Re-creative interpretation and the autonomy of law

Even those who agree with me so far may still think that there is room for a theory of interpretation. My argument against a theory of legal interpretation was directed at its moral end. It leaves open the possibility that there can be a general theory of legal interpretation addressed at the other side of legal reasoning, that is answering the question: what should legal interpretation be like to establish the law faithfully as laid down by legitimate legal authorities? As you know, many theories of interpretation aim to do nothing more. But I think that here too the quest for theory is misguided. There is no room for a general theory of 're-creative' interpretation, ie of that aspect of the interpretive task which aims to establish the meaning of authoritatively binding legal standards.

The thought that a theory of 're-creative' interpretation is possible and needed appears compelling only if we overlook two important points. First, it overlooks the fact that law-makers know the ways in which their law is interpreted. Second, it overlooks the fact that 're-creative' interpretation cannot be comprehensively separated from innovative interpretation. Let me explain them in that order.

First, law makers know the ways in which their law is interpreted. This is no mere observation of common political realities. It is a necessary implication of the very idea of someone making law. Making law is an intentional activity. One does not make law except through acts committed in the knowledge that they will make law. And one cannot make law intentionally if one is totally in the dark as to which law one is making. If someone decrees that my next five words will change the law of the United Kingdom, but in a way I have no way of knowing, it would be a gross distortion of the idea of law-making to call me the maker of the law establishing a public holiday on the first of August every year by having written 'but in a way I have', as I just did. Law-making does not

---

[26] I do not wish to imply that there may not be apparently persuasive arguments to show that the objectivity of evaluative discourse must depend on such theories even if the objectivity of other areas of discourse does not. These matters cannot be considered here.

imply knowingly making the law one intended, but knowingly making a law that one could have known one is making.

Therefore, law-makers can always know the meaning of the law they make. Moreover, the law they make must be the law they are understood to have made. It is simply the standard made by their law-making act when understood as such acts are normally understood in the context of their making. Meaning, as we know, is a public and social phenomenon. Words and actions have the meaning they are taken to have. So law-makers know the way their actions will be interpreted. Since they know that, they can, when making a law, take those actions which they know, or can establish, will be understood to be making that law which they want to make.

It follows that it does not matter which way law-making actions will be interpreted. Provided there are established ways or conventions for interpreting them they will ensure that the law-makers' intentions become law, that the law is as the law-makers intended it to be.[27] This argument shows that there is no need for a theory of 're-creative' interpretation. Whichever way the law is interpreted the condition that it should be interpreted in part in a way which retrieves its intended meaning is met.

If the first point shows that a theory of 're-creative' interpretation is unnecessary, the second shows that it is futile. You will remember that the prominence of interpretive reasoning in legal reasoning results from the fact that in the law the two aspects of legal reasoning, that is establishing the content of authoritatively endorsed legal standards and establishing the (other) moral considerations which bear on the issue, are inextricably interwoven. This means that there is no point in a theory of 're-creative' interpretation which will identify interpretations which do no more than state the content of existing norms.

In some areas such a theory is not merely futile, it is also impossible. The impossibility of separating the re-creative from the non-re-creative elements in interpretation is starkest in the case of interpretations through the performance of plays, music, opera, etc. There is no performance which merely captures an original without also being an expression of the performer's view of it or attitude to it. There is no pure re-creation in performance. Other kinds of interpretation display the same inseparability though usually in a weaker form. It would be going too far to claim that there cannot be a statement of any aspect of the law which merely reiterates its existing content,

---

[27] For the full argument to this conclusion see chapter 11, 'Intention in Interpretation'.

without adding to it or deviating from it. But clearly many standard legal interpretations do add or deviate. They are not merely re-creative. They are meant to do more than merely restate the authoritative standards. They are meant to apply them to a concrete or a hypothetical case or type of case, and in doing that to resolve any ambiguities in the authoritative standards, to develop them or concretize them. Hence the futility of a theory of 're-creative' interpretation which will identify successful and purely 're-creative' interpretations.

This argument leaves open the possibility of a weaker theory of 're-creative' interpretation, that is one which will identify which of the not purely 're-creative' interpretations is faithful to the authoritative standards the interpreter has to follow. But such a theory is not necessary, as my first point has established. All one needs are conventions of interpretation of one kind or another.

E. Interpretation and power

I will conclude by considering two consequences of the argument I have presented, which may be mistaken for objections to it. First, that I exaggerate the degree to which law-makers can know the way the law they make will be interpreted. Second, that my argument leads to the absurd conclusion that it does not matter in what ways the law is interpreted.

Obviously there are severe limitations on the ability of the law-maker to know how the law will be interpreted. First, the conventions of interpretation may be uncertain and indeterminate. There may be rival conventions on certain issues, and the application of others may be uncertain. Second, the conventions may change with time. Both points are valid. They demonstrate that legislation is a matter of degree. It is a cooperative enterprise between legislators and the authoritative interpreters of their legislation.[28] Where the conventions of legislation are

---

[28] A different issue is raised by the fact that the interpretation depends on moral issues. True, the interpretation should be morally correct, and the legislator can have correct knowledge of morality, at least insofar as it bears on his actions. However, for the reasons set out earlier, legislators cannot know in advance what is morally correct in all the circumstances to which their law is relevant. Hence they are denied complete knowledge of the implications of their law. But that does not mean that they do not know what law they are enacting, which is all that is made necessary by the very idea of legislation. That requirement is satisfied. It does not extend to ability to acquire complete knowledge of all

ambiguous, uncertain, or unsettled there will be points on which the legislation is incomplete. To the extent that its meaning depends on resolving the ambiguities and uncertainties, authoritative interpretations which resolve them have a law-making effect. They complement the original law-making act.

So the legislator's inability to know exactly how the law will be interpreted is no objection to my analysis. It shows the strength of the analysis that it highlights central features of our experience with the law. In showing legal standards to be a product of creation and re-creation, of continuous development rather than a product of a single act of legislation, the analysis enables us to face another crucial aspect of the law. Typically the law survives its creator. This is seen dramatically when we consider, for example, the constitution of the USA which is into its third century. Clearly by now its validity cannot rest merely on the authority its framers once had. The same is true of ordinary legislation, and of common-law doctrines. Many of them outlive the authority of their original makers. How then are we to understand their continued validity?

The authority of the original legislator is important in providing the grounds for believing that those subject to the law would be doing the best they can do if they conform to it. Since the law is continuously re-created through the authority of its interpreters with time it is their authority, rather than that of its original legislators, which provides the grounds for holding it to be binding on its subjects, to the extent that such grounds exist.

This consideration is particularly forceful once the law becomes established, that is once it becomes embodied in the practices and ways of life of people, commercial enterprises, and organizations. In that case its very status as embodying the common practices of its subjects gives it weight, to the extent that it deals with matters where the interest in co-ordination is paramount. One could say[29] that in those cases people do not really have reason to comply with the law as such. Rather they have reason to conform to the common practices. It is all the same true that the law marks the divide between those common practices which enjoy legal-institutional support and those which lack it. It marks out

---

the implications of the law, a task which is impossible not only where moral issues are in question.

[29] Indeed in *The Authority of Law* I said so myself.

those practices that the courts and the law enforcement agencies will take action to protect and preserve, those where individuals who lose by the fact that others deviate from common practices can hope to recover their loss through legal machinery.

In as much as the law serves as a guarantor of common practices there is no surprise that it can become detached from its original source in an act of legislation or in its original endorsement in a precedent-setting judicial decision. In such cases its continued endorsement by legal institutions in charge of its enforcement guarantees, when they act well, its readjustments to dovetail with the ever-developing and changing social and commercial practices that it protects and enforces.

Finally, let me turn to the second possible objection which says that in my argument I belittled the importance of a choice of different ways of interpreting the law. After all I denied that any method of interpretation is more successful in establishing the original content of the law as laid down by legitimate authority than any other. It appears that I may believe that we may entrust the choice of a method of interpretation to luck.

In fact nothing can be further from the truth. First and foremost much interpretation has to do with finding morally acceptable solutions to problems of conflicting interests. But let us put this fact on one side, and focus on other factors which may affect choice of methods of interpretation. All I was claiming is that any established method of interpretation will enable the law-makers to draft laws which will have the meaning they want the law to have. Some of my comments already indicate how this claim should be refined. We saw that to the extent that existing methods of interpretation are ambiguous, uncertain, or unsettled they set a limit to the ability of legislators to legislate.

Law-makers can draft provisions for the interpretation of their laws, and can draft the laws themselves in ways which will minimize the ambiguities and uncertainties. But given that the law has the meaning it has when interpreted by the established methods, if those methods are ambiguous and unsettled so is the law they establish.

This means that ambiguities and uncertainties in the methods of interpretation limit the legislative powers of the law-makers. At the same time they increase the power of the courts or other institutions with power authoritatively to interpret the law. The choice of method of interpretation is an important device for the distribution of power among organs of government. Other things being equal,[30] the more certain and predictable the application of these methods is, the greater the power of those who make the standard, and the smaller the power of its authoritative interpreters. The allocation of power to different organs of government is a matter of great moral and political consequence. It is a matter for the constitution of the state concerned. The choice of methods of interpretation is part of the constitution of every state.

---

[30] The main factor which need not be equal is the power of the court to overrule and modify a rule of law whose meaning is clear.

5

The Problem of Authority: Revisiting the Service Conception[1]

The problem I have in mind is the problem of the possible justification of subjecting one's will to that of another, and of the normative standing of demands to do so. The account of authority that I offered, many years ago,[2] under the title of the service conception of authority, addressed this issue, and assumed that all other problems regarding authority are subsumed under it. Many found the account implausible. It is thin, relying on very few ideas. It may well appear to be too thin, and to depart too far from many of the ideas that have gained currency in the history of reflection on authority.

Criticism can be radical, rejecting the service conception altogether. Or it can be more moderate, accepting the service conception or some of its central traits, especially the normal justification thesis, as setting necessary conditions for the legitimacy of authority, but denying that they constitute sufficient conditions. Most commonly, moderate critics argue that legitimate authority, at any rate legitimate political authority, presupposes a special connection between rulers and ruled, a special bond that is overlooked by the service conception. My purpose is to revisit the problem of authority, and to examine moderately critical claims, or some of them. I will start by explaining in the first section some background methodological points. Section II will briefly restate the service conception and the way it deals with the problem of

[1] In writing this chapter I benefited from oral or published comments on my ideas by more people than I remember. Among those to whom I owe a debt of gratitude are Jules Coleman, Ronald Dworkin, Leslie Green, Herbert Hart, Scott Hershovitz, Heidi Hurd, Michael Moore, Stephen Perry, Donald Regan, Philip Soper, Jeremy Waldron—most of whom will find my response to the comments inadequate.

[2] Some of the basic ideas appear in J Raz, *The Authority of Law* (Oxford: Clarendon Press, 1979); the main elements of the service conception are set out in J Raz, *The Morality of Freedom* (Oxford: Clarendon Press, 1986).

authority. Section III develops the service conception and elaborates some of its implications by dealing with a series of only loosely connected questions and doubts to which it is open. Section IV examines in general terms the argument that authority, at any rate political authority, presupposes a special link, missing in the service conception, between government and the governed. Section V considers the possibility that such a link is forged by consent, whereas section VI comments on the possibility that the link is constituted by identification with or membership of the political community (or some other group).

I. Some Methodological Observations

A few observations about the general approach to start with.

First, authority, political obligation, and obligation to obey the law: Some writers think that the so-called political obligation is to obey the law, and that one has an obligation to obey the law if and only if the law or legal institutions have legitimate authority. That is a mistake, and it is so even if we confine our attention to legal authorities alone. Political obligation is the broadest of the three notions, signifying the obligations members of a political community have towards it or its institutions and political order, in virtue of their membership. That includes much more and much less than an obligation to obey the law. More—because it includes some duties to be a good citizen in ways that have little to do with the law. They will be duties to react to injustice perpetrated by or in the name of the community, to contribute to its proper functioning (eg. by voting and by being active in various other ways), and more. They require less than obeying the law, for much of the law has nothing to do with the political community. If I pick my neighbour's apple and eat it, I may be breaking the law, but I am unlikely to be doing any harm to the polity. Obligations to obey the law need not depend on the legitimacy of its authorities. There could be various reasons, including moral reasons, to obey the law in a country whose legal authorities are not legitimate. Considerations of stability and the protection of vested interests are often thought to provide such reasons.[3] Finally, it is worth mentioning that we have political duties that do not depend either on membership in a political community or on being subject to its laws. Rawls's duty to

---

[3] Various legal systems recognize such reasons by having doctrines giving legal effect to de facto authorities.

uphold and support just institutions is of this kind, applying to all of us, regarding any just institutions, wherever they are.[4] This chapter deals exclusively with the nature of authority.

Second, power and right: In our common use of the concept of authority, power and the right to it intermingle. Any attempt to separate them is bound to be somewhat artificial. Yet it must be made, for they seem to be interrelated in some systematic way, which invites describing their distinctive contributions to the concept of authority. My suggestion was that even the notion of a *mere* de facto authority (i.e. one that exercises power over its subjects, but lacks the right to it) involves that of legitimacy. What makes mere de facto authorities different from people or groups who exert naked power (e.g. through terrorizing a population or manipulating it) is that mere de facto authorities claim, and those who have naked power do not, to have a right to rule those subject to their power. They claim legitimacy. They act, as I say, under the guise of legitimacy.[5]

On the other hand, I suggested, legitimate authorities are not always de facto authorities. Arguably, the legitimate government of Poland in 1940 was the government in exile in London, which did not enjoy power over the population of Poland.[6] The resulting methodology applies to the clarification of other concepts too: there is a class of normative concepts that have a secondary use in which they indicate a claim by their users, or some of them, that they apply in their primary, normative, sense, a claim that may be erroneous. The most important concept of this kind is that of a (normative) reason.[7] A reason for an action is a

---

[4] See J Rawls, *A Theory of Justice* (rev edn, Cambridge, Mass: Belknap, 1999) 293–294.

[5] Even those who do not claim a right to rule do—exceptional cases apart—claim that they may act as they do, that their actions are defensible. But they do not claim that those over whom they wield power owe them obedience, ie have a duty to obey them. They are content with being able to make them obey, by credible threats or in some other way.

[6] Possibly the government in exile enjoyed some de facto powers (there was a Polish army—also in exile—that recognized it, etc), but its legitimacy did not depend on its possession of that power. Its legitimacy depended, however, on a non-normative fact, on being recognized as legitimate by the bulk of the Polish population and by some other countries. In other circumstances legitimacy may depend on the chance of the government gaining effective control. This enables one to keep the distinction between authority without the power to use it effectively, and someone who is entitled to have authority (say, was duly elected) but does not have it (because, for example, he was not admitted to the office to which he was elected). Contrast with this case a parent who has authority over his child even though he lacks power over him.

[7] I qualify them as 'normative' to distinguish between them and explanatory reasons, which are simply facts or events that explain how or why things are.

consideration that renders its choice intelligible, and counts in its favour. But when I say 'my reason for leaving was that I was afraid of missing the last bus', I indicate what reason I believed at the time I had for leaving (the fact that I will miss the last bus if I do not leave), though I am not committed to the fact that there was in fact such a reason.

If that is right, then the concept of legitimate authority has explanatory priority over that of a mere de facto authority. The latter presupposes the former but not the other way around. From here on 'authority' refers to legitimate authority.

Third, concept possession and its application: It is not literally true that 'authority' is a concept that applies only to people who think that it applies to them. There can be authorities who do not claim to have authority. However, as just explained, de facto authorities do claim to have legitimate authority, and as will be seen below, political authorities generally do so. The question arises whether it is a condition of adequacy of an explanation of the concept of authority that those who have authority at least implicitly accept the explanation as correct. (Alternatively, can one accept an explanation of the concept as of limited validity, as applying only to people—perhaps in authority, or perhaps subject to authority—who at least implicitly take it to be a true explanation?)

No. If people dispute an account of authority that is otherwise well supported, they make a mistake. The service conception is an account of authority, which includes an explanation of what it is to have authority, to be subject to authority, when one has authority or is subject to it, and like questions. The account is not about what people think it is like to have authority or to be subject to it, but of what it is to have it or be subject to it. It is compatible with claims that people have different beliefs on these matters, though it follows from the account that theirs are mistaken beliefs. Does it follow that they are guilty of a conceptual confusion? Worse, does it follow that they do not know their own language? Of course not. If they have false beliefs about authority (not merely about the powers of people who actually have authority) then they have the concept of authority, they have some understanding of what it involves. But their understanding is partial, and in part incorrect. Our understanding of concepts usually is. It leaves plenty of room for mistakes and disagreements.[8]

---

[8] See chapter 3, 'Two Views of the Nature of the Theory of Law: A Partial Comparison'.

Fourth, hopes of neutrality: Some writers take their task to be to provide an explanation of normative concepts, such as 'authority', which is normatively neutral, that is consistent with any possible normative view.[9] It is not clear whether there is a sense in which this can be a reasonable demand. If it is satisfied only by explaining normative concepts exclusively in non-normative (or non-evaluative) terms, it amounts to a requirement of semantic reduction of all the normative concepts to which it applies, and in that form there is no reason to accept it as a general methodological requirement. Alternatively, it may be taken to require that, while explanations of normative concepts may rely on other normative or evaluative concepts, these must be ones which anyone, whatever their normative or evaluative beliefs, is committed to accept as possibly[10] having true (or valid) instantiations. So understood, the requirement gestures towards a semantic reduction of thick normative or evaluative terms into thin ones. It is not clear, however, that many normative terms meet this requirement. It is doubtful that many thick concepts can be reduced to thin ones.

Perhaps the neutrality requirement should be taken as a matter of degree: the closer an explanation comes to satisfying it, the better it is, other things being equal. After all, explanations that meet the requirement, or rather concepts that they successfully explain, can be accepted and used by people whatever their normative beliefs.

Some people suppose that the explanation of authority should be normatively neutral in a different sense. They think that the explanation of authority should be such that it is possible for the propositional form 'X has authority over Y' to have true instances, that it is possible for someone to be a legitimate authority over others. Let me call the first kind of normative neutrality 'explanatory neutrality', and the second kind 'existential neutrality'.

Existential neutrality has the advantage that it does not conflict with the view that there can be legitimate authorities, a view that is very widely held, and has been throughout history, wherever people had views on the topic. People can make mistakes, including normative mistakes, but an explanation of a concept in wide use and more or less universally believed to have applications, which, in combination with true

---

[9] For example, if a correct explanation of dishonour entails that (1) those who acted dishonourably deserve to be killed, and (2) that anyone who betrayed a trust acted dishonourably, then this explanation is inconsistent with my normative views.

[10] In the non-epistemic sense of 'possibly'.

normative beliefs, entails that it has none, has a tall task of explaining how it is that people are so mistaken.

It is possible to exaggerate the difficulty of the task. First, it is possible to explain how people are generally mistaken about the possibility of legitimate authority without attributing to them a gross misunderstanding of the concept. Their mistake, if mistaken they are, may be in some of their normative beliefs, rather than in their conceptual understanding.[11] Second, concepts have a history, and the conditions of their persistence or identity through time are, at best, very vague. Hence it may be that the impossibility of legitimate authority is the impossibility of there being instances of our current concept of authority. Possibly, under some ancestors of our concept, legitimate authority was possible. The reverse is also possible, and even more likely. One source of pressure towards concept change may have been a growing realization that the concept then prevailing has no instances (eg if ever the concept of authority was such that it had to derive from divine authority, then recognition of the impossibility of divine authority may have encouraged change in the concept, a change that made it possible for it to have instances, at least in the eyes of the people at that time).

The account I offer has instances. But the hurdle of running against popular opinion can be higher or lower. For example, my account has the consequence that political authorities are likely to have a more limited authority than the authority many, perhaps all of them, claim to have, and that people generally believe that they have. This still requires explaining why people are so mistaken,[12] though since the mistake attributed is less far-reaching, the burden of explanation is much less.

My previous comments explained what advantages I find in both explanatory and existential neutrality. They fall short of making either a methodological principle. I suspect that the demand for explanatory neutrality is impossible to meet (ie explanations that meet it, if there are such, are otherwise faulty). There is not much plausibility in it. We do not expect all scientific concepts, for example, to be explanatorily neutral

---

[11] Out of abundance of caution, let me amplify here: there is no implication in the points above that an explanation of a concept to be correct must be one generally available to those who have the concept. There are many aspects of a concept that its users may not be aware of, and many mistakes about it they may make. The claim was merely that there would need to be a good explanation of how a mistaken belief in the possibility of instances of the concept, in our case a belief in the possibility of legitimate authorities, came to be so widespread.

[12] A point made to me privately by HLA Hart.

in the sense of their instantiations being consistent with all possible scientific theories. Some scientific concepts may be theory-transcendent, or they may be more or less theory-transcendent. But many are not. *Mutatis mutandis*, the same, I suspect, is true of normative concepts. The same considerations would rule out the requirement of existential neutrality. Special cases apart, it is not a requirement we normally impose on the explanation of other concepts, and it seems unmotivated to impose it on normative concepts generally or on authority in particular.

The hope for neutrality may express itself in a requirement that the account of authority should explain what follows when someone has authority, but will not include anything about the conditions under which one may acquire or hold authority. For this requirement to make sense, it has to be the case not only that whoever offers the account does not write about the conditions under which one does hold authority, but also that nothing follows from the account regarding the conditions that make one an authority. This seems to be an impossible requirement to meet: how could it be that the way to justify a claim that one has authority is not affected by, indeed not guided by what has to be justified, namely the consequences of having authority?

Still, there is a difference between the two parts of the account of authority. One can reasonably expect an account of authority to specify, however abstractly, all or at least the central consequences of having authority. However, beyond saying that the conditions under which one holds authority are those that justify ascribing authority—namely, ascribing to one's actions the consequences that follow from having authority—it is not clear that one can reasonably hope for a complete specification of those conditions. If one provides some sufficient conditions for having authority, the question arises: can it be established that no other conditions establish one as an authority? Establishing a negative existential is notoriously difficult, and while I tried to make the account that follows exhaustive, I do not have an argument to show that it is.

Fifth, concept possession and the limits of its application: The remark about the historicity of the concept of authority calls for a couple of brief clarifications. It implies two possibilities: first, that there was a time when the concept did not exist at all, and second, that our concept is a descendent of earlier concepts. It is plausible to think that both are realized, which explains how the term is used: sometimes to refer to the whole series of concepts that are the ancestors of our concept, sometimes to our concept alone.

Does it not follow that there is a wider concept, which is used whenever we use the term in the first way, ie to refer to what I called the whole series of ancestral concepts? And is it not the real concept of authority? Yes and no. Yes, for there is such a general concept. No, because it is misleading to identify the general concept with the concept of authority *simpliciter*. The main reason is that the way, and I think the only way, in which the broad notion can be identified is as I did identify it, ie historically, as the concept that applies to all instances of what I called 'our' concept of authority and those of its ancestors (rather than by its ahistorical features). 'Our' concept is the concept of authority, if only because it is our point of access to all its ancestors, which are identified by their relations to it.

It is also true that we need the wider concept, or rather that we regularly rely on it. For example, and crucially, there can be no de facto authority among people who do not have the concept of authority, for to have de facto authority is, among other things, to claim legitimate authority. It follows that when we talk of the de facto authorities existing in the middle ages, or in fifteenth-century Japan, or in Ancient Persia, we rely on something like the broad concept: there were at that time people or bodies with power over populations who claimed authority over them, using here the appropriate ancestor of our concept, or the wide concept, which includes all ancestors.

One concept is an ancestor if the successor concept emerged as a modification of the ancestral one and retained sufficient similarity to it, either in its features or its function. The relationship is not typically one of similarity alone. It contains a contingent causal component. Typically when that does not exist, as when we find in a different culture a causally unrelated but similar concept, we would identify it just like that: 'They,' we would say, 'also had a concept like (or similar to) our concept of——.' On the other hand, similarity is part of the ancestral relationship, for otherwise we would have no criteria to distinguish between a concept being modified by a successor and one rejected in favour of an alternative.

Needless to say, since the broad concept is identified by its relations to our concept and its ancestors, and since 'our' concept can change over time and acquire more ancestors, the overall concept we have now is different from the one we had, or will have, when 'our' concept was or will become different.

Sixth, explanation and advocacy: I keep referring to 'our' concept of authority. But is there such a thing? Are there not several concepts, all of them descending from the very same ancestors? Quite possibly so. Each person when using the concept of authority uses his concept, and should allow for the possibility that there are several. That does not lead to an explosion of concepts. The reason is simple: in the use of concepts we allow that we are ignorant about many aspects of them, that we may use them incorrectly, and that their character is determined by the rules governing their use in the community, rules whose complete understanding may elude any or indeed all of us. In allowing the possibility of at least partial ignorance regarding the nature of our concepts, we recognize that concepts are social beings, owing their features to a community of speakers in ways that may elude any one of them, or indeed all of them. This means that our concepts are not very idiosyncratic, that there are common concepts, even though we may not know all their features.

Needless to say, if there are a number of concepts of authority prevalent in a single society, they are likely to be competitors. The boundaries between them are fluid, and those who use each claim merit for it, and (when aware, if only dimly, of the existence of the others) find reason to prefer it to the others. This means that each explanation of a concept can also be used in the battle of concepts, where there is such a battle; that is it can be used to advocate the merits of one concept over its competitors.

The indeterminacy of concepts is another factor forcing all explanations to enter, if successful, into the advocacy business. Explanations may strive to replicate the indeterminacies of the concepts they explain, but it is almost impossible to replicate them perfectly, and the success of the explanation will inevitably exercise some influence towards changing the concept to make it conform to its explanation.

II. The Service Conception in Brief

The service conception is driven by two problems, one theoretical and one moral. Starting with the common thought, which broadly speaking and with appropriate qualifications and amplifications I endorse, that authority is a right to rule, the theoretical question is how to understand the standing of an authoritative directive (as I shall call the product of the exercise of the right to rule). If issued by someone who has a right to rule, then its recipients are bound to obey. The directive is binding on them and they are duty-bound to obey it.[13] But how could it be that the

---

[13] Authorities do much more than impose duties. But arguably whatever they do— confer powers or rights, grant permissions or immunities, change status, create and

say-so of one person constitutes a reason, a duty, for another? Is it that easy to manufacture duties out of thin air?

The moral question is how can it ever be that one has a duty to subject one's will and judgement to those of another? Of course, we are affected by others and by the actions of others in innumerable ways. We often act to induce others to help or not to hinder us, to collaborate with us in common enterprises, to avoid hurting us or to turn their actions to our advantage. But the case of authority is special. Directives issued by authority aim to constitute reasons for their subjects and are binding on their subjects because they are meant to be so binding. If we recognize a duty to obey them we recognize that they have a right to command us, not only to affect the circumstances that shape our opportunities and the obstacles on our path. Authorities tell us what to intend, with the aim of achieving whatever goals they pursue through commanding our will. Can one human being ever have such normative power over another? Can it ever be right to acknowledge such power over oneself in another?

The theoretical problem is similar to the one that promises (and all voluntary undertakings) present. By promising, we impose on ourselves obligations that we did not have before, and we do so simply by communicating an intention to do so. In exercising authority we impose on others duties that they did not have before, and we do so simply by expressing an intention to do so.[14] How can actions communicating intentions to create reasons or obligations (for ourselves or others) do so just because they communicate these intentions?

The beginning of the answer is to note that fundamentally there is nothing special in such a case. Various of our actions incur obligations. Conceiving and giving birth to a child is often assumed to be one such case. Infringing other people's rights is another (it generates an obligation to make amends, etc). Claims that we have an obligation because of what we did, or because of how we acted, are true, if they are, by virtue of general reasons for people who acted in certain ways to have certain reasons or obligations. There are, it is assumed, general reasons for

terminate legal persons (corporations and their like), regulate the relations between organs of legal persons, and much else—they do by imposing duties, actual or conditional. I will therefore continue, as writers on authority generally do, to discuss the problem of authority in relation to its right to impose duties.

[14] In both cases, sometimes the person placed under an obligation already had an obligation to perform the same act. 'An obligation that he did not have before' does not mean an obligation to do something which until then he had no obligation to do. The obligation is new, even if another obligation to perform the same act already exists.

anyone who has a child to look after it, a general reason for anyone who violates another's right, to compensate them, and so on. Promises and authorities are no exception. Not every time someone acts with the intention of undertaking an obligation towards someone does he or she make a binding promise. A promise is binding only if the promised action is of a class regarding which there are sufficient reasons to hold the promisor bound by his promise. That means that to be binding, promises must meet many conditions: the promisor must be capable of knowing the meaning of his action, he must be capable of having a reasonable understanding of its likely consequences, and, most importantly, (1) the act promised must belong to a class of actions such that it enhances people's control over their life to be able to make such promises, and (2) the act must not be grossly immoral, etc. A promise to be a slave is not binding, nor a promise to make someone else a slave, and so on.

The theoretical question regarding the nature of authority is answered in a similar fashion. A person can have authority over another only if there are sufficient reasons for the latter to be subject to duties at the say-so of the former. That, of course, while probably right, does not tell us when one person has authority over another. It does not establish even that anyone can ever have authority. But it states what has to be the case if some people have authority over others. That is all that one can ask of a general account of authority, namely that it establish what it takes for there to be legitimate authority, rather than that it should show who has authority over whom and regarding what. That latter task is a matter for evaluating individual cases. But of course, a general account of authority can, while still not establishing who actually has authority, say much more about the conditions under which people are subject to authority. In particular we would expect it to address the moral problem with authority, namely, how can it be consistent with one's standing as a person to be subject to the will of another in the way one is when subject to the authority of another?

The suggestion of the service conception is that the moral question is answered when two conditions are met, and regarding matters with respect to which they are met: First, that the subject would better conform to reasons that apply to him anyway (that is, to reasons other than the directives of the authority) if he intends[15] to be guided by the

---

[15] Perhaps I should say 'tries' rather than 'intends' to cover cases where even though one intends to be guided by the authority one will fail to do so because of one's weakness

authority's directives than if he does not (I will refer to it as the normal justification thesis or condition). Second, that the matters regarding which the first condition is met are such that with respect to them it is better to conform to reason than to decide for oneself, unaided by authority (I will refer to it as the independence condition).

Simple examples of regulations regarding dangerous activities or materials illustrate the point. I can best avoid endangering myself and others by conforming to the law regarding the dispensation and use of pharmaceutical products. I can rely on the experts whose advice it reflects to know what is dangerous in these matters better than I can judge for myself, a fact that is reinforced by my reliance on other people's conformity to the law, which enables me to act with safety in ways that otherwise I could not. Of course, none of this is necessarily so. The law may reflect the interests of pharmaceutical companies, and not those of consumers. If that is so it may lack authority over me because it fails to meet the normal justification condition.[16] But if it does meet the normal justification condition it is likely to meet the independence condition as well. Decisions about the safety of pharmaceutical products are not the sort of personal decisions regarding which I should decide for myself rather than follow authority. They do not require me to use any drugs, etc, and in that they are unlike decisions about undergoing a course of medication or treatment where we may well feel that I should decide for myself, rather than be dictated to by authority.

I said that the two conditions solve the moral question about authority. But in what sense do they do so? Several objections can be anticipated. The independence condition, it may be objected, merely restates the problem and does not help with its solution. The whole point of the moral problem is that acting by oneself is more important than anything. What advance is there in stating that authority is legitimate only where acting by oneself is less important than conforming to reason?

Another objection to the independence condition has it that it suggests that one can compare the importance of conforming to reason

---

of will, and would therefore do better to ignore the authority and try to conform to background reasons. There are probably endless refinements of this kind, which I will not try to provide, and which are probably impossible to enumerate.

[16] For the purpose of the example only, I disregard the complicating fact that the law's authority is wider than regarding the possession and use of pharmaceutical products. This raises the question of the unit of assessment in determinations of the legitimacy of authorities, which is discussed below.

with the importance of deciding for oneself, independently of authority. But this, says the objection, cannot be done: the two are very different, incommensurable concerns. There is never an answer to the question which of the two is more important? I doubt that this objection is valid. It seems to be premised on the thought that the concerns that underlie reasons with which we should conform and those that underlie the reason to act independently of authority have nothing to do with each other. But that is not so.

Some of the reasons for relying on one's own judgement derive from the need to cultivate the ability to be self-reliant, simply because often one has no one else to rely on. The clearest case is the way parents should allow their children freedom to decide for themselves on a gradually expanding range of matters, in spite of knowing that they, the parents, would make a better choice for their children were they to take over deciding on those matters. This is the way children learn how to decide for themselves and become self-reliant. There are other reasons to decide for oneself. Certain matters are, by the social forms of various cultures, to be decided by oneself. For example, while in some forms of marriage parents choose the partners, in others neither parents nor anyone else are expected to have any say in the matter. In such cases one cannot have the relationship, or engage in the good or the activity, unless one does so oneself, not through an agent, nor by following a superior.

The former case for self-reliance (parents and children) is instrumental where the end is to secure what conformity with reason will, in the long run, secure; the latter case (marriage) depends on the fact that there are reasons that can only be satisfied by independent action.[17] Both of them trace the concerns behind independence back to concerns with satisfying reasons. The thought that the two concerns never meet and must be incommensurate is unjustified. The question of the role of what I called independence also involves other, perhaps more fundamental considerations. We are not fully ourselves if too many of our decisions are not taken by us, but by agents, automata, or superiors. On the other side, sometimes it is our duty, our moral duty if you like, to accept authority. Sometimes—for example, on the scene of an accident—coordination, which in the circumstances requires recognizing someone

---

[17] I turned to the notion of second-order reasons to express such situations. They involve reasons to act for a certain reason, and the faculty of reason discharges its function when we conform with that second-order reason.

as being in charge of the rescue, is essential if lives are to be saved. We must yield to the authority, where there is someone capable of playing this role. There are in the political sphere many less dramatic analogues of such situations, where a substantial good is at stake, a good that we have moral reasons to secure for ourselves and for others but that can in the circumstances be best secured by yielding to a coordinating authority. These cases justify giving up deciding for oneself, and pose no threat to the authenticity of one's life, or to one's ability to lead a self-reliant and self-fulfilling life. None of this denies that often the two concerns, one satisfied by conformity with reasons, the other by acting on one's own judgement, may be radically different, and the cases for conformity or independence may be incommensurate, with the (uncomfortable) result that whether one is then subject to authority is undetermined.

The other objection to the autonomy condition cannot be dismissed so easily. It should be met not by a refutation but by a deflection. Indeed, the independence condition does little to solve the problem. That is not its task. It merely frames the question. Part of the answer to the moral challenge to all authority is in the first condition, which says that authority can be legitimate if conformity with it improves one's conformity with reason.[18] It provides the key to the justification of authority: authority helps our rational capacity whose function is to secure conformity with reason. It allows our rational capacity to achieve its purpose more successfully. These observations express a way of understanding our general capacity to guide our conduct (and our life more broadly) by our own judgement. The point of this general capacity is to enable us to conform to the reasons that confront us at any given time. It is conformity achieved by the exercise of one's judgement. We value the ability to exercise one's judgement and to rely on it in action, but it is a capacity we value because of its purpose, which is, by its very nature, to secure conformity with reason. The point is perfectly general. The value of many of our capacities should not be reduced to the value of their use. But, even where their value also reflects the value of the freedom to use our capacities or not,[19] it depends on the value of their successful use.

The value of our rational capacity, ie our capacity to form a view of our situation in the world and to act in light of it, derives from the

---

[18] For the sake of brevity I'll use this and other similarly inaccurate restatements of the first condition.

[19] In fact, while we can manipulate ourselves through substance abuse or in some other way into losing, for a short or a long period, the use of our rational capacity, it is not one that we can use or refrain from using at will, as we can our capacity to read books.

fact that there are reasons that we should satisfy, and that this capacity enables us to do so. It is not, however, our only way of conforming to reasons. We are, for example, hardwired to be alert to certain dangers and react to them instinctively and without deliberation, as we react to fire or to sudden movement in our immediate vicinity. In other contexts we do better to follow our emotions than to reason our way to action. These examples suggest that the primary value of our general ability to act by our own judgement derives from the concern to conform to reasons, and that concern can be met in a variety of ways. It is not, therefore, surprising that we find it met also in ways that come closer to obeying authority, such as making vows, taking advice, binding oneself to others long before the time for action with a promise to act in certain ways, or relying on technical devices to 'take decisions for us,' as when setting alarm clocks, speed limiters, etc.

Both being guided by our emotions and being guided by our judgement (not necessarily mutually exclusive conditions) are constituents of some activities and relationships that are valuable in themselves, resulting in cases where the independence condition of legitimacy is not satisfied. By the same token, there can be other forms of activities, joint activities and enterprises, which are valuable in themselves and that inherently involve yielding to decisions taken by others. The conditions of legitimacy are open to different views about what is and what is not valuable and worthwhile. They merely state how conclusions on such issues bear on the question of authority.

In postulating that authorities are legitimate only if their directives enable their subjects to better conform to reason, we see authority for what it is: not a denial of people's capacity for rational action, but simply one device, one method, through the use of which people can achieve the goal (*telos*) of their capacity for rational action, albeit not through its direct use. This way of understanding matters is reinforced by the fact that in following authority, just as in following advice, or being guided by any of the technical devices, one's ultimate self-reliance is preserved, for it is one's own judgement which directs one to recognize the authority of another, just as it directs one to keep one's promises, follow advice, use technical devices, and the like.

Of course, authority is special in the way in which it restricts one's ability to act independently. The service conception expresses that thought by the thesis that authoritative directives pre-empt those reasons against the conduct they require that the authority was meant to take into account in deciding to issue its directives. Those subject to the authority are not allowed to second-guess the wisdom or advisability of the authority's directives. A simplified description of typical situations explains the point. There are reasons with which we should all conform, say regarding safe driving. In the absence of the law (or other authoritative directives) telling us how to drive (by imposing speed restrictions, traffic lights, road signs, etc), we would have tried to drive as safely as we can. The law of the road is meant to enable us to drive more safely (i.e. to conform better to the background reasons), and it does so by directing us to do things that otherwise we might not have done. Where the law leaves driving decisions to us, we are still guided by those background considerations. But where it intervenes to require certain ways of driving, we are bound to obey it, and are not allowed to question its force, even while we are, of course, allowed to question its wisdom and advocate its reform. This is, roughly, what I mean when I say that legitimate laws, and the directives of legitimate authorities generally, pre-empt the background reasons that might militate against the authoritative directives and replace them with their own requirements.[20]

The pre-emptive force of authority is part and parcel of its nature. It cannot succeed as an authority (ie succeed in improving our conformity with reason) if it does not pre-empt the background reasons. The function of authorities is to improve our conformity with those background reasons by making us try to follow their instructions rather than the background reasons. Authorities cannot do so without at least the possibility that their directives will sometimes lead us to act differently than we would have done without them. In itself, while this requires that the authority's directives must be capable of changing what we ought to do, all things considered, it does not specify in what way they impact on what we have most reason to do. The pre-emption thesis explains that: it reflects the thought that authorities are able to function in the way described because their decrees are the product of decisions by agents who themselves are set on determining what it is that we ought to do, and direct us to do so. They constitute legitimate authorities when doing

---

[20] I do not wish to indulge in excessively detailed analysis, but it is worth noting that there are two kinds of reasons the pre-emption thesis affects: First, it pre-empts reasons against the conduct required by the authoritative directive. Second, it pre-empts reasons that do not necessarily bear on the pros and cons of behaving as the directive requires, but that do militate against the desirability of issuing the directive. These may be that the matter should be left to individual discretion, or that the directive will have undesirable side-effects that make it undesirable, and so on.

so will in fact achieve the result of conforming better to reason (while respecting what reasons there are for us to determine our actions by our unhindered judgement). The fact that this is how they operate indicates that when they are legitimate their decrees should replace the background reasons. They pre-empt them. How much is pre-empted? What count as background reasons? They are the reasons that the authority was meant to consider in issuing its directives, provided, of course, that it acts within its legitimate power.

The pre-emptive standing of authoritative directives shows why the moral question about the law is a serious one. It shows what truth there is in the saying that in accepting authority we surrender our judgement to the authority. At the same time the solution of the theoretical problem shows that, in spite of its special character, authority, when subjected to the normal justification and the independence conditions, is just another case of the world confronting us with reasons for action. The theoretical puzzle was 'how can people create reasons by acting with the intention of doing so?' The answer is that this is so when considerations that are independent of human will make it so.

Yet again we see the analogy (as well as the difference) between authority and promises. Both yield reasons generated by actions designed to do so, a fact that gives both of them their puzzling air, and both can do so because considerations independent of human will validate such creation of reasons. Therefore, in following both, we follow reason, and thus exercise our judgement—though in both cases we do it at one remove—by accepting, through our judgement, the binding force of acts (promises, directives) that pre-empt our freedom to act for some of the background reasons. It is true that only authority involves accepting the directives of another. But if the two conditions are right, even authoritative directives, just like promises, are binding because, and where, they improve our powers by enabling us to conform to reason better than we could without them.

III. Refinements and Elaborations

So far I have tried to sketch the outlines of the service conception and to explain how it contends with two basic problems about authority. Its success in dealing with them is the main case for believing that it is along the right lines. But to establish itself the account has to deal with a whole host of additional difficulties. In this section I will briefly look at a range of difficulties, reflection on which leads to refining the account, as well as displaying some of its strengths.

A. Can we be subject to several authorities at the same time?

Of course we can. The more difficult question is whether we can be subject to more than one authority regarding the same subject matter at the same time. The normal justification thesis is based on a contrast between how I would act if unaffected by the authority compared with how I would act when trying to follow the authority. In the context, this is ambiguous. Does it mean 'how I would act when not influenced by any authority?' or 'how I would act when not trying to follow this particular authority?' The first question allows for the possibility that we are subject to several authorities at the same time and regarding the same matter. This is as it should be. We can be subject to the authority of our parents, of our schools, and of the law, for example, at the same time, and regarding the same issue.

When subject to several authorities with similar or overlapping jurisdictions, certain matters may be regulated by one authority, while the others remain silent on them. We should, in such cases, follow those who issue directives on the matter. When several authorities pronounce on the same matter and their directives conflict, we must decide, to the best of our ability, which is more reliable as a guide. Often there are co-operative relations among authorities. The law recognizes the authority of schools and of parents, for example, and lends them legal authority, by directing the relevant people to obey them, or by enforcing their directives through legal procedures. At other times authorities may be hostile to each other, directing their subjects not to obey, and more generally not to co-operate with the working of other authorities. In such cases the question whether a given authority's power extends to exclude the authority of another is to be judged in the way we judge the legitimacy of its power on any matter, namely whether we would conform better to reason by trying to follow its directives than if we do not.

B. Pre-emption and acting for the best reasons

Often we have more than one sufficient reason to do something. An authoritative directive may direct us to do something that we should do for independent reasons anyway. For example, I may have promised a friend to drive slowly and the law also instructs me to drive slowly. If

I drive slowly, I may do so because of the promise alone, not being aware of the law or not caring to obey it, or I may do so because of the law alone, or because of both, or for yet another consideration that appears to be a cogent reason, but may not be.

Such situations raise no problems. But the law involves a different kind of over-determination. By law we must not murder, but we also have an independent reason not to murder, namely respect for human life. This case is typical of many. Another kind of over-determination is somewhat different. We have a reason independent of the law to contribute our share towards meeting the cost of maintaining communal services. The law imposes a duty to pay tax as a way of doing so. Independently of the law, we do not have a reason to pay the precise sum we owe as tax. But once the law is there we have two reasons, we may want to say, to pay the sum that we owe as tax (we can disregard here that the tax law is likely to serve other purposes as well). One is our obligation to obey the law, the other our duty to contribute to the cost of community services.

Ideally, we would refrain from killing exclusively out of respect for people's lives, and not at all out of respect for the law. Ideally, we should pay our tax because we owe it as our share towards the cost of community services, as well as because the law demands it. Is this consistent with the pre-emption thesis?

A proper understanding of pre-emption removes any suspicion of a problem. A binding authoritative directive is not only a reason for behaving as it directs, but also an exclusionary reason, that is a reason for not following (ie not acting for) reasons that conflict with the rule. That is how authoritative directives pre-empt. They exclude reliance on conflicting reasons, not all conflicting reasons, but those that the law-maker was meant to consider before issuing the directive. These exclusionary reasons do not, of course, exclude relying on reasons for behaving in the same way as the directive requires. Think about it: authority improves our conformity with reason by overriding what we would do without it, when doing so would not conform with reason. So, assuming that it is entirely successful in its task, it need not and does not stop us from following the reasons on the winning side of an argument. It must, however, if it is to improve our conformity with reason, override our inclination to follow reasons on the losing side of the argument. Hence the pre-emption excludes only reasons that conflict with the authority's directive.

So when an action is rightly required by authority (ie when there are conclusive reasons for it, independently of the authority's intervention), we may (in both senses) do as we are required either because we are so required, or for the reasons that justify the requirement, or both. Sometimes, as in the case of the prohibition of murder, doing as required by authority for cogent reasons other than that the conduct is so required, is the better option. There will be other cases, for example, cases in which the directive issued by authority is mistaken or unjustified. It requires some action, the performance of which, while supported by some authority-independent reasons, is not sufficiently supported to require that action, not if the directive requiring it is ignored. This can be consistent with the directive being binding on us. Even legitimate authorities make mistakes. In such cases we should conform with the directive, and the ideal case is one in which we do so because we are required to by the authority and not because of the other reasons that support the action.

The tax example was different because we do not have a reason independent of the law to pay exactly as required by law and to pay it to this precise authority, even though once the law is in place the reason that justifies passing it is a reason for doing as it requires, which is distinct from the general duty we have to obey a legitimate authority. In such cases the best option is to act for both reasons, ie for both the law and the background reason for it.

In what sense are these options best? All that is required of us is to conform to reason, and it does not matter for what reason, or imagined reason, we do so. However, not only what we do but why we do it tells something about us. It is regarding such judgements, judgements about the agent, about what kind of person he is, how he conducts himself and so on, that the actual reasons that led him to action matter.

C. Conflicting reasons

Authoritative directives are not always conclusive reasons for the conduct they require. They can be defeated by conflicting reasons, or by conflicting directives. The reasons that can defeat them are those they do not exclude. The question is of some importance when considering the law. Typically, one rule of law does not exclude another of the same rank (in the sense in which constitutional rules, primary legislation, delegated legislation, and common law are of different rank). Rules of law exclude many non-legal considerations, though legal systems typically allow some to count and sometimes to override legal requirements. But they do not exclude other legal rules of the same rank. I will say that legal rules constitute prima facie reasons for the conduct they prescribe.

When legal rules conflict, how is the outcome to be decided? There are many devices to which the law appeals for assistance. The problem arises when no formal device is available or sufficient. The question is whether the relative merits of the background reasons, those for and against each of the rules, count in the correct determination of each such conflict. It appears unreasonable to ignore these background reasons, for to do so leaves no option but to take all rules of the same constitutional rank as counting in the same way and to the same degree towards the outcome. Given that one rule may be a trivial one, say some minor tax regulation, while the other may be a matter central to the protection of fundamental rights, it would be unreasonable to take them to be of equal importance. Yet does not the thesis that authoritative directives exclude reliance on conflicting considerations mean that one is not allowed to assess the true importance of a rule, which would involve assessing both reasons for and reasons against it, and these include reasons for and against the conduct it prescribes?

However, the pre-emption thesis implies rejecting both alternatives. As mentioned, it excludes reference to the background considerations and thus precludes a proper assessment of the importance of the rule. However, it does not follow that all rules of the same constitutional rank must be seen as of the same importance. Just as the authority makes the law, so it does, or at least can, indicate its importance in its eyes. There are various ways of doing so, mostly implicit, some more explicit, like preambles and other legislative material. Other indications are implied in the language the law was expressed in and the context of its legislation. To the extent that judicial practice instructs courts to resort to these devices, they are recognized as legally binding and have authoritative standing.

There is no denying that such considerations are unlikely to determine all questions that may arise about the importance of each legal rule. Nor can all issues arising out of conflicts among legal rules be determined by prioritizing some over others. Often, instead of following one rule rather than the other, practical conflicts should be resolved by finding the option that satisfies the conflicting rules to the highest possible degree. That follows from the nature of practical rationality, which requires that when reasons cannot be completely conformed to, they should be conformed to, to the highest possible degree. This will require courts confronted with conflicts of this kind to find such an optimific outcome, which will involve an understanding of the point of the conflicting rules. We already saw that this is consistent with the service conception.

Even so, not infrequently in different rules of law conflicts, the law does not contain the resources to resolve the conflict. It is indeterminate regarding the issue, usually leaving such decisions to the discretion of judges, ie to their judgement about the real merit of the different rules, a judgement that goes beyond what the law determines.

D. Reason and knowability

It is a matter of dispute whether a factor not known by some agents, or not knowable by them, can nevertheless constitute a reason for those agents. Whatever is the truth on that general question, there are independent reasons for thinking that someone or some body can be an authority only if the fact that the two conditions are met can be known to its subjects. The point of being under an authority is that it opens a way of improving one's conformity with reason. One achieves that by conforming to the authority's directives, and (special circumstances apart) one can reliably conform only if one has reliable beliefs regarding who has legitimate authority, and what its directives are. If one cannot have trustworthy beliefs that a certain body meets the conditions for legitimacy, then one's belief in its authority is haphazard, and cannot (again special circumstances apart) be reliable. Therefore, to fulfil its function, the legitimacy of an authority must be knowable to its subjects.

In stating this argument I assumed that whenever one can form reliable beliefs that the conditions for legitimacy are met, one can also have knowledge that they are met. I was also relying on the fact that, generally speaking, the only reliable way of conforming to authority is through having a reliable belief that it is an authority, and therefore should be obeyed. This assumption helps with defining more precisely what has to be the case for the legitimacy to be knowable. Since the point is to improve conformity with reason, there is at least a rough measure of how important such improvement is. The more important it is, the more extensive inquiries about ways of achieving it are indicated. The indicated degree of inquiry sets the limit to knowability: it is knowable if an inquiry of that kind would yield that knowledge.

We engage in such assessments every day of the week. We regularly need to decide how far to pursue an inquiry in the hope of coming to a more reliable or more nuanced conclusion about what is the right course of action on various occasions. When the issue is of importance we extend our inquiries and deliberations well beyond what we do when the matter is relatively trifling. The same kind of consideration applies to establishing the existence of authorities. How much it can be expected to improve our conformity to reason, and how important the matter is, establish what inquiry is reasonable to undertake. When reasonable inquiry will not reveal the case for authority, that case, if it exists at all, is unknowable. It follows that people are not subject to any authority regarding those matters.

This argument is used here to establish not merely that it is not rational, or not worthwhile, to carry on with the inquiry about the existence of certain reasons, but that those reasons, authoritative directives, do not exist. There is no authority over the matter, because to exist, authorities must be knowable. This extension of the argument is not surprising. The service conception makes the legitimacy of authorities turn primarily on their value in achieving something beyond them, ie conformity to background reasons existing independently of them. In general we have no reason to pursue the means unless they are worth pursuing, given the cost of doing so relative to the importance of the ends. To give one simple example: I suppose that I can get you to give me five pounds by giving you ten pounds on condition that you give me five pounds in return. But (special circumstances apart) I have no reason to pursue this means to that end, no reason at all. It is not merely the case that I have a reason that is defeated by the cost of pursuing the means. The case of authority is not exactly the same, but it is analogous: obeying Jane, let us say, would help me better to conform with reasons that apply to me. However, I cannot know that without pursuing an inquiry that would be irrational to pursue. It follows that I have no reason to obey Jane, and it follows from that, that Jane has no authority over me.

E. Smallest class

There are other epistemic constraints on the conditions of legitimacy. They constrain the application of the substantive conditions. For example, suppose we can establish that we will conform better with reason if we follow authority regarding matters in a certain domain, let us say matters dealt with in work-safety regulations. Does the authority's power extend over the whole domain or is it limited to part of it only? The normal justification condition may be taken to mean that it has authority over the whole domain. But that encounters the objection that the domain can be artificially extended (eg by adding to it safety at home) without any reason to believe that we actually do better in the extensions themselves (eg we may be better judges of safety in our homes than whoever is the authority over safety at work). The extended domain may still meet both conditions of legitimacy simply because the narrower domain meets them, and the disadvantages of the extension are not bad enough to cancel out the case for the authority.

The solution to this conundrum is, I believe, that a person or body has authority regarding any domain if that person or body meets the conditions regarding that domain and there is no proper part of the domain regarding which the person or body can be known to fail the conditions.

F. Burdens of inquiry and decision

The second, independence, condition of legitimacy is premised on the thought that it is important that people decide for themselves how to conduct their lives, and that, especially in some areas, they should do so with only limited reliance on direct advice, let alone commands, from others. We do not fully live as autonomous persons if we do not decide for ourselves. It does not follow, of course, that we always enjoy doing so. Some people find the burden of decision hard to bear. They prevaricate, get depressed, feel oppressed and pressured, and, of course, often decide unwisely, often deciding almost arbitrarily in order to relieve themselves of the burden of decision.

Not everyone suffers from an aversion to taking decisions and assuming responsibility, though most people feel the burden. We are tempted to think that one is not a responsible agent if one does not, as it shows a lack of seriousness about one's actions. Be this as it may, everyone has to carry the burden of inquiry. It makes demands on our attention, energy, time, and resources. It may impose a strain on our relations with others, and so on. To be sure, the process of purposeful inquiry, of working one's way towards a decision, can also be enjoyable and rewarding in its own right. But given that its primary purpose and justification is that it contributes to a good decision, one cannot expect the rewards to match the burdens, and sometimes the burdens far exceed the rewards.

There are ways of reducing the burdens of decision and inquiry, and some of them involve shifting the burden onto others. The practice of relying on professional advice has grown in recent times, perhaps in parallel with a decline in the family as a source of advice and support in decision making. Submitting to authority is one way of reducing the burdens. It can be justified only if it is consistent with the independence condition of legitimacy (though when the psychological vulnerability to the burden is extreme it may be justified to mitigate the condition to relieve the burden). The normal justification condition, however, is better understood broadly to allow that meeting the burdens of decision and inquiry is one of the benefits authorities can bring.

G. Respect and other reasons

We can accommodate the burdens of decision and inquiry in an account of legitimate authority, either through an appropriate reading of the two conditions, or by recognizing these burdens as additional factors bearing on legitimacy, factors that modify or add to the two conditions. I do not believe that it is possible to enumerate exhaustively the considerations that can bear on the legitimacy of authority, or for that matter on the justification of any other normative institution that is widely accepted and is enshrined in social practices. Such institutions do sometimes have core purposes or points, but once they are recognized and are followed in practice they become enmeshed in other practices and concerns, which lead them, without deflecting from their primary justification, to accrue additional purposes and justifying reasons.

One such factor arises out of the way in which, in many societies, some authorities become the primary visible expression of institutions to which they belong, and in the name of which they function. Political and legal institutions with legal authority are a case in point. In many countries superior legal authorities are identified with the state or the country or the nation and speak in their name. Where this is so, respect for and identification with the state, country, or nation may be expressed in respect for legal authority, and that in turn takes the form (among others) of trusting these institutions, taking it on trust that they have authority to do what they do, not questioning their conduct too closely to see whether they exceed their authority, etc. Trust is a general mark of respect, and a natural one. If respect for the state, country or nation is desirable, which sometimes it is, and if it is appropriate, given the circumstances of the society in question, for it to express itself through respect and trust in its legal institutions, then a certain slackening of vigilance regarding the two conditions of legitimacy is also acceptable. That is, in such cases, while the conditions themselves are unaffected, people would be justified in maintaining that the government has authority on evidence that would not be sufficient to reach such conclusions but for the trust they have in the government.

I do not maintain that people have a duty to trust and respect their government in that way. That would be like claiming that they have a duty to have someone as their friend. The respect we are concerned with here is not the basic respect we owe every person. It is respect arising out of identification with the country, and there is no duty on anyone to identify with any country. The claim is simply that that attitude is sometimes (ie when certain moral conditions are met) appropriate.

Does it show that sometimes people who trust the government are justified in believing that the government has authority when it does not, or does it show that sometimes the government has authority over such people even though it does not have authority or has only a more limited authority over people who do not trust it? One can argue either way. On the one hand, it may be thought desirable to separate epistemic from substantive considerations, and to have an account that tends to make governmental authority independent of individually variable factors such as trust resulting from identification with the country. On the other hand, as we saw, the service conception does incorporate epistemic elements into the conditions of authority, and, as we shall see, it allows for considerable variability in the extent of governmental authority over the population over which it claims authority. So it may be that the better view is to regard identification as affecting the conditions of legitimacy, and not merely the occasions on which it is justified to believe that they are met. This way the account is closer to familiar (and rational) attitudes that people have to authority.

H. Pre-existing reasons and concretization

The account may appear unduly restrictive. It may appear to exclude any power for governments to improve the economic conditions of their citizens. For example, the authority may do so by imposing taxes and using the revenue to subsidize training, which is useful for full employment and for economic development. Neither I nor other inhabitants have reason to impose taxes or subsidize training in the country. But that is a misperception. To the extent that the inhabitants of a country have reason to improve their own economic situation, they will have reason to do so through a common authority in those matters where that authority will be capable of achieving that goal better than they can do so by acting independently of it.

Does it mean that I do have reason to raise taxes? Not necessarily, but the question stems from overlooking the fact that typically reasons do not come singly, rather they are nested. Typically, we have one reason because conforming to it is a way of advancing another reason. The more general reasons apply as a standard background to our activities, and are less affected by changing circumstances, whereas the more specific reasons that nest in them tend to apply during shorter periods and depend on conditions that are often liable to change. My reason to improve my economic situation is an example of a relatively general reason, not likely to disappear until my retirement or even later, though its urgency and force may change over time. A reason to change employment may derive from it. I may have reason to change employment in order to improve my economic condition. But it is a more short-term reason, which may disappear if, for example, I am offered promotion by my current employer, or through other circumstances.

People assigned the task of helping us do so by conforming to or realizing some reasons that apply to us, reasons we have ourselves. These reasons have others nested in them, which set out ways of realizing them. But those nested reasons need not be reasons for us. That is, those helping us may have good grounds for pursuing the goals set by reasons that apply to us in ways that are not open to us. Indeed, as the service conception of authority illustrates, they may be assigned the task of helping us precisely because of that. Through their intervention we acquire new ways of realizing the goals set by the general background reasons, and thereby new reasons to take the actions that will do so.

There are various other ways in which the suppleness of the service conception can be underestimated. In giving the following examples I do not wish to endorse their cogency. I mention them just to illustrate the power of the service conception. For example, someone may believe that people, members of a certain group, have a duty, perhaps a religious duty or a duty of loyalty arising from some historical circumstances, to obey some person or institution. In that case the normal justification thesis is easily satisfied. By obeying that person or institution one is discharging that duty. Or suppose that members of a certain group, perhaps an ethnic group, have a duty to obey someone who can command the allegiance of the group, a sort of national duty for the glory of the nation. Again, if anyone can command the allegiance of the group then that person will satisfy the conditions of having authority under the service conception. Or suppose that one has a duty to obey whoever wins a lottery; again the conditions of the service conception would be met regarding anyone who wins the lottery. Some people believe that one has a duty to obey anyone who is elected by the majority. Again, that is no problem for the service conception. If that is so it simply shows that the conditions of the service conception are met regarding anyone who is so elected.[21]

I. Coordination and metacoordination

A major, if not the main, factor in establishing the legitimacy of political authorities is their ability to secure coordination. Some writers, commenting on this fact, have gone further and argued: (1) that the sole (or only major) function of political authorities is to coordinate the conduct of those subject to them for the achievement of some goods; (2) that coordination being secured via a Lewis-type convention does not require an authority with a right to rule: all it requires is the ability to make salient certain coordinative outcomes; and (3) that it follows that political authorities, as such, do not enjoy a right to rule.

Such views overlook quite a number of facts central to the functioning of legitimate political authorities. First, that they can satisfy the normal justification thesis not only by securing coordination, but also by having more reliable judgement regarding the best options, given the circumstances, and that in their normal activities, expertise and coordination are inextricably mixed. Second, that the coordination that political authorities should secure and often do, is rarely the sort of coordination constituting the solution to a Lewis-type coordination problem. Coordinating the actions of many agents means nothing more than making or enabling them to act in such a way that they all play diverse roles in some possible plan of action that is likely to yield some sought-after results. This kind of coordination cannot generally

---

[21] It is of course no accident that my account of authority makes no special reference to democratic authority. I do not believe that democracy is the only regime that can be legitimate, nor that all democratic governments are legitimate. That is not to say that democratic governments do not have, in many countries, unique claims to enjoy some qualified or limited authority, either through their ability to produce beneficial results or because of their ability to give expression to people's standing as free, autonomous agents, or whatever other values they serve. It seems to me, however, of vital importance that we should not fall prey to the current, and much abused, democratic rhetoric, and maintain a clear-sighted and critical perspective on the nature of democratic institutions, and that we should preserve our ability to recognize the limitations of democratic regimes as well as acknowledge the possibility that what pass for democratic regimes could completely lack legitimacy.

be achieved via a Lewis-type convention. Third, one reason for this is that the need for coordination and the means for achieving it are not necessarily generally known and are often a matter of controversy. Fourth, that since the goals people actually have need not be desirable, coordination aimed at securing these goals need not be desirable either. The coordinated schemes of action that political authorities should pursue are those to which people should be committed, or those needed to secure goals that people should have, which are not always the goals which they do have. Fifth, that typically, when the political authority is otherwise legitimate and reasonably successful, it will also be rightly taken, at least in some areas, to be an authority on the second-order question of when coordination is in place.

IV. The Qualification Objection

One possible reaction to the service conception is that it misses its target. It describes the conditions under which an authority is a good-enough authority. It articulates tests of success for authorities, but it does not explain what it is to be an authority. It describes the conditions that have to hold if an authority is to be capable of successfully discharging its tasks, but it is not and cannot be the case that everyone who can discharge a task well has that task. Not everyone who can be a good prime minister of a country is the prime minister of that country, not everyone who can be a good teacher in the primary school of my neighbourhood is a teacher in that school. Moreover, no one is a prime minister or a teacher just in virtue of the fact that they can perform the task well. Something else has to happen to give them the task, to make it their task.

To evaluate this point we should contrast theoretical and practical authority. Theoretical authorities are experts whose knowledge and understanding of the matter on which they are authorities is both exceptionally extensive and remarkably systematic and secure, making them reliable guides on those matters. Their word is a reason for holding certain beliefs and discarding others. In that, it is like testimony: the reports of witnesses about the events on which they report. But expert advice is very different from witnesses' testimony. First, normally their advice does not report their perceptual beliefs or the content of their experiences. (The exceptions are cases where what we see is hard to understand, where experts may be useful in telling us what we and they see.)

Rather, it reports inferential beliefs, conclusions they draw from evidence derived from their own experience or that of others. Secondly, and as a corollary, their advice does not depend on their advantageous situation relative to the matter under consideration: unlike the testimony of witnesses, they need not have been at the right place at the right time to see or otherwise witness the events they report about. They derive their conclusions not from observation, which requires an advantageous position, but by inference from evidence, including testimony, and that does not require enjoying a privileged or advantageous position relative to the events on which they advise. As a result, while testimony bears only on past events, experts can also predict future events.

These differences account for the normative differences between witnesses and experts. With witnesses all we have to do is assess the reliability of their report: the quality of their eyesight, weather conditions, their attention at the time, their distance from the events reported, etc. With experts none of these questions normally arises. What is at issue is their ability to draw conclusions from the evidence. Often it is knowledge of the theory, say some scientific theory, and at other times it is breadth of experience and depth of understanding that establish their credentials as experts, ie as people who can reliably infer one thing from another. Once their authority as experts is established, it follows that our non-expert evaluations of the same evidence cannot reliably challenge theirs. I see the piece of meat at the butchers, and its colour makes me think that it is not fresh. But I do not have experience or theory to back me up. My expert friend reassures me that the meat is fresh, and I just yield. If I accept my friend's expertise, relative to me, I have no choice. Theoretical advice pre-empts the reasons for belief that I would have relied upon otherwise. Just as with any practical authority, the point of a theoretical authority is to enable me to conform to reason, this time reason for belief, better than I would otherwise be able to do. This requires taking the expert advice, and allowing it to pre-empt my own assessment of the evidence. If I do not do that, I do not benefit from it.

Theoretical authority resembles practical authority in its point (to improve conformity with reason) and in being pre-emptive, as well as in being relational both regarding who has to take an authority's word as authoritative, and regarding what matters: it is possible that I should take this expert's word as authoritative, because he knows much more than I do, but you have no reason to do the same, as you know as much as he does on these matters.

These similarities notwithstanding, there are significant differences between theoretical and practical authorities. I noted that, unlike testimony, some expertise can be the basis of predictions of future events. But it cannot change anything. The ability of practical authorities to improve coordination, a factor entirely absent from the activities of theoretical authorities, makes them subject to derived reasons[22] to secure pre-existing goals in ways not otherwise possible. They can, as a result, change things in the world.

Furthermore, and it hardly needs saying, theoretical authorities, experts, cannot order us to believe one thing or another, and cannot impose duties to believe—the nature of belief and belief formation excludes such duties. Belief formation, just like actions, is responsive to reasons, but only actions, and not the formation of beliefs, involve the will. Duties exist only when (but not always even then) the response to reason involves the will.

These points are associated with important differences of idiom. For example, some people are authorities on eighteenth-century farming methods, but they do not have authority over anyone. I know nothing about eighteenth-century farming methods and should take what they say as authoritative, but they do not have authority over me. Similarly the notion of legitimate authority is confined to practical authority. People may or may not be experts in or authorities on eighteenth-century farming methods. But they cannot be de facto authorities or legitimate authorities on the subject. Finally, only regarding practical matters can we say that someone has authority, or lacks it. In theoretical matters, someone either is or is not an authority, but no one has authority.

What have these points to do with the critique of the service conception, with the claim that it mistakes an analysis of when an authority is good at what it is doing for an analysis of what it is to be an authority? At first blush, they may suggest that the critique is correct regarding practical authorities, but mistaken about theoretical authorities.

Since theoretical authorities cannot possess or lack legitimacy, and cannot impose duties (not even duties to believe), they cannot require an additional condition beyond those of the service conception. If they are qualified as authorities, they are authorities. In fact, even the

---

[22] Note that it is not merely that authorities create new reasons by issuing directives. This is true of theoretical authorities as well. Their very existence opens up opportunities, and thereby subjects them to new derived reasons, reasons to satisfy previously existing reasons in new ways.

epistemic condition we noticed before, namely that their possession of authority is knowable to those over whom they have authority, does not apply to theoretical authorities, which have no authority over anyone. The greatest expert on eighteenth-century farming methods may be a solitary scholar unknown to the academic community and unrecognized by anyone. He is still an authority, just in virtue of his knowledge of his subject. Nothing more is needed.[23] So the objection fails regarding theoretical authorities.

Practical authorities, on the other hand, impose duties on people. They have authority over people. They have normative powers over people. To be authorities, so the argument goes, they need more than the capacity to function well. They need to be made authorities, not necessarily by being appointed to the job, but something like an appointment has to be there.

However, the admission that the objection fails regarding theoretical authorities seems to me to establish that it fails altogether. It is implausible to think that what is a successful analysis of what it is to be an authority in theoretical matters makes no contribution at all to an understanding of the notion of authority, of what it is to have practical authority. Possibly, the differences between the two kinds of authority mean that it is a successful analysis of one kind, and only a partial analysis of the other. But it is implausible to claim that it has nothing to do with the analysis of the other. There is another reason to doubt the objection. It seems implausible to think that one can be a legitimate authority however bad one is at acting as an authority. If the primary point of authority, practical authority included, is to improve conformity with reason, it is implausible to think that someone who contributes not at all in that respect, someone who in fact makes us act more against reason than we would do had we not tried to follow him, can have legitimate authority.

We can therefore reject the objection. But another more modest objection is just around the corner. It says that regarding practical authorities, given their ability to change things, to impose duties and confer rights, the service conception furnishes only part of their analysis. It states a necessary condition for being an authority, but not a sufficient one.

---

[23] Of course normally we cannot know that he is an authority unless someone else attests to it. But it seems best to assign the implication that no one who is totally unrecognized can be an authority to the pragmatics of discourse.

This objection is more plausible. But to succeed it needs to meet one doubt: the differences between theoretical and practical authorities may lead to differences in what has to be established to confirm that they do meet the service conception's criteria for legitimate authority. Would not those differences be sufficient to show that not everyone who can be a good authority has practical authority?

Confining the discussion to political authorities, we know that a major part of their role: improving public services, personal safety, security of contracts, and other commercial transactions, requires them to be successful in coordinating the conduct of large numbers of people. That ability is not enough for the performance of such tasks, but it is necessary for it. It follows that only bodies that enjoy de facto authority (ie that are in fact followed or at least conformed with by considerable segments of the population) can have legitimate authority over all these matters. Hence there cannot be an unknown political authority. Similarly, there cannot be a political authority that does not exercise its authority, ie does not issue directives that impose duties, confer rights, etc. We can contrast this with theoretical authority: our expert in eighteenth-century farming methods may never give any advice or express any opinions on the matter. It is enough that he could, for his authority depends on his knowledge, not on his power over people, his ability to make them modify their behaviour to conform to his directives, as does the legitimacy of political authorities.

Finally, but most importantly, given how things are in our world, governments of the kind we are familiar with can only succeed in meeting the conditions of legitimacy (according to the service conception) if they have the authority to use and are successful in the use of force against those who flout certain of their directives. There is no need now to establish what are the general conditions for the rightful use of force by governments. For our purposes it is enough that such a right must exist for a government to meet the two conditions of legitimacy, and that it must be effectively used. This is an additional, double obstacle on the road to the possession of legitimate governmental authority. It is a normative obstacle: justifying the possession of a moral right to use force; and a factual obstacle: being de facto able to use it effectively. No such conditions need be met by theoretical authorities. Does not the existence of these conditions show that the service conception explains not who would be good had he been given authority, but who really has authority? At the very least they show that the service conception recognizes and has some account of the difference between being qualified to hold authority, and having authority. The question is whether its account is adequate. That question is still open. But the accusation that it simply confused qualification for authority with authority fails.

V. Consent

Let us examine one contender for this missing element: the consent of the subjects. On the view to be considered, the conditions of the service conception need to be met for consent to confer authority on anyone. To have authority, a person or body must meet the necessary qualifications for holding authority. The two conditions of the service conception state what the qualifications are, and therefore, to qualify for having authority anyone must meet them. But actually to have authority over another requires the consent of that other as well.

Most commonly, however, the claim that all authority derives from consent is taken by its advocates to be based on other considerations, independent of the preceding argument. To use the familiar slogans, it cannot be—people say—that one person is subject to the will of another except by his own choosing, expressed by his consent to be subject to that authority.

Some people take this view to be an application to the case of authority of a broader thesis, namely that no obligations bind anyone except by their own will. I will have to disregard that view, which takes us too far afield for the present occasion. I will focus on the more limited view that at least all people who are persons, who are autonomous agents, cannot be subject to the will of another except by choice. No one can have authority over us and tell us what to do without our consent.

We nevertheless assume that there can be duties without the consent of the person bound. I have a duty to respect others, which does not depend on my consent to respect others, let alone on my consent to an obligation to do so. For what, then, is consent a prerequisite? One line of argument will have it that no obligation whose discharge affects a person can be valid without his consent. But that seems highly implausible. Other people's obligation to respect me, not to kill me, as well as their duty to protect the environment, for example, affect me quite deeply, and they nevertheless have them regardless of my consent. Nor, it seems plausible to think, can I release them from these obligations. I cannot release them from their obligation to protect the environment, for its impact on me is not central to its justification. But nor can I release people from their duty to respect me, or my humanity, as Kant would have said, even though I am central to its justification. To be sure, my consent can turn acts that would, without it, breach that duty, into innocuous acts. For example, by giving you my car as a gift I turn your driving away in it from theft to a permissible handling of your own property. But the effect of my consent presupposes the existence of a prior duty, and its scope (Can I consent to be killed? Or to become a slave?) is determined by that duty, which itself exists independently of consent.

So we turn to the most plausible suggestion: namely that no one can intentionally impose an obligation on a person without the consent of its subject. This idea is supposed to tie up with the ideal of personal autonomy. What makes obligations intentionally created by another a special case requiring consent? It cannot be the content of these obligations, for the demand for consent is not made to depend on the content of the obligations. It depends on their source. Given that only one thing is known of the source, namely that it is supposed to be an authority, the demand for consent seems to depend on the general relationship that is indicated: a relationship of one person being subject to the will of another.

Do you have the impression that we have come full circle? Have we not considered that precise point? Was it not the moral question that was answered earlier? If that answer was good, and nothing was said to indicate otherwise, why are we back with it? Presumably there is a residual feeling that the earlier reply did not cover all aspects of the moral problem. What is left? How are we to find it? The way to an answer was indicated earlier. We saw that consent is a source of obligation only when some considerations, themselves independent of consent, vindicate its being such a source. And those considerations would also determine what kind of consent is required to legitimize the authority and determine over what matters it will reign.

Oddly, it is this test that I find no way of meeting. The moral question was about the legitimacy of one person being subject to the will of another. But that problem cannot be solved by consent. Suppose you say to me: 'I impose on you an obligation to come to my party tomorrow' (and you may add: 'provided of course that you agree'), and I reply 'I agree'. I definitely consented to come to your party. I may even have promised to do so. But clearly whatever you said, you did not impose an obligation on me. The obligation is entirely my own creation. You may have invited me in a funny way, or expressed a strong desire that I should come, again in a funny way. But you did not obligate me to come.

Now suppose you say to me: 'You will have an obligation to do whatever I tell you to do' or 'Whenever I tell you to do something that in my judgement you should do anyway, you will have a duty to do it, provided you now agree to this.' If you tell me something like that and I agree, then while until I agreed, and at the moment of agreeing, I was not subject to your will, once I agree I am subject to your will. It is analogous to becoming a slave. I was free, and I lost my freedom. Here, I was independent of your will, and now I am subject to your will. Of course it is not the case that I am subject to your will because I want to be. I may have wanted it when I consented. But once I consented, what I want becomes immaterial. I am subject to your will whether I want to be or not. Does not that raise the moral problem, rather than answer it?

Still, as I said, the feeling persists that the solution to the moral question given before left some of our concerns unanswered. It saw the issue as one having some other person decide for one rather than deciding for oneself. The emphasis was on 'not deciding for oneself.' It showed that there is no objection to that, that we should approve of that when it makes us conform better with reason. The argument drew analogies between authorities, agents, mechanical devices, and so on. And that is where it falls short. It did not notice that while they are all cases of not deciding for oneself, there is a difference between these cases and that of authority, for only authority involves subjecting our will to that of another, and that is not merely a matter of not deciding for oneself.

Let us concede that the problem exists, that perhaps the solution offered so far ignores it. It remains the fact that consent does not solve the problem. It can solve the problem only when there is a reason for such consent to bind us, and there is none, other than the one that can dispense with consent but cannot explain why a single act of consent can subject us for life to the will of another, ie that the authority will make us better conform to reason. It should be noted that in denying that consent is necessary for legitimacy, I am not denying that it has some significance. I suspect that the way it is treated in the law of some countries shows that it is regarded as significant, but not to the legitimacy of an authority. Naturalized citizens and the holders of some offices of state are often required to express formal consent, though not necessarily to the legitimacy of the authority. Since the law claims authority over all of us but requires consent from some only, it does not regard consent as necessary for its authority. But the requirement of consent may show that it is taken to express some more specific attitude(s) that are taken to be required in some contexts in particular. Beyond the law we may feel that consent makes a difference: 'now (having consented) you have only yourself to blame', we sometimes say. I cannot inquire here into such possibilities, but will simply reiterate that, for the reasons given, they do not establish that consent is a condition of authority.

Perhaps, however, the popularity of consent-based explanations of authority has something to tell us. Perhaps while being mistaken, it points in the right direction. The question is a question of appropriation. The aspect of the moral problem we are confronting is not the limits to one's freedom that the law or other authoritative directives pose. It is that the limits are imposed deliberately, and that they are imposed by another. They are not limits set by me. Consent explanations appeal because they seek to make the limits the agent's own. They are chimerical because they fail to do that. They remain imposed limits, deliberately imposed by another. My historical consent cannot have the significance placed on it; it cannot make the limits my own.

What we need, you may think, is another way of explaining appropriation, of explaining how the commands of authority can lose the character of subjection of one person to the will of another. That is where the search for collective identities begins.

VI. Collective Identities

The flaw in consent accounts is that they fly in the face of reality. They claim that what is not mine is mine, in spite of the patent fact that it is binding on me regardless of my will, and often against my will. The best that can be said for them is that they make each of us slaves of our own decisions when young. But there is another way. A rule or directive may be neither imposed on me by another nor made by me. It could be made by 'us', by a collectivity of which I am a part. The simplest and least controversial examples derive from limited collective enterprises. We, six friends, may go on an adventure trip together, or organize a party or a conference together. And we may decide, by mutual consultation, what to do in pursuing our joint venture, decisions that bind each and all of us. While none of them is made by me, none of them is imposed on me by the will of another. They are made by us. Is it not an additional necessary condition of the legitimacy of authority that it acts for a collectivity so that its directives are not imposed on members of that group, but are their decisions, collectively taken, perhaps through their agents or representatives?

A. Are authorities acting for the people?: collectivities and collective actions

There is discourse about collectivities, their identity and action, and how we relate to them when we say 'we', meaning Oxford University, 'did this or that' or 'hold these ideals high,' etc. This is comprehensible discourse, therefore it has truth conditions, and there are states of affairs in virtue of which such statements are true or false.

I have no general reason to think that there are no practical authorities, ie authorities with a right to rule or command, which are not the organs of collectivities in the way in which governments are the organs of countries or of states. But it may well be that cases in which authorities act for collectivities and are organs of collectivities are typical. They may be the paradigm in relation to which we understand all authorities. So let us allow that point, necessary for the success of the thought that the answer to the moral problem is that authorities' actions are our actions.

This is not the place to investigate the truth conditions of propositions about collective action. But one aspect of such an investigation is important for our purpose: is it the case that a university, a country, a government, or whatever other collectivity, is *my* university, country, or government only if I identify with it?

The notion of identification is both important and obscure, but I think that there can be no doubt that the answer to the question is negative. Oxford University is my university whether I identify with it or not. Your country is your country whether you like it or not, whether you are alienated from it or not, and this government is the government of all the people of this country however much they hate it. There were times in the past when many Anglo-Irish did not identify with Eire and its government. They did not regard it as their state and their government. But Eire was their state, and its government was their government. Not infrequently we find in a country individuals or groups that do not and cannot bring themselves to identify with their country or to regard its government as their own. They will not use the language of 'we', as in 'we just changed the law to make it harder for asylum seekers to stay in the country'. Their refusal, often their inability to use such locutions, is highly significant, but it does not change the fact that that is their country, their law, and their government.

B. Is the moral problem solved when the authority's action is ours?

The fact that people can be alienated from their countries, that they may refuse to talk of what 'we' did when talking of their countries, raises severe doubts about the contention that the answer to the moral problem is that the commands of authorities are our commands, even while we are their subjects. Tell this to the people who are alienated from their country or from their regime. Tell them that it is they who passed the laws that they regard as anathema, etc. It is a sad form of trickery to think that its being the authority of their country makes its command their command in any sense that solves the moral problem.

One response to this point is to say that there is a different sense of belonging, of a group being ours, of its actions being our actions, a sense that does bridge the gap we are looking at. Maybe. There may be a sense of belonging to a country, or identification with its regime (ie its political constitution), a sense that would enable people to affirm that the actions of authorities they identify with are their actions— thus dissolving the moral problem. The question is: does this mean that the legitimate power of authorities is limited to people who so identify with the collectivities that the authorities represent? Does it mean, for example, that the Anglo-Irish who did not identify with Eire and its government were not subject to its authority, that they were not subject to the law of Eire?

The problem of the limits of the state's authority is even more far-reaching. We tend to believe that states have some extraterritorial jurisdiction, and that in any case they have territorial jurisdiction over all people within the boundaries of the state. But we do not expect visitors to identify with the state or the regime. It may be a good thing if the population of a country identifies with it, and with its regime. But there is no reasonable argument to deny that where the state has any legitimate authority at all its authority reaches beyond ruling those who identify with it.

Identification may play an important role in a theory of legitimacy in another way. It may be said that it is a requirement of the legitimacy of the state, and of its authorities, that it would be reasonable of its citizens to identify with it. Identification, the thought is, is not a brute fact, it is an attitude, which like beliefs, emotions, and desires, is responsive to reasons. There are, or can be, reasons to identify and reasons not to identify. Hence sometimes identifying is reasonable and at others it is not.[24] It is, so it may be claimed, a condition of the legitimacy of an authority that it will be reasonable for its subjects to identify themselves with it. That may be so, at least in the case of some authorities. But not surprisingly I believe that the service conception provides the conditions for the fulfilment of this requirement (the others having to do with the relations of the individual to the authority or to the body in the name of which it acts). So that thought offers neither a criticism of nor a supplementation to the service conception account of authority.

C. Must legitimate authorities be also acting for collectivities and does it matter?

This brief argument relies on the fact that people, including us, who believe that political authorities can ever be legitimate, hold views about their legitimacy in many concrete cases that cannot be reconciled with the view that political bodies have legitimate authority only over people who identify with them, or with the regimes for which they act. It is open to some to maintain that we should revise our beliefs about the scope of authority. My sense is that this would be a mistake. The problem of appropriation, to which identification is supposed to be the answer, is a misguided question. It is not part of our normal understanding of authority that its actions are the actions of its subjects. On the contrary, the normal understanding is that authority involves a hierarchical relationship, that it involves an imposition on the subject. The service conception explains how and when such power can be justified, at least in the sense of being for the good. The quest for a solution to the appropriation problem is perhaps best seen as an aspirational ideal: it would be good, desirable, to have the bulk of those subject to a political authority identify with the regime for which it acts. But identification should not be thought of as a condition of legitimacy.

---

[24] Some people would say that sometimes one should or one has a duty to identify, though I doubt that.

6

About Morality and the Nature of Law

I. On the Necessary Connection Test

Two innocent truisms about the law lie behind much of the difficulty we have in understanding the relations between law and morality. *The law can be valuable, but it can also be the source[1] of much evil.* Not everyone agrees to these truisms, and there is nothing inappropriate in challenging them, or examining their credentials. They are, however, truisms in being taken by most people to be obviously true and beyond question. In other words, they express many people's direct reactions to or understanding of the phenomena, an understanding which is open to theoretical challenge, but has to be taken as correct absent a successful theoretical challenge.

There is no conflict between the truisms. People and much else in the world can be the source of both good and evil. Trouble begins when we ask ourselves whether it is entirely contingent whether the law is the source of good or ill in various societies, or how much good and how much evil there is in it. There has, of course, been enthusiastic and persisting support for claiming that the connection between law and morality is not contingent. The support comes from contradictory directions. Some strands in political anarchism claim that it is of the essence of law to have features which render it inconsistent with morality. Hence the law is essentially immoral.[2] A clear example of this in recent times has been Robert Paul Wolff's argument that the law in its nature requires obedience regardless of one's judgement about the merit

---

[1] I say that the law can be the source of much evil, meaning that the evil is brought about by human beings, but that the law often plays a causal role in bringing it about, in facilitating its occurrence.

[2] This normally means that 'legal authorities' do not have moral authority, and the law they make and enforce is not morally binding on us, at least not as it claims to bind. This allows that the law can also be a source of good in ways which fall short of possessing authority.

of the obeying conduct, and that this is inconsistent with people's moral autonomy which requires them to take responsibility for their actions and to act only on their own judgement on the merit of their actions.[3] Diametrically opposed to this variant of anarchism is, for example, a variety of Thomist natural law views which regard the law as good in its very nature.[4]

Both sides of this particular dispute admit that the law can do some good (even according to the anarchists), and that it can be the source of evil (even according to the Thomists). Anarchists can admit that some laws are sensible. They can admit that their directives can create valuable options not otherwise available, and that people ought to conform to them, so long as they do not do so because they were ordered, so long as they conform only where, in their judgement, they should perform the legally required act, regardless of the fact that they have a legal duty to perform it, and of course, so long as the law is not coercively enforced. Thomists can admit that the law can be corrupted and put to evil use by governments, or by some of their officials. All they need insist on is that such aberrations are exactly that, namely aberrations, not to be confused with the normal case.[5]

Some of my observations will bear on these views, but my aim is to focus first on a preliminary question: should we, as is common,[6] make the question 'is there a necessary connection between law and morality?', a litmus test for the basic orientation of different theories of law? It is common to call those who show negative in the test, including John Austin, Jeremy Bentham, Hans Kelsen, and HLA Hart, *legal positivists*, and to regard Thomas Aquinas, Michael Moore, Philip Soper, and Ronald Dworkin as *natural lawyers*, for no other reason than that they show positive when the litmus test is applied.

Arguably there is no harm in any classification. Any similarity and any difference can be the basis of a classification, and most classifications would do no greater harm than being boring because they would be insignificant. The harm is done by proceeding to make the division

---

[3] RP Wolff, *In Defense of Anarchism* (New York: Harper & Row, 1970), discussed in part I of *The Morality of Freedom* (Oxford: OUP, 1986).

[4] For a modern version see J Finnis, *Natural Law and Natural Rights* (Oxford: Clarendon Press, 1980) esp chs 1 and 10.

[5] See Finnis, op cit. A similar view is held by a number of other, non-Thomist contemporary legal philosophers. See, eg, Dworkin, *Law's Empire* (Cambridge, Mass: Belknap Press, 1986).

[6] But see J Gardner, 'Legal Positivism: 5½ Myths' (2001) 46 American Journal of Jurisprudence 199, 222ff, rightly rejecting this view.

between 'legal positivists' and 'natural lawyers', so defined, the basic division in legal philosophy. For there can be no doubt that there are necessary connections between law and morality. This makes it appear as if 'legal positivism' is mistaken, that is as if any 'legal positivist' theory is false, and every natural law theory, even if mistaken on some issues, recognizes the truth of a deep and contentious thesis. And of course it follows that all the theories which deny any necessary connection between law and morality include at least one false proposition. However, as it happens it does not show that they contain more than one false proposition, because the theories concerned do not build on their mistaken denial of a necessary connection, and all their main theses about the nature of law remain intact. Correspondingly, the truth shared by all natural law theories, so understood, is a relatively trivial thesis, which lends no credence to what is of interest in them.

This shows that the question of a necessary connection is a bad litmus test. Rather than offering a useful key to the typology of legal theories it leads to confusion. To be sure, clarifying the relations between law and morality is rightly seen as central to the explanation of the nature of law. But unless we ask the right questions about that relationship we will not reach illuminating answers.

Here are three examples of necessary connections between law and morality:

- (Following Hart,[7] but without trying to be faithful to the details of his argument): given human nature and the conditions of human life (especially mutual vulnerability and relative scarcity), necessarily no legal system can be stable unless it provides some protection for life and property to some of the people to whom it applies.
- Given that only living animals can have sex, necessarily rape cannot be committed by the law nor by legal institutions (though they and the law can sanction it, and legal institutions can be accomplices to it).
- Given value pluralism,[8] necessarily no state or legal system can manifest to their highest degree all the virtues or all the vices there are.

The first of these is a natural necessity. The other two can claim to be conceptual, a priori necessities. Either way they are necessary connections,

---

[7] *The Concept of Law* (2nd edn, Oxford: Clarendon Press, 1994), 193 ff.

[8] Defined as the existence of a plurality of values which cannot be instantiated in the life of any single human being, and relying on the fact that the realization of various incompatible values and virtues requires supportive societal conditions (see my *The Morality of Freedom*, ch 14).

for natural necessities—those which exist because of basic features of the world, for example because it is governed by the natural laws which do in fact govern it—are sufficiently secure to merit the attention of the theory of law, assuming that they are not trivial in nature. The three necessities enumerated suggest ways of generating many more true statements about necessary connections between law and morality (the law cannot be in love, and therefore cannot have the virtues of true love, etc). Many of them are of little interest. But regardless of what interest they hold, they show that the existence of necessary connections between law and morality cannot really be doubted, at least that it should not be doubted, and that it has little bearing on important issues which may divide writers like those I mentioned above.

II. On the Necessary Obligation to Obey

Some writers claim, of course, that there are other types of necessary connections between law and morality, which have greater significance for an understanding of their relations. Here are a few examples of such *claimed* or *alleged* necessary connections which appear to be of a kind, to belong together:

(1) Necessarily, everyone has a duty to obey the law of his country.
(2) Necessarily, everyone has a reason to obey the law of his country.
(3) Necessarily, if the law is just all its subjects have a duty to obey it (or, alternatively, a reason to obey it).
(4) Necessarily, if the government of a country is democratic all its subjects have a duty to obey its law (or, alternatively, a reason to obey its law).
(5) Necessarily, one has an obligation to support just legal systems.

Clearly, these claimed necessary connections show, if true, something important about the relations of law and morality. This is, perhaps, most clearly seen in (1).[9] Some people regard it as the real divide between so-called natural lawyers and so-called legal positivists. However, there are natural lawyers who do not uphold it, and in any case (as will be briefly observed below) it does not follow from the basic assumptions of Thomist natural law. (1) claims that the law is a source of moral duties

---

[9] The difference between (1) and (2) relates to the nature and stringency of the moral requirement the law creates. I will make nothing of this difference and my references to (1) should be read as references to either (1) or (2).

in the way in which one often thinks of promises as a source of moral duties:[10] just as one has a moral duty to do what one promises, and therefore every promise creates a moral duty, so one has a moral duty to do what the law demands of one, and every law imposing another legal duty imposes or creates a moral duty.

This does not mean that (1) claims that any legal duty adds to the number of things one has a moral duty to do. Just as one may promise to act as one morally ought to act in any case, so the law may impose a legal, and therefore a moral, duty to do what one ought to do, or has a moral duty to do, anyway. In saying that every new law creating a legal duty creates a new moral duty we mean only that the obligation to act in the required way acquires a new ground, one which will remain in force even if the others do not exist, or if they cease to exist.[11]

On this view the law is part of morality just as promising is part of morality. It is natural for those who doubt the soundness of such a view to think that the main objection to it is that it underestimates the ability of the law to do evil, and to be immoral. After all if law is part of morality, how can it be immoral or do evil? I suspect, however, that on its own this objection lacks force. There are two ways consistent with a general obligation to obey all law, in which the law can fall short of moral ideals, and they allow for the possibility of considerable evil perpetrated by law.

First, we must allow that any account of the nature of law will apply to central cases, and will allow for degenerate cases of law. To give a related example, there are states like the Vatican, which do not display some of the central characteristics of states, and yet it would be pointless to debate whether they are states or not, or to take them as

---

[10] Moral duties (as well as reasons, values, etc) do not in general have sources. They can be explained, and it is possible to establish what duties people have. But their explanations, and justifications, or grounds, are not 'sources'. Promissory and legal duties are among the few types of obligation which have sources, ie the acts of making promises and laws.

[11] Even that is not strictly necessary. It is possible for the moral standing of a law to be conditional on its content being morally required anyway. Compare this case with, for example, a child being told by his parents to obey his minder if at lunch-time he tells him to have his lunch. We can imagine that the child should have his lunch anyway (would have had ample reason to have it had he been left alone), and that implicitly the parents intimate that the minder need not be obeyed if he instruct the child to do something the child has no reason to do anyway. Still the minder's instructions to the child are binding on him and we understand that (and would understand similar laws) as meaning that they reinforce the reason or obligation the child has anyway. Once instructed, not doing what one ought is a wrong in an additional way, for an additional reason.

counter-examples disproving the correctness of otherwise sound characterizations of states. We simply acknowledge them as marginal cases of being a state. Similarly, with the law, there can be legal systems which are so regarded conventionally, yet which are exceptional or degenerate cases of legal systems. It would be a mistake to deny that they are legal systems, but also a mistake to take them as disproving otherwise sound characterizations of the law.[12]

I do not mean to say that no single example can be a decisive counter-example. Any characterization which will fail to apply to the law of France, or of the United States, for example, will be defective just in virtue of this fact (though still possibly better than all known alternatives). But some legal systems can reasonably be taken to be marginal or degenerate cases of law.[13]

John Finnis and Dworkin,[14] both espousers of a general obligation to obey all law, emphasized the possibility of marginal cases of law to which the duty does not apply. There is, however, yet another way in which the law of a country may do evil even if there is a general duty to obey all its laws. That way is open to those who support the duty to obey by content-independent moral reasons. These are reasons which depend not on the claim that each and every one of the laws of all legal systems is morally meritorious in a way which imposes a duty of obedience on all its subjects, rather they depend on general virtues and moral properties of legal systems as a whole, which justify a duty to obey each of their laws, just because they are laws of that system. If that is the foundation of the general obligation to obey then it is compatible with considerable moral failings. It is compatible with many of the laws of the system and many of its institutions being morally defective, or worse.

This is a point of general importance, which I will return to later in the chapter. The law as a whole can have moral properties because its, or the majority of its, components, especially its laws or rules, have them. These are its aggregate moral properties. But it also has what I will call systemic properties, properties which belong to the law or legal system

---

[12] For a brief explanation of the theoretical character of accounts of concepts like that of the law see *The Morality of Freedom* ch 3 (regarding the concept of authority), and chapter 3 of this volume, 'Two Views on the Nature of the Theory of Law: A Partial Comparison'.

[13] I am assuming what some people find problematic, that vague concepts can have essential properties. This is possible so long as those properties admit of vagueness, or if they apply or can apply to a greater or lesser degree, and their vagueness or degree of application is among the factors which make the concept to which they belong vague.

[14] In *Natural Law and Natural Rights* ch 1, and in *Law's Empire*, respectively.

as a whole but not in virtue of being aggregates of the properties of its component parts.[15] The necessary moral properties of the law as a whole may be systemic, allowing for a good deal of shortcoming in the moral merit of its individual norms.

The fact that the general duty to obey may depend on systemic features of the law does not, of course, show that it is compatible with a proper conception of how evil the law can be, and of how much injustice and oppression, etc it may cause. It is unlikely that the systemic moral qualities of the law are entirely independent of, entirely unaffected by, the moral qualities of the content of the law, that is of the moral content of the laws which constitute it. How are we then to assess the claim that there is a general obligation to obey?

The issue turns, naturally enough, on what are the main essential systemic features of the law, and especially what are its essential systemic moral properties. The commonly accepted answer is that they have to do with the institutionalized character of the law, and its reliance on the use of force. I will follow this line of thought, and will consider the law's use of force to be but an aspect of the kind of institution it is, ie as an aspect of its institutional character.[16] The institutions necessarily involved with the law are institutions of adjudication and law enforcement. In most societies they also include law-making institutions, that is those with power to make perfectly general laws, and not only, as with institutions whose power is limited to adjudicative and law-enforcing functions, particular laws or legally binding directives.

The case for the moral character of the law, understood as a quest for its systemic moral properties, rather than for the moral properties

---

[15] One needs a more precise way of marking the distinction between systemic and aggregate properties. One could define emergent properties as simply properties of the whole which are not properties of any of its parts. In this sense being wise is a property of a human being, which is not a property of any part of a human being (except metaphorically), though it may be a function of those properties. The distinction I am after is different. It is meant to exclude properties of the whole which are 'simple' mathematical functions of the properties of the parts, properties which it is tempting to say are mere modes of representing properties of the parts. I have in mind properties of a whole which, for example, it possesses simply because there is a property which either all, or a threshold number or proportion of its parts have, or because it is the average or the mean of the properties of the parts. These may differ from proper systemic properties only in degree, only in the indirectness or complexity of their dependence on properties of the parts. But the difference matters.

[16] Those who put the emphasis more on the use of force by the law sometimes refer to its monopolization of the use of force. But that, read simply, is false. Law can be and usually is consistent with a good deal of 'private' use of force, ie use of force by people and organizations other than law-enforcing ones.

of each and all its binding standards, is the moral case for having legal authorities, of the law-making and law-applying varieties.

There is such a case. It is a Thomist case. Versions of it have been expressed in recent time by various writers.[17] Broadly speaking, it goes thus:

First, human life goes better when subjected to governance by (conscientious) authority. There is, in other words, a job to be done, a task to be discharged, a need for authority to regulate interactions in human societies.

Second, whoever is in a position to discharge that job has the moral authority to do so. That is, whoever has de facto political power and legal control has legitimate power. For, on the one hand, only those with de facto political power and legal control can perform the job. Only they can meet the moral need for human societies to be governed by authority. And, on the other hand, possession of de facto power is sufficient to make them able to perform that job.

The argument has the right shape: it does not rely on the alleged moral quality of each and every law. Rather, it acknowledges that bad, including morally bad, laws can be laws. The argument relies on the systemic moral qualities of the law, from which an obligation to obey laws, including bad ones, can be derived. But its conclusion can easily be exaggerated. It cannot be used to establish that those who have de facto power and legal control have legitimate authority, a right to the power and legal control that they possess, which is what has to be established to vindicate a general obligation to obey the law in any country, as is asserted by (1).

Any obligation to obey the law that it can establish must be doubly qualified. First, since it derives the authority of the state or the government from the fact that it can fulfil a job which needs doing, that authority must be limited to a government which *discharges the job successfully*. The authority of the government cannot derive from its ability to discharge the needed job; rather, it must depend on success (or the likelihood of success) in doing so. Second, the legitimacy of the government which derives from its success (actual or likely) in performing a job which needs doing must be confined to its actions aimed at

---

[17] Anscombe, 'On the Sources of the Authority of the State', *Collected Papers, Vol. III, Ethics, Religion and Politics* (Oxford: Blackwells, 1981). It is also adopted by Tony Honoré in *Making Law Bind* (Oxford: Clarendon Press, 1987). A more specific and detailed argument of the same family is advanced by Finnis in *Natural Law and Natural Rights*, chapters 5 and 10. My rendering of the argument above differs in some respects from that of those writers, but shares their basic approach.

discharging this job. The argument cannot endow governments with a general authority, an authority to do whatever they see fit, as it must if it is to vindicate a general obligation to obey as in (1).

Let us say for the sake of argument that governments have power to keep the peace, enforce a fair system of property and contractual rights, and make sure that no one suffers (non-voluntarily) from serious deprivation. Arguably, this does not cover the regulation of the consumption of tobacco or its advertising (those who do not eat in smoke-filled restaurants will avoid the effects of tobacco, etc). It would follow that governments which do regulate the consumption and advertising of tobacco exceed their authority, and there is no obligation to obey the laws they make without authority.

Once we subject the criteria of legitimacy to a success condition (to accommodate the first qualification), and a relevance to the needed job condition (to accommodate the second) only those who make a reasonable success of the morally sanctioned task of government, or stand a reasonable chance of succeeding in it, enjoy legitimate authority. Propositions (3) and (4) above contain conditions which may meet the success condition. A just state and a democratic state is a state which succeeds in at least some of its tasks. The justice condition may meet at least some aspects of the concern expressed in the relevance condition. Arguably a state cannot be just if it exceeds its proper jurisdiction, if it strays into areas not its own.

These matters have been much written about, and cannot be resolved here. I will mention briefly, however, that there are two familiar rejoinders to the line of reasoning pursued thus far. One claims that it has gone too far, that there is no need for the success and relevance conditions, while the other claims that the justice or democracy conditions are not sufficient to establish success and relevance and therefore not sufficient to establish even a qualified obligation to obey the law. The first rejoinder is based on the thought that any conditions on the authority of states or governments will undermine, if generally believed and acted on, their ability to discharge the task which justifies their existence. This is essentially an empirical argument, and I see no reason to give it general credence. Possibly this danger exists in some special situations, but there is no reason to think that it exists always. I say that partly because of some anecdotal knowledge that governments can function reasonably well even when their population is critical and alert, and will withdraw recognition from measures thought to be unjust or anti-democratic, and partly because there is, as will be mentioned below, a separate duty to uphold and support just institutions, which, if generally believed, will obviate the danger this first rejoinder relies on.

The second rejoinder, that the conditions of the government being just or democratic do not suffice to establish an obligation to obey, is more plausible. The problem is that being just, or being democratic, when they are systemic properties of the law, are consistent with individual laws being unjust, or pointless, or oppressive. The question is: is there an obligation to obey such a law, for if there is not there is no obligation to obey the law generally. One answer, and obviously there are many others which I will just have to ignore here, is that it is necessary to support a just institution, a just government, and legal system. This is again an empirical question, and I believe that there is plenty of evidence that the better argument is different. Just governments and legal systems, generally speaking, work better with less than perfect compliance. This statement should not be misread. I do not mean that a few murders are better than none. I mean that there are many laws regarding which occasional breach by their subjects, and the occasional turning of a blind eye by the authorities make them achieve their goals with fewer injustices, and less friction with resisting populations. Besides, though here one's sense of justice may cloud one's impressionistic empirical judgement, a population ready to defy pointless, unjust, and oppressive laws does more to preserve the just character of governments and their laws than a docile population willing to eat whatever it is dished out.

A proper doctrine of authority should be based on the task to be done argument, qualified by the success and relevance conditions. Adequately formulating these conditions is no easy matter.[18] What appears clear is that they set a test which is far from trivial and that it is not that difficult to find governments which fail it completely (ie have no legitimate authority at all) or partially (ie have some legitimate authority, but less than they claim to have). This means that there is no chance that the 'general obligation to obey', or 'a general obligation to obey just or democratic legal systems' theses are correct.

III. Systemic Moral Properties of the Law

There is a general mistake undermining theses (1) to (4), a mistake which it is not too difficult to spot: they attempt to derive a moral

---

[18] I made my suggestion in *The Morality of Freedom* ch 3.

property which applies equally to each and every law from systemic moral properties of the law as a whole, or of some kinds of legal systems. Admittedly, there is no general reason to think that premises about the systemic moral properties of the law, perhaps afforded by appropriate moral or other premises, will not yield conclusions pointing to moral properties of every single legal norm. Some trivial conclusions come readily to mind (eg the law of every just legal system has the moral property of belonging to a just legal system). But without additional premises, which I cannot see, no significant conclusions like (1) to (4) seem possible.

Perhaps a more promising route is to explore the systemic moral properties of the law itself in order to establish what attitude to the law as an institution they require. An analogy with promises may guide us. The similarities between promising and the law are considerable. Both are ways of creating obligations by acts intended to do so—a fact often regarded as so mysterious that it has led to most ingenious writings attempting to explain away the mystery.[19] The Thomist type of explanation of authority helps here too. There is a good which binding promises can serve or achieve, and that is why they can be binding. That is, the practice of promising is a morally valuable practice because it is one which can achieve valuable goals.

It does not follow that all promises bind.[20] Promises given by incompetent agents (say young children, or incapacitated people) are not binding, nor are promises given under duress, or those in which the promisee undertakes to perform morally impermissible acts, and there are many others. Just as in the case of the law, we cannot infer from the systemic property of the promising practice (ie that it is a valuable moral practice) specific obligations to perform all promises. But needless to say, the very proposition that the practice of promising is a morally valuable practice asserts a necessary connection between promising and morality.

Is not the same true of the law? There are values that it can serve, there is therefore value in the law as a general institution. It is a morally valuable institution, just as promising is a morally valuable practice. That

---

[19] Often, as in the recent case of Scanlon's *What We Owe to Each Other* (Cambridge, Mass: Harvard University Press, 1998), by explaining away the fact that promising is a way of creating obligations by intending to do so. But see the effective criticism of his views by Liam Murphy, and by David Owens 'A Simple Theory of Promising' (2006) 115 *Philosophical Review*.

[20] In other words, the argument has to be hedged with qualifications when applied to promises, just as when applied to the law.

law is a morally valuable institution is part of its nature. There is a moral property, being morally valuable, which all law has by its very nature. So here we have another necessary connection between law and morality, and one which is of the kind writers in the Thomist tradition assert, and those in the so-called legal-positivist tradition deny. So much for the argument which uses an analogy with promising to establish a necessary connection between law and morality.

What are we to make of it? We should distinguish three claims (among others):

(i) Law, by its nature, is an institution which can be used to realize valuable ends.
(ii) Law, by its nature, is an institution with a moral task to perform.
(iii) Law, by its nature, is a morally valuable institution.

The first, claiming no more than that the law can be used for moral ends, seems unexceptional. Just about anything can be used for moral ends. Even Nazi gas chambers can be so used. They can be used, I imagine, even though perhaps not very efficiently, to kill some dangerous vermin.

The second claim, that law by its nature has a moral task, seems both true and more interesting. It does more than indicate a possibility of a morally laudable use for the law. It postulates that some specific (though possibly abstractly conceived) moral task is central to the law, essential to its being the type of institution it is. It is important to note what this claim does not imply.

First, it does not imply that it is morally or otherwise preferable to be governed by law than not to be subject to law, not even that it is preferable to be governed by a just legal system. Many anarchists, for example, who believe that it is much better not to be subject to law could agree to the claim that by its nature law has a moral task. Some anarchists, those who take any legal system to be radically immoral, will demur. But moderate anarchists who hold that it is better to be governed by other means than through the law may agree that if one is subject to law, that is governed by a legal system, that law has a moral task.

Second, it does not imply anything about the moral character of any actually existing legal system. It allows that legal systems can be radically evil. Nor does it imply anything regarding the likelihood that any legal system will be just or unjust, good or evil. It merely claims that there is a specific moral test by which (among other tests) any legal system should be judged.

Third, the claim does not imply that nothing but the law can have that task. It does not say that it is unique to the law. I doubt that there are important tasks that are unique to the law, in the sense that they cannot at all be achieved any other way.

Fourth, the claim does not imply that the law may not legitimately aim to achieve other aims than the specific moral task inherent in its nature.

The claim that law has, by its nature, a specific moral task, is nevertheless an important claim, as it sets the way in which we should think about the law. It sets a critical perspective for judging it. Just as we do not fully understand what chairs are without knowing that they are meant to sit on, and judged (*inter alia*) by how well they serve that function so, the claim is, we do not fully understand what law is unless we understand that it has a certain task, and is to be judged (*inter alia*) by how well it performs it.

While endorsing the thought that there are essential tasks the law is burdened with, I have been so far shy of identifying any. This chapter is meant primarily to be about the basic way of conceiving the connection between law and morality. In this regard identifying the possibility or likelihood that one such connection is that the law has moral tasks is all that is required. The specific identification of the tasks can be left to a more extended and substantial discussion in political philosophy. For what it is worth, however, let me state, rather briefly and dogmatically, what task I can see for the law. It arises out of the law's character as a structure of authority, that is a structured, coordinated system of authorities. Authorities are legitimate only if they facilitate conformity with reason. *The law's task, put abstractly, is to secure a situation whereby moral goals which, given the current social situation in the country whose law it is, would be unlikely to be achieved without it, and whose achievement by the law is not counter-productive, are realized.*

If the law has an essential task, does it follow that it is by its nature *an essentially valuable institution* (as per (3) above)? The analogy with promises would suggest so. But the analogy is flawed.

There are, among others, two important differences between promises and the law, differences which bear on the way we conceive of their relations to morality. First, promises are made voluntarily (if binding) by a promisor, and accepted, or not rejected by the promisee. They bind the promisor and no one else. The law could not be more different. Typically it is binding on people who did not make it, and had little influence on its content (even in a democracy, if only because the law binds successive generations, as well as those who voted against it). It is as if rather than binding himself the promisor were to impose obligations on the promisee who would be bound by them regardless of his agreement. That is why the law typically does, whereas promises do not, rely on coercion to improve the chances of compliance. Second, the law is not a promise, or a set of discrete promises, but a whole normative system, a system of interrelating norms with a network of institutions in charge of their modification and application.

The first point makes it reasonable to think that the law is more prone to abuse, to injustice and immorality than promises. But it is the second difference between them which is crucial. When we say that promising is a morally valuable institution (or practice) we are judging the abstract institution, not the way it is put into practice in one country or another. Perhaps in some countries most promises are of doubtful character. We imply nothing about that, nothing about the actual use made of promising, in saying that promising is morally valuable. Not so when we say that the law is a valuable moral institution. 'The law is...' is, in most contexts, short for the law of the country of which we speak. 'The law requires me to pay income tax' is not a statement about the abstract institution, but about UK law. When we do not refer to the law of a specific country we normally refer to the law of all countries, or of all countries today, etc.

Therefore, 'the law is a moral institution' means something quite different from 'promising is a moral institution'. The latter refers to an abstract moral institution, the former to the way it is actually implemented in history. But that is not a claim which can be warranted. While we can affirm that the law, as an abstract institution, as a kind of complex social practice, can be put to moral use, and that, where it exists, it has moral tasks to discharge, so that it is to be judged, among other ways, by its success in discharging them, we cannot say that in its historical manifestations through the ages it has always, or generally, been a morally valuable institution, and we can certainly not say that it has necessarily been so. To say that is to claim that by its very nature the law cannot be realized except in a morally valuable way. And that is not so.

IV. Conclusion

My ruminations so far did not yield very definite results. On the one hand, I argued that the denial of necessary connections between law and morality cannot be sustained. On the other hand, I contended that many of the claims of specific necessary connections between law and morality made by legal theorists are mistaken. My suggestion was that while there are necessary connections between morality and how the law is, the more significant necessary connections relate to the evaluative perspective which informs our thinking of how the law ought to be, rather than how it is.

It may be thought that the thesis that by its nature the law ought to be moral is empty or trivial, for everyone and everything ought to be moral. But that is not so. To be sure, nothing should be immoral. But it is not the case that the University of Oxford, or the city of Oxford, ought to be moral in the way that the law is. The intrinsic virtue of a university, ie what makes a university into a good university, is excellence in learning, research, and teaching. The intrinsic excellence of a city may be comfort, and the provision of certain services. What makes the law different, what makes its intrinsic excellence a moral excellence, is that it is a structure of authority, that it is in the business of telling people what they must do. Necessarily, the law claims to have legitimate moral authority over its subjects. Hence its intrinsic virtue is to have such authority. To say that is to say that its virtue is to be moral but in a special way, in meeting the conditions of legitimacy. Like cities and universities it too can excel in other ways, including in other moral ways. The possession of moral legitimacy is only its intrinsic excellence, the one it must have, not the only one it may, or ideally should have.

Let me instance one other important virtue the law may possess, in order to help bring out the difference between it and other possible excellences of the law, and the possession of legitimate authority. People, Aristotle reminded us, are social animals. People can prosper and enjoy a rich and fulfilled life only within human society, and that requires the existence of social groups, communities, of a variety of kinds. Perhaps no specific kind of grouping is necessary. Perhaps humans need not live in societies organized as they are today, with the familiar nation-states, and small heterosexual families. But a variety of types of social groupings, some larger and some more intimate, are needed to provide the background for fulfilled human lives. Let us accept such vague statements as being along the right lines. It can be claimed that the law is a constitutive element of some valuable forms of society, in today's world of a national society, which is valuable for human prosperity. It can be further claimed that identification with the societies one belongs to is needed to make one prosper by being part of them. Does it follow that, therefore, people should identify with the law, holding it in respect and esteem?

Not quite, for we are moving from necessary conditions for forms or aspects of personal prosperity to a conclusion taking them to be sufficient to require identification and respect. Still, it does follow from the very vague suggestion I articulated that the law, and society generally, could be worthy objects of identification and respect. If they are then identifying with them would be worthwhile. It is an additional virtue in a good legal system that it is a worthy object of identification and respect.

These are, as I said, very vague suggestions, but there is something to them. Generally, talk of 'the law', as in 'the law is a constitutive element of some valuable social groupings', refers to one or some or all of actual legal systems. And they may be immoral and unjust, lacking in legitimacy, and they may be a constitutive element of an inherently immoral grouping, rather than of a valuable one. We are here in the hands of human history, and no virtue is guaranteed. Moreover, it is not necessary for valuable social forms that they be constituted by law. There are national groups which do not form nation-states, and enjoy no special legal standing, and are none the worse for it. And so on. All we can say is that the law can be a valuable constituent component of valuable social groups, and if it is it has moral merit in being a worthy object of identification and respect. But we cannot say that it must be such a constituent component, or that it fails if it does not. On the other hand, all law must enjoy legitimate authority, or it fails in meeting its inherent claim to authority.

7

Incorporation by Law[1]

The truism that launched many theories about the nature of law—that law is a social institution—leaves, not surprisingly, many questions unanswered. One of the most important among them is the question of whether social institutions or more generally social practices can be understood in entirely non-evaluative terms.[2] Not penetrating to the same degree the heart of our understanding of law and of normative phenomena generally is another question left open by the truism, a question much discussed in recent years, namely whether moral principles can become part of the law of a country by 'incorporation'.[3] Though different, it may be thought that the two are interconnected in certain ways.

[1] This chapter includes material presented as the first of three Storrs Lectures at Yale in 2003.

[2] We lack a general term to refer collectively to all the concepts characteristic of practical thought. These include concepts belonging to virtue and character-related concepts (courage, etc), responsibility-related concepts (excuses, etc), value concepts (admirable, etc), normative concepts (ought, etc), and reason concepts (rational, etc). In previous times 'descriptive' and 'factual' were commonly used to designate those concepts that are not specifically practical. This, however, miscasts descriptions. ('This is John' is not a description of anything yet is supposed to be a descriptive sentence.) Designating non-evaluative propositions 'factual' implies that there are no evaluative facts, which is false. I will use 'evaluative' and 'normative' interchangeably to refer to all of them, as well as using them more narrowly to refer to items of the subcategories indicated above.

[3] That the idea is consistent with Hart's account of the law was intimated by him in his review of 'Lon Fuller, The Morality of Law in Hart' (1965) 78 Harvard Law Review 1281, repr in HLA Hart, *Essays in Jurisprudence and Philosophy* (Oxford: Clarendon Press, 1983) 361, and reiterated in the postscript to *The Concept of Law* (Oxford: Clarendon Press, 2nd edn, 1994) 250, though neither time did Hart stop to explore the meaning and implication of the idea; see D Lyons, 'Principles, Positivism and Legal Theory' (1977) 87 Yale Law Journal 415, at 423–424, and P Soper, 'Legal Theory and the Obligation of a Judge: The Hart/Dworkin Dispute' (1977) 75 Michigan Law Review 473. The point was embraced by J Coleman, 'Negative and Positive Positivism' (1982) 11 J of Legal Studies 139, and developed and defended at length by him in J Coleman, *The Practice of Principle* (Oxford: OUP, 2001). See, for a general discussion of the view, KE Himma, 'Inclusive Legal Positivism', in J Coleman and S Shapiro (eds), *The Oxford Handbook of Jurisprudence and Philosophy of Law* (Oxford: OUP, 2002).

My purpose here is to examine the question of how the law can be incorporated within morality and how the existence of the law can impinge on our moral rights and duties, a question (or questions) which is a central aspect of the broad question of the relation between law and morality. My conclusions cast doubts on the incorporation thesis, that is the view that moral principles can become part of the law of the land by incorporation.

I. Even Judges are Humans

This way of putting the question is not meant to be neutral. Legal theorists tend to start at the other end. They do not ask how law impinges upon morality, but how morality impinges on the law. It may be natural for legal theorists, being as they are focused on the law, to start with the law and ask what room it makes for morality. I will suggest that this way of conceiving the question of the relations between law and morality has contributed to some important mistakes. A better way of motivating reflection on the relations is to start with morality. That is why I have entitled this section 'Even Judges Are Humans'. In being human, they are subject to morality. That is the only fact the title is meant to convey.

A. The scope of morality

Why are judges, and humans generally, subject to morality? This is due to the nature of morality. It has no doctrine of jurisdiction setting out its conditions of application. It applies universally to all agents capable of understanding it.[4] Suppose that by the rules of the university, no one should use offensive language about any member of the university. It makes sense to say: that rule applies only to students of the university and not, say, to their parents, for the university has no jurisdiction over the parents of its students. I do not mean merely that it has no jurisdiction to discipline them if they break the rule. I mean that it has no jurisdiction, no power to make rules applying to them. It has no jurisdiction to bind them.

By way of contrast, let us suppose, for example, that morally, if I learn about a person's intentions in confidence I should not tell people about

---

[4] And for agents, understanding it implies the capacity to be guided by it.

them. If so, then it makes no sense to say: Morally speaking, I should not tell people about his intention, but luckily morality does not apply to me. It has no jurisdiction over me. If I know that it is morally wrong of me to tell people, and so on, or even if I do not know it but can know it, then it does apply to me.

Some may think that morality has a doctrine of jurisdiction and that I have just stated what I take it to be—morality applies to all agents who are capable of understanding it. But this is a misunderstanding. Reasons are considerations by which agents' behaviour is to be guided. They apply only to agents who can, in principle,[5] be aware of their existence, for otherwise those agents cannot be guided by them. Hence the fact that moral reasons apply to people and not to lions is not a result of any doctrine of jurisdiction, nor is it a reflection of any aspect of the content of morality. It is simply a consequence of the fact that moral reasons are reasons.[6]

To repeat, that is why judges are subject to morality. Morality, unlike the law or the norms governing the university or any other social institution, is not a system of rules. Talking of morality is just a way of talking of some of the reasons that people have. They apply to whomever they address. Not all moral reasons apply to everyone. Some apply to pregnant women only, some to parents, some to teachers. Their scope of application is determined by their content. If they are reasons to respect one's children, then they apply only to people who have children. When I say that judges being human are willy-nilly subject to morality, I do not mean that all of them ought to respect their children. Only those who have children ought to do so. That goes without saying. It does not deny that they are all subject to morality.

B. On points of view

I assume that no one denies that morality applies to judges. The question is how to understand this statement. Some may say: of course morality applies itself to judges; from the moral point of view, judges are

---

[5] A weasel word disguising the difficulty of specifying the strength of the 'can in principle' in that condition.

[6] Other moral properties, such as generosity and conscientiousness, apply to agents in virtue of their propensity to react to moral reasons or the way they did or failed to do so adequately. Some properties make objects or events morally fortunate or unfortunate, and they may apply to things that are not moral agents, but they too ultimately derive their meaning from their relations to circumstances in which rational agents confront choices.

morally bound just like anyone else. But the moral point of view is just that—one point of view among many. The question is whether morality applies to judges or to others from, let us say, a prudential point of view; that is, whether it is in their self-interest to be guided by morality. Or one may ask: Is it the law that morality applies to judges? Are they legally bound to follow morality?

To examine the standing of such questions we need to spend a little time looking at the notion of a normative point of view or a normative perspective.[7] Several uses of 'a point of view' are helpful and unproblematic. They can be divided into two types. The first consists of discourse where the effect of the qualification 'from this and that point of view things are thus and so' is to bracket the question of truth: from a Christian point of view, or from a Kantian point of view, or from the point of view of cognitive science things are thus and so—implying that if Christianity, or Kant's theory, or cognitive science are true, then this is how things are, but without committing to their truth.[8] The second type of use isolates different aspects of a problem, often as a way of helping with thinking about it and advancing towards its solution. For example, we may say 'from the economic point of view it would be good for the university to close the philosophy department, as its alumni rarely earn much money and the loss of their donations to the university would not hurt it much; from an academic point of view, however, this would not be justified'. We can then proceed to a decision of what would be right, all things considered.

Discourse of any possible point of view can serve this second function, that is indicate that the considerations referred to need not be the only ones, nor need they be the ones that carry the day.[9] But there are some points of view reference to which cannot be used to serve the first function, that of suspending the question of truth. This is obvious if you think of artificially defined or 'made up' points of view such as 'from the point of view of valid reasons, you have reason to do this

---

[7] The views that follow apply to non-normative points of view as well, but I will not be concerned to establish that.

[8] Though of course one is committed to it being truly so from that point of view. Note that the truth conditions of propositions from a point of view (so understood) are not the same as those of the corresponding material implication; for example, 'if Christian doctrine is true then...'. For one thing, they assert not merely that the from-a-point-of-view proposition is true but that (in this example) it is Christianity that is the ground of its truth. Besides, the falsity of Christianity, far from guaranteeing the truth of the proposition, has no bearing on the question of its truth.

[9] Barring some artificial creations such as 'from the decisive point of view'.

and that'. Valid reasons are real reasons, and once you have committed yourself that you are talking about valid reasons, you can no longer say 'but I do not know if there is any reason to do so'. Contrast this with 'from a Catholic point of view, I ought to give it to him'. Saying this need not imply belief that there is any reason for me to give it to him. The Catholic point of view may be false, that is the specific doctrines and beliefs of the Catholic Church may be false or, if true, only accidentally true, that is not true for the reasons Catholic doctrine gives for them. So it is perfectly intelligible to say 'from a Catholic point of view you ought to give it to him, but I really do not know whether you have any reason to do so'.

There are many terms that can indicate a point of view when used in the second way but cannot indicate a point of view when we talk of the suspension of the question of truth. For example, if I say 'from the point of view of my own interests, there are reasons for the first option', my statement is qualified by recognition of the possibility of other conflicting interests, but I cannot continue my statement with 'but I do not know whether there is any reason at all for that option', for I have already said that there are: my interest furnishes reasons for it.

Morality is another perspective reference to which cannot be used to suspend truth. 'Morality' is used to refer only to true or valid considerations. In saying this, I merely clarify the sense in which I will use the term. While it is the sense in which it is used when considering the relations of law and morality, it is not the only sense in which people use the term. When Dolittle answers Pickering's reprimand 'Have you no morals, man?' with 'I can't afford them',[10] he suggests that morals, like breeding, are fineries that only the moneyed classes can afford. But that is not the way the term will be used here.

C. The legal and the moral points of view

Sometimes, when reasons for and against an action conflict, there is no rational determination to the conflict. Neither of the conflicting reasons defeats the other. Most commonly this is the case when the conflicting reasons are incommensurate. Not uncommonly incommensurate reasons arise out of diverse values. Sometimes, for example, there is no right answer to the question of whether it is now more important for

[10] GB Shaw, *Pygmalion*, in *The Complete Plays of Bernard Shaw* (London: Odhams, 1934) 729.

the government to increase its investments in education or in health services. These are familiar facts, born out by analysis.

Some people, including some philosophers, go further and assume that there is never a rational way of concluding what one may, all told, do when reasons of certain different kinds, say moral reasons and reasons of self-interest, point in different directions. If from a moral point of view one ought to take an action that self-interested reasons indicate one should avoid, then there is no conclusion regarding what one ought to do, all things told. Some people assume that that is so when legal and moral reasons are concerned.[11]

These claims involve two mistakes. They suppose that it is rational to perform an action, that is that it is rationally all right to perform an action, only if reason requires its performance (in the sense that entails that there are reasons for it that defeat all reasons against it). On this view, it is not rational to pick a tin of Heinz baked beans from a supermarket shelf unless it is the only tin of its kind. If there are more than one placed conveniently, then there is no more reason to choose one of them than to choose any of the others, and therefore it is not all right, rationally speaking, to choose any. This is obviously absurd. It is rationally all right to perform an action so long as the reasons for it are not defeated, for example so long as the reasons against it are not more stringent. Therefore, if an action is favoured by one reason and opposed by another and neither of them defeats the other, then it is right both to perform the action and to refrain from it, and that is so whether or not the two conflicting reasons belong to the same point of view or to different points of view.[12]

The second mistake is the assumption that legal and moral reasons constitute points of view in the same way. Whatever else the law is, it consists, at least in part, in man-made norms, that is it takes itself to impose duties on people and to do so in virtue of decisions taken by governmental institutions with the intention of imposing duties on people, including people other than those taking the decisions.

Some people tend to think that in democratic countries people are bound only by laws that they themselves made. But those who live in democratic countries know that they are bound by laws made a

---

[11] This may have been Hart's view in his later work; see HLA Hart, *Essays on Bentham* (Oxford: Clarendon Press, 1983).

[12] The only alternative I can see is to deny that reasons which belong to a point of view have any bearing on what one ought to do, all told. But if so, it is not clear in what sense they are reasons at all.

hundred years before they were born and that their children are bound by laws that they had no say in, and they themselves are bound by laws whether or not they participated in the process leading to their enactment, let alone being bound by them whether or not they supported or opposed them.

It is well understood that no one can impose a duty on another just by expressing his will that the other have that duty. If governments can do so, this can only be because and to the extent that there are valid principles that establish their right to do so. Those principles, the principles establishing the legitimacy of man-made laws and of the governments that make them, are themselves, whatever else they are, moral principles. They may also be principles deriving from people's self-interest. For example, Hobbesians think that all morality derives from self-interest and that all moral principles are also principles of indirect self-interest. They may also be legal principles. I do not wish to prejudge the question of what does and what does not belong to the law. All I am saying is that whether or not the principles that endow governments with legitimacy are legal principles, they are moral principles.

How do we know that? By their content. They are principles that allow, perhaps even require, some people to interfere in important ways in the lives of others. Valid principles that have such content are moral principles, or nothing is. I do not believe that morality is a unified systematic body of principles. But whatever else we grace with the title 'moral', principles that impose, or give people power to impose on others, duties affecting central areas of life are moral principles. That much about the nature of morality is clear.

The result is that we cannot conceive of the law as a normatively valid point of view contrasting with morality. Perhaps it is possible to think of reasons of self-interest as a distinct point of view contrasting with that of morality. But that, if possible, is possible only because self-interest is thought to be a ground of reasons independently of morality. It is not similarly possible to think of the law as a ground of reasons independently of morality. Given that much of it is man-made, at least man-made legal duties bind their subjects only if moral principles of legitimacy make them so binding.

We can of course suspend judgement on whether the law is binding on its subjects, on whether legal rules do provide anyone with the reasons they purport to establish. We can thus treat the law as a normative point of view in the way in which we might treat Muslim morality as a distinct normative point of view, that is if it is legitimate or valid, then we have the reasons that, according to it, we have. But in that sense the law does not conflict with any other normative considerations, since when so treated, it is not assumed that it includes or creates any normative considerations.

D. The law presupposing morality

Far be it for me to claim that all legal systems do enjoy moral legitimacy, which means that legal duties are really duties binding on people rather than being the demands governments impose on people. All I am saying is that when it is assumed that any legal system is legitimate and binding, that it does impose the duties it purports to impose—and I will generally proceed in this discussion on the assumption that the legal systems we are considering enjoy such legitimacy—in such cases we cannot separate law from morality as two independent normative points of view, for the legal one derives what validity it has from morality.

This, then, is finally the full answer to the question of why judges are humans too, why they are subject to morality: they would not be subject to the law were they not subject to morality.

Let this reply not be misinterpreted: it does not deny that we can discuss and describe the law from a detached point of view. We can talk of a legal system that is practised in a country and of its requirements and implications without making any assumption that they have normative standing.[13] Such discourse, free of the assumption of the normative standing of the law, is the equivalent of talking of what people demand of others without implying that these demands have any normative standing, that the others have reason to comply with them as they are intended to do. But—and this is my point—where the law is normatively valid, it is so in virtue of a moral principle, and therefore *if we take the law to be normatively valid we cannot construe its requirements as constituting a point of view independent of morality, a point of view that represents a separate normative concern that has nothing to do with morality, and then ask whether it recognizes morality as applying to its officials.* The boot is on the other foot; the question is whether morality, which applies to all humans simply because they are humans, has room for the law. How can morality accommodate the law within it?

---

[13] I take this view to have been Kelsen's position.

II. The Puzzles of So-called 'Incorporation'

A. The puzzle

But before we turn to examine this question (which can only be examined cursorily in this chapter), it is fitting to consider some questions that the truism that judges are human, and as such subject to morality, may raise. I argued that we cannot counter the claim that judges are subject to morality by saying that from a moral point of view they are, but not necessarily from a legal one. For the legal point of view cannot be contrasted with morality in that way. If they are bound by law, that is because they are morally bound by it. Morality comes first. Does it mean that it is the law that judges are subject to morality? In a way I want to say that that does not make sense. The law cannot empower morality. It is the other way round. It is empowered by morality. But it would be wrong to leave matters at that. Surely the law can instruct judges not to follow morality, and it can instruct them to follow it, and it can do either or both in more discriminating ways. That is, it can instruct judges to decide some issue by reference to morality and not to do so in other cases, or to decide some cases with special reference to some parts or aspects of morality, for example fairness between the parties, or the public interest in safety, and so on.

In other words, how does the view that judges are humans too square with legislation or precedents that at least appear to exclude morality or with legislation or precedents that appear to incorporate morality?

B. Exclusion before inclusion

As it turns out, inclusion is made possible by the ability of the law legitimately to exclude and modify the application of morality. So let us start with a few remarks regarding exclusion. Tempted to be provocative rather than accurate, one may say that the very existence of the law, even of morally legitimate law, means the exclusion of morality. Think about it: judges are bound by morality. So, absent any law, they would decide the case on the basis of moral considerations. Does it not follow that where there is law, it either makes no difference to their decisions or it forces them to deviate from what they would do on the basis of morality alone—that it in effect excludes morality? Is it not the case that whenever the law makes a difference to the outcome, it excludes morality? If it is the purpose of the law to make a difference to our life, does it not follow that its realization of its purpose depends on its ability to exclude morality?

Few people endorse the view that the law purports to make no difference to what we should do. But no one feels embarrassed by my paradoxical inference. First of all, it will be pointed out that the law is binding, by my own admission, only if it is morally legitimate. (I do not, of course, mean that only then is it legally binding. I mean that to say that it is legally binding implies that it claims to be morally binding, and that it is binding only if it is morally binding, and that it is taken to be binding as it claims to be only by those thinking it to be morally binding.) To repeat, the law is binding only if morally legitimate. It would follow that if it is both legitimate and excludes morality, there is no problem, for the exclusion is morally permissible.

It may be relevant here to mention that morality is not a seamless web that is either in or out. We simply refer to some of the myriad considerations that apply to us as moral considerations not because they have a common origin or purpose or some systemic unity but simply on account of their content, for example, that they are considerations requiring us to take notice of the interests of others, regardless of our own aims and interests. For value pluralists it is a commonplace that moral considerations conflict in a variety of ways, that right action requires compromises between various moral concerns, and that sometimes it requires edging some out in favour of others. When we think of the special responsibilities of judges, we are reminded that they are analogous in some respects to the special responsibilities of teachers, doctors, parents, friends, and others, in that each one of those roles requires prioritizing some moral concerns at the expense of others. The rights and duties of a doctor vis-à-vis his or her patients are different from the rights and duties we have vis-à-vis strangers, and they partly displace them. There are ways of acting that are permissible between strangers but not between doctor and patient.

I am not suggesting that the way the law affects the application of morality is closely analogous to the way roles, such as those of doctors or lawyers, affect it. I bring up the analogy simply to illustrate the more general point, namely that the application of abstract moral principles is affected and modified by special institutional arrangements such as roles. I have previously tried to describe the way the presence of legitimate authorities affects the application of moral principles[14] and will be brief and schematic here.

It is time to abandon the dramatic metaphor of the law excluding morality. What happens—and remember, we are talking here of morally legitimate law only—is that the law modifies the way morality applies to people. True, the result is that some moral considerations that apply absent the law do not apply or do not apply in the same way. But barring mistakes and other malfunctioning that can occur even within a just and legitimate system, the law modifies rather than excludes the way moral considerations apply and, in doing so, advances, all things considered, moral concerns rather than undermines them.

I will mention three ways in which this happens. First, the law concretizes general moral considerations, determining, for those to whom it applies, what bearing these considerations have on their lives. It takes away from individuals the right and the burden of deciding in various circumstances how morality bears on the situation—what exactly it requires. For example, what form of dealings in a company's shares is proper for its directors or employees; what information a doctor need disclose to a patient before the patient's consent can count as voluntary and binding on him or her.

Second, in giving moral considerations concrete and public form, the law also makes their relatively uniform and relatively assured enforcement possible, making reliance on them more secure and preventing unfairness in relations between conformers and non-conformers.

Third, it makes moral goals and morally desirable conditions easier to achieve and sometimes it makes possible what would be impossible without it.[15] The simplest and most written-about way in which the law achieves such goals revolves around its ability to secure coordinated conduct that solves, so to speak, what are known as coordination problems and prisoner's dilemma problems. But there is much more to this story than these relatively simple tales. Even fairly straightforward legal institutions, such as contract law, enable the creation of business relationships that would not exist outside institutional contexts. Needless to say, neither corporations nor intellectual property could exist, except in rudimentary ways, outside the law. These may be taken to illustrate

---

[14] See, eg, J Raz, *The Morality of Freedom* (Oxford: Clarendon Press, 1986) chs 2–4.
[15] That is, without some institutional background, not necessarily without this legal system.

the ability of the law to facilitate desirable economic relations and activities. But they and other legal institutions do much more. They made the whole urban civilization as we have known it over the last century or two possible—large numbers of people living with relative anonymity side by side, enjoying freedoms and rich civic amenities together and at the same time separately, each by her or himself, an urban civilization of the kind the world has not known before and is unlikely to enjoy for much longer.

C. When is incorporation not incorporation?

There is much more to be said about the ways the law modifies morality by making the realization of ideals possible. But let me turn to the question of so-called incorporation. Article 1(1) of the German Constitution provides: 'Human dignity is inviolable. To respect and protect it is the duty of all state authority.' The first amendment of the US Constitution says, among other things, that 'Congress shall make no law... abridging the freedom of speech', assuming, as it is generally assumed, that the freedom of speech referred to in it is not the freedom of speech existing in the common law before the passing of the Bill of Rights, but a moral right to free speech. This Amendment, too, is often taken as an example of the incorporation of morality by law.

Such instances of apparent incorporation raise the obvious question: What effect can they have, given that judges are subject to morality anyway? Before I consider it, let me answer another question which my terminology was bound to raise: Why do I call these cases 'instances of apparent incorporation'? Are they not clear instances of incorporation? The answer is that they are not. That is, they are not cases of incorporation if 'incorporation' means legislating or otherwise making a standard into a law of the relevant legal system by a rule that refers to it and gives it some legal effect.

UK and USA statutes give legal effect to company regulations, to university statutes, and to many other standards without making them part of the law of the United Kingdom or the United States. Conflict-of-law doctrines give effect to foreign law without making it part of the law of the land. Such references make the application of the standards referred to legally required, and rights and duties according to law include thereafter rights and duties determined by those standards. But they do not make those standards part of the law. They no more become part of the law of the land than do legally binding contracts, which are also binding according to law and change people's rights and duties without being themselves part of the law of the land.

There are many diverse forms of giving effect to standards by reference to them. An interesting, relatively recent example illustrating that diversity is the United Kingdom's Human Rights Act 2000, which states in its first article:

1. (1) In this Act 'the Convention rights' means the rights and fundamental freedoms set out in—
   (a) Articles 2 to 12 and 14 of the Convention,
   (b) Articles 1 to 3 of the First Protocol, and
   (c) Articles 1 and 2 of the Sixth Protocol,
   as read with Articles 16 to 18 of the Convention.
   (2) Those Articles are to have effect for the purposes of this Act subject to any designated derogation or reservation.

Does this article make 'the Convention rights' part of UK law? Its language is cautious and qualified. The rest of the act specifies what legal effects the rights have in UK law. For example, Article 3 states:

3. (1) So far as it is possible to do so, primary legislation and subordinate legislation must be read and given effect in a way which is compatible with the Convention rights.
   (2) This section—
   (a) applies to primary legislation and subordinate legislation whenever enacted;
   (b) does not affect the validity, continuing operation or enforcement of any incompatible primary legislation; and
   (c) does not affect the validity, continuing operation or enforcement of any incompatible subordinate legislation if (disregarding any possibility of revocation) primary legislation prevents removal of the incompatibility.

Had a statute said 'So far as it is possible to do so, primary legislation and subordinate legislation must be read and given effect in a way which is compatible with the edicts of the Pope or with the writings of Kant', we would not have been in the least tempted to think that through it either the edicts of the Pope or the writings of Kant have become parts of the law of the land, though beyond doubt they would have been given by that imagined act some legal effect.

I think that the cumulative effect of the various articles of the Human Rights Act entitles one to say that it incorporates 'Convention rights' into UK law, that is that UK law now includes those rights.[16] But I hope that these remarks show that decision on this issue is not straightforward and that not everything which looks like incorporation is incorporation. They also show that the difference between making a standard part of the law and merely giving it some legal effect without making it in itself part of the law of the land does not lie in the language of the 'incorporating' legislative measure—that it depends in part on our general conception of what a legal system is and how it relates to normative standards outside it, such as foreign law, moral considerations, or the constitution and laws of non-state organizations.

Perhaps I should add that the distinction between what is part of the law and what are standards binding according to law but not themselves part of the law is particularly vague. That is not surprising given that we do not often need to rely on it. Though sometimes there are procedural differences regarding, say, judicial notice and rules of evidence and of presentation that do or do not apply to standards that are part of the law or merely enforceable according to law, much of the time the practical implications of a standard are the same either way. That is not to say that we can dispense with the distinction or that it is of no importance. So long as we maintain that what is required according to law is made so by law, we cannot dispense with it, and so long as the law maintains its place at the heart of the political organization of society and remains a focus of attitudes of identification and alienation, the distinction has an importance way beyond any legal technicalities.

I believe that so-called 'incorporating' reference to morality belongs, with conflicts-of-law doctrines, to a non-incorporating form of giving standards legal effect without turning them into part of the law of the land. To see the reasons for this view, we need first to examine the legal effect of such references.

D. So-called incorporation as modulated exclusion

So back to the main question: What is the point of provisions giving effect to moral considerations if judges are subject to morality anyway? The point is that such references help the law modulate its intervention in and modification of the way moral considerations affect us. I will use

---

[16] Though they do not have the same effect or force in UK law as if they were enacted in a straightforward way nor the same effect that they have in other countries that have embraced the European Convention on Human Rights.

three examples to make the point. As a general rule the law, as we have seen, can modify the application of moral principles to its subjects. The law is, however, a complex institution, a complex *set* of institutions. Which legal organs have such powers? As a general rule, all lawmaking institutions have the power to modify moral considerations and can use this power whenever they make new law. In fact the making of law implies the use of such powers.[17] So-called 'incorporation' of morality modulates the application of this general rule.

My first example has to do with the truism that the law-making functions are unequally distributed among various bodies. Some are federal and some are state, some legislative and some judicial, some are superior to others. All such divisions imply limits on the law-making powers of some institutions. One way in which they are set is by establishing a conflict rule prioritizing the rules made by one body over those of others when the two conflict. Hence Congress cannot make law which is at odds with the Constitution. When the Constitution 'incorporates' a moral consideration, such as freedom of speech, it sets limits to the power of Congress and other law-makers to modify this aspect of morality. References to moral considerations in constitutions are typically not cases of the incorporation of morality but blocks to its exclusion or modification by ordinary legislation.

My second example concerns the common practice of coupling such constitutional provisions with judicial review. Judicial review not only makes the block to the exclusion or modification of constitutionally protected moral considerations by legislation enforceable; in addition in conferring on the courts powers to enforce that block, it gives them, when adjudicating on the compatibility of legislation with the constitutionally protected moral considerations, the power to modify the application of those moral considerations themselves. So a second use of so-called incorporation of morality into law is to allocate powers among law-making institutions.

Legislative reference to moral considerations has various other legal functions. My third and last example is again both typical and simple. It is the legal equivalent of the multi-stage decision procedure we are all familiar with in our lives. When I was last looking to move house,

---

[17] Qualifications are in place here for a law may be newly made yet old in content, being a mere restatement of 'old' law, and it can, though more rarely than we tend to imagine, merely restate moral precepts as they are without any modification and without any implications (for the process of enforcement and implementation) that modify the application of moral considerations.

my final decision to buy and move to the apartment where I now live was not taken all at once but in stages. At least three are easily discernible. First, I decided how much I could afford to spend. Then, in light of that decision and other factors, I decided on the neighbourhood in which to buy an apartment. Finally, I collected information about available accommodation within my price range in the chosen neighbourhood and chose the one to buy on the basis of a whole slate of functional and aesthetic considerations. Each of the first two stages terminated with a partial decision about what apartment to buy (an apartment costing no more than about..., an apartment in this neighbourhood) that narrowed the options I considered in the next stage. Each stage brought to bear considerations that did not play a part in the previous stage (or played only an indirect part). And, crucially, each stage terminated my deliberations about the impact of some reasons, which were not revisited in the later stages. We resort to multi-staged decision procedures often. They make life simpler, improving our ability to reach reasonable decisions.

Institutions have additional reasons to use such procedures. Some institutions are better than others in assessing some aspects of the decision. Political accountability demands that certain institutions will take part in the decision, but they are too burdened with work to be able to consider it thoroughly. It may be best to let them set a framework that will be filled out by others. Some of the information that may be helpful will not be available until nearer the time when deciding from scratch will no longer be rationally possible, and sometimes it may be advisable to delay some aspects of a decision until nearer the time of its implementation. Typically we find that such considerations furnish at least part of the justification for delegating legislative or regulatory powers to subordinate bodies and agencies and to the courts. Such delegation occurs whenever a standard is set but is to be implemented in a way that is sensitive to certain moral concerns; for example, the doctrine of contract determines who can make them and under what conditions they are valid but adds that contracts against public policy will not be enforceable, delegating to the courts a residual power to set aside contracts on grounds of public policy.

References to morality in this context indicate to the courts or the regulatory agencies or delegated legislature that while the maker of the law has considered moral and other considerations and found that they justify the legislated standards, it did not consider, or did not exhaustively consider, the impact of the so-called incorporated moral

considerations, and it is for the court or regulator and so on to do that.[18]
Again, what appears as incorporation is no more than an indication
that certain considerations are not excluded. The courts cannot gainsay
the legislation and set it aside because they think that a better standard
should be endorsed. The legislation bars them from doing so. It in effect
excludes their access to the moral considerations on which the legislator
should have relied in passing the act. But they can supplement or modify
the standard set by the act in light of the non-excluded considerations.

To conclude, judges are humans, and they are subject to morality
without any special incorporation of morality, as are we all. What appear
as incorporation are various instances of non-exclusion.

III. Inclusive Positivism and the Boundaries of Law

The discussion and conclusions of this chapter relate to one of the oldest
and most important questions in our quest to understand the nature of
the law: the question of its relation to morality. One of its aspects is the
question of the boundaries of law, and especially the boundary between
law and morality. I tried, in the course of the discussion above, to avoid
prejudging that issue, the question of the boundary between what is
and what is not part of the law. My preliminary remarks on 'so-called
incorporation' explain why the problem of the boundaries of law is an
unprofitable focus for a jurisprudential discussion. Yet I also remarked
that the distinction between what does and what does not belong to the
law is inescapable, an inescapable conclusion of any sensible theory of
the law. It is worth dwelling a little further on the nature of the problem
and its difficulties.

As noted above, for the courts the difference between standards they
have to apply because they are the law of the land and those they have to
apply 'merely' according to law often makes no practical difference, with
the consequence that they do not bother to establish sharp boundaries

---

[18] A very simple illustration (drawn to my attention by T Endicott) is in practice
direction 25.13 of the Civil Procedure Rules (in the UK) which says: 'The court may
make an order for security for costs under rule 25.12 if (a) it is satisfied, having regard
to all the circumstances of the case, that it is just to make such an order.' Clearly it
might just as well have said 'the court may, in its discretion, make an order for security
for costs . . .'. In that case, too, the court would have had to do what is just. The language of the rule merely reminds courts that their discretion was not curtailed. It does not
'incorporate' anything.

to the notions. It is true that that is not always the case. Standards such as foreign law, rules of other organizations, private agreements, and their like sometimes occasion the application of different rules of evidence, or of procedure, or general doctrines constraining the validity of one kind of rules and not of others (eg being subject to federal constitutional doctrines if but only if they are the law of the land, or being subject to public policy doctrines only if they are not). For people whose thinking about the law is focused exclusively on the practice of the courts, it may appear that that is all that can matter to anyone. They may doubt that the distinction is needed at all. To the extent that we find it in our thinking about the law, in our legal practices, it is, they would claim, of mere local interest and without any theoretical significance.

The law is, however, not merely a set of guides for court decisions. It is a political institution of great importance to the working of societies and to their members. From this point of view a British person cannot say 'Polish law is my law' just because it will be followed by British courts when their conflict-of-law rules direct them to do so. The distinction between standards that the courts have to apply and those that are the law of the land is vital to our ability to identify the law as the political institution it is.

Vital distinctions are not necessarily sharp ones. It may be that in many cases we have to resist the temptation to adjudicate whether a matter is part of the law or merely to be followed according to law. It makes no difference, we may say. You could take it either way. Or we may feel that neither view can strictly be proclaimed to be correct.

Is not the so-called incorporation of morality a case of this kind, where it is six of one or half a dozen of the other? On the contrary, it seems to me that the question of the status of the incorporation of morality provides a good case study showing the need to attend sometimes to the question of the boundaries of the law, and the way that need arises only in the service of other issues, rather than because there is an inherent importance in fixing such boundaries for their own sake.

When the question is the relation between law and morality, it seems inevitable that different claims about this relationship will imply different demarcations of the boundary of law, at least in the interface between it and morality.[19] So long as we allow that it is possible for a population

---

[19] Of course, a society or a culture that does not have the concepts of morality and of law does not have a view about their demarcation. Such a society may even be subject to law. The existence of a legal system in any country does not depend on the possession of the concept of law by the population of that country. But it does not follow, of course,

not to be governed by law, there must be a difference between legal stand-ards and those which are not legal, not part of the law. If a population has law, then it has a normative system that can fail to exist.[20] Morality, on the other hand, cannot fail to exist or to apply. Moreover, in any country subject to law there are moral rights and duties that are not legal rights and duties, or at least there can be such. Hence there is a boundary between law and morality. Hence there are boundaries to the law.

A simple-minded view has it that the law is marked by its connec-tion with certain institutions and that there are two ways in which it is so connected: first, only standards, norms, enacted or endorsed by certain institutions (law-making institutions, among them courts) are law and they are law because they are so endorsed. Second, only stand-ards, norms, that apply to certain institutions (law-applying institutions, among them courts) are law. Any theory that endorses the simple view will tend to regard the connection between law and morality as largely contingent, though it need not and should not deny that there are some necessary connections between law and morality.

The main alternatives to the simple view abandon the first condition of legal validity. They find only one necessary connection between law and social institutions, the connection to law-applying institutions, with almost always an exclusive concentration on the courts. There is a large number of possible variations on that theme. One could, for example, argue that the law consists of all the norms that the simple view acknow-ledges but in addition contains also the moral principles that apply to the conduct of legal institutions, such as courts. Rules such as *audi alteram partem*, for example, are, on this view, part of perhaps every legal system, regardless of whether they are followed in it or not and regard-less of whether they were made into law by its legal institutions, simply because it is a moral norm binding on institutions such as courts of law. Another variant of this approach holds that the law consists of all the norms that the courts ought to apply. These may include those standards that the simple view recognizes, and they may include the moral stand-ards that apply to the courts. But they include more, namely, standards regardless of whom they apply to, which the courts have a moral duty to follow, or something like that.

that in that country there is no boundary demarcating the limits of law, distinguishing between what is part of it and what is not. The argument in the text applies to it as well.

[20] I rely on the view that the law exists, where it does, as a normative system; that is that there are no single, stand-alone laws that are not part of a normative system.

Both alternatives to the simple view allow that moral norms are part of the law just because they are moral norms, yet both—and they are just two prototypes among many—respect the institutional nature of the law by acknowledging that moral norms are part of the law only if they are connected specifically to legal institutions. The views known as inclusive legal positivism seem to be closer to the simple view in that like it they insist on the dual connection between legal institutions and legal standards—legal standards are made so by legal institutions as well as being applied and enforced by legal institutions. In fact, they can lay claim to being pure advocates of the simple view: if, according to them, a legal standard requires appropriate sections of the population to follow it and the courts to apply a certain standard, then it is part of the law. And if the legal standard so-called incorporates moral standards, then those moral standards are part of the law. If there is a law that stipulates that one ought, in all dealings with people to whom one does not owe special responsibility, to observe all the moral requirements that apply to dealings between strangers, then the moral standards setting out these requirements have become part of the law. I will call this version of the inclusive legal positivist thesis the incorporation thesis.[21]

The conclusions of the earlier part of this chapter pose a difficulty for the incorporation thesis. If morality applies to people and courts alike anyway, then we are all, courts included, bound by it even before its incorporation. In what way can incorporation turn it into law? The fact that the incorporation thesis is the purest expression of the simple view counts against it rather than being a point in its favour. We know that the simple view is too simple. We know that Polish law is not part of Greek law just because Greek conflict-of-law rules direct people and courts to follow Polish law on certain occasions.

The incorporation thesis claims that moral standards turn into law simply because of their incorporation. It seems to lack the resources to distinguish between law directing us and the courts to follow some foreign law or to obey the rules of some associations, and so on, and the incorporation of morality. In fact it has a special difficulty with the

---

[21] These remarks apply only to what Himma, above n 3, calls the sufficiency condition of inclusive legal positivism, that is to the view that so-called 'incorporation' can turn morality into law. I do not, in this chapter, consider in any way the case for or against the view that the validity of legal norms may depend, whether because some other law so determines or for other reasons, on their being consistent with some non-legal norms, moral or other.

latter, for morality applies anyway, and the incorporation thesis suggests that it applies only if incorporated.

The argument of this chapter has shown that so-called incorporating laws have their point—that their effect is not to incorporate but rather to prevent the exclusion of morality by law. This deprives the incorporation thesis of another possible argument, namely that it alone can make sense of the existence of laws that appear to incorporate moral standards. On the contrary, it cannot explain their function. Given that morality applies anyway, their function cannot be to incorporate it. None of this *proves* that the incorporation thesis is false. But it raises serious doubts about it, doubts that its supporters have not yet confronted successfully.[22]

---

[22] I raised essentially the same question in *The Authority of Law* (Oxford: Clarendon Press, 1979) 47 n 8, though I did so rather briefly and without the supporting arguments above.

8

Reasoning with Rules

What is special about legal reasoning? In what way is it distinctive? How does it differ from reasoning in medicine, engineering, physics, or everyday life? The answers range from the very ambitious to the modest. The ambitious claim that there is a special and distinctive legal logic, or legal ways of reasoning, modes of reasoning which set the law apart from all other disciplines. Opposing them are the modest, who claim that there is nothing special to legal reasoning, that reason is the same in all domains. According to them, only the contents of the law differentiate it from other areas of inquiry, whereas its mode of reasoning is the one common to all domains of inquiry.

Those of a moderately cynical temperament will not be surprised at the popularity of the ambitious view among lawyers. After all, the more special the law is the more justified are the high fees which make the law inaccessible to all but the rich in so many countries. However, we will not engage in such sociological ruminations. Whoever stands to gain or to lose from the existence or absence of special legal modes of reasoning, the only question to be explored here is whether there are such distinctive modes of reasoning.

Not surprisingly, there is some truth in various rival positions. The most important point to make on the side of modesty is that the core of logic is not domain-specific, nor could it be. Numerous arguments establish this point. I will sketch one. Rules of inference are not independent of rules of meaning, nor of rules for the attribution of content to concepts and propositions. On the contrary, they are part of the factors that fix the meanings of terms and the content of concepts. The content of concepts is determined in part by the inferential relations that apply to them. That 'a is green' entails 'a is coloured' is part of what determines the meaning of 'coloured' and of 'green'. Therefore, if law, morality, physics, and medicine, for example, are each subject to different rules of logic then either they employ distinct terminology or they use the same terms in different meanings. In fact while some terminology is special to different domains (eg 'quarks', 'resulting trust') for the most part we use one and the same language in all domains, and it would be preposterous to suggest that the same words bear different meanings when used by doctors, lawyers, bus conductors, accountants, etc.

However, not all modes of reasoning belong to the core of logic. Regarding the rest it is more plausible to assume that some differences between domains may exist. Much of what is often called 'inductive reasoning' consists in following congeries of rules based on localized experience, or localized probabilities. Perhaps there are domain-specific modes of reasoning consisting in non-deductive rules of warrant. The law applies to all aspects of life. Therefore, legal arguments incorporate modes of reasoning from all domains of thought. But they may add to them. There may be some additional modes of reasoning special to legal thought.

By its nature the law has features that greatly affect the character of legal reasoning. I have in mind three: that the law of every country constitutes a system of law, that it consists, if not entirely then at least to a marked degree, of norms or rules, and that applying it and following it require or presuppose interpretation. It would be wrong to suggest that these features are unique to law. They are shared by a number of the major religions and by other social organizations. They mark all institutionalized normative systems, and to a lesser degree they can also be present in other normative domains. But they are central to the law, and they can be claimed to give a special character to legal (and religious, etc) reasoning. The systematic nature of law, its dependence on rules and on interpretation: these three features of the law are closely interrelated and, being structural features, they can rightly be said to affect modes of reasoning common to legal reasoning. In other words, legal reasoning is just like any other reasoning, but in addition it manifests features which express the structural, one may say formal, characteristics of the law.

As you see I find what is special in the law in some of its structural-normative features. Many would prefer to single out some of its social-institutional features. The two levels of analysis are not unrelated. The structural-normative aspects of the law affect its social-institutional character, and of course the influence works the other way round as well. There is no reason to be deterministic about the relations between these two aspects of the law, no reason to assume a one-to-one correlation between them. Their relations are, and have long been recognized as, a subject of great interest which we understand very incompletely. This is only one of the reasons for focusing here exclusively on the structural-normative features which I mentioned.

Of the three—rules, interpretation, and systematic character—the first, rules, is the most basic. Because rules play a central role in the law, it has a systematic nature, and interpretation plays a crucial role in legal reasoning. To understand this we need to understand what is so special about rules, and how they determine modes of reasoning.

How do rules figure in practical deliberation? How should they affect action, and the justification of action? It seems that rules are reasons for action. A person may well give the fact that his action is required by a rule as his reason for performing it, and an action may be justified because it conforms to a rule. Yet rules are unlike most other reasons. Most reasons are facts which show what is good in an action, which render it eligible: it will give pleasure. It will protect one's health, or earn one money, or improve one's understanding. It will relieve poverty in one's country, or bring peace of mind to a troubled friend, and so on. What is the good in conforming to a rule?

This is the question I want to explore here: how can it be that rules are reasons when they do not point to a good in the action for which they are reason? I will call the phenomenon to be explained *the opaqueness of rules*.[1] I will concentrate on one type of rule, rules which are man-made, and which require conduct unconditionally.[2] My central case will be rules which are deliberately made as rules. What is true of them is true of other man-made rules, but may not be true of other reason-constituting rules.

Not all rules are reasons. Some 'rules' mark regularities, as when we talk of what we do as a rule. Regularities may, but need not, be reasons.

---

[1] So, a reason is opaque, in the sense intended here, if a complete statement of it fails to show what is good about the action for which it is a reason. But, one may object, does not the fact that the reason is required by a binding (or valid) rule show what is good about it? Not so. As will be made clear below, that only shows that it is required, that we have a reason to perform it. It does not show in what way the action is good. In other words, being the action required by a binding rule is a normative, not an evaluative property of the action. Admittedly, one may claim that the fact that there is a reason for an action makes it, *pro tanto*, good. But then here the evaluative follows the normative, rather than being its ground. The opaqueness of rules is that a complete statement of a reason does not disclose any good quality in the action which may explain why there is a reason for the action.

[2] Much of what will be said below applies, with self-explanatory modifications, to other types of rules, especially to other types of legal rules, and need not be discussed here.

In other words, qua regularities they are not reasons.[3] 'Rules' are sometimes used to mark any normative proposition, that is any proposition stating what ought to be done,[4] especially those which are natural expressions of common opinion. Such rules are not reasons either. They are statements (true or false) of what we have reason to do, but we have these reasons independently of the rules. Many rules are recipes. They are instructions on how to do things: how to bake a cake, assemble furniture, impress an audience, untie knots, find one's way out of a maze, or win at chess. Such rules state conditional reasons. That is, they are not themselves reasons, and the reasons they state are reasons only for those who have some other reason. You have reason to bake this way if you have a reason to bake a cake, for that is how cakes are baked.

Closer to the rules central to our concern are those which are sometimes called 'constitutive rules'. The rules of chess, ie those that determine which moves are allowed rather than how to win at chess, are said to be constitutive of the game. It is often said that constitutive rules are not reasons either. I think that they are, but they are (that is their existence constitutes) conditional reasons. They are reasons to behave in this way or that, reasons why you must behave this way and that, if you are to play chess, and therefore, if you have reason to play chess.

Many constitutive rules are themselves man-made, but not all. Many of them are conditional reasons, whose condition can be avoided. One can avoid playing chess and at least in principle one can avoid a country, or a profession. Some constitutive rules are different. The rules of mathematics and logic are—in the old terminology—rules or laws of thought, constitutive of thinking (or of central kinds of thinking). We do not make them, and we cannot avoid them, at least we cannot avoid observing some of them, so long as we continue to think. But they too may be regarded as setting conditional reasons, even though the reason cannot be avoided by anything less than opting out of all rational thought.[5]

[3] Another way of making my point is this: every fact can be a reason, in the sense of being part of an explanation of why some action, belief, emotion, etc was appropriate to the occasion. But facts do play different roles in such explanations. Good-making or bad-making properties, and rules, are what I call 'operative reasons' (see J Raz, *Practical Reason and Norms* (Oxford: OUP, 1999) 33–34), and what J Dancy calls 'favouring reasons': *Moral Reasons* (Oxford: Blackwell, 1993).

[4] Or what must or should, or may or may not be done, etc.

[5] See on the rules of rationality in my *Engaging Reason* (Oxford: OUP, 2000) ch 4, where these conclusions are qualified. Notice that the claim is not that we cannot avoid complete compliance with the rules of logic or of thought generally. We all violate them

So, let me return to the rules that I will focus on. These rules are unconditional reasons, and they are man-made. I said that the question to focus on is how can rules be reasons,[6] given that on their face they do not point to any value in the action for which they are reasons, given that they are opaque. One reply is that the question is based on a false assumption. All normative statements[7] (and they are rules, by one use of the term) are opaque. They state what we have to do. It is evaluative statements[8] which state what is good about doing this or that. There is no puzzle about the opaqueness of normative statements. My puzzle derives from the claim that rules, some rules, are themselves reasons,[9] and not merely statements of what we have reason to do. Its solution is in the denial of the premise. If rules are never reasons, the puzzle disappears.

This last statement has to be acknowledged. However, we should start from the assumption that rules are reasons, for they are commonly treated as such. If, however, the assumption leads to conundrums and paradoxes it cannot be secure until they are laid to rest. In proceeding to explore the puzzle of the opaqueness of man-made rules I will be undertaking to defend the thought that rules are reasons, as well as to explain how they can be reasons in spite of their opaqueness.

The puzzle of the opaqueness of rules is made more acute when added to another: how can it be that people can create reasons just by acting with the intention to do so? This second question is bound to sound familiar. It arises in other cases not involving rules. Most prominently, it arises regarding contracts or agreements, but also, of course, regarding promises, and all other voluntary undertakings. Moreover, undertakings and agreements too are opaque. Does the fact that I promised to stay awake tonight show that there is some value, some good in my staying awake tonight? At the very least we can safely say that if it does it is not

from time to time. The claim is that the reason that conditions their application is not readily avoided, that nearly all have that reason most of the time. These rules are conditional on a reason to live as a rational, ie thinking being, while one is alive.

[6] Throughout the rest of this chapter I use 'reasons' to refer to unconditional reasons. Rules which are conditional reasons are opaque only in not disclosing on their face what are the reasons on which they depend. Once these are known the good they serve is made evident.

[7] That is, statements that we must, or should, or ought to, etc, do this or that.

[8] That is, statements that this or that has some properties which entail that it is good or of value.

[9] Strictly speaking it is not rules but their existence which are reasons. I will, however, adopt the shorthand of referring to rules as reasons.

in the way that the fact that I will be awake by the bedside of an ailing friend does. The similarity between man-made rules, agreements, and undertakings helps in answering the second question and through it, it helps in answering the first, which is our main question.

One analogy between agreements, undertakings, and the sort of rules I am focusing on is that of all of them we can ask two different, and relatively independent, questions. The questions will be idiomatically expressed in different ways in different contexts, but they all are versions of the following. (1) Are they binding, valid rules (agreements or undertakings)? These questions are equivalent to 'ought one to conform to them?' (2) Are they good, wise, justified rules (agreements or undertakings)?

A rule, or a promise, or an agreement can be binding, and it may be wrong to break it, it may be a valid reason for action, and yet it may be a bad rule, which should never have been made, and which should be changed as soon as possible. Rules, agreements, and undertakings allow for a potential normative gap, a gap between the evaluative and the normative, that is between their value and their normative force.

Contrast this with 'ordinary' reasons. That a novel is insightful and subtle is a reason to read it. We cannot here drive a wedge between the evaluative and the normative, between the two questions: 'is it good?' and 'is it binding or valid?' If being insightful and subtle are good characteristics of novels then they are reasons. There is no gap between being valid reasons and being good or of value, between the normative and the evaluative, as there is in the cases of rules, undertakings, and agreements.

Why the difference? It is plausible to think that the explanation has to do with the fact that rules, undertakings, and agreements are man-made. Since they are man-made they cannot be reasons unless they pass an appropriate normative test. Not everything which someone intends to create as a reason for himself (as with promises and personal rules) or for others (as with other kinds of rules) is such a reason.

This observation is correct, and may be relevant to an account of the place of rules in practical reason, but it cannot explain the separation between the binding character of rules and their goodness or justifiability. Why not have one test: if rules, agreements, and promises are good and wise then they are binding, and if not then they are not? To explain why deficient rules, agreements, and undertakings can, nevertheless, be binding we need to rely on something more than the fact that they are man-made.

To explain the normative gap we should start by noticing its contours and effects. First, the gap is not absolute, nor could it be. When we ask 'what makes rules bind?' the answer will revert to evaluative considerations.[10] The rules of the Mastergame chess club may be binding because it is *better* for the affairs of the club to be governed by its committee than to be organized some other way, or be left in chaos.

It is possible, of course, that that is not so, and that while the rules which give the club committee power to make rules for the governance of the club are binding, they are not good rules. It may be better to leave matters to a general meeting rather than have them decided by the committee, for example.[11] If so then this is yet another manifestation of a *limited* normative gap. This time the gap exists regarding the constitution of the club, that is those rules which set up the committee, and govern its rule-making activities. To explain why the rules of the constitution of Mastergame are binding, that is to explain why they have *normative* force, we have to rely on *evaluative* considerations. These may be, for example, the desirability of not upsetting arrangements which, defective though they are, have governed the running of the club for some time, given that the harm that would be occasioned by a disorderly attempt to overturn them is too great. Were the harm caused by disregarding the rule establishing the committee small, and the advantage of organizing matters some other way significant, and the prospect of securing the better way good, then the rules establishing the committee would not have been binding. *Normativity is ultimately based on evaluative considerations*, but in a way which leaves room for a normative gap.

[10] Some writers believe that the explanation of what is binding does, at least sometimes, derive from a range of considerations which are altogether independent of evaluative considerations. They are sometimes called deontic considerations. Nothing I say in this chapter refutes this supposition. It shows, however, that the very binding nature of rules and the phenomena associated with it do not depend on the supposition being correct.

[11] I am skirting around a point which must be mentioned, however briefly. I assume in the text above that rules can be justified by what I call below content-independent considerations, relating, for example, to their mode of origin even independently of the validity of any rules authorizing this mode of the generation of rules. This seems to me true in principle. However, most legal systems observe doctrines of the rule of law, with the consequence that rules are valid in law only if they arise in accord with a legal rule about the proper ways for making law (some original constitutions being the only officially acknowledged exception). My observations in the text are not meant to challenge such rule of law precepts, only to indicate that they are not required by the nature of rules.

How can that be? Notice the considerations which justify rules in this example: a rule saying that members are entitled to bring no more than three guests to social functions of the club. The considerations which establish that it is binding do not turn on the desirability of members having a small number of guests, nor on the desirability of members having the option to bring guests, but on the desirability of the affairs of the club being organized by the committee which laid down the rule. It is, in other words, an instance of what I call (following Hart) *a content-independent justification.* It is content-independent in that it does not bear primarily on the desirability of the acts for which the rule is a reason. Here we see clearly how rules differ from other reasons. The insightfulness and subtlety of a novel are reasons for reading it because they show why reading it is good. But the considerations which show why the rule is binding, ie why it is a reason for not bringing more than three guests, do not show that it is good not to bring more than three guests.[12] They show that it is good to have power given to a committee, and therefore good to abide by decisions of that committee. But that can justify a variety of rules: to have an annual championship competition, to admit new members by a simple majority in a postal vote of all members, to levy a membership fee of £50 a year, etc. Moreover, typically, though not without exception, the very same considerations could justify contradictory rules. They could justify a rule saying that membership will be confined to residents of the district, and a rule that

---

[12] There are various ways of trying to give a more formal characterization of content-independent reasons, or justifications. Some of them may well yield different concepts. The text above suggests breakdown of transitivity of reasons as a mark of content-independent reasons, a point to which I return in the text below. In general, if P is a justification of Q, which is a justification of R, then P is a justification of R. But the justification of a rule is not, in and of itself, a justification for performing the action which the rule requires. It justifies giving the makers of the rule power to make the rule, and no more. Of course, indirectly it justifies the action which the rule requires, as being an action in accordance with a rule which is thus justified. But, unlike content-dependent justifications, it does not justify the action without these additional mediating premises. Put another way, the justification we consider, like all justifications of rules, is *prima facie* justification of the acts which fall under the rule. In as much as Roberta's act was to avoid bringing more than three guests it was justified, because that is what the rule required of her. Overall, of course, matters may be different, for her act has other features as well, some of which may condemn it. All *prima facie* justifications are description-sensitive. The lack of transitivity is that the reasons for the validity of the rule are not in themselves reasons for performing the act required by the rule, as described in the rule. In this rules are the exception to the norm that the reason for a reason for an action is a reason for that action (under the same description). To explore fully the credential of this test goes beyond the ambition of this chapter. It will require, for example, a way of distinguishing conditional reasons from content-independent reasons.

membership will not be limited to the residents of the district, etc. They are in this sense content-independent.[13]

Do you feel that I am going around in a circle? I stated at the outset that my aim is to explain how rules can be reasons even though they do not show that the acts that they require are desirable or of value, even though they are opaque. Now I have proclaimed as a great discovery the very same fact as if it explains why rules display a normative gap, that is a gap between the normative and the evaluative.

Nevertheless, I believe that we are making progress. First, notice that *the thesis about the content-independence of the justification of rules*[14] goes further than *opacity*, the feature I set out to explain. That was that *rules* are reasons even though they do not show the value of the actions for which they are reasons. The content-independence thesis makes things worse by adding that even *the justification* of rules does not bear on the desirability of the actions for which they are reasons.[15] Doubling the puzzle makes it easier to solve.

Secondly, by showing the centrality of the features to be explained we improve our understanding of rules. We can see now that the *opaqueness of rules* is a result of their *content-independence*, and their content-independence is an aspect of *the normative gap* rules display between the normative and the evaluative. By tying all these features together we show them to be robust and central to rules. Of course, we still have to explain them.

---

[13] It is important not to confuse content-independence with unlimited jurisdiction. A justification can be, and typically will be, both content-independent and limited. The club committee cannot be authorized to commit or order others to commit murder, etc. It is, if you like, content-sensitive in that it does not allow for any content whatsoever, while being content-independent, in not being specific to one rule. What makes a justification content-independent is not whether it can justify more or less possible rules, but that the considerations which constitute it do not bear on the desirability of having rules with the content of the rules which they can justify. That there are other rules which, because of their content, the justification does not show to be binding is immaterial.

[14] Strictly speaking not rules, but their justifications are content-independent. For the sake of brevity I will, however, refer also to rules as content-independent.

[15] Perhaps I should add here 'under that description'. The justification of rules bears on the desirability of actions required by the rules when they are described as 'actions required by the rule', etc. That is not a description of action which can be used in the formulation of the rule ('the rule is that one ought to do whatever this rule requires', even though true, is not a way rules can be informatively formulated). Put precisely, then, the claim is that the justification of the rule does not bear on the desirability of any action required by the rule, under any description which can be used to formulate the content of the rule informatively.

But what does it mean that we have to explain them? After all, rules are what they are. The task of analysis is to explain their central features. Having isolated three, their content-independence, their opaqueness, and the normative gap, and having shown that they are interconnected, we can go on to describe other of their features. But what sort of request is it that we explain them? What more need be said? Of course, analysing rules in these terms does not mean justifying them. We have not shown which rules are binding, nor that there are any rules which bind. But surely the justification of rules is not our task. The problem is not that it is a normative task. The problem is that it is impossible to justify rules in general. We can consider the justification of this or that rule or group of rules and that cannot be done outside a specific context.

To this we should reply: yes and no. True, there is no question of providing a general justification of rules. Some are not justified and are not binding. Possibly, those that are binding are to be justified in arguments of varying patterns, which cannot be exhaustively described in advance. Yet more needs to be said to explain the opacity of rules. At the very least we must show how it is possible for people to believe that rules are binding. For without such an explanation the rest of the analysis is suspect. People do make mistakes and many believe in the validity of rules which are not valid at all. Yet unless we can show how it *can reasonably* appear to people that some rules are valid the analysis will be in jeopardy. It is unlikely that so many people, perhaps almost everyone, have normatively similar beliefs, all of which are totally irrational.

Showing how it could be plausible for people to believe that some rules bind is likely to amount to showing, at the very least, that it is possible for rules to bind, and also to pointing to some circumstances under which they do bind.

So we are back with our question: how can rules be reasons when they are opaque? To understand this we need to find a focal point which will open the way from delineating the features of rules to their possible justifications. That focal point is likely to be their content-independence. The content-independence of rules readily explains their opaqueness. It also explains the normative gap. Since the justification of the validity of a rule does not depend on the value of the act the rule is a reason for a normative gap opens. The question then is: how can justification be content-independent?

For a content-independent justification to be possible there must be reasons for an agent to behave in a certain way other than the value of the behaviour in question. Let us move away from rules (undertakings or agreements) and take an example of content-independent justification for a particular act on a particular occasion. Suppose that you are asked why you walked to work along Marylebone High Street today, rather than along Baker Street. You may say that the former has more attractive shops and buildings and is less noisy than Baker Street. This would be a content-dependent explanation. But suppose you said: because I always do. That reply is content-independent. It shows nothing good about walking along Marylebone High Street. The problem with it is that it is not clear in what way it points to a reason at all. Why should one do what one always does? Depending on the circumstances an explanation may be readily forthcoming. It may be, for example, that you find choosing a route every morning (should it be Baker Street? Or Gloucester Place? Or Marylebone High Street? Or Upper Montague Street followed by Montague Square?) tiresome. Sticking to a routine is a way of not spending time and energy deciding, when the difference in the merits of the different realistic options does not appear to justify the effort and worry that deciding would involve.

It is obvious that the justification is not entirely content-independent. Had the margin of merit between the different options been greater then the reason for choosing the route might have been inadequate. Yet clearly the reason is content-independent in not bearing on the quality of the route chosen. We can therefore examine this case, and consider how some of its features can apply to rules. What enables the content-independent justification to work is the existence of a personal routine of going to work along Marylebone High Street. The very same reason for the desirability of a quick decision, free from detailed consideration of the different options, would have been to no avail but for the existence of the routine (or something to take its place).

As a rule, normative justification, and justification in general, are transitive.[16] If A justifies B and B justifies C then A justifies C. So if there is reason to read the novel because it is a good novel, and if it is a good novel because it is insightful and subtle, then that it is insightful and subtle is reason to read it. And so it goes on. If the novel is insightful because it vividly sheds light on a deep emotional conflict which is usually denied and misunderstood, then that it sheds such light is a reason why it is good, and therefore also a reason for reading it. The

---

[16] As remarked above, I assume that the justifications concerned are *prima facie* justifications and therefore that they are description-sensitive, in the same way that explanations are description-sensitive.

opacity and content-independence of rules mean that transitivity does not hold. That it is good to uphold the authority of the committee is a reason for the validity of its rules, including the rule that one may not bring more than three guests to social functions of the club. But the desirability of upholding the authority of the committee is not a reason for not bringing more than three guests (not, that is, under this description).

The lack of transitivity in justification seems to me to be among the most important features of rules. They are not, of course, alone. Undertakings and agreements display the same feature. The promise to go to Paris is a reason to do so, but the reason the promise is binding (eg the desirability of people being able to bind themselves) is not a reason to go to Paris (nothing about the value of being in Paris or of travelling there). It justifies going to Paris only indirectly. The same justification could have justified staying away from Paris, had one promised to do that.

Some thirty or more years ago much philosophical ink was spilt over whether rules make a difference. One party insisted that having rules as a reason for action makes no difference for the guidance and evaluation of action, whereas the other party argued that it does. In the terminology I have here developed, those who denied that rules can make a difference relied on the general transitivity of reasoning to argue that rules cannot yield different conclusions from those which would follow without them, for they can only transmit the force of reasons we have anyway. Those who opposed them knew better, but only a few of them realized that the explanation lies in the breakdown in transitivity which is a result of the content-independence of the justification of rules, and of their opaque character. That is why rules, at least man-made rules, can make a difference to practical reasoning, and why when valid they are rightly said to be reasons in their own right rather than merely statements of reasons we have independently of them. This then is what we may call *the autonomy thesis*. It says that rules make a difference. If valid, they constitute reasons which one would not have but for them. While the considerations which justify a rule exist independently of the rule, they do not constitute the same reason for action that the rule constitutes.

You will realize of course that in proceeding with the analysis and identifying further features of rules we are continuously restating the question, or rather stating further and closely related questions. We have not yet answered it. I believe, however, that we have finally found the question which provides the best avenue towards an answer. To explain how it can be that a rule can be a valid reason, even though it is opaque, we need to explain how it is that rules can be autonomous. Once we explain how there can be reasons which are autonomous, in the sense explained, we will have the answer to our question: we will understand why reasons can be opaque.

Some people think that the very idea of autonomous reasons is incoherent, or at least that it is logically impossible for such reasons to be valid. After all, the autonomy of rules is an expression of the breakdown of transitivity and that means that the force of some reasons does not carry through. It is thwarted by other considerations which in themselves are reasons neither for the action concerned, nor against it. Think of the chess club example again. There may be a reason for a member of the club to bring more than three guests to a particular function. He cannot do so because the rule forbids him. The rule is a reason against the action, so everything looks ordinary. But the reason for the validity of the rule is the good of having the committee regulate the club. And that is not a reason against bringing four guests to the function. Small wonder that rules are opaque. They do not show what is good about the action they require for they do not in fact rely for their validity, for their force as a reason, on anything which makes the action they require good. (Notice that it is the same with agreements and undertakings: the reason is that you are committed, rather than that what you are committed to has any value.) So we have in the rule a putative reason against four guests which does not depend on there being anything wrong with four guests but which stops one from acting on reasons for having four guests. Is not that irrational? Does it not follow that there cannot be binding rules?

Some have thought that to dissolve this apparent paradox one needs to invoke considerations of a different order altogether, considerations which are not subsumable under the category of the good. They are sometimes identified as deontological considerations. I will say nothing to refute the thought that there are normative considerations which cannot be subsumed under the good. I do not believe, however, that they need to be invoked to explain the autonomy or any other feature of rules, or to account for the possibility of plausibly believing in the validity of some rules. So far as the considerations we examine here are concerned, all can be explained on the assumption that the normative derives entirely from the evaluative, that reasons depend exclusively on values.

Long ago[17] I suggested that rules, rules of the kind we are considering, are not simple reasons but a structure of interrelated reasons. They are, first, reasons for the acts they prescribe, but they are also, second, reasons not to act for some competing reasons. The rule that no more than three guests may be invited by a club member is, first, a reason for members not to invite more than three guests, and also, second, a reason not to act on some reasons for inviting a fourth guest. I call the second kind of reasons exclusionary reasons (for they exclude action for some reasons) and I call the rule itself a protected reason, because the reason for the action it prescribes is protected by these exclusionary reasons.

Any complexity of this kind is unwelcome. Why do I think that it helps to explain how rules function? Take again our humble and long-suffering example. I repeatedly said that the reason for the validity of the rule is that it is best if club affairs are regulated by the committee which made the rule. That is presumably because, on the whole, if members follow the judgement of the committee their actions will track reason better than if they act on their best judgement without taking account of the judgement of the committee. Usually when this is the case it is so through a combination of two factors. First, the good judgement of the committee. And secondly, the fact that it can secure desirable coordination among people, which, left to their own devices, the members are less likely to secure. These factors are not a reason against inviting a fourth guest. But they are a reason for not second-guessing the decision of the committee. So if the committee, having had the opportunity to weigh the pros and cons of imposing the no-more-than-three-guests rule, has approved it then all members have reason not to challenge that judgement, and that means that they have reason not to act on the reasons for or against bringing a fourth guest. Rather, they should regard the rule as displacing the reasons which the committee was meant to consider in issuing the rule. That is what I mean when I say that the rule is an exclusionary reason.

Obviously it is also a reason for the action required by the rule. In all it is a protected reason for that action. If this example can be generalized, and I believe that it can, then we have an explanation of why rules are opaque, content-independent, autonomous reasons for action, and how they can be rational even though they violate the transitivity of reasons. I finally call this an explanation, for it includes an account of how it is

---

[17] In *Practical Reason and Norms*, n 3 above, and in subsequent writings.

33-34

possible for rules to be valid. More than that, it makes it clear that often rules are valid protected reasons. QED.[18]

Armed with this skeletal analysis we can make its meaning and implication clearer by considering a few of the contexts in which we may find some valid rules. An obvious and very important context consists of all those cases where there is a good case for enabling people, organizations, or other agents to pre-commit themselves. To achieve its purpose pre-commitment must achieve closure: once the commitment is made it is to be adhered to. Absolute closure would mean that the commitment is to be adhered to however much circumstances change, whether or not one changes one's mind, and whether or not one realizes that one made a mistake in making the commitment. Arguably, no valid commitment can be absolute. There are no circumstances which would warrant absolute commitments. But a pre-commitment need not be absolute. It may be designed to achieve closure so long as the situation does not change radically, or closure from change of mind motivated by considerations of one kind or another, and so on. But how can any pre-commitment be rational? Does not reason require reassessment of the proposed action just before it is undertaken? My suggestion is that it works because when there is a case to enable an agent to pre-commit himself, the pre-commitment constitutes an exclusionary reason for not acting on those considerations that the pre-commitment was meant to exclude (subject to emergencies, or whatever other exceptions reason imposes on the power to pre-commit).[18]

Pre-commitment is useful, sometimes even necessary, in a large variety of contexts and for a number of reasons. It can facilitate forward planning, it can enable coordination, it extends people's abilities to form ties with others, and also their ability to enter into mutually profitable arrangements with others. Finally, it is a prerequisite of many arrangements based on a division of labour between different agents. Pre-commitments take many forms: promises, vows, and agreements are familiar cases. So are personal rules (to have only two cigarettes a day, or to go jogging daily) and decisions.

Some people regard rules made by authorities as pre-commitments. They regard communities as agents and governments as their agents. Laws passed by the government are seen as commitments of the community. This may be the right way to think of some communities,

[18] There are alternative explanations, but I believe that they are either equivalent to mine, or fail to account for all the aspects of pre-commitment.

but for reasons we need not go into here, it seems no more than a fiction when considering most states today. This does not mean that legal rules cannot be binding. Governments have useful, and in the conditions of our life essential, functions in securing coordination, overcoming collective action problems, and utilizing hard to master information for the benefit of their communities and beyond. There is much more to be said about rules of political communities, such as legal rules. I will leave the subject with a couple of comments on rules and disagreements, and rules and division of power among legal institutions.

There are many sources of disagreement. Hobbesian and market-oriented theories tend to regard all disagreements as expressions of conflicts of interests. This is an exaggeration, but no doubt many disagreements do result from conflict of interests. Many political theorists of left-liberal persuasion emphasize the prevalence of disagreements about morality and about values more generally. The disputes about abortion, surrogate motherhood, the rights of gays and lesbians, and many others are predominantly, though perhaps not exclusively, such disagreements. But there are other sources of societal disagreement. Disagreements can arise between people who share the same values and whose interests do not conflict. They can arise, of course, because of factual disagreement: for example, economics is far from a secure science, and disagreements about the likely effects of various social or technological changes lead to disagreements about governmental policies. Finally, disagreements are liable to arise where reason suggests that people should coordinate their conduct but it allows for various schemes of coordination, without judging between them.

The actual situation is much more complicated than this thumbnail sketch suggests. Not only are the causes of disagreement often mixed, but in addition it is often far from clear what they are. People faced with a problem of coordination where reason under-determines the solution may believe that the problem is of disagreement over values, etc.

Where the law is concerned another complication looms large: the coordination the law aims to achieve is multi-layered: to coordinate not only the conduct of individuals but that of legal institutions as well. These institutions themselves are inter-related in complex ways: electorates, legislatures, executive and administrative bodies, central and provincial bodies, as well as complex hierarchies of courts and tribunals, all have to function in an orderly and co-operative fashion.

These brief reminders of what we all know connect with the analysis of rules, as autonomous, opaque reasons. To some degree the sensible reaction to disagreement is to avoid common policy and common action which relies on the disputed beliefs. Often that is neither possible nor desirable. Yet common action requires some measure of agreement, at least on the part of the officials who may be involved in implementing the disputed measures. Moreover, in general it is desirable that common actions shall command agreement. Rules allow agreement in the face of disagreement. They do so by allowing for agreement on the decision procedure in spite of disagreements about the measures it should yield, or because of agreement on measures, in the face of disagreement about their justification.[19] Again we can see how rules are the inevitable backbone of any structure of authority, of which the law is a paradigm example. We can also begin to see how the centrality of rules, and of the factors which justify it, make interpretation crucial to much legal reasoning, and make much interpretation concerned with giving effect to the systematic nature of law. These too are concomitants of the fact that the law is a structure of authority. But that is a matter for another paper.

---

[19] A point well highlighted by Cass Sunstein in various publications. See, eg, CR Sunstein, *Legal Reasoning and Political Conflict* (New York; Oxford: OUP, 1996).

PART III

INTERPRETATION

9

Why Interpret?[1]

This chapter is about legal interpretation, but not about the question: how to interpret the law. Rather, its aim is to make us consider seriously the question: Why is interpretation central to legal practices? After all not all normative practices assign interpretation such a central role. In this regard the law contrasts with morality. The reason for the contrast has to do with the status of sources in the law. There are no 'moral sources', while legal sources are central to the law. Legal interpretation is primarily—I will suggest—the interpretation not of the law, but of its sources. To understand why interpretation is central to legal practices requires understanding the role of sources in the law: the reasons for having them, and hence also the ways in which they should be treated. I will show how reflections about these topics connect with some traditional jurisprudential puzzles, such as the relations between law and morality. Are there gaps in the law? Is the law or its interpretation objective or subjective?

I

We—legal theorists—write a lot about interpretation. Mostly we inquire into the methods of interpretation used or to be used in law. But we do not often ask why interpret at all? You may think that interpretation is so deeply established in law that there is no point in raising the question. Interpretation is here to stay. That is indeed so, but it is an objection to the question only if it is understood as a sceptical question: Would it not be better if legal practices were not bound up with interpretation as they are? That, however, is not my question. Mine is a quest

[1] I am grateful to Jeremy Waldron, Kent Greenawalt, David Leebron, Jules Coleman, and Liam Murphy for comments on a draft of this chapter.

for understanding: what can we learn about the nature of law from the fact that interpretation plays such a crucial role in adjudication?

Let me mention five issues raised by the importance of interpretation in legal practice:

First, law is often compared to morality, and the relation between law and morality is one of the persistent puzzles which preoccupy legal philosophy. Interpretation[2] is not essential to morality nor to our moral practices, but is essential to our legal practices. Why this difference? Can it illuminate in any way the question of the relations between the two?

Second, it has become a common tenet of our understanding of the law that it is meant to provide common standards for the guidance of the people of a political society. Political societies are societies in which acknowledged authorities are empowered to act for the society, and in particular to decide how the people in that society should behave in matters where there may be disagreements on principles or conflicts of interest among members of the society. This aspect of the law suggests that it typically consists of publicly proclaimed standards which are meant to be available to those subject to them so that they can be guided by them. But interpretation is possible only when the meaning of what is interpreted is not obvious. Therefore, if interpretation is central to the law it must be doubtful whether the law can be available to its subjects.

Third, some theories of law claim that the law is necessarily incomplete, that there are legal propositions which are neither true nor false. For example, according to these theories there are modes of conduct regarding which it is neither true nor false that they are lawful, and there are other gaps in the law, gaps regarding rights, status, and so on. Theories which emphasize the incompleteness of the law usually argue that courts have a dual function: to apply law and to create new or revise old law.[3] The prevalence of interpretation, however, seems to belie this view. Interpretation straddles the divide between the identification of existing law and the creation of a new one. Where interpretation is concerned that distinction does not apply. Rather than sometimes

---

[2] Contrary to the suggestions of some writers. See M Walzer, *Interpretation and Social Criticism* (Harvard: Harvard University Press, 1987).

[3] Strictly speaking incompleteness of the law implies only that apart from their duty to apply law, courts also have the duty to settle disputes not settled by law. It takes additional arguments to establish that the courts can also make new law, and a separate argument still to show that they have authority to revise existing law. But such arguments are commonly advanced by theorists who accept the incompleteness of the law.

identifying the law as it is and sometimes making new law the courts seem always to interpret it.

Fourth, just as the validity of the distinction between identifying existing law and making a new one is inconsistent with the role of interpretation so is the widespread belief that the law is necessarily incomplete. Were it incomplete the courts would not be able to decide cases by interpreting the law. In fact—so some claim—all cases can be decided by legal interpretation and therefore the law is complete.

Fifth, and last, contrary to the view of many who believe that while moral matters are perhaps subjective, the law is objective, the fact that what is law is a matter of interpretation shows—according to some— that, since any object of interpretation allows for multiple interpretations, the law is subjective, that law, like beauty, is in the eye of the beholder.

These problems, and others like them, are not new. Various accounts of legal interpretation have been offered, each with its own solution to some of these problems. Some of these accounts may be true. It is quite likely that all of them contain some grains of truth. However, we cannot have confidence in any of them until we understand why interpretation is so central to the law, for only then will we be in a position to evaluate the different accounts of legal interpretation.

My aim here is the modest one of doing what I have started to do: to raise the question and convince you that it is a distinct question, not to be confused with the commonly discussed question of how one should interpret the law. As I've just said I do not believe that the question 'How to interpret?' can be answered without an answer to the question 'Why interpret?'

Legal theorists have tried to advance our understanding of legal interpretation by comparing it with interpretation in other spheres.[4] Such analogies can be very helpful in two respects: First, in exploring the nature of interpretation in general they help us avoid mistakes derived from assigning features specific to interpretation in one field to interpretation as such. Second, by comparing and contrasting interpretation in the law and elsewhere they help us understand what is specific to legal interpretation, the ways it differs from interpretation in other spheres. I too will draw analogies with interpretation in other fields, first to illustrate a few general features of interpretation and then to reflect on the special nature of legal interpretation.

---

[4] S Fish and R Dworkin have been particularly influential in their use of analogies between law and literature.

II

The general features of all interpretation which help understand how to deal with the question 'Why interpret?' are trivially obvious: First, every interpretation is of an object. Second, there can be good and bad (or better and worse) interpretations. Some interpretations are correct or incorrect (rather than good or bad). The general point, however, stands: Interpretations can be objectively evaluated regarding their success as interpretations. Third, there can be competing yet good interpretations of the same object. Often what passes for several interpretations does not amount to an affirmation of interpretive pluralism. Several interpretations may illuminate several different aspects of the same work. For example, one may concentrate on the iconography of a painting, the other on its formal structure. Both can be integrated in a single more complete interpretation of the painting. Interpretive pluralism is manifested by the fact that several competing interpretations can all be good interpretations: for example, that both Glenn Gould's and Wilhelm Kempff's interpretations of Beethoven piano sonatas can be excellent. Fourth, interpretations are judged good or bad by their ability to make people understand the meaning of their object.

I say that these features are trivially obvious even though some of them have been, and are being, keenly contested. Some people, for example, dispute that any interpretation can be truly said to be good or bad. They dispute that the success of interpretations is an objective matter. But features of concepts can be trivially obvious and in dispute at the same time. It is trivially obvious that the statements: 'I now realize that I was wrong in thinking that Richter's is the best interpretation of Liszt's Sonata in B-minor. In fact Brendel's is better,' are meaningful English statements. It is trivial—in other words—that it is part and parcel of the practice which constitutes the concept of interpretation that the success of interpretations is an objective matter. Those who dispute the objectivity of interpretations do not, or at any rate should not, deny that. As an analysis or description of the practice of interpretation their denial of the objectivity of interpretation flies in the face of obvious features of our practice. But it may be right, and it certainly should be taken seriously as a denial of the very possibility of our practice. Of course in a sense the practice exists, we interpret and we judge interpretations to be more or less successful. But for our practice to make sense and to have a point it has to be coherent, and its presuppositions have to be true. Claims that interpretations are not, and cannot be, objective challenge either the coherence or the presuppositions of our practice, and claim that the practice of interpretation cannot really make sense, or cannot really have a point unless it is changed to be a practice of subjective opinions: unless the practice we now have, which understands interpretations as objective, is reformed.[5]

It has to be admitted that the reforming nature of some philosophical accounts is not always clear. Some are motivated by a global, metaphysical worldview, for example by some form of physicalism. In trying to impose that picture on various philosophical issues, like that of the nature of interpretation, they sometimes vacillate between attempts to understand the phenomena in light of their metaphysical picture, claiming that the phenomena readily fit their picture and need no reinterpretation (such claims being sometimes accompanied by blindness to the very basic features of our practices), and claims that our concepts need reforming to conform to some allegedly true metaphysical doctrine; and there are other variants on these themes. For example, the objectivity of interpretation is sometimes challenged not in the cause of reforming our practices, but in denial that our practices treat interpretation as objective. Such denials are sometimes based on gross misunderstandings of our practices (e.g. equating statements like 'Brendel's interpretation is better than Richter's' with 'I (the speaker) like Brendel's performance better than Richter's').

Sometimes, however, philosophical denials of truisms like the four I mentioned are motivated by suspicion that claims that interpretation is 'objective' are not mere reports of aspects of our practices (eg that it is possible to like Richter's recording better than Brendel's, yet think that Brendel's is the better interpretation, or that considerations which may force one to admit that one was mistaken in judging Richter's to be the better interpretation may have no bearing on the correctness of the assertion that one likes his performance better). Philosophers sometimes suspect talk of objectivity to be deeply committed to a metaphysical picture which they reject, and therefore they deny that interpretation is, or can be, objective, not minding one way or another whether our practices

---

[5] Some may claim that they do not challenge our practice, rather that our understanding of the practice is their target. But that is a mistake. The practice includes commonplace observations like 'How can you say that the film is about the condition of modernity? It is pure entertainment and nothing more.' This is what it is for it to be an objective practice, ie a practice which admits of judgements of the success of interpretations, and regards them as either true or false.

establish its objectivity. As these remarks make plain I have little sympathy with this philosophical temperament. Metaphysical pictures are, when useful at all, illuminating summaries of central aspects of our practices. They are, in other words, accountable to our practices, rather than our practices being accountable to them.

I do not deny that some of our concepts may be incoherent. But while dogmatic conceptual conservatism is misguided, moderate conceptual conservatism is in place. Moderate conservatism postulates for any concept a presumption that that concept is coherent. In this chapter I will proceed on the basis of that presumption, and will find no reason to think that it is rebutted in the case of 'interpretation'.

In itself moderate conceptual conservatism does not resolve the tensions between various aspects of our concepts. And these tensions are the main difficulty in our attempt to develop an account of interpretation as a coherent activity. Particularly troubling is the tension between the objectivity of interpretation and interpretive pluralism, given the last of the mentioned features, namely that interpretations are judged by their success in elucidating or illuminating the meaning of their object.

Why should the fact that there can be several good interpretations of the same object be thought to be in tension with the objectivity of interpretation? There is no conflict or tension between pluralism and objectivity as such. There is, for example, no conflict between the existence of a plurality of distinct values and their objectivity. The conflict results from the fact that an interpretation is good only if it illuminates the meaning of its object. But as the meaning of the object is one, how can there be many good yet competing interpretations? If interpretations are subjective then the problem does not arise. In that case the meaning is in the eye of the beholder, and anything goes.

III

The way out of this *impasse*, the way to reconcile the existence of a multiplicity of competing interpretations with objectivity turns on the point which is often put metaphorically by saying that 'the meaning of the object is not in the object'. The helpful suggestion in the metaphor is this: if interpretation depends in part on something outside its object then possibly there are a plurality of such additional objects, and they will account for the plurality of good interpretations. Subjectivism, with its claim that any interpretation goes, is but one extreme way of understanding the metaphor. According to it the way any interpreter sees the object of interpretation at any time, as expressed in the interpretation, *determines* its meaning. That is why all interpretations are equally good. But the metaphor itself allows for more sensible accounts which identify other factors as those which in part determine the meanings of objects, and thus their proper interpretations.

This having been said I cannot but add that the metaphorical contrast between the internal and the external has often been the grave of good sense. First, there are those who take it to be an explanation rather than an obscure picture in need of an explanation. Second, sometimes the element 'external' to the object, and relevant to its interpretation, is said to be the conventions of interpretation or of meaning prevailing among one group of people or another.

The triumphalism which often accompanies this suggestion, and the implication that conventions were overlooked in pre-post-modern analysis is somewhat surprising. Since the decline of magic no one has ever doubted the dependence of language and other carriers of meaning on conventions. But in any case this suggestion would not do for it misconceives the relations between meaning and conventions of meaning. The existence of conventions of meaning in a certain population indicates that they all regard the same things as having the same meaning. Such conventions are necessary for communication, and indirectly they are necessary for anything to have meaning at all. But conventions are not grounds justifying one interpretation rather than another. Admittedly we can correctly say that 'sister' means female sibling, and add that everyone understands 'sister' to mean female sibling. That everyone so understands it *shows* that this is its right meaning but it is not *a reason* for it being the right meaning.

Contrast the following interpretive exchange about Shaw's play *Pygmalion*:

Interpreter: It is a play about transformations, and especially about the transformation of Eliza from a wild teenager into a mature woman.

Sceptic: Why do you say that? Why not prefer a more romantic interpretation?

Interpreter: Because my interpretation makes better sense of the relationship between Higgins and Eliza.

Here the reason supporting the interpretation 'it makes better sense of a relationship between two characters'—assuming for the sake of argument that it is a good reason, and adequate to its task—not only shows that this is a good interpretation of the play. It not only points to a presupposition of this being the meaning of the play, it also explains what makes it the meaning. And it makes it intelligible that it is the meaning of the play. It is what I'll call a constitutive reason. A constitutive reason is the fact (or facts) which makes the interpretation correct, and therefore the facts the understanding of which (whether conscious or not) enables one to understand the interpretation. *Since interpretations are successful to the extent that they illuminate the meaning of their objects they should be supported by constitutive reasons which show how they do so.*

Though time will not allow exploring the matter, this web of precepts: that interpretation is of *meaning*; that it not only establishes what the meaning is, but makes it transparent, that is *intelligible*, and that therefore interpretation is backed by *constitutive* reasons—marks the kind of interpretation we are interested in, the kind of interpretation which advances understanding and which is the special repository of art criticism, the humanities, and the social sciences. *For as far as we know there is meaning in the world only where it was invested with meaning by human beings.*

This fact probably accounts for the tenacity of the view that interpretation consists in retrieving the author's or the agent's intention. For if interpretation is of meaning and meaning is the result of human agency, does it not follow that it is the result of human intentions and therefore that the successful retrieval of those intentions is the mark of a good interpretation? As we know, this inference is invalid. Intentional action creates more (as well as—quite often—less) than is intended. What counts is what we express in our actions, and what the products of our actions express.

Shifting from talking of the meaning of actions, practices, or their products to what they express does not solve the puzzles of interpretation. However, since what we express is not necessarily what we mean to express it shows at least one way in which the meaning of what we do is not exhausted by what we intend it to mean. Yet from a broader perspective concentration on what actions or their products express commits the same fallacy that the intentionalist is guilty of. Both understand interpretation as a process of retrieving the meaning invested in the object by its creator.

Subjectivists by contrast stand at the other extreme. In holding that meaning is in the eye of the beholder they regard the receiver rather than the creator as the sole origin of meaning. Common sense suggests that both are wrong. The anthropocentric aspect of meaning and interpretation means that they are responsive to facts about human nature, as historically constituted, and to human interests. Neither of these is under the voluntary control of anyone.

So here is my summary preliminary statement of the key to interpretation: *an interpretation successfully illuminates the meaning of its object to the degree that it responds to whatever reasons there are for paying attention to its object as a thing of its kind.* This summary statement requires much careful unpacking, too long to undertake here. I will, however, return to it and modify it at the end of this chapter.

Think, by way of illustrating my point, of different reasons people may have, or believe they have, for understanding history. Some may view it as divinely ordained, and may study it to understand God's message to man as it reveals itself in history. Others may believe it to be deterministically dictated by physical/biological/economic factors and they may turn to history in order to predict the future. Others still may be interested in history as a repository of stories and characters they can identify with, regarding history as the font of their own identity. It seems plausible to suppose that these different reasons for historical interest: to understand God's message to man, to predict the future, and to make/discover one's own identity—it is plausible to suppose that these reasons will lead to somewhat divergent interpretations of various historical events and processes. Hence pluralism.

I am not using this example as an argument for pluralism. It is merely an illustration of the way different reasons for paying attention to history would lead to different interpretations of history. Hence it is no objection that it is unlikely that all three reasons I mentioned are valid ones. It is possible for them to be good reasons, and they may be valid simultaneously. This is all one needs to be able to use them—as I did—to illustrate the way a diversity of reasons can lead to interpretive pluralism, which is, of course, entirely consistent with the objectivity of interpretation: Reasons in general, and interpretive reasons are no exception, are objective factors, about which we can be right or wrong.

There are other ways in which the dependence of interpretation on reasons for paying attention to its object leads to interpretive pluralism. Given any single reason for paying attention to the object of interpretation there may be several different interpretations which satisfy the reason in some way and to some degree so that none of them is better than any of the others. This is another topic it is impossible to explore further here.

IV

With these general remarks in mind we can turn to the issues of legal interpretation. Interpretive pluralism understood by reference to the variety of reasons people have to be interested in the object of interpretation offers not only the possibility of a plurality of interpretations of any one object in any of the areas where interpretation is a central mode of understanding: law, the arts, sociology, and history in particular. It also opens the possibility that there are reasons which determine the nature of interpretation in one of them and are alien to the others. What then can we say about the reasons for the centrality of interpretation to legal reasoning?

Clearly there are *prima facie* reasons to think that they differ from the typical reasons which prevail in other areas. While law is like art in that typically it is made to be interpreted,[6] history, again typically, is not made to be interpreted.[7] This helps explain how the reasons for historical interpretation differ from reasons for artistic interpretation. Works of art can be created specifically in order to provide an object for the exercise of interpretive imagination. It would be a bizarre motive for a person to perform an act of historical interest with the sole aim that it be the object of interpretive imagination. In this respect law is of course like history and unlike art. There are other fairly obvious ways in which legal interpretation differs from art interpretation. It may be a matter of the taste of a particular period, but at least in some cultures novelty in art interpretation is valued in itself. The great interpreters are—other things being equal—those who can make us see the work interpreted in a new light. Think of Peter Sellars' interpretation of

---

[6] See on the relations between art and its interpretation my 'Interpretation without Retrieval', in A. Marmor (ed), *Essays on Legal Interpretation* (Oxford: OUP, 1995). See also A Danto, *The Transfiguration of the Commonplace* (Harvard: Harvard University Press, 1981); A Danto, *The Philosophical Disenfranchisement of Art* (New York: Columbia University Press, 1986). For example, in the latter book Danto observes that 'indiscernible objects became quite different and distinct works of art by dint of distinct and different interpretations, so I shall think of interpretations as functions which transform material objects into works of art' (39).

[7] Some historical events are caused with the intention that they will be understood in certain ways by some people: members of the government, those eligible to vote in the next general election, workers in manufacturing industries, etc. But few are caused with the intention that they will be interpreted in certain ways by the general public, now and in the future. When this happens we say—usually disapprovingly—things like: 'The president is now concerned only with his place in history.'

The Magic Flute set under a spaghetti junction in Los Angeles, or Jonathan Miller's *Rigoletto* set in Chicago in the 1920s. The very fact that we can talk of Sellars' *Magic Flute* or Miller's *Rigoletto* makes the point. There is no analogy for this in the law.

In legal interpretation we value—other things being equal—continuity. We also value authority, legal development and equity.[8] Continuity, authority, legal development, and equity provide the four foci of legal interpretation. But it is continuity and authority which hold the key to the question of my chapter, to the question: 'why interpret?' and in reflecting on them we may come closer to an understanding of the issues to which the question gives rise.

There is little need to belabour the role of authority in the law. The law is an institutionalized normative system, and in being institutionalized it is based on recognizing the authority of institutions to make, apply, and enforce laws.

Is not continuity merely a by-product of the legal role of authorities? Not at all. The importance of continuity in the law is manifested most of all by two central features. First is the fact that legislation and precedents remain binding long after their authors lost power. The life of the law is not bounded by the life of the law-makers. This endows the law with a considerable measure of continuity. Second, there is the role of legal doctrine. Legal doctrine provides a glue which binds different legal regulations together. It smoothes and polishes the law, regularizes what would otherwise be deviant, irregular aspects of legislation or precedents. Of course, these features are no barrier to legal upheaval in countries which undergo fast political change or suffer political instability.

What the law is, and how stable it is, are ultimately contingent on the circumstances of the country concerned. But these two features which in one form or another are present in all legal systems create a systematic bias in favour of continuity which is inherent in the law. They also show how continuity transcends and conflicts with authority: The first point shows how continuity extends the life of laws beyond the period during which they are to be respected through respect for the authority which issued them. The second point, the role of doctrine, shows how continuity can conflict with the power of legal authorities, and set limits to it.

---

[8] I am using 'equity' in a narrow sense to refer to considerations which affect the way rules are applied in particular circumstances, sanctioning deviations from 'the letter of the rules', which are not meant to lead to a modification or development of the rule.

These observations point to the inherent importance of continuity and authority in the law. They do not justify their importance, nor do they explain the function they perform. Nor do they show why they rather than legal development and equity help explain why so much legal reasoning is interpretive. To do all of that it is necessary to reflect on the essential role of the law in society—in as much as it is capable of being ethically justified. There can be no doubt that it is inherent in law that it aims to be ethically justified, and that every legal system claims to be by and large ethically justified. Since to understand the law we must understand the way the law understands itself, that is the way its officials and others who accept its legitimacy understand it, we must understand it as it would be understood by people who see it as ethically justified, at least in the sense that it is ethically right to obey it,[9] and therefore we must understand it as if it were so justified.

It follows that a general theory of legal interpretation, that is a theory which claims general validity, and is not merely an account of interpretation in one country or one family of countries, is necessarily based on the assumption that the law is justified, at least in the sense that it is justified to obey it. Its application depends on the assumption being correct, which it may not be. In that sense there is no theory of interpretation which is strictly speaking universal. The universal theory of interpretation is not a theory of how to interpret all law in any legal system. Rather, it is a theory of the interpretation of justified law only.

Can there be a general theory of legal interpretation, even one confined to justified legal systems? To be sure, the specific goals pursued by the law of any country are many and diverse, and that remains the case even if we restrict our concern to ethically justified systems only. But diverse as they are they share certain general characteristics: I hope that you will bear with me if I venture to offer a very brief and simplified sketch of a couple of points which emerge from this line of exploration.

First, all the measures adopted by law are measures which at the time and place at which the laws which embrace them were made were right for the law to embrace, or at least it is justified to treat them as if this condition is satisfied. If the condition is not satisfied then the laws embracing these measures will not be justified or it would not be

---

[9] One may consistently believe that it is morally justified to obey a law which is morally defective, and in need of reform.

justified to obey them (i.e. to treat them in practice as if they are justified, i.e. as one would treat laws which are justified), as we assume that it
is. This condition means that—other things being equal—the justification for treating laws as valid derives from the authority of their makers.
The laws pursuing the goals should be understood in a way which
accurately reflects the intentions of the law-makers in making them. The
reasoning behind this principle is simple: The very notion of practical
authority is that of a person or body deliberately deciding how things
should be done. The normal justification of authority assumes that people are better able to conform to reason by following the decisions made
by the authority. It follows that the law laid down by authority is that
which it meant to lay down, the law it intended.

Second, while the initial validity of a law normally derives from
the authority of its maker, this cannot explain its continued existence
beyond the point where that authority's rule runs. Take a law made at
the beginning of last century. No account of legitimate authority can
yield the conclusion that we are now subject to the authority of the long
defunct maker of that law. Yet the law it made may well still be valid, and
following it may be ethically justified. I suspect that the considerations
which account for this fact include the ethical importance of continuity. Continuity is ethically welcome for a variety of reasons, one being
the need to provide people with common standards for the guidance of
the members of the political society. This requires that the standards be
relatively stable.

V

This thumbnail sketch, oversimplified as it is, is I think along the right
lines and helps in seeing the role of our question 'why interpret?' in an
account of interpretation. Interpretation is of an object and is in place
when there is reason to be attached to the object. When it comes to
the law, that is to morally legitimate law, the thumbnail sketch shows
that that reason is the moral respect we owe to the object of interpretation. This is not the general reason for interpretation: the reasons for
our concern with the interpretation of history, and with the meaning of
historical events, are not due to respect for history. Nor is art interpretation motivated by moral respect for works of art. In as much as legal
reasoning is interpretive it is so because of moral respect for the law,
and for its sources.

Authority and continuity: the two factors which explain the reasons for the importance of interpretation are systematically related: To the extent that the law arises out of respect for legitimate authority, legal reasoning must establish the law as laid down by authority, that is it must rest on an interpretation of the decisions of legal authorities which accord with the intentions of those authorities. To the extent that the law arises out of the need to secure continuity, legal decisions are binding even when their authors no longer have authority. The content of these decisions is established by interpreting them as they were interpreted when the reasons for paying them attention were based on respect for the authorities which took them.

Authority and continuity provide the key to the question 'why interpret?' and as such they also guide us in how to interpret: We should interpret in ways responsive to the reasons we have for interpreting. But there are—as I have already indicated—other factors which though they provide no help with the question 'why interpret?' are crucial to the question 'how should we interpret?'. These are the role of the courts in the development of law and equity.

Since to be justified the law must be just to the people it is applied to, equity has an inescapable separate role in the application and enforcement of the law.

Just as justice requires the presence of a relatively stable framework of familiar principles by which individual and social life are governed, so it requires that the application of the principles to specific cases should be mediated by equity, to make sure that no injustice results from their application. For it is impossible to have general rules the application of which may not on occasion lead to injustice if not mitigated by equity. Equity is not always manifested through interpretive reasoning. Jury decisions in common law jurisdiction, which are rendered without making their reasons public, are an example of a mechanism which allows for the operation of equity, allowing it to take place not through interpretation.[10] However, equity can also be manifested in the way courts or others interpret authoritative decisions when confronted by the specific circumstances of a case litigated before them.

The moral need for equity to inform interpretation, combined with the tendency of institutions to develop routines, ie to develop a common

---

[10] Juries are expected to reason about the law, even though their reasoning is not made public. This means that in discharging their duties they do interpret the law. However, the absence of a requirement to make their reasons public enables them to rely on considerations of equity outside an interpretive framework.

law—broadly understood—generate the fourth major factor fashioning interpretation: the role of courts in the development of the law. Here too, just as with equity, different jurisdictions have different traditions regarding the ways the courts contribute to the development of the law. But that they have such a role is pretty universal.

The need to consider changing and developing the law to improve it, to adapt it to changing conditions, and to do justice to the litigants in the case before the court is a major influence on the way the law is interpreted. It is not, however, part of the answer to the question 'why interpret?'. On the contrary. So far as that question is concerned considerations of equity and the role of the courts in developing the law are considerations which militate against assigning interpretation a major role in legal reasoning. In themselves they would suggest that legal reasoning in the courts should have the same character as legislative reasoning. If these considerations were the dominant considerations dictating the character of judicial reasoning then it would have been the same as the reasoning on which legislation in parliaments or subsidiary legislative agency is based.

This point is worth pondering. It illustrates how the question 'why interpret?' is distinct, and should not be confused with the question 'how should we interpret?' It shows how factors which play a major role in determining the character of legal interpretation—equity and the role of the courts in developing the law—play no role in explaining 'why interpret?'. The reasons for conducting so much of legal reasoning as an interpretive reasoning are respect for authority and the case for continuity, and especially the first. The need for continuity plays a similar role in legislative reasoning, without giving it interpretive character. It is only in combination with the courts' respect for authority that it supports interpretive reasoning.

So the factors which determine the character of legal interpretation divide into two: authority and continuity, which provide the reason for interpretation as well as contributing to the determination of its character, and equity and the development of the law, which in themselves are no reason to interpret at all, but given that we have reason to interpret they contribute to the determination of its character. Moreover, the two types of factors are forever in conflict: authority and continuity militate towards a broadly speaking conservative attitude in interpretation, equity, and legal development—towards an innovatory attitude. This tension—in one form or another—is typical of all interpretation. Understanding it, and its sources, is at the centre of understanding what makes interpretation what it is.

VI

The conflict between the conservative and the innovatory factors in legal interpretation takes us back to some issues left behind earlier in this chapter. First, my preliminary statement of the nature of successful interpretation (see p 231 above) was cast in terms of the reasons one has for paying attention to the object of interpretation as a thing of its kind. It may seem that this characterization leaves no room for any considerations to govern the conduct of interpretation which are not also reasons for interpreting in the first place. According to this understanding one cannot maintain that equity and legal development are reasons which guide the interpretation of the law while denying that they provide reasons for interpreting the law.

I think that both the objector and I are correct on this matter. We simply need a further distinction to reconcile the two opposing claims. Given that authority and continuity provide reason to pay attention to the law, equity and legal development become additional reasons to pay it attention in a certain way, or in the light of certain considerations. They are secondary reasons for interpreting the law, dependent on the primary reasons, in that had there not been the primary reasons which determine the need to interpret the law, the secondary reasons would not have been reasons for interpreting it at all. But given that there are primary reasons for interpretation, they attract, or generate, additional, secondary reasons for interpretation. My earlier characterization of a successful interpretation refers to all the reasons for paying attention to the object of interpretation, be they primary or secondary. In the discussion of legal interpretation, however, I drew the distinction between the conservative reasons which motivate interpretation in the first place, and the innovatory reasons which are secondary reasons for interpretation.

The conflict between the two groups of considerations takes us back also to the five issues about the nature of law with which I started, and to which I will briefly return in these concluding remarks. The dependence of law on authority explains why much of legal reasoning is interpretive, whereas moral reasoning is not. Morality is not based on authority. The dependence on authority leads to the need to interpret the decisions of authority: and that is the basic object of legal interpretation. The other factors I mentioned—continuity, equity, and

legal development—are all factors in the interpretation of authoritative acts and decisions. One often neglected question is what is legal
interpretation an interpretation of? Is it an interpretation of the law,
of legal texts, or legal acts? No doubt all of these are subject to interpretation on one occasion or another, and no doubt often it does not
matter which is being interpreted. But some clarity is gained by being
clear as to what is the primary object of legal interpretation. If authority and continuity provide the answer to the question 'why interpret?'
then the decisions of legal authorities are the primary objects, and
through interpreting them we gain understanding of the content of
the law, which they create.

This reveals what some would regard as a paradox: If legal reasoning
establishes what the law is by interpreting authoritative decisions this
can only mean that its purpose is to reveal the intention of the authorities which took these decisions. It follows that there is no room in legal
interpretation for equity or for considerations of legal development.
This apparent paradox accounts for some misguided theories of law:
Some emphasize the innovatory aspect of interpretation and—under the
influence of moral subjectivism—tend towards subjectivist pluralism
in their understanding of law. Others restrict legal interpretation to its
conservative elements, which are usually crudely understood in theories
such as originalism. Others still, realizing rightly that interpretation is
neither wholly conservative nor wholly innovative, deny that the distinction between identifying existing law and creating a new one is coherent,
or that it plays a central role in the functioning of courts of law. But no
one has succeeded in offering an account of interpretation which does
not rely—openly or surreptitiously—on that distinction in explaining
legal interpretation. Nor can such an account be found. The distinction between identifying the law and changing it is basic to the law, and
central to any coherent understanding of judicial decision-making. It is
equally important to realize that both aspects—the conservative and the
innovatory—are present in legal interpretation just as they are present
in the interpretation of *Hamlet* or of *Don Giovanni*. It is equally crucial
to understand that the two elements introduce a tension into the factors which direct judicial decisions, a tension which expresses itself in
the problems I mentioned at the outset: How can the law form a stable
guide for people's actions if it is subject to innovatory interpretation?
How can there be a fact of the matter as to what the law is if there can be
a plurality of valid interpretations?

These are good questions which require carefully balanced answers. The questions arise out of the fundamental conflict in legal interpretation I have diagnosed. Their answers lie in recognizing the inescapability of this conflict in the law. It arises from the fact that due to the basic nature of human societies law and adjudication must fulfil several functions, and therefore even an ideal law cannot fulfil all of them in an ideal fashion.

10

Interpretation Without Retrieval

When interpreting we explain, show, or display the meaning of the object of interpretation ('the original', as I will refer to it). Interpretation is therefore often thought to be retrieval, a process of retrieving and elucidating the meaning the original has. After all, if interpretation is a display or an explanation of the meaning of an original, that original must have meaning to be capable of being interpreted, and interpretation is the retrieval of that meaning, making it plain to those who might be unaware of it. The role of an author's, or, more generally, a creator's intention in interpretation is closely connected with the retrieval picture. If interpretation is retrieval it is often tempting to think that the only thing there to retrieve is the intention of the creator.

The purpose of this chapter is to show that the ideas associated with the retrieval picture are mistaken or misleading. I have chosen to concentrate on interpretation of works of art, music, and literature for two reasons. First, such works are among the paradigmatic objects of interpretation. Secondly, we are all familiar with good interpretations of such works which are innovative, and therefore appear to be at odds with the view of interpretation as retrieval.

I will offer an abstract account of the interpretation of works of art, music, and literature[1] which can, I hope, be modified to apply to other standard objects of interpretation (eg the law, historical events, rituals, and social customs). That account allows for a more balanced view of the different ways in which authors' intentions can play a role in interpretation.

I. Levels of Meaning

It is convenient to distinguish broadly between three types or levels of question about the meanings of works of art and literature. At one

[1] I will often use 'art' in its broad sense to include music and literature.

end there is the question of the significance of the fact that a work of a certain kind was created, or became popular at a certain time, as well as other questions about its reception and influence. These questions shade into historical issues, which may not be about meaning and interpretation at all, or which may concern the interpretation of a culture or its mood at a particular time. Those of them which deal with the interpretation of the work of art call for conserving interpretations, that is they deal with interpreting how other people interpreted the work: 'What did the Romantics see in the Don Giovanni story?', 'How did attitudes to McCarthyism influence the reception of Miller's *The Crucible* at the time of its first performance?', and so on. This level of meaning has little to contribute to our enquiry.

For the purposes of this chapter I will distinguish two levels of meaning which I will call 'deep' and 'basic' meaning, though one should not make anything of the choice of these terms. The basic meaning of a work concerns the question of the subject of the work ('a portrait of Alexander VI') or its literal content ('Is this Salomé holding the head of John on a platter?', 'What do the words of a poem mean?', and so on). The identification of a work's subject and literal meaning does give rise to interpretive issues and there is an understandable feeling that if nowhere else surely here the author's intention reigns supreme. Take portraiture: is it not the case that if Giacometti makes a sculpture which he declares to be the portrait of Annette then a portrait of Annette it is? It is made so by being baptized by him as such, and nothing else counts. I will return to this argument later. To begin with I will focus on the deep level of meaning. It is captured by observations such as: 'the painting portrays the compassion of the Christian victors towards the vanquished Muslims', 'the play contrasts the new sophisticated metropolitan culture with the crudity of the traditional mores of the provinces', 'the music is an expression of the passion of love, followed by the depths of despair when it is not requited', and so on. This distinction between the levels of meaning and interpretation is not a sharp one, but it can render useful service for many purposes, including ours. The deep, more than literal meaning is the subject of most discussions of the meaning of works of art. 'Why did Hamlet turn against Ophelia?'; 'Did Hamlet's delay in revenging his father expose an ambivalence in his attitude to his father?', etc. These questions are the standard stuff of critical discussions in art and literature. Are such questions illuminated by the picture of interpretation as retrieval? Are they to be settled by reference to the author's intention?[2]

II. From Intention to Expression

If interpretation explains or displays the meaning of the work being interpreted, what meaning can a work of art have other than that given it by its creator? One answer which springs to mind is both right and inadequate. Meaning, we may say (indeed people have said), just like beauty, is in the eye of the beholder. The performer or spectator, in interpreting the work, is displaying or explaining a meaning which he sees in it.[3] This is correct as far as it goes, and the implication that the meaning he sees in it may not have been put there by the author, or anybody else, may be correct as well. But it is false to conclude that the interpreter can find any meaning whatsoever in the work. Interpreting a work of art differs from reacting to it as to a Rorschach test, or from being inspired or moved by it to have or express certain thoughts, emotions, or attitudes. A sculptor may be inspired by the grain of a block of marble in carving a piece of sculpture out of it. But that would not make the sculpture into an interpretation of the block of marble.

Part of what is missing is an intention to interpret.[4] But what is that intention if not the intention to display, state, or explain the meaning of the work, that is the meaning it in some sense already has? So we are back to square one. If interpretation requires an intention to bring out the meaning the work has is it not a process of retrieval, and what can there be to retrieve other than what was put into the work by the intention of its author?

The first step towards liberation from the power of the intention paradigm is to note that even interpretations which take the creator's attitudes as the key to success are not confined to viewing interpretation as a retrieval of the author's intention. We need to distinguish the

---

[2] Whether or not every work of art has meaning at one or both of these levels is a question which will not be taken up here.

[3] To guard against the mistaken assumption that the interpreter must believe that the work has one correct or best interpretation I refrain from saying that he explains or displays the meaning he sees in it.

[4] In 'Morality as Interpretation: on Walzer's *Interpretation and Social Criticism*' (1991) 101 *Ethics* 392, I have argued that one interprets only if one intends to do so (under this or some other description).

meaning of a work to its author, the meaning he intends it to have, and the views, emotions, attitudes, and so on that he expresses in it.

The meaning of a work to its author can differ from the meaning he intended to express in it in several ways. It may mean something to him because of his memories of events in his life associated with the time of its creation, or publication, and so on, or because of its success with the public, or because of his ultimately unsuccessful struggle to express his vision of this or that in it. It may come to be for him a record of his failure or success. Typically the work may also mean something to the author because of what it and the process of its making reveal to him about himself. Just as the work can mean something to its author, so it can mean various things to other people, who saw the work for the first time on their honeymoon, whose life was transformed by an experience in which it played a role, or in many other ways.

The question is whether what the work means to its author is special in fixing (at least in part) the meaning of the work. But in all cases what the work means to its author, just like what it means to anyone else, is distinct from, and external to, the meaning the work has. When someone says 'this work means a lot to me', or 'it has a special meaning for me', and we ask 'what does it mean to you?', the answer is not, nor can it be 'it means to me that Hamlet felt frustrated at having lost his mother a second time, first to his father and now to his uncle'. That may be (part of) what *Hamlet* means, and our interlocutor may be aware of that, but it cannot be what it means to him, nor what it meant to Shakespeare or to anyone else. It is rather the meaning he, or they, see in it.[5]

So the meaning of the work is different from what it means to its creator. Is it what he intended it to mean? Why should it be that? Presumably because that is what works of art and literature are. They are vehicles for people to express their views, attitudes, emotions, feelings about beauty, and so on. Whatever else art is, the argument goes, it is a framework, a language for self-expression and for communicating one's thoughts, feelings, and the like by expressing them. But if this is so then the author's intention does not always prevail in interpretation,

---

[5] Possibly this exaggerates the degree to which 'what does the work mean to X?' can only be answered by reference to X's personal experience of it and personal associations with it. This and kindred expressions range from a usage which excludes what X takes the work to mean, to a usage in which they refer primarily to the meaning which X believes the work to have (as in 'what did *The Sorrows of Werther* mean to the Romantics?'), and on many occasions they refer both to the meaning X believes the work to have, and to the personal associations connected with it.

for what authors of works of art and literature express in their work is not always what they intend to express. They may be surprised by what they learn about themselves from reading, watching, or listening to the works they created. A work can express guilt about one's attitude to one's parents which the author never suspected that he felt. (Is *Don Giovanni* a case in point?)

If the underlying thought is that art is a vehicle for self-expression then authors' intentions are important, but they by no means dominate interpretation. Should we then opt for the view that the work means that which the author expressed in it? If we do we should not do so for lack of rival ways of understanding the meaning of works of art. Clearly some interpretations can proceed without reference to what an author expressed, if only because we can interpret customs, rituals, ceremonies, and such things which do not have authors. Such ceremonies, rituals, and their like can be conveniently called 'cultural objects' to mark the fact that—in some sense yet to be explained—they possess their meaning within cultures. Flying or waving a flag expresses pride in or loyalty to one's nation only within a culture or against the background of a culture in which such acts bear this meaning.

One mistake to avoid is to regard the interpretation of cultural objects as a conserving interpretation. First, it is useful to remember that the fact that cultural objects have the meaning they have only against the background of certain practices does not mean that their meaning is the meaning they have in the eyes of any particular person, or of the majority of people in the society in which the practices obtain. The meaning of cultural objects is not to be reduced to a statistical fact. It is related to the meaning people believe cultural objects to have, but it does not follow that all aspects of their meanings are understood or known to everyone or to many. Secondly, while we can always look for conserving interpretations such as 'What did a work mean to the Victorians?', conserving interpretations are always secondary or parasitic on non-conserving ones. It is always possible that the two questions: 'What is the meaning of the work?' and 'What is or was the meaning of the work to this public or that, or at this period or that?' have the same answer.[6] But they are always two different questions. Ours is the former.

---

[6] It may even be a necessary truth that any statement of the form 'this is the meaning (or one meaning or part of the meaning) of the work' is true only if there is a public or a period for which it is its meaning. We will return to this question later.

Works of art, I will argue in the next section, are cultural objects and as such their interpretation is, in principle, independent of the intention of their creator. Later sections will qualify this conclusion. But before we embark on the main argument a brief clarification of its relation to the view of art as a vehicle for self-expression is in place. First, the strong view I have put forward above, that is that it is the essence of art to provide vehicles for self-expression, is at best misleading, and possibly wrong. It is wrong if it suggests that necessarily artists create artworks in order to express themselves. They can do so to fulfil a commission, aiming to meet detailed specifications and bringing only their skills to the task. They can make randomly produced works, or use 'ready-mades' in order to make theoretical points about the nature of art. And there are other ways in which the self-expression view understood in that way can fail. More importantly, whatever truth there is in it has to accommodate the following distinctions:

The attitudes, emotions, or views which the work expresses need not be those that its creator expressed in it, and what its creator expressed in it differs from those attitudes, emotions, and views for whose existence in the author it contains evidence. To start from the end, a psychologist, or just anyone who knows the artist or author, can find the work revealing in the way in which slips of the tongue or malapropisms are. In our actions, and in the products of our actions, we betray our thoughts and feelings in a variety of ways, and not only through expressing them. Furthermore, an artist can create a work or write a poem expressing passionate love or anything else without feeling such emotions or having such thoughts. As I have just remarked, it may simply be his commission to do so. It is then true that he has created a work which expresses these feelings and thoughts, and in a sense, that he has found a way, or invented a way, of expressing such thoughts or feelings. But it is not the case that he has expressed himself or his feelings or thoughts in the work. He expressed himself or his feelings and thoughts only if he felt or thought what the work expresses. So we need to understand what the work expresses, what it means, independently of what its creator expressed in it.

III. Works of Art as Cultural Objects

Works of art not only may become, they are meant to become cultural objects. It is the nature of works of art and literature that they are cultural objects, in the sense that they are judged by their success as cultural objects. Let me explain. One aspect of the concept of art is that works of art are meant to be of interest to people who are not merely interested in their creator. They are meant to be of a wider interest, in the sense that their success is judged by the degree and the way in which they do deserve such wider interest. A very bad work of art may still be of great interest to the friends or relations of its creator, for it may be every bit as revealing of his life or personality as a good work. No one else need pay it any attention, if—as we are assuming—it is a bad work of art in all relevant respects. Nor is the general significance of works of art, that is their interest beyond any interest in the author, to be confused with their significance as historical evidence of the mores of the time, of the language of their day, evidence of the eating habits, and so on, of one period or another. Their general significance, which makes them into cultural objects, is in what they express or represent, in their meaning when that is understood to exclude what they express about the author.

The fact that works of art are cultural objects with cultural meaning does not entail, but goes well with, a further feature of art, namely that they are meant to be understood in a relatively context-independent way. I should heavily underline the word 'relatively' in this sentence. Much of the meaning of a work of art may be missed by someone who is unaware of the fact that it was created under severe censorship, or shortly after widespread race riots, or in a literary tradition which valued allusions to Greek myths and literature, and so on and so forth. Context is highly relevant to the appreciation of the meaning of artworks. But the context which is relevant is the public context. The reader–listener–spectator is not expected to know that the work's creator has moved house, that his cousin has recently been divorced, or that his first child has reached school age. Such events may have greatly influenced the work he produced (and his biographers may dwell on them), but while the work may have special appeal to people who have experienced or are interested in changing places, divorce, separation, loss of love, joy in children, and the like, the meaning of the work must be available to those who have no knowledge of the circumstances of its creator. I will refer to this point by saying that the meaning of a work of art depends on its public context, but not on its private context. This means that its success is to be judged by reference to what it expresses as it can be understood without reference to the circumstances of the author's life.[7]

---

[7] Can there be a convention to the contrary, ie a convention that the work is to be understood as, say, a lament on lost love—and judged by the degree to which it is good as such, only if the author suffered such loss before writing the work? Not really.

The convention that the meaning of the work is to be available to people without reference to the private context[8] is consistent with the fact that artworks are necessarily works deliberately created by their authors. This may suggest an analogy with the general argument for the intention thesis regarding legislation.[9] Artists, like legislators know (when they do)[10] that the meaning of their work is that which can be gauged without regard to the private context, and therefore they will create works which have the meaning they intend when so understood. But the analogy, while valid, disguises a basic difference between artworks and legislation. This fundamental feature of art, that artworks are meant to carry meaning to people who have no interest in their creator, makes the intentions of the artists relatively unimportant. What counts is the work of art. If an artist attracts our admiration it is because he or she produces great art. We often suspect that some admire certain artworks for no reason other than that they were made by a famous or fashionable artist. But it is commonly agreed that this is a perversion of the proper appreciation of art. Even those who are guilty of it know as much, and disguise their true reasons, sometimes even from themselves.

An enactment, on the other hand, is binding not because its content is exceptional, but because it was promulgated by this person or body, which is endowed with authority to legislate. Legislation is to be interpreted in accordance with convention because this is the way of establishing the intention of the law-maker. Art is to be understood independently of the private context of its creation because what counts is its public meaning. If this meaning is the one intended by the artist, so be it. But if the work brings out something in the artist which even he is unaware of, and the expression of which is publicly perceived, and becomes crucial to the interpretation, that is to the common understanding of the work, this belittles neither this understanding of the work nor the work's merit.

This dual independence of art from the artist (its meaning is meant to be relevant to people who are uninterested in the artist, and is determined independently of the private context of its creation) is crucial to

---

[8] Though there is no denying that it may reveal itself more readily to those aware of the private context of its creation.

[9] I am here relying on chapter 11, 'Intention in Interpretation'.

[10] Which need not be the case. Many artworks were made in civilizations which did not have the concept of art, and did not conceive of them as art. Many works were created in civilizations which did have the concept, by so-called primitive artists who did not think of their work as art.

an explanation of the role of interpretation in determining the meaning of works of art. But it has to be supplemented by another feature. In the main the aspects of the context which determine the meaning of works of art can be divided into two: first, the state of the art in question; and secondly, other reflections on or representations of the meaning of human life, man's place in the world, and aspects of human experience. The relevance of the first type of contextual feature, which includes technical developments such as use of pigments, musical instruments, methods of projection such as perspective, or techniques of amplification, iconographic conventions, narrative techniques, and their like, is inescapable given that the arts are identified, classified, and therefore understood by their techniques and by the skills that they display. The relevance of the second type of feature derives in part from the public nature of art, that is, from its dual independence of the artist. This makes it natural to expect its meaning to be in the portrayal and expression of matters of relevance to human beings in general.

This consideration, however, does not fully account for the involvement of art with the 'higher' meanings of human life. It is an aspect of art which can only be explained historically, by reference to the way the concept of art developed. In the West the arts of the modern era, and the concept of art, grew out of the traditions of Christian art. In Medieval Europe what we recognize as art was, as life generally was meant to be, created for the glory of God. It re-enacted, and where appropriate celebrated, in icons the stories which embodied the meaning of human existence, and of divine existence and intervention. When in early modern Europe some of the crafts of the Middle Ages were separated in status and in the understanding of their meaning from the rest and elevated to the status of 'Art', they kept their significance as expressing and speaking about the meaning of human life, of the world, its tribulations and triumphs, social and metaphysical. The further they appeared to stray from this self-conception towards a view of art for art's sake only, the closer they approached it. For the art-for-art's-sake movement is associated, and not by accident, with the most extravagant claims ever made for art and artistic beauty as being the quintessentially human value, supreme in its ability to endow human life with meaning.

A resulting standing temptation is the 'high' view of art. It holds that the difference between 'art' and the crafts which lie outside its boundary is that it expresses and represents views on and attitudes to nature and to human life. But while much art does so, this feature cannot be used as part of its definition. The distinction between art and the merely decorative (allegedly the only aesthetic property of wallpaper, and all other 'mere' artefacts) does not apply to music and to some other areas in the arts. This having been said, it has also to be pointed out that art is biased towards the 'higher' meaning in a specific way: it is always legitimate to see any work of art as expressing an attitude to life or experience, to nature or God, if its content when seen against the context of its creation will bear this meaning. It is judged as merely decorative only if no such understanding of it is possible.

In this section I have argued that works of art are cultural objects, and that therefore their interpretation is relatively independent of the intentions of their creators. Being cultural objects in this context means that they can legitimately be seen as bearers of meaning for their culture, that is be judged as good or bad depending—in part—on their meaning (bad works of art, or insignificant ones, may have 'no meaning'). Having a meaning for a culture means being a suitable object of certain attitudes, responses, and uses. Meaning and interpretation are reciprocal notions. Interpretation is the elucidation of a meaning, and what has meaning which is not trivially obvious can be interpreted. It follows that an essential feature of the arts is that works of art can be interpreted. The arts come with interpretive traditions, the meaning of works of art can be perceived only by those who, through familiarity with these traditions, can interpret, that is come to understand, their meanings.

The connection between art and its interpretation is neither trivial nor accidental. It is no accident that one cannot interpret a kitchen sink in the kitchen, but that a kitchen sink in an art gallery, or otherwise presented or used as art, calls for interpretation. There is much more to art than interpretation, but there is no art without interpretation, and there is no art without a practice of the interpretation of works of art. The sense in which this is so has to be carefully stated. Clearly many works of art were created at times and in cultures in which there was nothing resembling our traditions of art interpretation. Many were created in cultures which did not recognize the notion of art itself. The good sense in the remark that there is no art without interpretation is that our understanding of art makes all works of art suitable objects of interpretation of a certain kind, art interpretation. Therefore, in recognizing works as works of art we recognize them as objects of interpretation of that kind, whether or not they were so regarded by their creators or by their early public. As a result, we can focus on these works in our attempts to understand the meaning of the cultures in which they were born and of life in those cultures.

IV. Basic Meaning in Art and Literature

Granting the argument of the previous section, is it not the case that meaning and interpretation there discussed presuppose a more basic meaning, meaning in the sense used when we say that the ermine in Leonardo's portrait of Cecilia Gallerani (in Cracow) symbolizes the sitter,[11] or that blue in Italian Renaissance Madonna paintings symbolizes the subject's virginity, or that 'vanished power of the usual reign' in TS Eliot's 'Ash Wednesday' refers to the speaker's declining powers at the end of his life. I will refer to meaning in this sense as the 'basic meaning' of elements of the work, and contrast it with the 'deeper' meaning of the work as a whole or of parts or aspects of it as discussed in the previous section.

The case for the sovereignty of author's intention seems stronger with regard to the interpretation of basic meaning. Two points militate in that direction. First, works of art and literature are intentional creations. In the normal case only what is made to be a novel or a poem or a painting and so on is a novel or a poem or painting and so on. As Duchamp's urinal reminds us, sometimes what makes a work of art is no more than that an object has been christened by its author (that is, its author as a work of art, who need not have made the physical object itself) *as* a work of art. It has been noted in the previous section that this point is not without exception. We are used to co-opting into art works produced in cultures or subcultures where the notion of art did not exist, or where the authors did not think of their creations as art. But this co-option can be understood only as an exceptional extension of the application of the notion of a work of art.

Secondly, the boundaries of the work are determined by its creator. Whether or not a piece of dialogue is part of *Henry V* depends on whether Shakespeare intended it to be part of that play. Given that Anselm Kiefer wanted the frame to be part of his painting, it is part of

---

[11] According to Kenneth Clark it is doubly symbolical of her identity: first, because the ermine was frequently used as Ludovico's emblem, and secondly, because the Greek for ermine has a punning reference to her name. Kenneth Clark, *Leonardo Da Vinci* (Harmondsworth: Penguin, 1939) 54. To understand this reference one had to know Greek and to know that Gallerani was Ludovico's mistress at the time of the painting. This shows the elasticity of the contrast between the public and the private contexts I have been relying on. Given that the portrait was painted for her, and was to be seen by her family and friends, what was common knowledge to them was the public context against which the portrait was to be interpreted.

the painting. Admittedly, the answer can be far from straightforward. Did Aristophanes intend his later revisions of *The Clouds* to be part of the play? He may have intended them to be part of a version of the play to be read, but not to be part of a performing version.[12] But that does not mean that the boundaries of the work are not determined by its creator. It merely shows that sometimes there is no simple answer to the question 'what are the boundaries of this work?'.

Given that works of art are meant to be intentionally created, and that their boundaries are created by their authors, can we make sense of the basic meaning of any work except by reference to its author's intention? The problem with this argument is that it runs counter to the basic feature of art highlighted in the previous section, that works of art belong to the domain of cultural objects, to be understood independently of the private context of their creation. This aspect of art applies to its basic meaning as much as to its deeper meaning.

In Italian Renaissance paintings of the Madonna the blue of her dress symbolizes her virginity. We know this because we know the public meaning of the iconography of those paintings. We need know nothing about the intentions of the painter. Admittedly, the assumption is that the painter knew that and used blue to refer to the virginity of the Madonna, but he may have been a hack painter who knew of the meaning of the colour but cared little. He may even not have known—though in fact this is unlikely. He may have painted her dress blue because that is how it is done, and his patron will complain if he does not follow convention. He may not have cared about what it signified, and may have had no intention of signifying anything. Regardless of that, the Madonna's blue dress in the painting does symbolize her virginity. The patron could not have complained that he was offered a painting of the Madonna lacking a reference to her virginity. He could not have complained that, though the dress was blue, it did not refer to her virginity for the painter did not intend it to do so.

We see in this the difference between art and the law. In the law, *prima facie*, the fact that the text is interpreted contrary to the law-maker's intentions denies it legitimacy. Its legitimacy derives from the authority of the law-maker to make the law it judged right to make. The application of this argument is both limited and indirect.[13] But it

---

[12] Aristophanes *Clouds* (ed KJ Dover, Oxford: OUP, 1958) xcviii. I am grateful to Dr Bulloch for having drawn my attention to this example.

[13] See, on the case for the role of intention in legal interpretation, Chapter 11 'Intention in Interpretation'.

is always there in the background of any interpretation of enacted law. Not so interpretation in the arts. The autonomy of works of art means that the author's intention can be said to be irrelevant to the interpretation of his work, except where there are special considerations to take it into account.

Can this conclusion be reconciled with the fact that works of art are intentional creations, whose boundaries are determined by their author? It can, for it leaves untouched the basic understanding of art and literature as fields of human self-expression, which is at the core of the fact that it is of the essence of art that works of art are normally products of intentional creation. Art bears a dual relation to self-expression. Being cultural objects makes works of art both works through which their creators can express themselves, and works which provide a focus for reflection, emotion, and even identification for their public. Members of the public express themselves through their relations to the works.

This statement should be cautiously interpreted. First, it does not subscribe to an expressionist view of art. It refers to expressing beliefs about the glory of god, the order of the angels, the piety of a donor, as well as to the despair of frustrated ambition or love, or of the futility of human life, or of the overpowering joy of conquest, and other more conventional subjects of expressionism in the arts. Secondly, it is not meant to deny that much art is created by craftsmen or even hacks who work to a formula and express nothing. Nor does it deny that many works never see the light of day, as they remain confined to drawers or cellars, and many others are stillborn, never becoming an object of contemplation or identification to anyone. Yet I am saying more than that sometimes they do serve as vehicles of self-expression to their author and public. That much is true about almost everything. Art works are meant to be vehicles of self-expression. They are evaluated in part by the degree to which they are good vehicles for self-expression.

This both assures the connection between works of art and their creator's intention, and secures their distance from it. It is open to people to make works which will express what they intend to express. That possibility is assured by the fact that they intentionally create the work and determine its boundaries. Since it is what they make it, they can—in principle—make it mean what they want it to mean. But to do that they have to take note of what makes works of art mean one thing or another, and in the light of that make the work so that it will have the meaning they want it to have. They cannot make it mean something just by intending it to mean that. Nor can they deny it a meaning simply by not having it in mind.

V. Interpretation as Discovery

The argument so far has undermined the case for author's intention as the foundation of interpretation. It has done little either to challenge the broader conception of interpretation as retrieval, or to explain the nature of interpretation of works of art. To do both we should concentrate on the test case of innovative interpretation. How is it possible? If interpretation is retrieval, how can it be new? If it is not, what is the difference between a novel interpretation of a work and reacting to it as to a Rorschach test?

The retrieval picture offers an answer through a threefold distinction: there are two ways in which an interpretation can be new, and one in which it cannot. It can be a new statement of a familiar meaning, a new way of articulating it. An illuminating simile, a striking phrase, a bold statement of a familiar meaning strikes home precisely because it articulates a familiar point in such a strikingly new way. This kind of novelty, novelty in articulation, is possible and often attractive. It is different from an innovative interpretation which assigns a new meaning to the work. Such interpretations are inconsistent with the retrieval picture. Interpretation is a retrieval of the meaning the work has. It cannot reveal in it a meaning it did not have before.

It is, however, the third way of being innovative which is the most interesting. An interpretation may do no more than retrieve the meaning that was always there, and yet its novelty may not be just in re-describing a familiar meaning in a fresh way. It may rather be a matter of revealing a meaning which was so far hidden. When *Hamlet* was first given a psychoanalytic interpretation that did not give it a new meaning. Rather, it claimed to display the meaning of the play by explaining Hamlet's motivation as it has always been—what else can it be? After all, the play has not changed with the advent of psychoanalysis. So the motivation of its characters and the meaning of its action cannot change either. An interpretation can only retrieve and disclose what is there already. It is innovative when that meaning was hidden from sight. There are innovative interpretations, but there are no new meanings. On the retrieval model, innovative interpretation is a discovery of a hitherto unknown meaning.

The case of the psychoanalytic interpretation of *Hamlet* illus-trates this idea. It is an example of how innovative interpretation is arrived at (at least some of the time). The 'discovery' of psychoanalysis makes possible novel interpretations of many works of art. We can now reinterpret *Hamlet* as the working out of an Oedipal complex, or something like that. It is fairly clear how innovative interpretations are possible in such cases: the discovery of the truth of some general theory, or just of a general truth about people, reveals that certain facts about the interpreted work which were not seen as significant before are significant. Interpretation consists in pointing to connec-tions and analogies. The test of a good interpretation is that those connections and interrelations are significant in terms of, or by refer-ence to, some general theory or general truths about people, society, or whatever. An interpretation is innovative if the significance of the aspect of the work highlighted by it has not been appreciated before, and this is most commonly due to the fact that the general truths were not known before.

Sometimes new interpretations are not prompted by new discov-eries of general truths, but by a novel realization of how some known truths bear on the events of a story or the features of some other works. We come to recognize that the work instantiates known general propositions in ways not hitherto realized. Sometimes authors deliber-ately disguise clues to the significance of their work, and only with time does their work yield its secrets.[14]

There is some truth in this picture of innovative interpretation as discovery. No doubt many new interpretations are new in the way described. Yet this cannot be the full story. It regards innovative inter-pretations as discoveries of hidden meaning. This was the meaning of *Hamlet* all along, although no one knew it until Freud. But the idea of hidden meaning, meaning hidden not from some but from all, is puz-zling. How can this be the meaning of *Hamlet* if *Hamlet* did not have that meaning for anyone? Can there be an expression in English that has a meaning which is hidden and unknown, awaiting discovery? Why should things be different with works of art? The idea of hidden mean-ing seems odd there as well.

---

[14] I am glossing over many complications: eg, does the significance of the Ghost in *Hamlet* depend on whether there are ghosts? Or is it the same whether or not there are ghosts, since it depends only on whether Shakespeare believed in ghosts, or perhaps whether he expected his audience to believe in them?

The discovery view of interpretation makes it too much like a scientific explanation or interpretation. The discovery of special relativity explains the deviation of Mercury from the course predicted by Newtonian physics. Here interpretation means just that: explanation of an event as an instance of a general law. But that is not an explanation of the meaning of the event. It is just an explanation of the event. The interpretations we are after are explanations of meaning. But if innovative interpretations can be arrived at simply by realizing how general truths are instantiated in the interpreted work, what is wrong with the discovery view of interpretation? What does it leave out?

We can be helped here by examining some of the ways in which interpretations can be criticized. Some criticism is fairly straightforward: our belief that a psychoanalytic interpretation of *Hamlet* is not a very good one may be due to doubts about psychoanalysis, or to a feeling that that interpretation leaves too much of the play outside its ambit, thus making it incomplete, or that the story of *Hamlet* does not fit analytic theory and does not warrant the construction put on it.

There is, however, an additional and far less obvious way of criticizing an interpretation. Imagine someone offering the absurdity of a physics-based interpretation of *Hamlet*. His interpretation consists in showing that all the events described in the play are consistent with physics and that all of them are instances of the laws of motion (speaking being interpreted as mouth and lung movement for this purpose, and so on). All our interpreter says—let us assume—is true. We are still entitled to say that his is no interpretation of the play at all. Why not? Because it altogether misses the meaning of the play. If this is right then a psychoanalytic interpretation cannot be a good interpretation just because it is true that the actions depicted in the play instantiate truths revealed by psychoanalysis. To put the point in other words: a psychoanalytic interpretation can be rejected as bad, or even as no interpretation at all (that is, as very bad) even though it is a true explanation of the motivations of the personae in the play, just as a physics-based interpretation can be rejected as no interpretation at all even though it is a true explanation of the physical events in the play. I am not saying that the two interpretations deserve the same verdict. I am saying that if they do not, then the difference between them is to be accounted for by factors which still elude our grasp. And while they do we are still ignorant of what innovative interpretation, and therefore what interpretation in general, is.

VI. Innovative Interpretation

It is tempting to say that we have all the pieces of the jigsaw puzzle in place. Our only problem is that we do not—at least I do not— understand the most important among them. My ruminations so far suggest that an interpretation is an explanation of the work interpreted which points to connections and interrelations among its parts, and between them and other aspects of the world, so that it (1) covers adequately the significant aspects of the work interpreted (that is, does not relate just to one part of a novel, or just to one of its themes, and so on), and is not inconsistent with any aspect of the work; (2) it shows the elements of the work to be instances of some general truths; and (3) in doing the above it elucidates the meaning of the work. The more successful it is in meeting these criteria the better the interpretation.

At least in one respect this way of elucidating the nature of inter- pretation is on the right lines: it proceeds by setting criteria for excel- lence as an interpretation, rather than by setting necessary and sufficient conditions for anything being an interpretation. There are no such necessary and sufficient conditions. At the limit the boundary between a very bad interpretation and one which is not an interpretation at all is usually pointless to draw or argue about.[15]

Yet this characterization includes both too much and too little. It includes too little because it overlooks how the way an interpretation affects the value of the work interpreted contributes to the evaluation of the interpretation itself.[16] The evaluation of works of art depends only to a limited degree on their interpretation. A large component in the evaluation of works of art is the degree to which they are skilfully executed, the degree to which they meet internal criteria of excellence for that genre of art. (When it comes to randomly produced art the two aspects of this test come apart: the generic criteria for the success

[15] Though sometimes it is clear that something is no interpretation, and is not a bad interpretation. For example, if it is not intended to be an interpretation. Though the fact that an interpretation must be intended as such is the closest we get to a necessary condition, it is not strictly speaking one. If someone says 'this is a splendid interpreta- tion of *Hamlet*', meaning 'this would make a splendid interpretation of *Hamlet* were it presented as such', he is not to be charged with abuse of language. Language has a way of stretching itself.

[16] The recognition that that is so is the core of Dworkin's view of interpretation. His mistake is not in emphasizing the importance of this factor, but in ignoring others, as well as in assuming that there is normally only one correct interpretation.

of the product are no longer criteria for skill in its execution.) But to a degree the evaluation depends on the importance of the subject matter of the work. If a work is merely a display of a minor aspect of human relations then it is less valuable than, or not as excellent a work of art as, one which deals with the fundamental dilemma of human life, if there is such a dilemma.[17] At the same time an interpretation which shows the work's meaning as dealing with what is more important is, *pro tanto*, a better interpretation than one which shows it as dealing only with what is less important.[18] Disagreement about what is important and what is not is a constant source of disagreement about which interpretation is better.

Where the characterization of interpretation I offered goes too far is in insisting that showing that aspects of the work are instances of general truths is the only way of showing or explaining its meaning. This is hardly consistent with performances being interpretations, and generally there are other ways of bringing out the meaning of a work than by showing it to be an instance of some general truths. Not all explanations refer to or presuppose exceptionless general truths, at least not in any significant way. Explanations of human action by reference to people's reasons and motives notoriously defy such generalizations. An interpretation of an artwork will include an explanation of the work. But any pattern of explanation will do.

All this is helpful and relevant. But we are still short of a general characterization of what counts as showing or explaining *the meaning* of the work. But is there really a problem here? All we need—you may say—is an explanation of what it is for a work of art to have a certain meaning. Once we understand that, there will not be any problem about interpretation left. An interpretation is whatever makes one understand that meaning. That is true as well. Right at the outset I insisted on the close connection between interpretation and meaning. If we understand either of these concepts we understand both. But it follows that to explain one is to explain both: we cannot be deemed to have explained interpretation without explaining meaning, at least to a degree.

There is a simple, though perhaps not altogether perspicacious, way of elucidating the missing element in our account. An interpretation is

---

[17] Notice that the beauty of a work of art is not the most fundamental category for its evaluation. The importance of its subject does not affect the beauty of an artwork, but it does affect its excellence.

[18] These points further elaborate the presumption noted in the third section of this paper, that any work of art is fair game for 'profound' interpretations.

an explanation of the work interpreted which explains why it is important, to the extent that it is. This shows what was right in the idea that a
novel interpretation can arise out of a discovery of some general truths.
Since any interpretation is an explanation of the work it can become
available as new discoveries are made. Yet, as we have seen, and as this
augmented account allows, not every explanation, however successful
as an explanation, is an interpretation. It is an interpretation only if in
explaining the work it also elucidates, makes plain, why it is important,
to the extent that it is. The physics-based explanation of *Hamlet* I dreamt
up earlier fails that test.

The following is an attempt to integrate all the points made so far:
an interpretation is an explanation of the work interpreted which
highlights some of its elements and points to connections and interrelations among its parts, and between them and other aspects of the
world, so that (1) it covers adequately the significant aspects of the
work interpreted (that is, it does not relate just to one part of a novel,
or just to one of its themes, and so on), and is not inconsistent with
any aspect of the work; (2) it explains the aspects of the work it focuses
on; and (3) in doing the above it elucidates what is important in the
work, and accounts—to the extent that this is possible—for whatever
reasons there are for paying attention to the work as a work of art of its
kind. The more successful it is in meeting these criteria, and the more
important the meaning it justifiably attributes to the work, the better
the interpretation.

In brief:

An interpretation is an explanation of aspects of the work, which accounts for reasons
to pay it attention as a work of art of its kind.

My reference to 'reasons to pay it attention as a work of art' is meant to
exclude primarily whatever reasons there are to pay attention to the work
as evidence about the character or life of its author, or of other people,
or of the practices of a period which it portrays, and so on. It assumes a
concept of art defining what counts as an appropriate attitude to it, what
kind of reasons could be reasons for attending to works of art. This stops
the definition from being too subjectivist. Different people have different reasons, and the definition allows for that. But only certain reasons
are proper reasons for attending to art as art, and that puts a limit to the
degree to which variations in the reasons different people have lead to
different interpretations. Even so this way of understanding interpretation offers the beginning of an explanation of why several incompatible

interpretations may attract each person. Developing this explanation requires further discussion of the subjectivity of interpretation—a topic which cannot be undertaken here.

Instead, let me note that this account implies that some of the variety of good, though possibly incompatible, explanations, while appealing to some people quite properly and legitimately, leave others cold. An interpretation is a good one if the explanation it produces displays valid reasons for (some) people to pay attention to the work of art. But people differ, and while all have to concede that the interpretation is good, for it displays reasons why some people (say children) may do well to pay attention to the work, these are not reasons for them (not being children themselves), and therefore they have no interest in the interpretation.

A spirit of intolerance often makes people deny the validity of interpretations they have no interest in. But clear-sighted people know better. They know that a good interpretation may be so because of the way it displays reasons which some people have to attend to the work, and they know that there is no need—indeed that it would be foolish—to deny an interpretation's value just because it holds no interest for them.

VII. The Instability of Interpretation

The characterization of interpretation offered above is very abstract. It requires careful fleshing out to illustrate its application to various forms of art, and careful adaptation to be applicable to the interpretation of objects other than works of art. One respect in which the account is both specific to the interpretation of works of art, and at the same time seriously incomplete, is in its reliance on the existence of genre-defining standards, and ways of identifying which genre the work belongs to. I believe, though the matter cannot be investigated here, that the interpretation of works of art essentially presupposes that works belong to kinds with their own defining standards of excellence.[19] Only by reference to the work's genre can the reason to pay attention to it be identified. If it is a psychological novel then a psychoanalytic interpretation may be acceptable, while if it is a religious allegory such an interpretation would be like one showing that everything in the novel can be

---

[19] Thus giving rise to the theoretical and—more painfully—the practical problems of understanding and appreciating genre-breaking works.

explained by reference to physics: a true statement which is no interpretation at all or, at any rate, a bad interpretation which misses the point of the work. Interpretations bring out reasons to pay attention to the work, to the extent that there are any. But—to repeat—not every reason will lead to an interpretation. The evidence the work provides for the culinary habits of its time is not relevant. The relevant reasons differ from the irrelevant ones in being reasons to attend to the work as a work of art of its kind. Hence an understanding of art and its genres is presupposed.

Naturally, works may belong to more than one genre, which is another source for the possibility of a multiplicity of good and incompatible interpretations. The account I have offered makes it plain that the interpretations and meanings of works of art are not only potentially many, but that they can and do change. They change when the reasons for attending to the work change. The reasons people have change because their circumstances change. The reasons people in modern post-industrial societies have for being interested in the works of classical Athens are not those of the Renaissance, nor those of Athenians of the Periclean period. For those Athenians the art of their day did not reveal—as it did to the people of the Renaissance—a culture lost for many generations, nor did it disclose to them—as it does to us—the source of so much Western art of the last two millennia. As one work influences another, or influences people's lives or perceptions in certain ways, it acquires new meanings, that is as prefiguring later development. These are but some of the innumerable ways in which the reasons for attending to a work of art may change.

The process of change is not a process of accretion. Some reasons lose their force. A period piece is a piece which portrays and illuminates, sometimes brilliantly, matters which preoccupied a certain period, and which may be of no interest any more. Most works of art have their 'period aspect', that is a meaning for their generation which they do not have for later generations. Works of art acquire new meanings, and shed some of their old meanings.

Does this make interpretation and meaning subjective? No. It makes them—in a sense—relative. To have meaning is to have meaning for someone. I say that this makes them relative in a sense, for we commonly use the terms 'meaning' and 'interpretation' in a non-relativized sense. This is the sense in which I am using the terms, and which enables me to say that the meaning of works of art changes. In a relativized sense the meaning does not change. The meaning of Periclean art to the Athenians at the time of Pericles remains the same, as does its meaning to the Renaissance, or to the nineteenth century. If we understand 'interpretation' and 'meaning' in a relativized sense, new meanings emerge but none die. So are 'meaning' and 'interpretation' relative or not? They are both, or rather we follow both a relativized and a non-relativized use of the terms.

Apart from the fact that the reasons people have vary with their circumstances, the reasons which count as relevant for the interpretation of art change with changes in the notion of art. The names of some 'schools' in the arts suggest such changes: Expressionism brings with it a new understanding of what art is about and how it is to be understood; the use of *objets trouvés,* or collages of ready-made items, and so on, effects a transformation in our understanding of the meaning of art, as does the emergence of op-art, the use of strobes, and so on.

Do these reflections on the instability of interpretation, on the fact that interpretations, as well as co-existing with their rivals, come and go, presuppose that interpretations are imposed on the work rather than discovered in it? And does it follow from this that judgement of how good an interpretation is has to be subjective, expressive of one's own feeling, rather than objective? Not in the least. Judgement of the value of interpretations is no more subjective than is judgement of the value of cars, even though in both cases the reasons why it is good to attend to the work or to have the car are, in an obvious sense, not in the work but in the circumstances of one's life, for example, in one's daily need to travel long distances.

VIII. The Rejection of Retrieval

The normative character of interpretation, its dependence on reasons, by explaining the possibility of change refutes the picture of interpretation as retrieval. Too many writers have triumphantly exclaimed that the meaning of a text is not 'in the text itself', on the ground that marks on paper, and so on, are meaningless except in the context of a linguistic practice, which requires the existence, at one time or another, of a population sharing an understanding of the same linguistic practices. This trivial point, never disputed by anyone, has nothing to do with the sense in which the interpretation of a work of art can be new in that it shows the work to have a meaning which it did not always have. If all there was to say was that works of art also have meaning only if there is a society whose practices establish artistic genres and the standards which apply to them, then the retrieval picture would be accurate, and there would be no truth in the thought that meaning is in the eye of the beholder.

What defeats the retrieval picture is the normativity of interpretation, its dependence on reasons, and the fact that those reasons may vary, and change. Two difficulties with this suggestion should be mentioned. First, how can the meaning of a work change without the work itself changing? Secondly, the problem raised above: how can an interpretation be new? Must not the meaning of anything be on the surface, that is known to those who know the relevant 'language'?

Our concepts are complex and flexible. We should not be captives of some features of our concepts to the exclusion of others. To be sure, Hamlet's motivation cannot change, except as Hamlet himself changes in the course of the play. That is why some new interpretations, for example a psychoanalytic interpretation, are discoveries about Hamlet's motivation. But these, like all interpretations, are relative to a certain perspective on the work, a certain set of reasons for seeing it as interesting. The perspectives can change as our reasons for taking an interest in the work change. We can understand Hamlet as representing the loss of orientation of a person who, under the influence of a new culture (that of the Renaissance in this case), loses the secure bearing that the culture he was brought up in gave him, and suffers a collapse of self-confidence, a collapse which is made manifest by the murder of his father and the hasty remarriage of his mother.

This interpretation comes from a different perspective than the psychoanalytic one. Here the interest is not in individual psychology, but in the interaction of culture and sense of self. From this perspective interpretive points are made which are, if true at all, true of Hamlet in a timeless way—which have always been true of him. The play has not changed, and what is true of it was, so seen, always true of it. But the perspective itself is new. This interest in the play is new, and therefore the interpretations offered from this perspective are new. With the emergence of this perspective the play has acquired a new meaning. Since meaning is relative to a normative perspective, it can change as that perspective changes. Our concepts are rich enough to accommodate both ways of thinking of meaning: as timeless, from one and the same perspective, and as changing, with the change in perspective.

Perspectives emerge with changes in culture and in the conditions of life. Being normative, they emerge as new reasons for new interests emerge. Revolutionary interpretations capitalize on that. They are offered by those whose view of the work is infused by the new perspective before it reaches others, or before it finds articulation in the hands of others. They capture the significance of the work from this newly emerging perspective. Their interpretations may themselves hasten that emergence, and affect the direction and content of the new perspective. Less revolutionary, but still novel, interpretations bring a perspective which by now is well established in the culture to a work which has not yet been seen in that light. There is here a wide range of different cases for the study of cultures to explore. They all display the varied and subtle combinations of the familiar and the novel, the range of ways in which meaning is there, and the interpretation merely articulates it, and the ways in which the articulation can itself be seen as contributing to the meaning, as in part investing the work with a new meaning—the sense in which the interpretation of works of art is part and parcel of the creative artistic enterprise.

The interpretation of works of art may be thought to be unique in this respect. Surely, the interpretation of history does not invest history with a meaning; history is not made through its interpretation, but by the people whose history it is. Art is special in that it is part of its nature—captured by the presumption in favour of interpretations which show the interpreted work to bear on important issues—to be a mirror to our lives and world. History and law are not mirrors; they are there, made by those who forged them, and are merely to be understood by those who interpret them. Or are they? The account offered here applies directly to the interpretation of works of art only. It requires careful modification to apply to other objects of interpretation. But, I believe, the similarities between different domains of interpretation are at least as striking as the differences.

11

Intention in Interpretation

The relevance of legislative intention to legal interpretation has become a matter of political debate. Perhaps this is as it should be. There can be no doubt that the role the courts assign to legislative intent in legal interpretation has significant political consequences. Arguably those consequences should affect the role intention is given in interpretation. That is, whether or not intention should play a role in legal interpretation and what, if any, role it should have are matters partly to be determined in the light of the political consequences of such decisions. I will return to this point towards the end of this chapter. But for the most part the political controversy surrounding the role of intention in interpretation is irrelevant to the argument of this chapter. Its main theme is the role intention must have, the role it cannot fail to have, in the interpretation of legislation. It is an argument about what the courts have no choice but to do, about what they cannot fail to do so long as they follow legislation. Where necessity reigns, considerations of moral and political desirability have no role to play.

There is no denying that many interpretive practices are parochial. In some jurisdictions the writings of distinguished legal scholars are an aid to interpretation in the sense that an interpretation which is consistent with them is to be preferred to interpretations inconsistent with them. In other countries the writings of such scholars cannot even be cited in court. In Britain 'there is a *prima facie* presumption that Parliament does not intend to act in breach of international law, including therein specific treaty obligations'[1] and the interpretation of statute is affected by it. Other countries may follow different practices. Some countries will allow parliamentary debates to serve as aids for interpretation. Others exclude them completely or allow them only

---

[1] Diplock LJ (as he then was) in *Salomon v Commissioners of Custom and Excise* [1967] 2 QB 116, at 143.

in a very limited way,[2] and so on and so forth. This chapter, being a jurisprudential reflection on intention in legal interpretation, will not consider practices of interpretation specific to some legal systems or to some types of legal system (common-law systems, or civil-law ones, etc). Its aim is to explore an aspect of legal interpretation in as much as it sheds light on a theory of law. The question 'what is the law?' is intertwined with the question 'how is the law to be interpreted?' This does not mean that there must be universal conventions of legal interpretation with content specific enough to provide concrete answers to interpretive questions. Even if there are such specific interpretive universals, their study does not exhaust the topic of this chapter. For even if there are no concrete universal rules of interpretation, it is more than likely that the varying conventions of interpretation of different legal jurisdictions display common characteristics which are necessary features of legal interpretation. Whether they are unique to it, or whether they are shared by the interpretation of music or other forms of interpretation, will remain—so far as the argument of this chapter goes—an open question.

I. Some General Characteristics of Interpretation

'Interpretation' is closely related to explanation. On many occasions of their use the two notions are interchangeable. A clear exception is performing interpretations—that is, those interpretations which consist in the performance of a play, opera, or musical composition, a dance performance, or a reading of prose or poetry, and so on. It is, therefore, tempting to think that 'interpretation' is multivocal. It can mean either an explanation (perhaps an explanation of a certain type) or a performance. But such a conclusion is premature. It is equally possible that 'interpretation' is univocal, and is closely related to explanation or to a certain kind of explanation in a way which applies to performing interpretations as well. After all, a performance may have the effect that an explanation has—that is, it makes one understand the work performed. It is something like this last path that I will explore.

Yet it is unpromising to base an enquiry on an examination of 'interpretation' in the raw. The boundaries of the proper use of the term

---

[2] For a recent change in the English rule concerning the use of such materials, see *Pepper v Hart* [1992] 3 WLR 1032.

are too fluid, and language is too tolerant of what the intolerant might regard as deviant uses to make the enquiry into 'interpretation' in the raw philosophically—as opposed to lexicographically—rewarding.[3] Therefore, while the investigation in this chapter will be of interpretation, ordinarily understood, as it is practised in the law, I will take the liberty to concentrate on the notion as used to convey an activity which has a special role in the humanities, being perhaps the most distinctive way of reaching an understanding of history or works of literature or of the visual arts. This does not commit one to the view that, when used without such connotations, or in other contexts (eg 'the best interpretation of the experiment suggests that...') the term bears a different meaning or is susceptible to a different analysis. All it means is that—following a respected tradition—I will take the way interpretation can be regarded as a way of reaching understanding of especial importance in the humanities to be the focus of the exploration to follow. Whether the interpretation of experiments and the like fits the analysis will be marginal to our concerns.

In following this course we will not be regarding 'interpretation' as a technical term. My aim is to isolate for special attention a type of context, or a kind of use of the term and its derivatives, which we are all familiar with and have an intuitive understanding of, the sort of understanding acquired with mastery of the meaning and correct use of the term in English. I will have nothing to say of the use of the term in some philosophical writings which can be taken seriously only on the assumption that in them 'interpretation' is taken to be a term of art with stipulated meaning. In this chapter 'interpretation' bears its natural meaning, and a typical context of its use is being investigated.

Perhaps the following four elements can be taken as relatively uncontroversial focal features of interpretation which, so long as they are not taken as either necessary or sufficient conditions, can help direct attention to some of its most significant features. They are—it should be added—elements towards an explanation of interpretation as the activity of interpreting. The product of that activity, when it is successful, is an understanding of what has been interpreted. It seems to me that, as designating a product, 'interpretation' has a wider, and a less distinctive use than in its use to designate an activity.

---

[3] Even less is there a philosophical interest in studying interpretation as used as a term of art in jurisprudential or some other discipline. Since interpretation became the flavour of the decade, the term has been used to convey any meaning which takes anyone's fancy.

(1) Interpretation is of an original. There is always something which is interpreted. In fact, in many situations there is more than one candidate for interpretation. Legal interpretation, for example, is mostly likely to be of the law, or of a practice, or of an act (of legislation, or giving judgment) or of a statute or judicial decision, or of their text or language. Much confusion is occasioned by writers failing to identify clearly the original of the interpretation they or others advance or criticize.

(2) An interpretation states, or shows (eg in performing interpretations) the meaning of the original.

(3) Interpretations are subject to assessment as right or wrong (correct or incorrect), or as good or bad (or some approximations of these, such as 'almost right'). I will often use 'valid' as a term which straddles the divide between the two types of assessments. They are judged as right or wrong, good or bad, by their success in stating, showing, or bringing out the meaning of the original. Such judgements are to be distinguished from the assessment of the success of an interpretation by other dimensions. For example, an interpretation can be said to be clear, accessible, etc when judged by its success in effectively conveying the meaning it identified; it can be said to be interesting, stimulating, etc when judged by the quality of the meaning it brings out or explains.

(4) Interpretation is an intentional act. One does not interpret unless one intends to interpret. What my friend said to me last night can be an interpretation of a dream I had last week. But he did not interpret my dream. I may have done so if I took his words to provide an interpretation of the dream.[4]

---

[4] I have discussed the point briefly in 'Morality as Interpretation: on Walzer's "Interpretation & Social Criticism"' (1991) 101 *Ethics* 392. Take, for example, a counter-instance. John says: 'Many Members of Parliament are revolting.' Jill overhears him. When Jack asks her what John said, she answers: 'He said that many Members of Parliament are repellent.' This tells us how she interpreted John's utterance. But she did not intend to interpret. She merely intended to relay the content of John's remark to Jack. Does it show that interpretation need not be intentional? Not if one focuses on the area of its use I mentioned. In this example, suggested to me by Timothy Endicott, to whom I am grateful, interpretation just means understanding. It does not refer to any activity at all. It is false that Jill interpreted John's remark to Jack. It is true that she interpreted (= understood) John to mean repellent when he said 'revolting'. This would have been true of her even had she said nothing to Jack. Her remark to Jack was not an interpretive remark (and was not intended as one). It merely revealed to those who heard her (and who knew enough of the context) how she interpreted (= understood) John. The marks of interpretation are meant to capture the meaning of the interpretation as a kind of activity

Interpretations differ from other ways of relating to an original—for example, by being inspired by it, in being explanations, or elucidations of the meaning of an original. A sculptor inspired by the grain of a block of marble to create the statue he sculpts is not interpreting the block.[5] When a statue inspired by a block of marble or a play inspired by a parliamentary row is judged as good or bad, it is not so judged by its success in explaining the meaning of what has inspired it.

One special type of interpretation can be dubbed conserving interpretation. A conserving interpretation is one which holds itself a success or a failure by the degree to which it succeeds in retrieving, or restating, the meaning the original had for someone, or its meaning in a culture at some past time. An interpretation is conserving if it seeks to explain or display the meaning of the original for its author, if it had one, or its meaning for its original audience, or some other reference group. Not all interpretations need be conserving interpretations. I can explain what an original means: 'autodidact' means self-taught. In offering that explanation I am not saying that it is what it means to you or to anyone in particular. This is just the meaning of the word. In that sense my explanation is not a conserving one. At the same time it is plausible to think that nothing can have a meaning unless it has that meaning to someone. Meaning is revealed. Meaning can be hidden from some, but not from all. Of course, no one need be capable of articulating the meaning of an original for the original to have that meaning, and possibly no one need be able to perceive the meaning of the original in all its aspects. Its meaning maybe a composite of, or an abstraction from, the meaning it has for various people. But it seems to make no sense for something to have a meaning without meaning that or something like that to someone or other. What can it mean to say that 'geap' means salvation even though no one has ever known that it does until I discovered the fact today?

So interpretation can be conventional—that is, one which sets out the meaning people (ie people at the time and place of the interpretation) commonly understand the original to have, without being conserving. It is conventional if, in explaining the meaning of the original, it agrees with the common view. It is conserving only if it sets out to explain the

---

(sometimes no more than a mental activity) through which one gains understanding. It does not apply to 'interpretation' when it is used interchangeably with 'understanding'.

[5] Someone can be inspired by an event to write, let us say, a play which offers an interpretation of that event, but not all inspirations lead to interpretations.

meaning the original has for a reference group which may or may not be 'the common view of people nowadays'.

Some interpretations are novel or innovative. This can be in one of two ways. An interpretation may be new or original in explaining for the first time the meaning the original has (or had at some previous time or for some different group). The meaning is not new. It is the conventional meaning of the original. But it has never been explicitly articulated or explained, at least not in this way. In that sense a conventional (as well as a conserving) interpretation can be new or original. I will reserve the term 'innovative' to designate interpretations which show the original to have a meaning other than the meaning it commonly has for people (or had for people in the past). The very possibility of innovative interpretations is problematic. How can one reconcile the following three propositions which I have asserted? (1) What an original means is what it means to some people or group. (2) An innovative interpretation shows the original to have a meaning other than the meaning it commonly has. (3) An interpretation is no free creation; it explains a meaning which an original has. The dissolution of this puzzle belongs to another occasion.

These remarks point to a further complexity. If what is interpreted can have various meanings, then there may be several different, but valid, interpretations of it. To clarify this thought we can be helped by a further distinction. Two interpretations will be said to be compatible if they can be combined in one more complex and comprehensive understanding of the original without rendering it self-contradictory. One interpretation of a novel, for example, may emphasize its social significance, as a portrayal of the rise of a new industrial class, with a distinctive voice. Another interpretation may emphasize the psychologically complex reactions of the heroine to her father, and their effects on the rest of her life. A third interpretation may focus on the way the author uses and transforms the 'authorial voice' as a narrative technique. While in the way we talk of these things we would say that each one of these literary critics has a different interpretation of the novel, for all we know there is no conflict between them. If so, they can be combined in a broader, more comprehensive view of the novel. When this is possible, the interpretations are compatible.

Incompatible interpretations offer conflicting views of the original. They cannot be regarded as complementary parts of one 'complete' or 'exhaustive' interpretation.[6] So interpretations which attribute to the

---

[6] I put these words in quotation marks, for there are independent reasons, to emerge later, for denying the possibility of an interpretation being complete or exhaustive in the sense of there being nothing else which is both compatible with it and true.

characters of a novel inconsistent motivation and take them (ie those characters) to be consistent are incompatible. When what is interpreted can be performed and the aspects of the performance which the different interpretations call for cannot be combined in one performance, the interpretations are inconsistent. So, if one interpretation of a poem requires reading it in a certain way which is inconsistent with another interpretation, then the two are incompatible. Must at least one of any two incompatible interpretations be mistaken? As we saw, this is not necessarily so. If an original can have several meanings, then possibly two incompatible interpretations can both be valid. They are both valid if each succeeds in revealing one of the meanings of the original.

With this distinction in hand we can suggest that an interpretation is judged to be correct or incorrect, right or wrong, when judged by a standard which excludes the validity of more than one of incompatible interpretations. Interpretations are judged good or bad when judged by a standard which allows for the validity of incompatible interpretations.

Interestingly we do not talk of an interpretation being true, though it can be true to the original or to something else (the approach of the interpreter's teacher, for example). At the same time interpretive propositions ('Hamlet was jealous of his uncle') can be true or false, and their truth or falsehood depends on whether the interpretation they offer is right (or good). When they are true and the interpretation they express is uniquely correct, their truth is straightforward. The truth of an interpretive statement expressing (an element of) a valid interpretation which admits the validity of incompatible interpretations must, on pain of contradiction, be understood as relative to the interpretation. For example, one may say: 'According to a psychoanalytic interpretation of Hamlet his paralysis of action was due to a conflict between a desire and a sense of guilt for having it.' In this example we have an unconditional truth of a relativizing statement. More commonly, the interpretive proposition asserted will include no explicit reference to the interpretation of which it is a (partial) expression.

How incompatible interpretations can be valid and what it means to say that they are is another task which will remain undischarged by the end of this chapter. Their resolution is not necessary for the examination of the role of intention in interpretation. To avoid any misconstrual of the conclusions that follow, it is important to chart some elements of the wider picture at the outset. The possibility of innovative interpretations, and the possibility that several mutually incompatible interpretations are all good interpretations, are familiar from our general knowledge. My aim in the above terminological clarifications was to acknowledge these facts. They set some hard questions for an account of interpretation, questions which cannot be explored in this chapter. But the questions are not whether there can be two incompatible and valid interpretations. We know that sometimes this is possible. The questions are when is it possible and what does it mean to say that one work has two meanings? Is meaning found or imposed on a work? How can an interpretation be both true to an original and innovative? These are questions of how to understand the familiar facts about interpretations. They do not doubt their existence. This is why it is important to acknowledge them even in this chapter which provides only a beginning of an account of interpretation.

II. Intention

A. The simple argument for the intention thesis

Some writers have asserted that all interpretations are necessarily of an authorial intention, or alternatively that interpretations of any original are valid only if they capture the intentions of the authors of that original. Some mean by this literally what they say—that is, that nothing which does not admit that it is to be judged by how well it conforms to the authorial intention counts as an interpretation. Others regard the point as merely formal. Something counts as an interpretation only if it is appropriate to present it as revealing an authorial intention even though this need not be taken literally. It can refer to a fictional author of an original which is not the product of any authorial intention, as when we interpret a practice by reference to the intention of the people. It can also refer to a fictional author when interpreting an original with a real one. For example, it can advance an interpretation of a statute as correct because it represents the intention an ideal legislator would have had had he enacted that statute.[7]

I find this view contrived and unhelpful. Commentators who advance an interpretation of the cultural trends of the 1980s do not think of

---

[7] See, among others, S Knapp and W Michaels, 'Against Theory' (1982) 8 *Critical Review* 723; S Fish, in—among other places—*Doing What Comes Naturally: Change, Rhetoric and the Practice of Theory in Literary and Legal Studies* (Durham: Duke University Press, 1989) 296, and 'Play of Surfaces: Theory and Law', in G Leyh (ed), *Legal Hermeneutics: History, Theory and Practice* (Berkeley, Calif: University of California Press, 1992); A Marmor, *Interpretation and Legal Theory* (Oxford: OUP, 1992).

them as expressing anyone's intentions, nor do people who learn of such interpretations regard them as revealing any intentions. They explore the meaning of cultural trends, and of their causes and effects. Of course, whenever we talk of the meaning of something we can imagine a real or fictional being who intends to make whatever it is which has this meaning. Sometimes presenting interpretations in such terms is fun. At other times it is not. But, unless real intentions are involved, talk of hypothetical intentions of fictitious people is rarely of any real significance. It does not advance our understanding in any way.

Arguably legal interpretation is concerned only with originals (constitutions, statutes, precedents, the texts in which they were formulated, legal rules and doctrines, and the law itself) which are creatures of human acts intended to create constitutions, statutes, precedents, etc. But this cannot be taken for granted at the outset. And at least one exception to the rule stands out. Legal and judicial practices are possible objects of legal interpretation and, while they are a function of intentional human acts, they are clearly not necessarily (in fact hardly ever) created by anyone taking action to create just them, i.e. to create practices with the characteristics which the practice which emerged has. Still, given that for the most part legal interpretation is of the products of deliberate creation, there is little surprise that a natural contender for 'the theory of legal interpretation' is the contention that the purpose of legal interpretation is to establish the intentions of the law-makers. I will call the extreme version of this view the *Radical Intention Thesis*. It says:

An interpretation is correct in law if and only if it reflects the author's intention.

There is a lot wrong with this doctrine. But it is not guilty of all the objections raised against it. This means that, even though it has been very ably discussed by many writers,[8] it needs looking into again. Three types of objection are commonly raised against the thesis. First, there is no reason to base interpretation on author's intention. Second, it is in principle impossible to establish the relevant authorial intention, and often no such intention exists. Third, as practised by the courts and sanctioned by judicial practices, interpretation does not consist in, or does not consist exclusively in, establishing authorial intent.

---

[8] Among those that I found particularly helpful are GC Maccullum Jr, 'Legislative Intent', in R Summers (ed), *Essays in Legal Philosophy* (Oxford: Blackwell, 1968); R Dworkin, *A Matter of Principle* (Cambridge, Mass: Harvard University Press, 1985) ch 3.

The first class of objections is clearly wrong. But there is enough truth in it to make us move to a much more limited thesis. I will comment on it first, returning to the others only in Section II (last subsection). There is a strong reason for interpreting statutes and precedents and the like in accordance with their author's intentions. It may help in explaining the case if I begin with a mistaken explanation of that case. Think of the interpretation of statutes as a central case. Some will say that there is a democratic argument in support of the Radical Intention Thesis. Democratic theory, the argument goes, requires that the law shall be determined by the will of the people as expressed by their democratically elected representatives. Therefore, since statutory law is the law as established by the interpretation of statutes, democratic theory requires that statutes be interpreted in accordance with the intentions of the democratically elected members of the legislature. I have put the argument in a very crude way. Much that is wrong with it can be readily set right without denting its force. But it runs against one major problem. It applies only to democracies (really only to democracies of a certain type). The law exists in many non-democratic countries, and, as we are seeking a general understanding of legal interpretation of the law created by law-making acts, this argument will not do. At least it will not do as it stands. It has to be generalized to apply to non-democratic regimes as well. This should not be difficult. It takes no more than pointing out that, whatever the justification—real or supposed—of entrusting law-making powers to any institutions it will not make sense unless the laws made by those institutions are the laws they intend to make. The following is a statement of this generalized argument:

To give a person or an institution law-making powers is to entrust them with the power to make law by acts intended to make law, or at least undertaken in the knowledge that they make law.[9] It makes no sense to give any person or body law-making power unless it is assumed that the law they make is the law they intended to make. Assume the contrary. Assume that the law made through legislation bears no relation to the law the legislator intended to make. For this assumption to be at all imaginable the legislator must be unaware of what law will be made by his actions. If he can predict that if he does one thing tax will be raised by a certain amount, and if he does another thing tax will be cut

---

[9] Typically, law-making powers come with an obligation to exercise them with deliberation. Such duties can play their role in judicial review of legislative action. But these are contingent features. The argument does not rely on their presence.

by a certain amount, for example, then he will take that action which will have the effect he wants to have—that is, the law he makes will be the law he intends to make.

So to assume that the law made by legislation is not the one intended by the legislator, we must assume that he cannot predict what law he is making when the legislature passes any piece of legislation. But if so, why does it matter who the members of the legislature are, whether they are democratically elected or not, whether they represent different regions in the country, or classes in the population, whether they are adults or children, sane or insane? Since the law they will end by making does not represent their intentions, the fact that their intentions are foolish or wise, partial or impartial, self-serving or public spirited, makes no difference. It would have been otherwise had there been some invisible hand mechanism, or a voting procedure, which secures desirable laws independently of the beliefs and intentions of the legislators, or possibly as a function of these beliefs and intentions but a function which does not match any of their intentions. But no such mechanism exists,[10] and our concept of legislation is moulded by the shape of institutional arrangements we know of or think possible in the real world. Hence, the very idea of law-making institutions is that of institutions which can make the law they intend to make. No alleged justification of law-making institutions which does not include that assumption can make sense. None can be believable.

This being the best general argument I know of supporting the view that interpretation should reflect the law-makers' intentions, it has to be conceded right away that it falls short of vindicating the full force of the Radical Intention Thesis. The argument supports the conclusion that

To the extent that the law derives from deliberate law-making, its interpretation should reflect the intentions of its lawmaker.

Let me call this the Authoritative Intention Thesis, in order to emphasize the way the argument supporting the thesis turns on our

---

[10] The only two kinds of invisible hand mechanism I am aware of—ie the democratic arguments which suggest that representatives tend to come to express the wishes of the people they represent, and the Hayek-type arguments to the effect that the common law has the advantages in efficiency of the market—assume that the mechanism works through the beliefs and intentions of the legislators and courts. Recently J Waldron suggested the possibility of three different explanations for an invisible hand mechanism. The fact, which for reasons of space cannot be argued for here, that none of them is plausible reinforces my conclusion. See 'Legislators' Intentions and Unintentional Legislation', in A Marmor (ed), *Interpretation and the Law* (Oxford: OUP, 1995).

understanding of the notion of authority and its conceivable justifications. It is a moot point whether the law rests entirely on the authority
of the law-maker(s). It seems fairly clear that this is not the case with
regard to customary law. It is far from clear whether the common law
is more like enacted law, with decisions becoming precedent if deliberately laid down as such by a court with an authority to bind itself or
other courts. Or whether the common law is really customary law, consisting of the practices of the courts. Nor is there any reason to think
that it is one thing or another. It could be a little of both, with perhaps
different traditions prevailing in different common-law jurisdictions.
Similarly, in countries with entrenched written constitutions coupled
with a doctrine of constitutional review, there is a case for viewing constitutional law not as enacted law but as a special, privileged, branch
of the common law. Whether this means that it escapes the scope of
the Authoritative Intention Thesis or merely means that the relevant
intentions are those of the constitutional courts depends on the way the
judge-made law of the country concerned is to be understood.

I will, therefore, abandon the Radical Intention Thesis as false
about the nature of law in general; while it may be true of some legal
systems, we lack any argument to believe it to be true of legal systems
like ours. Instead, whenever reference is made in the following pages to
the Intention Thesis, it is the Authoritative Intention Thesis that will be
under discussion.[11]

B. Value-presupposition of the authoritative intention thesis

Before I deal with objections to this argument, one of its presuppositions, which will feature prominently throughout this chapter, ought
to be highlighted. The argument from democracy was rejected because
of its reliance on a particular normative theory. That was seen to be a
fault, even if the theory it relied on is valid. Does it mean that a theory
of interpretation must be value-free? Not so. The generalized argument
for the Authoritative Intention Thesis presented above itself relies on
a normative premise. It is the assumption that, while the law may be

---

[11] For ease of expression I will refer interchangeably to legislation and to
law-making. It should be understood, however, that for present purposes 'legislation' should be broadly understood as involving no more than deliberate law-making.
Laying down a binding precedent is an act of law-making, and, while not in fact an act
of legislation, will be covered by the use of 'legislation' in the following pages.

morally indefensible, it must be understood as a system which many people believe to be morally defensible. While rejecting any explanation of the nature of law or legal interpretation which is true only if the law is morally good, we must also reject any explanation which fails to make it intelligible. This means that to be acceptable an explanation of the law and of legal interpretation must explain how people can believe that their law, the law of their country, is morally good.

It would be wrong to think that, since people's beliefs in the moral qualities of their law may be altogether misguided, the constraint on the acceptability of explanations of the law that I have described cannot be very significant. However misguided such beliefs can be, they must be recognizable moral or political beliefs, and not every attitude to, or belief about, other people or about social practices and institutions meets this condition. This generalized argument for the Authoritative Intention Thesis is an example of an argument with significant results for the understanding of the law which makes no stronger assumption than that the law is morally intelligible—that is, that people's attitude to the law is morally intelligible, that it is intelligible that they believe the law to be morally binding.

On its face, the assumption is not a moral assumption. It assumes neither that the law is good nor that people's moral beliefs about it are sound. Nevertheless, the assumption is normative for two reasons. First, the distinction between what is morally intelligible and what is not is itself a value-dependent distinction. One's view of morality colours what one finds morally intelligible. There is, of course, no direct connection between one's view of what is morally true and one's view on what is morally intelligible. Different and inconsistent moral views may agree at least on the main outlines of what is morally intelligible. That is the reason the notion of moral intelligibility can be helpful in an explanation of the law, a type of social institution characterized by being accepted, in spite of their differing moral views, by many who live under it as morally good. But none of this can disguise the fact that in the end the notion of moral intelligibility is itself a moral notion, one whose employment presupposes substantive moral views.

The other way in which the premise of the moral intelligibility of the law is a normative premise is revealed when we turn to the grounds for accepting it. They are that, while the law may be morally grossly defective, and even without any authority, it claims that it has (moral) authority and is, therefore, inevitably so regarded by those people who accept it as binding. That the law is morally intelligible follows from the fact that many of the people who live under it believe that it is morally sound or acceptable. If it is necessarily the case that the moral soundness or acceptability of any legal system is believed in by many of its subjects, then the law must be morally intelligible, for it must be intelligible that they have this attitude to their law. All this is consistent with the unfortunately all-too-familiar situation of large populations living under the yoke of oppressive law to which they feel no allegiance. It is true even if only the bulk of those involved in the administration of the law, in the running of the government, and some of those who benefit from it believe in the moral validity of the law.[12] Why must those involved in making or applying the law believe in its moral acceptability? Because the law purports to determine or reflect (moral) rights and duties of its subjects.[13] One cannot purport to do so unless one believes, or makes as if one believes, that one's actions indeed have the moral effect they purport to have. Saying this adds little to the premise that the law purports to determine or reflect moral duties, for one cannot act in a way which has this meaning without making it appear that one believes that the fact that the law has this meaning is justified.

This line of reasoning leaves room for the possibility that law-makers and courts and administrators are acting hypocritically when they make it appear that they believe in the moral acceptability of the law. But, quite apart from the fact that it is humanly impossible that they are all insincere, so far as our argument is concerned that does not matter. The law must be morally intelligible even for the people who man legal institutions to be insincere about their beliefs. Insincerity requires the same credibility as sincerity.

I have detailed the argument presupposed by the Authoritative Intention Thesis partly to bring out the assumptions leading to the thesis, as they tell us much about the nature of law, and partly to illustrate one of the ways in which they presuppose normative assumptions. The view that the law purports to reflect and determine morality itself

---

[12] It was, of course, central to HLA Hart's theory of law that a legal system is in force in a country only if 'officials' accept it (ie its rule of recognition), and, while in normal cases much of the population accepts it as well, this need not be so. Hart, however, did not believe that the acceptance necessarily expresses belief in the moral acceptability of the law.

[13] It purports to determine them when legislation purports to create a new right or duty. It purports to reflect moral rights and duties when legislation purports to incorporate into the law moral rights and duties which exist independently of the law. I and others have argued for this view too often in the past to argue again here. See J Raz, 'Law, Morality and Authority', *Ethics in the Public Domain* (Oxford: OUP, 1994).

relies on normative assumptions. Some of them concern the nature of morality (eg that a view on a moral issue is a moral view). Some are normative views about the nature of (intentional) human action (eg that, barring *akrasia*, it is done in the belief that the act is not against reason). Other normative assumptions presupposed here concern the purpose and therefore standards of success of explanations of social institutions and practices (eg that explanations which bring out the meaning of those institutions and practices for people who participate in them or in their activities enjoy a certain priority among such explanations, and that without them the practices and institutions are not properly explained). So the Authoritative Intention Thesis rests on a number of normative premises. So do the other conclusions to be reached below.

C. Whose intention? What intention?

Having abandoned The Radical Intention Thesis in favour of a more sensible version of the intention thesis, we can return to a brief examination of the other objections to it. Much ingenuity has been displayed in discussing what intention is referred to by The Authoritative Intention Thesis, usually by opponents of the thesis seeking to show that the multiple ambiguities prevailing on the subject foil any sensible defence of The Authoritative Intention Thesis. The most that can be salvaged, it is sometimes intimated, is a harmless fiction that legal interpretation establishes a fictitious author's intent. While there is no doubt that fictions can be harmless, they rarely advance understanding, and often help to obfuscate. In a jurisprudential discussion they are best avoided. The Authoritative Intention Thesis is helpful only if it refers to real intentions. Leaving on one side for the moment the question whether there are sufficient reasons to interpret deliberately-made law by the author's intention, the question arises, is there an author's intention which can be a guide to legal interpretation and can one know what it is? I will deal with these matters briefly, and will avoid the detailed arguments necessary to substantiate the conclusions reached below.

In particular I wish to say little on the epistemic question. There is no good general reason to think that we cannot know what was the intention with which past actions were performed. It is true that sometimes we are unable to have certain knowledge of people's intentions, but that does not affect the case for the Authoritative Intention Thesis. It shows that sometimes we may be unsure whether the interpretation adopted is correct. This is so whatever view of interpretation one takes.[14]

Much debate is occasioned by the fact that for the most part law-makers are institutions rather than individual human beings. How can institutions have intentions? The answer is that, if they can act intentionally, after much deliberation (e.g. 'after discussing the matter for seven hours the House of Commons approved the Bill as amended in committee'), they can have intentions. We find no problem in attributing intentions to corporations, groups, and institutions in ordinary life, and the law assumes that corporations and some other legal subjects who are not human beings can act intentionally. Some theorists believe that reference to corporate or institutional agents is mere shorthand for reference to individual agents ('the chairman of the board', 'one of the executive directors', 'the majority of the shareholders, voting in the general annual meeting', etc). This view (known as ontological individualism) is mistaken, but cannot be considered here.[15] I will continue to assume that institutions are agents who can act intentionally.

This allows one to entertain any of a number of theses regarding the relations between the actions of an institution and the actions of its members or officers. One thesis which has to be taken seriously is that an institution can act intentionally only in virtue of some human being(s) acting intentionally. That is, an institution acts only when some of its members or officers act, and it acts intentionally only if they do. I am not sure whether this thesis can be regarded as generally valid. (It may be, for example, that in some contexts an institution whose rules make certain consequences highly likely by securing the inaction, even the ignorance, of its members and officers may nevertheless be said to have intentionally brought about the consequences.) But the thesis seems plausible when applied to law-making, at least when law-making involves voting or other manifestations of endorsement, and I will rely on it. It is sometimes said that the intention of the members or officers is attributed to the institution. This way of putting the point may encourage the view that institutions do not exist and that reference to them is

---

[14] One may think that not all views of interpretation make it susceptible to doubt and liable to be mistaken to the same degree, and that there are good policy reasons to follow a method of interpretation which is less prone to mistakes and doubts. But, as will be seen below, the intention thesis is not a method of interpretation, and is not subject to this objection.

[15] See the excellent discussion in D Ruben, *The Metaphysics of the Social World* (London: Routledge, 1985).

but a shorthand reference to human beings. But we need not fall prey to this mistake by accepting the thesis that law-making institutions act only if their officers or members act, ie only through the action of their officers or members.

The question through whom do law-makers act is determined by their constitution. There is, therefore, no general jurisprudential answer to the question through whom do law-makers act. It depends entirely on who the law-makers are. And the answer to that question is also the answer to the question whose intention is 'attributed' to the institution. Some people find the fact that a legislature enacts a law if (normally) a majority of those voting vote for it a source of puzzlement. The majority is not a person. The people who constitute the majority on one occasion are not those who constitute it on another. None of this needs to be puzzling. It merely means that the actions and intentions of different people are attributed to the legislature at different times.

This leads to the next series of questions: which of the different intentions count? When people act intentionally, they display more than one intention. They intend to examine the contents of the fridge, to get to the kitchen, to leave the living-room, to walk, to traverse a certain distance, etc. A member of the legislature voting for a Bill may intend to curry favour with the electorate, to appear courageous and resolute to his children, to alleviate the distress caused to single parents (I am assuming that the Bill protects them in some way), etc. Which of all these intentions matters to the interpretation of the legislation? One may think that here as well the answer is a matter of the constitution of the law-making body. It determines what action has to be undertaken, and with what intent, for the action to be a valid law-creating act. Up to a point this is so. But this time more needs to be said from a jurisprudential perspective. The very notion of law-making is a general not a parochial legal concept. While each legal system can determine who, within its jurisdiction, has legislative power and how they are to exercise it, it cannot determine what is legislation. The clarification of that notion is a theoretical task. And it is a task which cannot be discharged without reference to a legislative intention.

Try to identify legislation without reference to legislative intent. Assume, for example, that an act is an act of legislation if, according to law, the result of its performance is that a new law comes into effect. This would not make it an act of legislation. Consider the possibility of a person legislating by eating a melon. If he does, then a law banning strikes comes into effect. It is a ridiculous example, for we are looking for examples of a phenomenon which while possible has no real-life instances. So let us assume that the legislature has passed a law decreeing that, if John Doe eats a melon before Christmas, then strikes will be banned. Were there such a law, it would be comparable to a law which stipulates that, should any region be struck by an earthquake force 6 or more, then its residents will be compensated by the government for any damage caused by the earthquake. That is, the event given legal significance (earthquake or eating melons) is not itself a legislative event. The legislation is done by Parliament in the usual way. It determines that the event will have certain legal consequences.

The example is meant to be understood on the assumption that John Doe is unaware of the legal power that his culinary habits have acquired. On that assumption, the fact that his action effects a change in the law, or in people's rights and duties, no more makes it into legislation than the fact that the occurrence of a natural event effects a change in the law, or in people's rights and duties, makes it a legislative event. Only acts undertaken with the intention to legislate can be legislative acts. The reason is that the notion of legislation imports the idea of entrusting power over the law into the hands of a person or an institution, and this imports entrusting voluntary control over the development of the law, or an aspect of it, into the hands of the legislator. This is inconsistent with the idea of unintentional legislation.[16]

Continuing with the same thought, we come to realize that legislation requires not merely intending to legislate, it requires knowing what one legislates. One is hardly in control over the development of an aspect of the law, if, while one can change the law by acts intending to do so, one cannot know what change in the law one's action imports. The natural suggestion is that legislators make the law that they intend to make, and they make that law by expressing the intention to do so. Following

---

[16] It may be that this condition is too strong. If the basic idea of legislation is that it entrusts to the legislator a measure of control over the law, then all that is required for an act to be a legislative act is that it be performed with the knowledge that it affects the law. That will enable the legislator to undertake it only if he is willing to put up with such change. I think that the balance of the argument favours the intention rather than the knowledge condition. But the two are difficult to prise apart in practice. For very cogent reasons, most legal systems insulate legislative acts—that is, they assign legislative effects to acts (voting, signing, declaring, etc.) which have no consequences (or as few as possible) other than those which follow from their legislative effects (or from the expression of an intention to legislate). Roughly speaking, typically an act of legislation has nothing to it except the expression of an intention to legislate. In these circumstances, there is no reason to legislate other than in order to legislate. Legislative acts are insulated precisely to achieve that effect.

standard work on speech-act theory,[17] and avoiding excessive technical complexities, this is to say that *A*, being an agent who has legal authority to make a law that *p*, legislates (i.e. makes it the law) that *p* (where *p* is a variable for the statement of the content of the law) by performing an action which expresses the intention that *p* become the law in virtue of that intention being manifestly expressed.[18]

But this characterization of the required intention is open to an obvious objection: surely legislators do not have to know the precise details of the legislation they vote for. Many of them are likely to know only its general outlines, and some of them may have very little idea of what they are voting for. The objection is based on a valid point, but it has to be interpreted with care. If, in the formula for the required intention, one substitutes for *p* a statement of the content of legislation, then the objection is valid, as it shows that this intention is not necessary for legislation. So, for the characterization of the required intention to be good, the parenthetical explanation to the effect that *p* is a variable for the statement of the content of the law has to be modified to make clear that, while the intention must identify the law being enacted, it need not identify it through a comprehensive statement of its content. The most relaxed form of this condition will be to say that there is some description, *p*, of the law such that a suitably authorized person legislates by performing an action which expresses the intention that *p* become the law in virtue of that intention being manifestly expressed.

---

[17] In particular the work of Grice and Strawson. See P Grice, *Studies in the Way of Words* (Cambridge, Mass: Harvard University Press, 1989) and PF Strawson, 'Intention and Convention in Speech Acts', in *Logico-Linguistic Papers* (London: Methuen, 1971).

[18] A couple of clarifications. First the statements that legislation makes it the law that *p*, and that a legislative act manifests an intention that *p* becomes the law, should be understood not to carry the normal implication that at the time of the act *p* is not, and/or is not believed to be, the law. An enactment can simply provide a new legal source (additional to existing ones or replacing them) for the law that *p*. Second, I referred to the intention that the very fact of manifestly expressing that very intention will be a source of law, because the publicity of the legislative act seems to be of its essence. But that publicity can be secret, with the legislation not being publicized to the general population. All that is denied is that legislation can consist in a private mental act. Following Grice one may think of legislation as requiring an intention that it be recognized as such, ie as an act of legislation or an intention to legislate. But that condition may be unnecessarily strict in this case, as well as in the case of some other speech acts. For a critical assessment of the application of the Gricean model to legislation, see H Hurd, 'Sovereignty in Silence' (1990) 99 Yale Law Journal 945. My own view is that Hurd shows the need to relax the conditions Grice asserts for communication to take place. Clearly the difficulties she points to affect not only legislation but other ordinary instances of communication (which are not face to face).

Is there always such a description? For the characterization to succeed in capturing the nature of the intention required for an act to qualify as a legislative one, it must be the case that whenever one legislates one intends, under some description, to make the law one is enacting. I believe this is so, and that the following description is present in all but the most anomalous circumstances.[19] A person is legislating (voting for a Bill, etc) by expressing an intention that the text of the Bill on which he is voting will—when understood as such texts, when promulgated in the circumstances in which this one is promulgated,[20] are understood in the legal culture of this country—be law.[21]

On this understanding the required intention is very minimal, and does not include any understanding of the content of the legislation. We can expect that this intention is almost universally present in acts of legislation.[22] But, as it is so minimal, someone may object that it is not enough to satisfy the rationale of the requirement, explained above, that an intention be present at all—that is, that legislation is an act of making that law which one intends to make. But the objection is unfounded. The minimal intention is sufficient to preserve the essential idea that legislators have control over the law. Legislators who have the minimal intention know that they are, if they carry the majority, making law, and they know how to find out what law they are making. All they have to do is establish the meaning of the text in front of them, when understood as it will be according to their legal culture assuming that it

[19] Notice that my claim here is stronger than is required by the thesis. It requires only that any legislator will undertake the act of legislation with some intention which meets the condition specified above. It does not require the existence of one intention which is present in all such acts.

[20] This qualification is vital. The law is—so to speak—the meaning of the utterance in a specific context, rather than of a text devoid of context.

[21] That intention is not to be equated with the intention that this shall be the law of the country. It is the intention that the Bill be a law, ie a *prima facie* legal reason, which takes effect alongside other—sometimes competing—legal rules and doctrines. To simplify I omitted to mention here the requirement that the intention be to make the Bill law by this very intention being openly expressed.

[22] The two exceptions are cases when one does not know that one is voting for a Bill, as may happen when accidentally operating the levers of a voting machine, or drunkenly going through the motions of voting, or when one knows that one's action is one of voting but one is doing it not in order to vote the Bill into law, but to escape a blackmailer or some other accidental consequence. As has already been remarked, legal systems go to great lengths to minimize the possibility of such cases occurring. They are therefore justified, given the interest in clarity on the question of whether an act of legislation took place or not, to presume that all acts of voting express an intention to legislate, in the sense explained. The very existence of such an absolute presumption makes it more likely that legislators will vote only when they have the relevant intention.

will be promulgated on that occasion. Of course, it is hard to imagine a theory of authority which will not demand much more—that is, which will not demand that authorities form an informed judgement about proposed legislation before endorsing it. But it is intelligible that the law would leave the judgement as to what exactly one needs to know and to intend in order to satisfy this moral requirement to the legislators themselves. Therefore, a legal system which does not require any more specific intention is intelligible.

As we saw, this characterization of the relevant legislative intent is the minimal intent required for an act to be a legislative act. Not uncommonly, the law will make the validity of law-making depend on additional mental conditions. One typical precondition for the validity of subordinate legislation in common-law countries is that it was adopted with the intention to promote one or another of a list of legally stipulated ends. When this is so, the interpretation of such legislation can rely on these further intentions as well. So the answer to the question which intention is relevant to the interpretation of enacted rules of law comes in two parts. The first refers to the intention specified above which is necessary for any act to count as a law-making act. The second part refers to the additional intentions, if any, which the law of different countries—through legislation, common law, or just in the accepted legal culture of the country—makes relevant to the interpretation of enacted law.

III. Interpretation and Legitimation

So far I have tried to put the strongest case for the Authoritative Intention Thesis that I am aware of. But the very argument for the thesis, the very form that argument gave the thesis, raises doubts about what exactly the thesis established. We saw that, as the argument for the Authoritative Intention Thesis is an aspect of the doctrine of authority, the intention by which legislation should be interpreted is the intention required to legislate. Only when its legislation is interpreted in this way does the authority really have control over the law. Barring consideration of the specific legal regulation of legislative practices in this country or that, that intention, to paraphrase the above, is the intention to say what one would be normally understood as saying, given the circumstances in which one said it. This may strike one as possibly true but not quite the helpful answer one was looking for.

Consider the following objection to the Authoritative Intention Thesis. Let it be granted that almost every legislator imaginable *can* have the standard intention stipulated by the thesis. But must they all have it? What is there to prevent any legislator from intending that the Bill he is voting for be understood as it would be understood if interpreted by the mystic code for the interpretation of sacred texts of the religious sect he belongs to? The answer is presumably that he cannot intend it to be understood in this way, for he knows that it will not be, and that one cannot, at least one cannot in these circumstances, intend what one knows will not happen. But, the objector will come back at us, should it be assumed that it will not happen? If his intention is known and if I am right in saying that legislation is intelligible only if it is interpreted by the legislature's intention, would courts and people generally be bound to follow the legislator's intention that the Bill be read in the light of the mystic code? Up to a point this line of reasoning is sound, but it does not constitute an objection to the Authoritative Intention Thesis. The legislator can make the mystic code the method of interpretation or some or all of his acts. All he has to do is express an intention that this be so. But, when he expresses that intention, he will be doing so by an act which will be interpreted as such acts are normally interpreted by the conventions prevailing at the time. That is, while legislators can change the conventions of interpretations, they must do so by expressing an intention to that effect, an intention which itself must be expressed in accord with the Authoritative Intention Thesis.

In the cycle of convention and intention, convention comes first. Not in the sense that we follow convention rather than intention, but in the sense that the content of any intention is that which it has when interpreted by reference to the conventions of interpreting such expressive acts at the time. And that is the case even with regard to an intention which, once expressed, changes these conventions.

Suppose we are enquiring not into the relations between intention and the law enacted through its expression, but into the relations between what people mean (ie intend to say) and what they say, and the answer is that they mean to say what they said. Even if this is true, it hardly helps one interpret what was said by reference to the speaker's meaning. This is indeed true. It exposes no flaw in the arguments rehearsed above. It merely indicates that the Authoritative Intention Thesis, while valid, plays no real role in the interpretation of legislation. We can begin examining this point by focusing on the interpretation of ordinary speech (or writing). Of course, people sometimes say things they do not mean, and mean to say things which they fail to say. These cases result from incomplete command of the language, momentary loss of control of the physical aspects of one's speech, or permanent impairment of such control, from momentary confusion of thought (as when one means to say 'the oven is on', and says instead 'the fridge is on', or in the case of unintentional spoonerisms). But it does not follow from this that when we speak we first intend to say something and then attempt to say it, so that it is always an open question whether one said what one intended. Rather, barring exceptions, like those listed, one means what one says. There is no more to having meant to say that p than that one said that p and none of the exceptions obtain. This should not be read as indicating the existence of some closed list of exceptions. An exception is any explanation of what went wrong which establishes either that one was trying or had formed an intention to say something and failed, or that one did not mean what one said even though there was nothing specific that one did intend.[23] But neither condition allows that normally saying what one intended is a matter of establishing a match between two independent variables, intention and action.

So the normal way of finding out what a person intended to say is to establish what he said. The thought that the process can be reversed mistakes the exceptional case, in which action misfires and one fails to say what one tries to say, for the normal case. The same is true of legislation, only more so. Given that normally legislation is institutionalized in a way which virtually removes the risk of a slip of the tongue, loss of physical control, and other explanations of misfired action, and given that any conceivable theory of authority puts a high premium on relative clarity in demarcating what counts as an exercise of authority and what does not, the possibility of having to go behind what is said to establish what was meant becomes very rare. For practical purposes it may altogether disappear.

It follows that, while the Authoritative Intention Thesis is valid, it does not provide an aid to interpretation. Once we know what the legislation means we know what the legislator meant. He meant that. Does it follow that the Authoritative Intention Thesis is true but empty? Not quite.

First, remember that legislators have several intentions. We are considering the minimal intention necessarily required for legislation, which I will call the minimal intention. Some legal systems may specify further intentions as relevant for interpretation—for example, the

---

[23] The point applies to the relation between intention and action in general.

intention to achieve certain social goals. In interpreting legislation in countries in which this is the case, their courts may be instructed to allow those intentions to override the minimal intention. That is, they may be mandated or allowed to determine that the law established by a statute is not what the statute says but what it would have said to give effect to those other intentions of the legislators. In the next section I will briefly discuss the argument that courts are always so mandated in democratic regimes.

Still, this reply does not rescue the Authoritative Intention Thesis from vacuity in so far as the minimal intention is concerned. Barring specific directions to the courts to take account of other legislative intentions, there is no way in which the process can be reversed and what the legislator meant be discovered by appeal to the minimal intention and independently of what it enacted. It does not follow, however, that the Authoritative Intention Thesis is empty. The Authoritative Intention Thesis is crucial for the legitimation of legislation. An enactment which is not interpreted as it was meant or intended to be cannot rest on the authority of the legislature (at least it cannot rest on that authority alone). But the Authoritative Intention Thesis is no use as an aid to or method of interpretation.

It would be wrong to think that, if the Authoritative Intention Thesis has 'merely' a legitimizing role and is not an aid to interpretation, it is of no consequence to the practice of interpretation, that interpretation would have proceeded in exactly the same way had the thesis been false. The thesis requires one to understand the legislation as meaning what the legislator said. What the legislator said is what his words mean, given the circumstances of the promulgation of the legislation, and the conventions of interpretation prevailing at the time.[24] But to say that the legislation has that meaning is to impose a severe constraint on it. Not every conceivable interpretation would meet this condition. Many theories of interpretation are inconsistent with that guide to interpretation. At the same time it is true that the Authoritative Intention Thesis is not itself a method of interpretation. Rather it refers the courts to the conventions of interpretation prevailing at the time of legislation.[25]

---

[24] Naturally, not all the interpretive conventions prevailing are relevant to the interpretation of what the legislator said. Some of them are conventions regarding when the meaning of the legislation can be disregarded in the light of other factors—eg changes in social or economic conditions, evidence of legislative 'mistakes' of one kind or another, or conflicting legal rules or doctrines.

[25] Those conventions, for example, may say that legislation is to be interpreted by the conventions of interpretation prevailing from time to time (rather than those prevailing

IV. Limits of the Authoritative Intention Thesis

The argument for the Authoritative Intention Thesis is consistent with the view that there may well be cases in which people believe that good law can emerge from human activities which are not designed to make law—typically from enduring social, judicial, or commercial practices. But the argument assumes that the occasions on which anyone might suppose that good law can emerge by legislation even though the law thus made does not conform with the intentions of the law-makers are so rare as to be negligible. The Authoritative Intention Thesis does not even purport to apply to practice-based law. But does it hold good for all legislated law? I will consider three realistic and partly successfully challenges to this assumption. None of them applies to all the cases of deliberately made law. But each of them applies to an important class of cases.

It is important not to mistake the character of the arguments against the Authoritative Intention Thesis. They do not refute the thesis. Rather they set limits to the justification for relying on it in legal interpretation, even where the only legal concern is that a certain piece of legislation be given effect. The Authoritative Intention Thesis, we can say, determines the basic conserving interpretation of all legislation; that is, it determines what counts as a successful elucidation of the meaning the legislation has when promulgated. The arguments to be canvassed below indicate conditions under which the best interpretation is not that basic conserving interpretation. They suggest that sometimes it is better to deviate from the basic meaning of the legislation. That marks their relation to the Authoritative Intention Thesis; they confirm it at the same time as justifying endorsing interpretations which deviate from it under certain circumstances.

The previous paragraph also marks the moral character of the arguments which follow. In this they differ from the arguments for the Authoritative Intention Thesis itself. Of course, invoking

at the time of legislation). If they do, then they defeat the distinction between interpretations which retrieve the original meaning of the legislation, as defined by the intention thesis, and interpretations which show it to have a meaning acquired at a later date. A legal system which follows such conventions guarantees that the legislator knows that his words may bear a meaning which he cannot foresee, even if he tries. As I pointed out above, this is inconsistent with the rationale of the doctrine of authority. However, as the next section explains, the force of legislation does not rest entirely on the authority of the legislator.

moral considerations in favour of one method of interpretation and against others is consistent with the discussion being part of general jurisprudence, provided that the considerations invoked and the conclusions they support have universal validity for legal interpretation in all legal systems. But it is important to be aware that in arguing for the Authoritative Intention Thesis, no moral reason for endorsing it was invoked. That was made possible by the fact that the thesis does not establish the case for interpreting the law one way or another. All it says is: to the extent that what one is doing is understanding the meaning of a rule as established by legislation, one must interpret it in accordance with the intention of the legislator (as identified by the thesis). It leaves it open whether or not there are adequate reasons to follow legislated rules. All it says is that, if there are such reasons, then to follow them interpretation should follow the Authoritative Intention Thesis.

Sometimes legislators lack authority or their legislation is so iniquitous that there is no adequate reason to follow the law they made. The examination of such issues belongs to the doctrine of legitimate authority and need not occupy us here. What follows assumes that the legislative authority is legitimate, and therefore that there are adequate reasons to follow its law, and to interpret it in accordance with the Authoritative Intention Thesis. But—the first two considerations which follow point out—sometimes the very reasons which support the Authoritative Intention Thesis also create a case for deviating from it in certain circumstances. The third consideration I will examine is more radical in nature. It claims that the reasons for the thesis run out in certain circumstances. When they do, the Authoritative Intention Thesis holds no sway. It loses its force because it depends on the reasons for obeying the legislator, and sometimes those reasons run out. They do—to repeat—not because the legislator has no authority, nor because we have no reason to obey legislated rules, but because in certain circumstances the reasons for obeying legislated law detach from the authority of the legislator.

A. Supporting coordination

In many cases it does not matter what the law is so long as there is a reasonably clear law on the issue. These are cases where the point of the law is to secure coordinating conventions. Sometimes important benefits to society as a whole (ie public and collective goods) or to some of its members can be best secured if people coordinate their actions, and sometimes a law indicating the way coordination is to be achieved is the most effective way of securing coordination. The law can make clear to people that the case calls for coordinated action, and reassure them that the number of defectors and free-riders will be limited.[26] Since it does not matter whether people coordinate their conduct around one scheme or another, it does not matter if the legislation laid down to achieve the coordination is interpreted as securing one scheme of coordination or another. Therefore, legislation which is solely designed to secure a coordinating convention need not be interpreted in accordance with the intention of the legislator. So long as it is interpreted in a way which secures a coordinating convention, it fully serves the legislator's intent, whether or not the convention it is interpreted to make legally binding is the one intended by the legislator. The same may apply to many cases where the interest in coordination, while not the only reason, is the dominant reason for the law.

B. Unmatching further intentions

Second, legislators typically have more than one intention.[27] One intention, other than the standard intention, seems relevant to the doctrine of authority. Sometimes the legislator may intend to secure certain social and economic results through making a certain law, the obedience to which and application of which will constitute or bring about these results. As we know, not infrequently this intention misfires. Because of a change in the social or economic situation, or because the legislator was labouring under a misapprehension as to what the conditions actually are or what the social or economic effect of the law, given that environment, will be, or because the legislator misunderstood the legal impact the statute will have, given the legal environment, doctrinal

---

[26] See my discussion of coordination and the law in ch 3 of *The Morality of Freedom* (Oxford: OUP, 1986) and in 'Facing Up' (1989) 62 *Southern Californian Law Review* 1154–1179. The relevance of the fact that a piece of legislation aims to secure coordination for its interpretation was pointed out by Marmor in *Interpretation and Legal Theory*.

[27] For a recent argument that sometimes the legislator's further intentions should count in support of an interpretation which conforms with them, an argument that I find in general very convincing, see Marmor, *Interpretation and Legal Theory*, ch 8. My concern in this section is parallel to Marmor's. It is not that the legislator's further intention should weigh in interpreting the law on issues on which the law lends itself to several interpretations, but that, when the legislator's standard intention conflicts with his further intention, his standard intention should not count when applying the law to cases where, should it count, its application is clear.

and bureaucratic, in which it will operate, or for some other reason, the statute, if interpreted in accordance with the legislator's standard intention, will not have the consequences the legislator further intended to secure. When this is so, it seems pointless to interpret the statute in accord with the legislator's intention. The doctrine of authority suggests that legislators were given authority to make the law they thought for good reasons to be right. When it becomes clear that the law does not, or will not, achieve the results which (according to the doctrine of authority) properly motivated its enactment, should not the courts interpret the law against the standard intention of the legislator and in accord with the legislator's further, but legitimate intentions?

An affirmative answer is far from a foregone conclusion. First, let us note that often no further intention of the right kind can be attributed to the legislating body. Either it had none (it may have acted for improper reasons, or for no reasons, or different of its members may have acted for different further reasons making it impossible to attribute any definite reason to the legislating body itself), or its reasons are impossible to discover with any certainty. In itself that consideration does not invalidate the above argument for overriding the legislating body's standard intention in favour of its appropriate further intention. It only shows that, if accepted, the argument will have limited consequences. Often it will be to no avail. But beyond that the fact that complicated factual issues about the actual intentions of legislators will have to be gone into is a powerful reason to reject the argument altogether. It may be much easier to determine the content of legislation when interpreted in accord with the standard intention than when interpreted in accordance with the appropriate further intention. Hence the chances of mistaken interpretation may be much increased if the latter course is followed. The will of the legislating body may prevail more often if its further intention is disregarded than if it comes to form the basis of interpretation. Second, while some of the legislator's further intentions may not be realized by the statute, possibly others are, and they may be sufficient to justify its interpretation in accord with the Authoritative Intention Thesis. When we know that the statute fails to match some further intentions, how do we know whether it does not match others? Third, it may be constitutionally inappropriate, and there may be many bad consequences to opening the question of the further intentions of the legislators in court. Private communications may become relevant evidence, etc.

The three counter-arguments can, however, be circumscribed if certain conventions are adopted—for example, the convention that further intent can be inferred only from a certain range of public documents. Perhaps our conclusion should be that, in principle, further intentions are an appropriate basis for interpretation in preference to the standard intention, provided measures to avoid the bad consequences indicated by the counter-arguments have been adopted. Naturally, the degree to which this has been done, and the degree to which courts may be authorized to rely on this argument, will vary from jurisdiction to jurisdiction depending on their law and their (legal) conventions. In some countries it may be deemed undesirable to give all or some courts the power to enquire into the social goals which the legislator was pursuing, on the ground that on balance this will lead to so many mistaken decisions as to make such power counter-productive, or because of considerations of the status or prestige of the legislature and the courts. But, so long as the argument above seems sound and so long as the courts' power to rely on it is not limited by law or convention, they should do so, subject to the assumption of guidelines to avoid the drawbacks indicated by the counter-arguments.

There is, however, a more powerful argument against reliance on such further intentions. The doctrine of authority does indeed entrust power to whichever authority has it so that it will use its judgement and pass the laws which achieve consequences it deems just or desirable. But it also requires reasonably clear demarcation of the way laws are made. If a law made in accordance with the constitutional procedures fails, when interpreted properly—that is, in accordance with the Authoritative Intention Thesis—to achieve its intended result, that cannot be a reason for the courts to interpret it in some other way. They have no reason to believe that the authority would have adopted a different law than the one it did in fact adopt were it convinced that that is necessary in order to achieve the result it wanted to secure by the law it did adopt. The law which achieves that result may have further predictable consequences which may have inclined the legislator to refrain from any measure rather than achieve its desired result at the cost of those further consequences. In many cases a further complication arises. There may be different ways of achieving the legislator's further intention, all of them with a variety of predictable and unpredictable further results. How are the courts to know which of these, if any, would have been endorsed by the legislating body had it been aware that its favoured law will not secure its intended goal?

To deal with the objection we need to distinguish two arguments in the proposed deviation from the Authoritative Intention Thesis: first, the argument that the courts should not follow the standard intention when it conflicts with the appropriate further intention; second, that they should interpret the law to give effect to the said further intention. The counter-argument is convincing in refuting the thought that the doctrine of authority requires giving effect to the legislator's further intention. It does not.[28] But the counter-argument does nothing to deny the force of the first argument, to the effect that the doctrine of authority does not cover cases in which the statute (correctly interpreted in accord with the Authoritative Intention Thesis) does not match the appropriate further intentions of the legislator. The doctrine is based on the belief that the legislating body has competence which makes its rulings worthy of obedience and respect. But, when that competence manifestly fails, the belief is refuted, and the doctrine of authority no longer supports the statute. It follows that, so far as the universal considerations of respect for authority are concerned, the courts are at liberty to deviate from the Authoritative Intention Thesis in interpreting the statute. It does not follow that they have to give effect to the legislator's further intention. They have discretion to offer an innovative interpretation, a topic to be considered in a separate paper.[29]

C. Old laws

The two limits to the Authoritative Intention Thesis showed that respect for the further intention of the legislator may, in certain conditions, justify deviating from the standard intention, or justifies indifference to such deviations. They are limitations on the Authoritative Intention Thesis imposed by taking note of the legislator's intention,

---

[28] Except in cases where the interpretation which serves the further intentions does not involve any consequences which any reasonable person could find undesirable and which are not also involved in giving effect to the act when interpreted in accord with the Authoritative Intention Thesis. When this condition is met, there is a case for following the further intention.

[29] Even with all the reservations here expressed, the notion of a 'legislator's further intent' is problematical. Arguably, an institution cannot have a legislative intention unless there are firm conventions for attributing to it the intentions of some individuals. Once this convention and all the other conventions necessary to overcome the objections to reliance on such intentions which were discussed above are in place, the further intentions are themselves incorporated in documents which should be regarded as part of the legislated text. Therefore, the intention they express is the standard intention, or a borderline case of it. Such doubts do not undermine the conclusions arrived at in this subsection. But they may show that the distinction between standard and further intentions relies on conventional ways of regarding intentions which do not have substantial theoretical justifications.

of that intention which the doctrine of authority makes relevant. The third limit has less to do with the legislator's further intentions. Like the second one, it casts doubt on the relevance of the standard intention because it casts doubt on whether respect for legislation always depends on the doctrine of authority.

When we think of the interpretation of recent statutes, the force of the generalized argument for the Authoritative Intention Thesis seems compelling. But when we think of a statute or a common-law decision 200- or 300-years-old, the force of the argument is less compelling. Consider the example of a democratic country. Being ruled by the will of those who were legislators 200 or 300 years ago is not everyone's idea of democratic government. For one thing, most countries which are democratic today were not democratic then. But, even if they were, there is no compelling reason to think that democracy includes the power of the majority of one generation to bind future generations. The fact that those future generations can repeal old legislation is no answer. Why should they have to spend scarce resources (and legislative time is a very scarce resource) to do so? Even though the matter requires more careful consideration than it can be given here, I would submit that the democratic argument does not justify interpreting very old law in accordance with the will of its law-makers. Furthermore, while not all countries are democratic, there are good reasons for thinking that whatever theory of authority they endorse will similarly fail to sanction the Authoritative Intention Thesis.

Perhaps this argument is too sweeping. Here is a counterargument. Some laws address standing human problems—as does, for example, the central core of the criminal law, or the basic doctrines of contract or property law. In such cases, the doctrine of authority may well vindicate the authority of any proper authority to bind future generations. If it is a good authority for its generation, the doctrine will say, then it is good for future generations as well, the reason being that the matters covered by the law of homicide, etc. affect all generations in the same way. The argument for the temporal limits of the authority of any legislator holds good only with regard to matters where changing opinions, tastes, or circumstances may make a difference to what is a sensible law and what is not.

The core of good sense in this counter-argument is undeniable. But the way it impacts on the interpretive role of the courts is less certain. A crucial question is: who has authority to establish the authority of old legislation? New legislation comes with the established authority of the legislator. No questions about the authority of the legislator arise there other than those which are handled by judicial review processes. But with older legislation the question whether it is a piece of legislation which still has the authoritative standing it once had must be confronted by the courts. Unless the specific jurisdiction in which they operate bars the courts from enquiring into the matter, they are bound to raise the question, as they should not follow a lapsed authority. This means that, in interpreting old statutes, questions of their binding force arise in ways they do not arise in interpreting recent statutes. Of course, the difference is a matter of degree and the freedom of the courts in interpreting old statutes increases gradually with their antiquity—other things being equal.[30] Moreover, even with regard to laws of standing relevance, one has to distinguish the core (a prohibition of homicide) from the details of the law or the offences or causes of action which it creates. While, regarding the core matter that the law deals with, the authority of the legislating body may be undiminished, its authority over details may not be as secure. This is, in fact, the most common case. Its manifestation is in the greater liberty the practices of interpretation of different legal jurisdictions allow the courts when they deal with older legislation. This freedom includes the freedom to interpret the law in ways which depart from the Authoritative Intention Thesis. Where the authority of the older legislation is affected by changes in circumstances since its adoption, this is consistent with the underlying rationale of the Authoritative Intention Thesis—that is, with the doctrine of authority.

As I said at the outset, none of the cases denies the force of the Authoritative Intention Thesis altogether. First, they do not deny that, where the doctrine of authority dictates that the courts should respect the authority of the legislature (or the authority of a higher court to lay down binding precedents), the Authoritative Intention Thesis normally holds good. They merely show that obedience to legislation does not always rest on the authority of the legislature alone, and that, where it does, some further intentions may justify disregarding the standard intention. Second, the loss of authority of old enactments is not sudden but gradual. One way this can express itself is by a legal practice according to which, as the time the legislation was passed recedes, the courts acquire more and more power to

---

[30] The very fact that the difference between recent and old is a gradual one makes the courts the appropriate authority to deal with its implications—though admittedly not every legal system need see it that way.

adjust it to changing social and economic circumstances. Third, in the normal run of things we would expect the courts to have plenty of reasons to respect the law as laid down by the legislator—that is, as interpreted in conformity with the Authoritative Intention Thesis—even after the reasons for respecting the Authoritative Intention Thesis no longer apply. The most obvious reason is that, in the normal course of events, by that time people's expectations have become fixed around the intention-based interpretation of the law, and these expectations should not be too hastily upset.

It is no good saying that, if the legislator adopted a practice not to respect the Authoritative Intention Thesis in the three classes of cases listed above, then no expectation would be formed and none upset. Given the uncertainty as to when the considerations we are canvassing take effect, any great readiness to upset the intention-based interpretation will indeed prevent expectations from forming, but it will be likely to do so in an inaccurate way. So sometimes people will be taken by surprise by the court's decision which upsets the intention-based interpretation when they did not expect it to do so. At other times, they will fail to rely on the intention-based interpretation even when they should rely on it—thus at least partially frustrating the aims of the legislation.

None of this shows that the courts should disregard altogether the force of the three arguments presented above. But it does mean that they should tend to err on the side of caution and to give weight to the intention-based interpretation even when it does not rest on the authority-oriented argument for the Authoritative Intention Thesis which is its foundation.

D. Interim conclusions

Why does interpretation play any role in adjudication? Should not the courts simply be guided by morality, and abandon any interpretation? This way of putting the question may mislead. Of course the courts should adjudicate disputes in a way consistent with morality. When they fail to do so, this need not be because they believe that they are not bound by morality or that they are bound by a code higher than morality which overrides it. When courts' decisions are inconsistent with morality this is because they are mistaken about what morality requires or permits them to do. The question is what is it about morality which requires courts to decide cases with the help of interpretive means? And what and how should they interpret?

The examination of the Authoritative Intention Thesis led to three principal conclusions. First, the interpretation of statutes, etc in accord with the authors' intentions is a universal feature of legal systems which recognize legislation as a source of law, for it is implied by the very notion of legislation. In other words, interpretation in accord with legislative intention is demanded by any realistically conceivable theory of authority.[31] Second, while the theory of authority shows that the legitimacy of legislated—that is, authority-based—law depends on it being interpreted in accordance with its authors' intentions, the guide to interpretation which the theory of authority indicates is reliance on the conventions for interpreting legislative texts of the kind in question prevailing in the legal culture when the legislation in question was promulgated. Intention legitimates, but conventions interpret. Third, and finally, the doctrine of authority cannot provide a complete and exhaustive basis for all the ways in which interpretive arguments feature in adjudication. It transpired that, even where the legal rules under consideration are enacted rules, the doctrine of authority, and with it the reliance on intention, does not cover all the grounds for the validity of these rules.[32]

Needless to say, where the legal rules concerned are practice-based rather than authority-based, and when, though they were laid down by authority, their interpretation by reference to conventions of interpretation is incomplete, or undiscoverable, because the conventions are irredeemably vague or ambiguous on the point at issue, interpretation has to find some other routes and a different justification (or be abandoned).

In other words, the doctrine of authority provides the foundation for the role of conserving interpretation in adjudication. In the practice of adjudication, interpretation features even where the doctrine of authority does not extend, and where conserving interpretation is either impossible or unjustified. The question of why and when should the courts use innovative interpretation as the morally correct way of deciding cases remains to be answered. Where courts' decisions are innovative (i.e. not based on respect for authority), why should they be interpretive at all?

---

[31] Authority based on revelation is probably the obvious exception to the rule. Throughout this chapter I disregard all theologically based doctrines.

[32] These arguments finally vindicate the abandonment above of the Radical Intention Thesis in favour of the Authoritative Intention Thesis.

12

Interpretation: Pluralism and Innovation

If I teach you the rules, you must interpret them anew
(Hans Sachs in Die Meistersinger von Nürnberg, Act 3)

A successful or good interpretation is a good or true explanation of something which has meaning because it explains or displays that meaning. Both the activity of explaining or displaying the meaning and its product are interpretations, and I will draw attention to the distinction only when there is a special point to make. As with many other activities and their products unsuccessful interpretations are also interpretations, though some interpretations are so bad as to be interpretations no longer.

An act or activity is one of interpretation if it is appropriate to judge its success by whether it is a good interpretation. Often what makes it appropriate so to judge it is the intention of the agent. But on the one hand other factors too may make it appropriate (most commonly if there is a practice which identifies the act as an interpretation then it is one whatever the agent's intention), and on the other hand, the agent's intention does not always suffice (eg when if taken to be an interpretation the activity would be such a bad interpretation that it is inappropriate to take it as such even though the agent meant it to be so taken and judged). There can be no exhaustive and informative specification of what makes it appropriate to judge an activity or its product by the standards which apply to interpretations, and therefore there can be no exhaustive and informative specification of what makes something an interpretation. What is of interest is what makes interpretations successful, what are the standards by which they are judged.

That all interpretations purport to explain or to display the meaning of an object, meaning by that that they are activities, or the products of activities, whose success is appropriately judged by their success in offering such explanations or displays, is a conceptual truth, and helps in directing the mind, but is not in itself very illuminating. 'Meaning' is, if anything, even more amorphous and protean than 'interpretation'. For example, the explanation of the meanings of words is the subject of semantics. Is semantics part of the study of interpretation?

Perhaps we should say that interpretations are displays or statements of meaning, other than that which is studied by semantics. This is not being perverse. It is trying to get at something which is at the centre of the study of interpretation in legal and many other contexts. Those interested in interpretation in this sense are not interested in what interpreters do, namely render in one language what is said in another. Nor are they interested in how interpreters can, in principle, succeed in doing what they do, which is, I take it, what Davidson studied when he studied radical interpretation. Semantics may help us understand that enterprise. But it does not help with the question: 'Can a translation of poetry avoid being an interpretation of the poetry translated?' When saying that translation inevitably involves interpretation in this context one is not saying that both interpreters and translators fail to do what they aim to do, ie render the meaning of the original. Rather, one is saying that translators are doing something other than mere translation, perhaps doing it inevitably, even when they would rather not do it. They are doing—and possibly doing well, something different.[1]

It is this notion of interpretation which I am interested in. I will claim for it that it is the notion of interpretation of interest to those thinking about or offering interpretations of historical events or periods or trends, and the like, as well as to those thinking about or offering interpretations of works of art in any medium or genre, and to those dealing with the interpretation of religious rites or texts and the like, and to those interested in legal interpretation. It is not what semantics is about, nor the interpretation of simple speech acts such as 'It is a hot day today,' said in the circumstances in which one may normally say such a thing,

---

[1] Our target concept can be narrowed still further. It excludes private meanings and associations (the two seem closely related). We are looking for meaning, not for the meaning an object has for a particular person. Private meaning is usually a matter of association of the object with some event or occasion in the life of the person for whom the object has that meaning ('The ring means a lot to me. It was the only gift I have from my grandmother,' 'This place means a lot to me, it reminds me of my first love'). Public meaning is symbolic, not causal, and involves at least in part conventions and rules of meaning.

nor in the interpretation of or the meaning of the results of scientific experiments, or of natural phenomena.[2]

I. Some Basic Features

An account of interpretation can be expected to answer three questions, the what, why, and how questions, namely what is interpretation? Why engage in it? How to do it?

Let us start at the beginning—what is interpretation?

We start with features of the concept evident from the standards people apply when using it, that is the standards by which they judge its correct use, ie from the practice of interpretation. It determines constraints on any possible account (though not necessarily rigid constraints). It also gives rise to the problems an account encounters.

Roughly characterized interpretation has seven marks:

First, it is an *explanation* or (in performance-interpretations) *a display* of its object.

Second, it explains an object by making plain its meaning.[3] Only what has meaning can be interpreted.

Third, some interpretations are good and some are bad, and some are better than others. This is not to say that all interpretations can be ranked by how good they are. Some are incommensurate.

Fourth, a good interpretation is one which explains the meaning of its object, and thereby the object that has that meaning, so that the intended audience does, if it tries, understand it.

These four features are probably true of interpretation in general. The special kind of interpretation I will be concerned with shares these four marks of interpretation, but has three additional ones:

Fifth, a good interpretation provides understanding, not merely knowledge. This in itself excludes the giving of a dictionary meaning, substitution of synonyms or near synonyms, and translation; that is it excludes semantic meaning.

---

[2] And it is a moot point whether the interpretation of dreams belongs with those, or with the interpretation I am writing about.

[3] Or, that they display the object in ways which make its meaning plain. I will not continue to rephrase my remarks about interpretation to make them apply to interpretations which display rather than explain. The adjustments required are not hard to find.

Sixth, interpretive pluralism: there can be more than one good interpretation of objects with meaning.

Seventh, some good interpretations are innovative, in a strong sense. That is they are not merely new in having been hitherto unknown to some or all. They are innovative in that the meaning they explain is not one the object had independently of them.

One important clarification: I will be talking of interpretations of a *kind* which can be innovative, and which allows for good conflicting interpretations. What matters is what is possible by the norms which set standards of correctness for interpretation, rather than the properties of any particular interpretation. The thought is that even non-innovative, conserving, or retrieving interpretations are affected by the fact that they are of a kind which allows for innovative alternatives to them.

II. The Puzzles of Pluralism and Innovation

There is a tame way of understanding the sixth mark. Often different interpretations, even by different interpreters, of, say, one novel can be combined as so many parts of one more comprehensive interpretation. Interpretive pluralism does not refer to this fact. Its point is that several *incompatible* interpretations of the same object can all be good. Understanding in what sense interpretations can be incompatible is not an easy matter, and I doubt that it admits of informative formal definition. Interpretations which cannot be parts of one interpretation are incompatible. I will assume that we have an informal understanding of the notion. Things are relatively easy in interpretation through performance. What cannot be done in one performance cannot belong to one interpretation.

If interpretation explains its object by explaining its meaning, how can incompatible explanations be true or good? Obviously, if the object has more than one meaning then there will be more than one interpretation of its meanings. However, just pointing to plurality of meanings, in the way that 'bank' means both the bank of a river and the bank in the High Street, makes it inexplicable what is special about interpretive pluralism at all. There is poignancy to interpretations which are incompatible with each other, but do not displace each other. That depends on the different meanings being related. They may be, for example, competing variations on a theme. But that is unlikely to be the only way in which there could be several good, though competing interpretations. In any case, the concept of meaning relevant here (that is the meaning which interpretations explain) is closely tied to the idea of interpretation. I suspect that we can explain it only by explaining (among other things) what interpretations are, and the other way round. Meaning and interpretation are reciprocal concepts, with no conceptual priority to one over the other, no possibility of explaining one independently of the other. So while explaining the possibility of pluralism is a major part of explaining the concept of interpretation which is our subject, we need another starting point to enable us to approach it.

Perhaps not surprisingly, the explanation of pluralism is closely tied to the explanation of innovation, and I will focus on the possibility of innovative interpretations to find the key to understanding interpretation. Innovative interpretations explain or reveal a meaning which was not there all along, such that the interpretation itself had something to do with the object having it. How can that be?

Suppose I offer an interpretation. If it is true then it was so before I offered it. After all it cannot be made true just by my say-so. If it is not true then my interpretation is not a good one. Either way there cannot be good innovative interpretations—if they are good they are not innovative, if they are innovative they are not good. A second objection relies on our notion of explanation: if an interpretation is an explanation then it cannot be innovative. Explanations are inert. They do not create or modify the object that they explain. In trying to explain what interpretations are I will concentrate on the two riddles of innovative interpretation. Their solution will, hopefully, provide the major part of the account of interpretation.

One preliminary point may help soften the appearance of a dilemma. Interpretations have a dual object: they explain the object and also its meaning, and they do the first by doing the second. Interpretations explain and do not change their objects. They explain their objects by making plain their meanings and so do innovative interpretations as well. What they affect is the meaning, not the object which has it. To give but one example: if cogent, Freud's interpretation of *Hamlet* ('Hamlet is able to do anything—except take vengeance on the man who did away with his father and took that father's place with his mother, the man who shows him the repressed wishes of his own childhood realized. Thus the loathing which should drive him on to revenge is replaced in him by self-reproaches, by scruples of conscience, which remind him that he himself is literally no better than the sinner whom he is to punish'[4]) casts new light on the play. But it did not change the play. That is clear enough regardless of one's judgement of its merits. No interpretation, however innovative, changes its object.

Innovative interpretations do, however, reveal a new meaning in their object. That reinstates the paradox. After all, it is natural to say that interpretations explain the meaning of their objects. If explanations are inert how can they affect the meanings that they explain? Admittedly, objects can be self-explanatory, and that can be literally true: they can be their own explanations. But relying on this point misses the source of the puzzle. In the first place, typically interpretations are offered to explain what is there independently of them, rather than in order to produce new objects which explain themselves. Second, and here we come to the heart of the matter, explanations can be good or bad, and they can be more or less good. Their success is determined by criteria, or rules for excellence in interpretations (ie in interpretations of the kind that they are). Surely these criteria are independent of the interpretations. If their validity has a temporal dimension then they are valid before the interpretations to which they apply are put forward, as well as independently of them. But if so then interpretations can be new only in the less radical sense: they are new because no one thought of them before, but they are not innovative. They reveal meanings their objects had all along, or at any rate before they were offered, and independently of the fact that they are offered. How, therefore, can there be innovative interpretations?

Furthermore, while—if the criteria deciding which interpretations are good have a temporal dimension, ie if these criteria may change over time—possibly innovative interpretations also change the criteria by which interpretations are judged, in itself that would not solve the puzzle either. Unless the change of criteria is arbitrary it itself must be responsive to other criteria, which designate some criteria as valid criteria by which to determine the quality of interpretations. And if so then the change of criteria can only be the mild one, ie the discovery of criteria which were valid all along, rather than the radical introduction of genuinely new criteria, and we are back with our puzzle.

We are in the grip of a fundamental dichotomy. So long as the criteria which determine how good interpretations are independent of the interpretations to which they apply they cannot be innovative

---

[4] *The Interpretation of Dreams* (trans A A Brill, 3rd edn, London: Allen & Unwin, 1932).

interpretations. If there are innovative interpretations then their criteria must determine how good an interpretation is not only by its (timeless) propositional content, but also by the character and the circumstances of the very act of advancing the interpretation. How can that be?

III. The Objects of Interpretation: Cultural Goods

The key lies in the nature of the objects of interpretations. Central to my account of interpretation is that typical objects of interpretation are what I will call cultural goods, namely things whose meaning depends on cultural practices.[5] They are 'goods' in a loose sense. They include things, relationships, activities, institutions, and more which can be good or bad. They are normative in that they are produced and maintained by activities aimed at achieving goals assumed to be valuable, or by activities which are seen as subject to norms assumed to be valid. Two main classes of such goods stand out. First, works of art, including literary works, musical works, and products of the visual arts. Second, social relations (such as the various forms of friendship), social events (such as weddings), and, more indirectly, social institutions.

One feature common to all cultural goods is that to benefit from them one needs to know of them. This is not true of all things of value. In general one need not have the concepts relating to sexual activity to enjoy sexual pleasure. The same goes for any purely sensual pleasure. Though it is significant that human cultures integrate many of the pure sensual pleasures in culturally recognized pursuits. But one needs some understanding of what a theatre play is to appreciate and enjoy a good play, and one needs some understanding of what friendship is to be a friend.

The reason is not far to seek. In all these cases we benefit from whichever good is in question by engaging with it, by acting in ways which are appropriate to it, with attitudes and expectations appropriate to it. We can do so only by directing our mind and actions in ways appropriate to that good, and that requires some appreciation of its nature.

---

[5] Bad, evil, and worthless cultural products are also open to the same kind of interpretation, but to simplify the discussion here I will disregard them. Cultural goods are only the 'typical' objects of interpretation, in the sense here explored, because once a type of normatively regulated activity is established it can spread itself beyond its proper sphere. The crucial claim is that untypical cases are parasitic, in their occurrence and understanding, on the typical ones.

The second feature of cultural goods is their dependence on culture. Arguably their existence, but certainly the ability to enjoy and benefit from cultural goods, what I will call having access to them, depends on the existence of social practices of engaging with them, benefiting from them and respecting them. My ability to read with understanding and pleasure Tolstoy's *War and Peace*, or to read or watch with understanding and pleasure Aristophanes' *The Clouds* depends on the existence, now or in the past, here or elsewhere, of a culture where people write, read, and discuss novels and plays.

The first feature of cultural goods helps in explaining the second. Access to cultural goods depends on sustaining practices because we can benefit from them only if we direct ourselves towards them, and that requires some understanding of what they are like. We acquire that understanding primarily through acculturation in, immersion in, societies where these values are recognized and engaged with, and secondarily through familiarity, personal or through testimony and other sources, with other societies or other periods, where such goods were recognized. Access depends on familiarity with sustaining practices because appreciating cultural goods is rich, complex, and nuanced, involving an appreciation of their relations to various other goods, and as such is too thick-textured to be transmitted by description only, let alone to be invented by a single individual.[6]

IV. The Argument from Relative Inevitability

The social dependence of cultural goods leads directly to one argument for the possibility of innovative interpretations. It is a familiar observation that one reason why innovative interpretation is sometimes possible is because it is sometimes inevitable. The inevitability is relative. It is normally possible to avoid offering any interpretation. The claim is that under some conditions, if good interpretations are offered, they cannot but be innovative.

I will pursue this argumentative strategy. This is how it goes: It can be assumed that if something has a meaning then its meaning can be explained. The assumption is not that a comprehensive and exhaustive

---

[6] These points are familiar from many discussions. For my contribution see *The Morality of Freedom* (Oxford: Clarendon Press, 1986) ch 12, and *The Practice of Value* (Oxford: Clarendon Press, 2003).

explanation is always possible, but that some explanation is. If it can be shown that it is impossible to interpret these objects except innovatively it follows that either they cannot be successfully interpreted or that good innovative interpretations of them are possible. Since we know that they can be interpreted successfully, it would follow that good innovative interpretations are possible.

The knowledge that they can be successfully interpreted is no more than knowledge that they can be explained. The existence of a flourishing practice of interpreting social events, social relationships, works of art, and other cultural products secures that knowledge. Hence, the practice of interpretation would, if the argument succeeds, also assure us that there are successful innovative interpretations.[7] In establishing the inevitability of good innovative interpretations in some cases, the argument opens the door for them in the generality of cases. So what has to be explained is how it is that some interpretations cannot but be innovative.

A thought familiar to lawyers, but perhaps paradigmatically exemplified in performances of music, plays, or any other work, is that the meaning of certain objects is not altogether determined, and that the indeterminacy forces one to adopt an innovative interpretation, that is one which does not simply represent the meaning of the object as it is independently of the interpretation. Let me explain the presuppositions of that thought in a little detail:

Think, by way of illustration, of the theatre. Typically, first, there will be various ways an actor can position himself, or move, various ways of speaking his lines, which make a difference to the meaning of the action, and a difference to the implied motivation and frame of mind of that character at the time of speaking, and in general. And second, the meaning of the character's action, his motivation, and frame of mind as portrayed by the text of the play is indeterminate as to which way of performing the role is correct. In such a case, given that to perform the play the actor has to act in one of the ways not required by the text, and given that each such way of acting will attribute to his character attitudes which the play itself does not, whichever way the actor acts will constitute an innovative interpretation of the play or of part of it.[8]

---

[7] Needless to say, the argument will also modify, though it will not abandon, the premises at the beginning of the previous paragraph: sometimes meaning can only be explained by changing it, etc.

[8] Though if that interpretation was offered before, say by Ellen Terry or Judy Dench, then so acting now will not be innovative (though if the actor does not know of the precedents she may think that it is).

We should note what this illustration does not show:

First, it does not show that all the ways of performing the play are acceptable. Some may be inconsistent with the text in ways which make them inadmissible.[9]

Second, it does not show that every time an actor speaks some lines, or moves on stage, he or she is interpreting the role, let alone doing so in an innovative way. They may not interpret at all, if the way they deliver the lines or move casts no light on the character, or on any other aspect of the play. Even if the piece of acting concerned does constitute a (partial) interpretation of the role or the play, it need not be innovative.

Third, the illustration is of a case where innovative interpretation is inevitable. There is no suggestion that such cases exhaust the instances of legitimate innovative interpretation. That is, I am not suggesting that a way of performing a role which is at odds with the character of the action or of the role as established by the text is always illegitimate, or would always constitute a bad interpretation.

Fourth, the inevitability of innovative interpretation depends on the existence of indeterminacy of meaning. But that indeterminacy is not in itself sufficient to necessitate innovative interpretation. Indeterminacy can be preserved by many interpretations, and sometimes it is essential to the success of an interpretation that it be preserved.

Fifth, nor is the fact that interpretation in performance requires one to adopt some manner of delivery, some mode of action, etc, which is underdetermined by the original sufficient to make innovative interpretation necessary. In simultaneous translation, for example, the interpreter often faces indeterminacy not only in choice of words, but also in intonation, speed of delivery, and the like. Nevertheless, so long as the interpreter speaks in a fairly even manner his manner of delivery is understood not to convey any message. It is not part of the interpretation.

The lesson of the theatrical illustration can be stated in terms which apply generally. Broadly speaking, innovative interpretations are inevitable where

- aspects of the meaning of the original are indeterminate;
- rules of meaning direct that various aspects of the interpretive statements carry interpretive messages; and
- such message-conveying aspects of the interpretive statements are inescapable when interpreting the original, even though they relate to indeterminate aspects of its meaning; and

---

[9] I am evading the question of whether, and how, interpretations are constrained by the text. In my view, if the matter is determined it is determined by local conventions of interpretation. More on this below.

- it is impossible for them to preserve the indeterminate contours of the original.

Crucial to this description of the inevitability of some innovative interpretations is that it is relative. It is relative to norms of meaning, norms which determine that the voice of a simultaneous translator is not significant, that the apparent relative age of actors in a play represents the relative age of their characters, whereas the apparent relative age of singers in an opera does not convey that meaning. These norms are rarely arbitrary. But they are contingent. They exist because of practices which sustain them, and they get transformed as the underlying practices change (e.g. in Britain it used to be that if an actor was black the character he or she was portraying was understood to be black; but that rule no longer exists).

The indeterminacies regarding the motivation or character of a fictional persona are not epistemic. Moreover, these indeterminacies need not be due to linguistic vagueness. It is not vagueness in the language of the play which makes us wonder about Hamlet's motivation at different points in the play. Rather, the inevitability as well as the possibility of innovative interpretation is a result (among other factors) of the fact that the objects interpreted and their meanings are cultural products.

Why are norms sustained by social practices, and the values they define, underdetermined? Norms sustained by practices exist only where there is common knowledge of the rules, and common acknowledgement, even in the breach, that they bind. That is, the sustained norms are those which the people whose conduct constitutes the practice regard themselves as following, or as bound to follow. The indeterminacy of these norms is the inevitable result of four factors.

First, norms sustained by social practices are often expressed in similar ways by many people, and these statements are vague to a greater or lesser degree.

Second, even where there is common knowledge of a norm, that is common agreement about its content, the agreement is not complete. It permits conflicting views an undefeated claim to be correct statements of the common agreement, which is therefore indeterminate.

Third, a point which elaborates a central aspect of the previous one, the meaning of each kind of cultural goods is governed by a field of meaning-norms. That is, their meanings are interdependent; they import each other and presuppose each other. The interdependence of the norms governing the meaning of cultural goods creates much room for unresolved questions, for indeterminacies.

The fourth reason for the indeterminacy of norms and values that depend on sustaining practices is the most important one for the resolution of the riddles of innovative interpretation. The content of the norms is limited to the content of the practices sustaining them. Let me explain through a comparison with people's beliefs.[10] What people believe is less than the content of the propositions we use to report their beliefs, at least if the content of a proposition includes all that is entailed by it. True, what is entailed or implied by a proposition I believe imposes rational constraints on me. For example, if something is entailed by a belief of mine then, in some circumstances, I will be irrational unless I believe the conclusion or abandon my belief in the premise. But that is far from saying that I already believe whatever my beliefs entail.

In a similar way, while the contents of a practice-sustained norm or value are expressed[11] in propositions they do not include all that those propositions entail. They include only such entailments as can reasonably be said to be part of the common knowledge of the content of the norms.[12] This feature contributes greatly to their indeterminacy. It means that various logical constructs and various normative arguments which could otherwise be relied upon to reduce indeterminacy cannot be relied upon unless they themselves are grounded in the common knowledge of the sustaining practice.

V. The Argument from Social Dependence

How successful is the argument from inevitability in resolving the riddles of innovative interpretation? The argument aims to establish that there are good innovative interpretations. If so then there is a solution

---

[10] A point I discuss in *Ethics in the Public Domain* (Oxford: Clarendon Press, 1995) 227–228.

[11] At least in part. I do not wish to consider here the difficult question whether the content of such norms or of the values they define, can be completely stated in propositional form.

[12] Common knowledge conditions are often taken to imply universal agreement. That is not my meaning. To use again the analogy with people's beliefs: people may not be aware that they believe something, and yet they do. For example, they do if it is such an immediate consequence of their beliefs that it is impossible to attribute to them belief in one proposition without the other. Similarly, in the social sphere the immediate implications of common knowledge are common knowledge, even if no one is aware of them. Not surprisingly given that common knowledge is a function of the beliefs and conduct of many people there are more ways in which aspects of it may elude people's awareness than in the individual case.

to the riddles. But that in itself does not explain the solution. The argument does, however, provide the material for the required explanation. The first riddle said: if the interpretation is a good one then it must have been good before it was propounded. Just putting it forward could not have made it good, or true. So put, the first riddle begs the question. If a good interpretation is innovative then the act of putting it forward must make a difference. It generates a new way of understanding its object.

But there was more to the riddle than simply begging the question: it is undeniable that if the interpretation is good then it must have been good before it was propounded. At the very least it must be the case that there is a time before it was put forward such that had it been put forward at that time it would have been good. That is, of course, consistent with the innovative character of the interpretation. It is just like saying that if I invent a new machine the invention would have been a good one had I or someone else made it earlier. We can accept that the same is true of innovative interpretation. It does not solve the puzzle. The point of the riddle is that the interpretation is made good by features of the object which were there all along. So why do we think of innovative interpretations as analogous to inventions rather than to discoveries which reveal to us what was the case all along? If features of the interpreted object make a good interpretation good how could advancing the interpretation affect its value or correctness? But if putting it forward does not contribute to its being good, how could it be innovative (rather than a discovery of what was there anyway)?

The features which establish that an interpretation is a good one are features of its object, and its context, as well as general truths, for example about human psychology. They are not limited to those aspects of the object and the world which are generally known or thought to be important. The determination of what meanings the object already has, and what meanings are new, does depend on the contingencies of the meaning-fixing norms, and of our knowledge of other matters (e.g. human psychology) relevant to the interpretation. A way of understanding any object of interpretation which was never thought of before is a new way of understanding, and the interpretation propounding it is innovative, simply because it was never thought of before. The fact that the features of the play or the ceremony or whatever the interpreted object is, which show it to be a good interpretation were there all along does not matter. The contingency of socially dependent meanings makes ample room for innovative interpretations which show new ways of understanding their objects, and in so doing establish new meanings for their objects.

Accepting this explanation one may still wonder why should the standard of innovation applying to interpretation resemble that of the invention of machines and devices, rather than follow the way we think of discoveries in science or mathematics? Interpretation through performance excluded, interpretations consist of propositions and are good if the propositions are correct or true, that is if they correctly state the meaning of their object. Those who bring new truths to our attention, or prove known truths for the first time, or in new ways, discover truths or proofs. Why are interpreters judged differently?

Formally the answer is that in putting forward their interpretations they affect, change the meaning of the object of their interpretation. In the cases we examined they determine some aspect of the meaning which was indeterminate before. But this formal reply does not yet dissolve the puzzle. Here is a way of restating it: if my advancing an interpretation (together with other factors) makes M the meaning of the interpreted object, then it must have been true all along that M would be a meaning of the object once advanced as part of an interpretation. That shows that M was a potential meaning of that object. Why should advancing it be something other than discovering that it is a potential meaning? And if advancing it, is just such a discovery then there is no real difference between being a potential meaning and being a meaning, and therefore while we can discover interpretations hitherto unnoticed, we cannot innovate, and we cannot through advancing interpretations affect the meaning of their objects.

The explanation lies in the fragility and changeability of (good) interpretations. Not only interpretations but the norms or considerations governing them, those which tell a good from a bad interpretation, change over time. As a result, and given, as I assume, that the future is open, i.e. that there is no definite set of future possibilities, there is also no definite set of possible interpretations (in the sense explained above). To see why this is so, to understand the fragility and contingency of interpretations, we need to examine the norms governing their success, and that takes us to the second of the three questions posed at the outset: why interpret? For the considerations which determine success in interpretation depend on the reasons for interpreting. To be brief and crude about it, given that the reasons one has to interpret are reasons to interpret well, those interpretations are good which satisfy the reasons we had to interpret in the first place. We will turn to that question in the next section.

First, a word about the second riddle of innovative interpretation: how can an interpretation be explanatory and innovative at the same time? The fact that innovative interpretations affect the meaning of the interpreted object helps with the second riddle too. It shows that innovative interpretations are not purely explanatory. They set a new meaning, a new way of understanding their objects. But innovative interpretations are explanatory as well, for they explain their objects with the aid of the new meaning that they advance.

It would be wrong to think that good innovative interpretations occur only when inescapable, or that they are regrettably necessary. Innovative interpretations are a welcome feature of our engagement with cultural goods. Indeed, the peculiarity of cultural goods is that the attitude to deviant behaviour implicit in their sustaining practices is not altogether negative. It is in the nature of cultural goods that people need to have some understanding of them to engage with them, to benefit from them and enjoy them. If, as I argued, innovative interpretations are sometimes inevitable then the implicit attitude of the sustaining practices to innovative interpretations cannot be altogether negative.

This remark should not be misinterpreted. I have not overlooked the fact that certain societies may require rigorous compliance with their norms, and be hostile to any deviation. Nor have I forgotten that many societies may be unaware of the fact that cultural goods depend on sustaining social practices, and may vary with them. I did not say that people accept the legitimacy of innovative interpretations, only that the nature of cultural goods requires such acknowledgement. This enables the emergence of attitudes which, however incompletely, recognize the dependence of cultural goods on traditions and practices, and recognize the resulting contingency underlying the existence of norms and meanings, and allow for pluralism of reasonable interpretations, as well as for the appropriateness, in some circumstances, of innovative interpretations. Clearly, if the root of innovation is in the indeterminacy of meaning then innovation is not complete. It always relates to existing meanings. At the minimum it incorporates them and transcends them. On other occasions it derives its force from flouting them. The analysis I offered here points the road to the explanation of such phenomena, to the explanation of the uses of interpretation.

VI. Why Interpret?

What is the point of innovative interpretations? Think of scientific interpretations or explanations. Surely the fact that there cannot be true incompatible interpretations is part of the reason why we are interested in them. Only because of this can they explain to us how things are in the world. If they allowed for incompatible good interpretations they would imply that maybe this is how things are, but maybe they are some other way. What good can pluralistic interpretations be? What purpose can they serve?

The puzzle does not disappear when we point out that interpretive pluralism presupposes a plurality of meanings. It is true that when the object of an interpretation has a plurality of meanings we cannot understand it except through a plurality of interpretations. Understanding a matter is a kind of knowledge, call it knowledge in depth, which differs from other kinds of knowledge in consisting in knowing how its object relates to its constituents and to its context, and in an ability to put this knowledge to use (picking out instances of concepts, following in action the implications of a proposition, etc). Understanding is knowledge which is rich and dense enough to be mostly implicit, that is knowledge which outstrips its possessor's ability to articulate it. Interpretations help us reach such understandings. The question is: what point is there in a plurality of meanings, or in the ability to innovate, to generate new meanings through interpretations? We know that sometimes a plurality of meanings is generated accidentally. But the practice of interpretation of cultural objects could hardly have developed as it did just to cater for such occasional accidents.

Some people demand a justification of, a normative defence of the practice of pluralistic interpretation. I feel that such demands are based on a misunderstanding of what justifications can and should deliver. Once it is established that pluralistic interpretations are a pervasive feature of human culture[13] what we need is an understanding of the function of such interpretations. Justification may be called for in specific cases. We may ask whether there is a good case for thinking that USA statutes, and not only the constitution, are properly subjected to pluralistic interpretation. But there is no room for justifying pluralistic

---

[13] I am inclined to say an inevitable feature of it, but we need not go that far. My claim above does not depend on inevitability. It is justified by pervasiveness.

interpretation in general, except in the sense of examining whether interpretive practices are based on false suppositions, or whether they are riddled with conceptual confusions. I hope that the argument of this chapter has exonerated them from some charges of confusion. Therefore, all we need, all we can hope for, is an understanding of the function of the practice of pluralistic interpretation.

We seek an answer to our second question: why interpret? The answer will be different for different domains. But the diverse answers have something in common. They all show the point of having room for variety within a more or less restrictive framework of continuity, which establishes a strong common backbone to diverse variations. Moreover, in all of them, I will suggest, the case for pluralistic interpretation is a case for innovative interpretation. Innovative interpretations are ways of combining tradition with renewal, general social forms with individual perspectives.

I will, very briefly and, I am afraid, inadequately, illustrate three different cases for variety within a confining common framework. They apply to the arts, to personal relationships, and to the law.

A. The arts

One feature of works of literature and art generally is that their meaning is independent of the biography and intentions of their authors. Many are interested in the lives of authors, composers, and painters. They help explain why they created the work they did. Some regard some authors as remarkable individuals, and their interest in their creations may be in part a way of learning more about their personality and life. After all we learn more about Shakespeare by reading *The Tempest*, than about the meaning of *The Tempest* from anything we know about Shakespeare. Sometimes the relations between biography and meaning are closer. Learning of Mozart's relations with his father made me aware of another way of understanding the meaning of the Commendatore to Don Giovanni in the eponymous opera. But I could have become aware of the very same possible interpretation by reading psychology, or by observing the relations between a friend and his father. Of course, commonly authors and artists hope that their work, or aspects of it, will be understood in certain ways. The way to do so is to make that the meaning the public will see the work to have when understanding it while relying on the common norms of interpretation (and not on diaries or other personal communications by the author or artist).

It is no accident that the concept, and practices, of art developed over the last three centuries positively encourage innovative interpretation, partly through norms which insulate, interpretively speaking, works from their background, and partly through norms which admit the legitimacy of innovative interpretations, even when they go against the existing meaning of the work. Minimally, this is a consequence of the public, and commercial, aspect of art and literature. But the development of art and literature over these centuries made them a sphere in which aspects of human existence and experience are portrayed, reflected upon, imagined (made real in the imagination), challenged, or reaffirmed. To play that role the relation of new to old is moulded and remoulded, through echoes of older work in new work, through the crystallization and the undermining of styles and genres, and through the interpretation and reinterpretation of works in light of the developing culture and human experience. Human imagination works against a constraining background. We need the old as a counterfoil for the creation of the new, which emerges either in opposition, or as variation on the old. As works of art became thought of as such, and their creation was conceived by their creators and their public as the creation of works of art, originality and creativity became a prized value, and the creative imagination was inevitably shaped, and both confined and inspired by the traditions of the various arts.

Furthermore, as artworks emerged as objects whose significance transcends their time, as works which can speak to people across the generations, we have come to think of works of art as objects inviting interpretations, as a treasure house of icons, of images and associations, with complex connections with people, movements, and ideas across the generations, whose interpretation and reinterpretation enables us to define ourselves within our history.

B. Personal relations

The role of pluralistic interpretation in other domains is clearly not the same as in the arts, which is predominantly a domain of symbolic meanings. Think, as a second example, of personal relations. Every culture recognizes a range of personal relationships, such as the relations of parents and children, or of friends. These relationships are constituted by norms which determine what conduct is appropriate between people in the relationships, between, for example, parents and children, as well as towards other people's children, etc. These norms also identify something more general: they determine what is expected to be the meaning of the relationships to their participants.

Our knowledge of these norms, that is of the nature of the relationship, guides our behaviour within it. Regarding voluntary relations, like those of friendship, they affect our willingness to enter into the relationship with this person or that. But, and that is the crucial point, they do not completely determine for each one of us the meaning of the relationship for him or her. That is done by each one of us.

The social forms of parent/child relations or of friendship or of relations between partners, etc create a framework by which, in entering into such relationships, we find ourselves bound. But the framework is always inchoate and flexible in two ways. First, it leaves room for many different, though overlapping, interpretations of the meaning of a relationship of that kind in general: of the meaning of the relations of parents to their children, etc. Second, it leaves room for each of us to work out the meaning of the relationships we are in for ourselves.

The combination of a stable framework with individually explored and established meanings is vital to social life. Given human nature it seems to me that social intercourse of the kind we are familiar with would have been impossible without a stable, though continuously changing, normative framework. Yet, without the flexibility of adjusting the framework to people's personal character, needs, goals, and imagination, the fixed forms of relationships allowed would have been oppressive to many, as indeed they are in many societies, including our own.

C. The law

Finally, I turn to the law. There is an obvious case for legal innovation and change within a stable, continuous legal framework. I will proceed in two stages. First, I will put the case for innovative interpretation. Then I will try to show how the general view of interpretation I adumbrated applies to legal interpretation as we know it.

The law is aware of the need for change, and for various methods of change. Innovative legal interpretation allows for change within continuity. It is particularly useful to achieve greater integration, and interstitial adjustment within existing legal frameworks. There are four general factors establishing the desirability of such interpretations, which goes well beyond the case for saying that it is sometimes inevitable.

First, there is the need for adjustment of the law, where existing law is defective.

Second, there is the need to integrate different legal norms and regulations into a coherent body of law, i.e. a body of law which makes doctrinal sense.

Third, there is the inevitable need to resolve conflicts and indeterminacies in the law.

Fourth, there is the need to integrate law and morality.

Let me make it clear that the list is not meant to be a 'theory of adjudication'. I am not making any claims about when courts have the right or the duty to engage in innovative interpretation. I am not saying that whenever one of these concerns is present they have such a right. Even cases of indeterminacy in the law need not always justify decisions based on innovative interpretation by the courts. There are two other alternatives: first, the courts can decline jurisdiction whenever they find that the law on any specific point is indeterminate. Second, they can reach a decision not through interpretation, but in some other way.

All I am saying is that the four concerns I identified present some reasons for empowering the courts to engage in innovative interpretation in cases to which they apply. Whether or not it would be right to endow them with such powers depends on further considerations, most prominently facts concerning the structure of law-enforcing and law-making institutions in each country, and the availability of alternatives to the courts resorting to innovative interpretations. The extent to which the courts in any country actually have such powers depends on the law in that country.

My aim was the modest one of illustrating how pluralistic interpretation *can* play a meaningful role in the law. As in the case of the arts and of personal relations, even where pluralistic interpretations are not inevitable there is still a case for them which derives from the role that innovative interpretations can play.

VII. The Role of Authority

My explanation of how innovative interpretation can play a positive role in the law did, however, rely on assumptions which have to be made explicit. There are two problems to notice: first, I have been regarding innovative legal interpretations as changing the law. Second, while saying explicitly that innovative interpretations provide for change confined within a continuing framework, I said nothing to show where this confinement comes from.

Innovative interpretations show us new ways of understanding their object. In doing this they establish new meanings, for meanings are no more than ways of understanding their bearers. Innovative interpretations can change the standard meaning of their object. The accretion of new meanings over time may obscure the original meaning of the object, which is what we normally mean when we say that its meaning has changed. Most of those concerned with it do not know its original meaning(s) and are only familiar with some of its new meanings. This is often the case with works of literature created hundreds of years ago which are still read, or performed.

But the process through which meanings change is incidental. It is neither the normal purpose nor the common effect of innovative interpretations to 'change' the meaning of their object, in the sense of leading to neglecting and eventually forgetting its previous meanings. The explanation of the roles innovative interpretations play in the arts and in personal relations made no reference to change of meaning. Rather, it was based on the thought that innovative interpretations are personal expressions of one's attitudes against a background, or within a framework of established meanings.

Works of art provide us with a store of images, ideas, plots, to which we can connect, which we can make sense of within the framework of our life, interpreting them in the light of our experiences, our imaginative inclinations. These interpretations are an integral part of the appreciation of works of art. They are mostly more or less innovative, but as they are personal they do not affect the standard meaning of the works, except occasionally, and mostly incidentally. The same is true of relations between parents and children, between friends and lovers, and so on. We negotiate our relations with others knowing what is expected, knowing not only the boundaries of the permissible, but, more fluidly, the various meanings different modes of conduct will have. Within these webs of public meaning we find room for our individuality. We make our relationships our own by making them different from the standard mould, and of course, for the most part we cannot avoid doing so, given the indeterminacies in the public formats. But here too, the personal meanings of our relationships are meant to be and to remain personal. On the whole they are not meant to change standard public meanings.

The role of legal interpretation is different. Or perhaps, I should say that it has an additional role. In many countries people's attitude to the law is bound up with their attitude to their government, or rather the regime under which they live. There can be countries in which such attitudes are affected by a fairly detailed knowledge of the law, and where interpretations of it fulfill a binding role, making individuals feel that they share in the principles governing their country, while giving it an individual meaning in or for their lives. Such attitudes may be more commonly addressed to some parts of the law, for example to the constitution.

But whether or not such attitudes are prevalent, legal interpretation has a different function as well, and it is a necessary feature of law that it has it. Law is a structure of authority, and central to its functioning is the interplay between legislators and other authorities on one side, and the courts, which are entrusted with delivering authoritative interpretations of its norms, on the other side. Judicial interpretations are authoritative in being binding on the litigants, whether they are correct or not.

The finality of judicial decisions is an essential feature of the law and of the judicial process. It expresses itself in doctrines like *res judicata*, and double jeopardy. In as much as judicial interpretation is part of the process aiming to achieve an authoritative decision, its role is the opposite of the role of interpretation of works of art or of social relations. Its role is not to allow for diversity and individuality within a relatively stable framework, but to secure uniformity if not of opinion at least in action. To fulfil their role courts' decisions need not be acknowledged as justified or correct, they have to be acknowledged to be binding.

The power of the courts to set binding precedents, as well as the emergence of judicial practices, respected as such by the courts, are no more than an extension of the power to settle authoritatively the litigation before the court: an extension of the power of the courts from authoritatively settling a particular cause of action to settling through their interpretive reasoning what is the law which will bind not only the litigants before them, but lower courts in the future, and through them bind all of us.

This is why innovative judicial interpretation changes the law. Interpretation in itself does no such thing. But the power of the courts to set precedents, and the contribution of judicial decisions to judicial practices, do mean that judicial decisions can change the law, and hence, when those decisions are backed by innovative interpretations, they do change the law.

There are a number of questions we face when confronting the law-making power of courts: how does its exercise differ from legislation? Why give courts such powers? Such questions have been studied to good effect by theorists. A complementary question is: given that courts have that power, is there any reason why they should, as they do, exercise it through interpretive reasoning? The list of four factors above was meant as a contribution towards an answer to that question.

VIII. The Limits of Interpretation

Just a brief comment on a matter which requires much more: one point is clear. For something to be an interpretation of a particular object, features of the object itself must be among the factors which determine whether it is a good interpretation or a bad one. Interpretations are guided by practice-based norms about the acceptability of various interpretive strategies together with features of the interpreted object. Unless the object contributes to the interpretation, in the sense that its features contribute to what make an interpretation good or bad, there is no ground to regard the interpretation as an interpretation of that object.

Since interpretations are explanations of meaning, the existing meaning of an object determines whether a proposed interpretation is good or bad. But that answer does not help with innovative interpretations. They show the object in a new light, and cannot be dismissed simply on the ground that they do not explain one of the object's existing meanings.

The question of what constrains an innovative interpretation is answered nevertheless in a similar way: it is constrained by the existing meanings and the norms of interpretation, which determine, even for innovative interpretations, which ones are good and which fail, though of course the relation to existing meanings is not one of reproduction, but of variation, contravention, etc, depending on the interpretive strategies acknowledged by the practice (literature, law, etc) in question.

One important conclusion is that the constraints on interpretation are always shifting. It is sometimes assumed that if the object of interpretation must constrain the interpretation, it follows that the constraining features must be ones which belong to the object once and for all, and constrain the interpretation in the same way always. That is a mistake. The constraints include the meanings of the object and they can change over time. Needless to say, the same conclusion follows from the fact that the norms governing interpretations are practice-based, and therefore subject to change.

IX. How to Interpret?

You will be aware of the fact that I have not yet addressed my third question which any account of interpretation must face: How is one to interpret? But in fact I feel that I have said the most important things about it. We learn how to interpret within a domain or a tradition by becoming familiar with the tradition and absorbing its ways, which include the freedom to innovate as understood within it. There are no useful universal recipes for interpretation. Theoretical reflection can help. But it helps in making us aware of the nature of interpretation, and the diverse reasons for engaging in it, not by providing us with recipes for correct interpretation. Sometimes, for example in the law, there are specific interpretive rules, but they are never exhaustive guides and they are local rules liable to change. The only true general guide is in understanding what interpretation is for.

13

On the Authority and Interpretation
of Constitutions: Some Preliminaries

I. What Kind of Constitution?

The writings on constitutional theory fill libraries. They are often
presented as, and almost invariably are, writings on the constitutional
practice of one country or another. Whether they offer an analysis of
current practices, doctrines that may justify them or critiques of these
practices, or suggestions for their improvement, they are valid, if at all,
against the background of the political and constitutional arrangements
of one country or another, valid for the interpretation of the constitution of one country or another. Few writings on constitutional interpretation successfully address problems in full generality; that is, few
offer useful lessons regarding the nature of constitutional interpretation as such. In part this is explained by the ambition of writers on
interpretation. Whether or not they mean their writings to provide an
account of current interpretive practices in their countries, they almost
invariably aim to provide an account of how constitutional interpretation should be carried out, an account of the correct method of constitutional interpretation. They also aim to present their conclusions in a
form that will be usable by lawyers and judges, and therefore in a form
that shuns very abstract formulations which presuppose much for their
interpretation and application. They aspire to help with the solution
to important constitutional problems facing their countries, and these
aspirations limit the relevance of their conclusions to one jurisdiction,
or a few similar ones.

But possibly it is not their underlying aspirations that limit the validity of most writings on constitutional interpretation. Possibly there is
no room for a truly universal theory of the subject. After all, the law,
including constitutional law, can vary from country to country, and

from period to period even in one country. Even the most basic understanding of the constitution and its role in the life and law of a country may be different in different countries. How can there be a theory of constitutional interpretation that spans all these differences?

Up to a point these doubts are well founded. A powerful case can be made to the effect that a substantive theory of constitutions and of constitutionalism has limited application. Its application is to some countries and to some constitutions only. One reason is that the notion of 'a constitution' is used in legal discourse sometimes in a thin sense and sometimes in a variety of thicker senses. In the thin sense it is tautological that every legal system includes a constitution. For in that sense the constitution is simply the law that establishes and regulates the main organs of government, their constitution and powers, and *ipso facto* it includes law that establishes the general principles under which the country is governed: democracy, if it establishes democratic organs of government; federalism, if it establishes a federal structure; and so on.

The thick sense of 'constitution' is less clear, and probably there are several such senses in use in different legal cultures. For the purposes of the present discussion I will regard constitutions as defined by a combination of seven features.

First, incorporating the thin sense, the constitution defines the constitution and powers of the main organs of the different branches of government. (This feature identifies the constitution as *constitutive* of the legal and political structure which is that legal system.)

Second, it is, and is meant to be, of long duration: It is meant to serve as a stable framework for the political and legal institutions of the country, to be adjusted and amended from time to time, but basically to preserve stability and continuity in the legal and political structure, and the basic principles that guide its institutions. (The constitution is *stable*, at least in aspiration.)

Third, it has a canonical formulation. That usually means that it is enshrined in one or a small number of written documents. It (they) is (are) commonly referred to as the constitution. (The constitution—we say when referring to this feature—is *written.*)

Fourth, it constitutes a superior law. This means that ordinary law which conflicts with the constitution is invalid or inapplicable. (The constitution is *superior law.*)

Fifth, there are judicial procedures to implement the superiority of the constitution, that is judicial processes by which the compatibility of rules of law and of other legal acts with the constitution can be tested, and incompatible rules or legal acts can be declared inapplicable or invalid. (The constitution is *justiciable*.)

Sixth, while there usually are legal procedures for constitutional amendment, constitutional amendments are legally more difficult to secure than ordinary legislation. (The constitution is *entrenched*.)

Seventh, its provisions include principles of government (democracy, federalism, basic civil and political rights, etc) that are generally held to express the common beliefs of the population about the way their society should be governed. It serves, you may say, not only as a lawyers' law, but as the people's law. Its main provisions are generally known, command general consent, and are held to be the (or part of the) common ideology that governs public life in that country. (The constitution expresses a *common ideology*.)

This characterization of a constitution (in the thick sense) yields a vague concept. Each one of the seven criteria is vague in application. To give but one example: Is it a condition of a country having a written constitution (condition 3) that there cannot be an 'unwritten' part of the constitution—for example, a part that is 'customary law'? And if the written-constitution condition is compatible with part of the constitution being unwritten, does it follow that Britain has a written constitution? Remember that while some of its constitution (in the thin sense) is customary or common law, part of it (eg the Bill of Rights of 1689, the Act of Union between England and Scotland of 1706, the European Communities Act of 1971) is written law. We know that in the relevant sense Britain does not have a written constitution. But that does not clearly follow from the characterization given, which is vague on the point.

But then the characterization is not meant to draw borderlines, but to focus discussion. Its purpose is to highlight the central features of constitutions—in (one) thick sense—features that explain why (some) constitutions (ie constitutions in this thick sense) give rise to theoretical questions that do not apply, at least not to the same degree, to other law. This chapter will consider some questions relating to constitutions in this sense. Some of the questions, even some of the answers, apply to constitutions that meet only some of the specified conditions, or meet them only to some degree. Indeed, some of them apply to ordinary (ie non-constitutional) law as well. But it is useful to discuss them in the constitutional context, and we will not be concerned with the degree to which the problems or their solutions apply elsewhere.

There would be little point in investigating in general terms thick constitutions wherever they are were it not the case that they play a major role in the life of more and more countries. Clearly, not all countries have a constitution in this sense. Britain today and the Roman Empire of old are but two examples of countries that do or did not. The absence of a constitution (in the strong sense) may be due to a variety of factors. One is that the country enjoys a level of political consensus that makes a constitution unnecessary. Such consensus means that everyone knows and accepts the framework of government, the distribution of powers among its organs, and the general principles guiding or constraining the exercise of governmental powers. These are, if you like, matters of understood conventions, with no mechanisms for their enforcement. A consensus of this kind can exist in a small country with a relatively homogeneous and stable population, enjoying relative equality of status and a stable economy. But it can also exist in a large country with a diverse population marked by considerable social and economic stratification if it is based on a culture of deference and enjoys stable social, demographic, and economic conditions.

Constitutions in the strong sense tend to exist in societies that enjoy relative stability within diversity and change. Such societies must have stability and a sense of a common identity sufficient to ensure the durability and stability of the constitution itself. But being large-scale societies, with many divisions of, for example, religion, class, and ethnic origin, they need the assurance of publicly accountable government, guided by openly administered principles, to strengthen the stability of the political structures and the authority of their legal institutions. A tempting suggestion is that the way to construct a theory of the authority and the proper interpretation of the (thick) constitution is to explore further the social, cultural, and economic conditions that justify it. Surely they hold the clues to an understanding of the nature and function of the constitution and therefore to its authority and interpretation. But the suggestion is misguided. No doubt such an inquiry will be very valuable. It will not, however, yield the hoped-for results. It assumes that the law, constitutional law at the very least, develops exclusively in response to the relatively stable aspects of the social conditions of the country to which it applies. As we know, this is far too rationalistic a view of the development of the law. Much of it depends on the ambitions of powerful personages, the political convenience of the hour. Fluctuating public moods and even temporary economic turns can lead to changes that remain in force many years after the conditions that led to them are forgotten.

Nor are matters any different with constitutions. The thought that their 'higher status' and their propensity for longevity make them responsive only to fundamental and lasting social conditions or social trends is mistaken. In 1995, to give but one example, influential voices in the British Labour Party called on it to put constitutional reform at the centre of its platform, because the economic situation in the country seemed to be improving and might favour the Conservative government in the forthcoming election. Similarly, it is arguable that the courts in Britain would not have been so active between the late 1980s and the mid-1990s in developing new doctrines in public law, leading to a series of humiliating defeats for the government, but for the fact that the Conservatives had been in power for seventeen years, meeting very little effective parliamentary opposition. Constitutional politics may not be the same as parliamentary politics, but they are not altogether separate either. Similar examples can be found in the history of other countries, including those with a constitution in the strong sense. Moreover, in our ever-contracting world the adoption of constitutions, and the way they develop, often owes more to fashion than to principle. Certain ways of understanding the constitution become fashionable, perhaps because of the prestige of the country that initiated them. It becomes politically expedient to follow fashion. More than we often like to admit is owed to this factor.

It may be objected that none of these facts matters to constitutional theory, which is a normative theory and therefore unaffected by mere contingencies. In a sense to be explored, a constitutional theory is normative. But that does not mean that it is or should be blind to the basic realities of life. That the adoption and development of constitutions are affected by a variety of short-term factors is no mere aberration in the life of one country or another. It is a universal feature of the political life of all countries with a constitution. Constitutional theory had better allow for that. A theory that condemns all such influences as aberrations to be avoided is too remote from this world to be much use in it.

We will have to come back to this point and explore it further. While the main exploration will have to await a more detailed discussion of the normativity of constitutional theory, we can begin here by making one relevant observation: A good deal of legal development (and this includes constitutional development) is autonomous. This means that its traditions crystallize into practices that are followed in decisions which develop constitutional law. These traditions may be informed by valid considerations, such as concern for the efficiency of government, or for the dignity of individuals, or for the relative autonomy of different regions. But the crucial point is that these considerations do not determine the outcome of the decisions they influence. These considerations will be respected by a variety of constitutional decisions. The decision actually taken is chosen out of habit, or out of respect for the constitutional practices and traditions of that country.

If that is right, and if the autonomous legal traditions of different countries rightly play a major part in determining their constitutional development, then a theory of the constitution cannot be based on social or economic or cultural factors. It cannot be derived from extraneous circumstances. It must allow a major role to internal legal considerations. Therefore, the reflections on a constitutional theory offered here proceed by examining the abstract central features of a constitution, the seven enumerated earlier and some of their implications. The theory abstracts from the possible impact of social conditions, for I assume that they will differ from country to country. I hope, however, that a theory of the constitution will provide the theoretical framework within which the effect of diverse social conditions can be assessed.

I believe that most of what needs saying about the nature of constitutions has already been said. This does not mean, of course, that matters are relatively clear and settled. The problem is not so much that the truth is elusive or obscure and has not yet been seen by anyone, as that a variety of misleading analogies helped lend plausibility to some misguided ideas. I will spend much of this chapter trying to explain why we should not listen to some false sirens.

We can start, though, by recalling one principle that seems to be common ground to many approaches to constitutional studies: Constitutional theory comprises two major parts, an account of the authority of constitutions and an account of the way constitutions should be interpreted. The first explains under what conditions the constitution of a country is legitimate, thus fixing the condition under which citizens have a duty to obey it. In doing that, it provides an account of the principles of political morality that underpin the constitution, in that they justify and legitimize its enforcement, if it is indeed justified. The theory of constitutional interpretation explains the ways the principles of constitutional interpretation in different countries are determined. A principle of constitutional theory that commands widespread support says that the principles of constitutional interpretation depend in part on the theory of constitutional authority. In determining the conditions for constitutional legitimacy, the theory of the authority of the constitution contributes to the determination of principles of interpretation. Unfortunately, this sound principle is also the source of many false analogies motivated by attempts to assimilate the authority of the constitution to that of other parts of the law.

II. The Authority of Constitutions

A. The authority of the constitution and the authority of its authors

It is tempting to think that the authority of law, of any law, derives from the authority of its maker. Customary law is allowed to be a puzzling exception. But consider enacted law—that is, law whose validity derives from the fact that it was made by a legitimate legal authority acting with the intention to make law. The paradigm example of this kind of law is statutes. They are valid because they were passed by a body authorized in law to pass them. If, for example, the legal validity of a regulation is impugned on the ground that the body that enacted it had no legal power to do so, the charge cannot be repulsed by a claim, however justified, that the rule the regulation embodies is nevertheless legally binding because it is a good rule, one that it would be sensible to follow. This does not mean that the merits of rules are irrelevant to legal reasoning. In appropriate contexts, such considerations can guide the interpretation of a statute or regulation whose legal validity is established on other grounds. In some contexts, the merits of having a rule of a certain kind may also justify the courts in adopting it and basing their decision on it, even if this requires overriding existing legal rules. The merit of a rule may also be grounds for giving it binding force, either through the courts, by turning it into a binding precedent, or by legislation. But the merit of a rule is not the sort of consideration which can establish that it is already legally binding.

I belabour this familiar point to bring out the fact, itself obvious, that the identity of the law-maker is material to the validity of the law, at least in the case of enacted law. It is plausible to think that only if the identity of the law-maker is the reason for the validity of the law can one make sense of this feature of enacted law. The fact that the law was made by that person or institution provides, on this view, the justification (at least at one level of justification) for holding the enacted rule to be valid in law. That means that with enacted law the authority of the law derives from the authority of its maker.

This is a powerful argument for the claim that the authority of constitutions derives from the authority of their makers. The argument is not that there is no other way in which law can have authority. Customary law shows that there are other ways of establishing the authority of law. Nor is the argument that anything which was made with the intention to make law must, if it is legally valid at all, derive its authority from the authority of its maker. That is not so either. In Britain, to mention just one example, a regulation laying down a rule may be *ultra vires*, in that the body which adopted it had no power to make law on that matter, and yet the rule which the regulation embodied may be valid, since it also happens to be a long-established common law rule. The argument lies elsewhere: Unless the authority of the constitution derives from the authority of its makers, there is no explaining the fact that it matters that it was made by one body rather than another. But surely it makes all the difference in the world that the constitution was adopted by those who did adopt it, and not by others. It is, we want to say, valid because it was so adopted. Does it not follow, by the force of the argument above, that its authority derives from the authority of those who made it?

As is so often the case, the short answer is both yes and no. To explain it, a longer answer must be given. But first we must dispose of a false answer waiting in the wings. Its interest lies not so much in itself, but in bringing us face to face with one aspect of the perennial question of the relations between law and morality. It may be claimed that the authority of constitutions cannot derive from that of their makers, for their makers, standing at the birth of their states, cannot have authority themselves. All authority derives from the constitution that they themselves made without prior authority to do so.

1. The nature of the authority of the makers of an originating constitution

To be taken seriously, this argument has to be confined to the few constitutions that can be called 'originating' constitutions. Most constitutions are not like that. They are made by legitimate legal authorities as part of a process of legal reform. Even constitutions that stand at the birth of a new independent country are often made in pursuance of legal authority conferred on their makers by the previous legal order in force in these countries, often a colonial regime. This is the way most of the countries of the British Commonwealth acquired their independence. But is not the argument cogent regarding those constitutions to which it applies? It is not.

The argument assumes that only those on whom authority has been conferred by pre-existing law can have legitimate authority. That is not, nor can it be, the case. Legal authority is itself a form of claimed moral authority.[1] The point is sometimes lost to sight, for legal structures transmit the authority to make law from one body to another. We are familiar with the fact that the law is a structure of authority, in which each legal authority derives its power from laws made by another. We rely on the authority of one to justify the authority of another. Only infrequently do we appeal to moral reasons to justify a claim to legal authority. This gives discourse about legal authority an appearance of being autonomous, technical, legal discourse. In a way it is. If the constitution and the other rules that establish legal authorities are morally justified, so are the authorities that they establish, and the laws made by those authorities are morally binding. This means that once the moral justification of those ultimate legal rules (ie those whose legal validity does not presuppose that of any other law) is established, or assumed, the moral justification of the rest of the law is—up to a point—established by technical legal argumentation. (This is so up to a point only, because, as was noted, the interpretation of the law may well involve further moral or other non-legal considerations.) Since much of the time legal argument is addressed to legal officials who accept the moral validity of the ultimate laws, and much legal argument explains (to clients or lawyers, or to any individual) what is the position in law—on the supposition that it is morally legitimate—regarding one matter or another, much legal argument is technically legal.

None of this denies the fact that the law claims to be morally binding and that on the whole only people who accept that claim, people who accept at least that it is morally permissible to apply the law (to tax people, to determine their property rights, or their right in and to employment, to imprison them, etc), serve in the authorities that make and apply the law. A theory of law is, therefore and among other things, a theory of the conditions, if any, under which the law is morally

---

[1] See, for an extended discussion, J Raz, *The Morality of Freedom* (Oxford: Clarendon Press, 1986) pt I and J Raz, *Ethics in the Public Domain* (rev edn, Oxford: Clarendon Press, 1995) essays 9 and 10.

legitimate and of the consequences that follow from the assumption that it is morally legitimate. That is also the nature of our investigation into the authority of the constitution. If the constitution is not an originating constitution, if it has been made by a body on which some other law (perhaps an earlier constitution) bestowed power to enact a constitution, then it may be morally legitimate if the law that authorized it is morally legitimate. But if it is an originating constitution, then the question of its moral legitimacy cannot turn on the legitimacy of any other law. It must turn directly on moral argument.

It follows that the argument that an originating constitution cannot derive its authority from the authority of its makers for they had no such authority is invalid. It is true that the makers of the constitution had no authority bestowed on them by other laws. But it does not follow that they had no authority, nor that the authority of the constitution cannot rest on their authority. They may have had moral authority, and it may be the reason for the authority of the constitution.

One may reply that, true as my observations are, they miss the point of the argument they were meant to refute. That argument, it may be said, is about the *legal* authority of originating constitutions, not about their moral authority. In a sense it is true that their framers did not have legal authority. (It is misleading to put the point in this form, but the technical considerations involved need not detain us here.[2]) The crucial point is that our interest in legal authority lies in how it establishes the moral authority of the law, or of parts of it. We are interested in the authority of law, if any, in order to establish whether we have an obligation to respect and obey it.[3] Moreover, the grounds for the authority of the law help to determine how it ought to be interpreted. Judges, perhaps more than anyone else, follow the law because they believe they are morally required to do so. There can be no other way in which they can justify[4] imprisoning people, interfering with their property, jobs, family relations, and so on, decisions that are the daily fare of judicial life.

---

[2] I discussed some of them in *The Concept of a Legal System* (2nd edn, Oxford: OUP, 1980) 29–32.

[3] The question of the authority of law does not exhaust the issue of political obligation, but it is a major part of it.

[4] Possibly, some hold judicial office for reasons of personal advantage even when they believe that it is morally wrong for them to do so. In some oppressive regimes we can imagine judges and other officials perpetrating immoralities out of fear for their life or the life of their families. In such circumstances it may be morally excusable to act as they do. But these are likely to be the exception, and I will disregard such cases in the present discussion.

It may be worth repeating that none of this implies that there is no room for more narrowly focused legal reasoning about whether any institution meets the purely legal conditions for the possession of authority. My claim is only that such an inquiry is of interest because it is embedded in a wider inquiry into the moral legitimacy of that institution's power. Nor do I claim that in any chain of reasoning about legal authority there will be a stage in which the moral considerations affecting legitimacy will be confronted directly or explicitly. Very often they are taken for granted. Nor is it, of course, my claim that whenever the legal conditions for legitimacy are met so are the moral conditions.

2. *The argument from the rule of recognition*

This may be an appropriate place to clear out of the way another misguided argument for the independence of the authority of the constitution from that of its authors. Some theorists who broadly follow HLA Hart's theory of law think that the constitution of a country is its rule of recognition, as that term is used by Hart.[5] Since the rule of recognition exists as a practice of the legal officials, it is, as it were, a living rule, a rule sustained by *current attitudes and conduct*, and not by what happened at the point it came into being. Hence, since the constitution is the rule of recognition, the constitution's authority derives from the current practice of the officials, and not from the authority of its makers.

This argument is easily refuted. For one thing, its conclusion can be turned around and used as a ground for rejecting its central premise: If the constitution is the rule of recognition, then its authority does not derive from the authority of its authors: since its authority does derive from the authority of its authors, it follows that the constitution is not the rule of recognition. There is no reason to prefer the argument to this reversal of it. This lands us in a tie. Fortunately, there are plenty of independent reasons which establish that constitutions are not the rules of recognition of their countries. No constitution can be, if that term is understood in the thick sense in which it is used here. For example, most constitutions may be amended or even repealed and replaced by others in accordance with procedures that they themselves provide. This means that they can be amended or repealed by enactment. The rule of recognition cannot be repealed or amended by an enactment. It can change only as the practice that it is changes. Customary law can be repealed and replaced by statute. There is nothing in the nature of

---

[5] See HLA Hart, *The Concept of Law* (Oxford: OUP, 1961; rev edn, 1994).

custom to prevent it from being changed by legislation. But once that happens, the law on the point is no longer customary. It is statutory. The rule of recognition, on the other hand, cannot give way to statutory law. It is and always remains customary.

Not only is it a mistake to identify constitutions with rules of recognition, but rules of recognition do not play the legitimating role that constitutions can play.[6] The rule of recognition is unlike the rest of the law. It is the practice—that is, the fact—that the courts and other legal institutions recognize the validity, the legitimacy, of the law, and that they are willing to follow it and apply it to others. As such it is unlike any other legal rule, including other customary legal rules. It is the point (one such point) at which—metaphorically speaking—the law ends and morality begins. It is the fact that enables us to separate legal from moral facts. If the rule of recognition exists—that is, if the appropriate practice of recognition is followed by the courts—then the law exists. But only if they are right in so conducting themselves is the law actually legitimate and binding, morally speaking.

Put it in different terms: Because we can identify a social fact of the judicial recognition of the law by the courts, we can establish that there is a law in a certain country and establish its content even if it is a morally bad and illegitimate system of law. The rule of recognition, being a social fact, enables us to identify the law without recourse to morality. But that is (by and large) all it does. It cannot be sensibly regarded as a conventional rule—that is, we cannot assume it to be a necessary truth that when a judge follows the practice of, let us say, applying acts passed by the Queen in Parliament as binding, he does so because all the courts do so, or because they all hold themselves duty bound to do so (even though they do). He may do so because Acts of Parliament enjoy democratic legitimacy, or for some other reason. The rule of recognition constitutes a normative practice, but not a conventional practice.

3. The argument from consent

Some people think that the only way in which some people can have authority over others is through the others' consent.[7] Since the constitution

---

[6] The views expressed in this paragraph and the next are at variance with Hart's own interpretation of the rule of recognition, as explained in the postscript to the revised edition of *The Concept of Law*.

[7] Other variants of the argument relate it to democracy rather than consent. The considerations advanced against the version considered in the text have to be adapted to apply to other variants of the argument.

is the source of legal authority in the state, its own authority must arise from the consent of the governed. If consent is the source of all authority, then this consent must be the consent of the living, the consent of those subject to the law as it is from time to time. Those who think that consent is the foundation of authority cannot tolerate the supposition that the current generation is subject to the law because it enjoyed the consent of the population living two hundred years ago. Hence, even if a constitution was adopted by a referendum, it is valid not because of the process by which it was adopted originally but because it commands the consent of the public as it is from time to time.

Some variants of this argument modify it to accommodate two objections: First is the fact that some people may refuse their consent by whim in a totally arbitrary or irrational way. When this happens, those who refuse their consent will not be subject to the law of the state. They can break the law with impunity. It seems implausible that it is that easy to escape the authority of the law, that people can escape its authority at will. Second, many people are never actually called upon to give their consent to the constitution. Many may have failed to consent to it simply because it never occurred to them that they should. Again it seems implausible that they will be exempt from the authority of the law. Both objections can be circumvented if one stipulates that the consent that gives rise to the authority of the constitution is not necessarily the actual consent of the governed. Rather, at least regarding those who did not in fact consent, it is the fact that they would have consented—had they been reasonable and rational people (but not necessarily exemplary moral people)—if they had been invited to do so. These variants regard authority as arising out of the hypothetical consent of the governed.

This is not the place to engage in a comprehensive discussion of the weaknesses of consent accounts of authority.[8] Suffice it to say that while in the respects mentioned accounts based on hypothetical consent are stronger than simple consent-based accounts, in others they are weaker: There is some normative force to the fact that one gives one's free and informed[9] consent to an arrangement affecting oneself, which hypothetical consent does not have. Consent, whether wise or foolish, expresses

---

[8] I have discussed them in 'Government by Consent', *Ethics in the Public Domain* 355.

[9] Meaning not that consenting was rational given the information, but that—judged in light of the information generally available at the time—the information known to the agent presented roughly a true picture of the (non-evaluative) features of the situation, in as much as they were relevant to his decision.

the will of the agent concerning the conduct of his own life. Whatever mess results from his consent is, in part at least, of his own making. Since his life is his own, it is relevant whether it is under his control or not, and consent shows that it is. So even if real consent is a source of authority, it is far from clear that hypothetical consent is. I know of no argument which shows that it is.[10]

In any case, *this* relevance of consent is not of a kind that can establish the legitimacy of any authority. Not being able to argue the case in full, let me give an analogy: Suppose that I consent to a boxing match with an opponent of far superior strength and skill. I am simply mad at him and lose my head in my desire to fight him. That I consented is relevant to what I can say later, when nursing my wounds. It affects the sort of complaints I can make (I can say to my friends, 'Why didn't you stop me?' but I cannot say to my enemy, 'Why did you fight me?'). It also affects any reasonable judgment of my character. But it does not necessarily establish that my enemy was right to fight me. He should have known that boxing is immoral and that my consent does not make it otherwise. He should have known that the fight will not be fair, given his superiority (he was not fighting in self-defence; it was an arranged fight). You may disagree with the judgments I am relying on here. Even so, you should agree that if they are true then my consent did not make my enemy's action right. The case of legitimate government is similar: My consent can bar me from certain complaints and can be material to judging my character. But it cannot endow the government with a right to govern if it did not have it—unless consent is relevant to its right in a way that is different from the one I was commenting on earlier. I will assume in the sequel that that aspect of consent is not relevant to our issue.

It is plausible to suppose that whatever merit there is in hypothetical-consent accounts derives from the fact that the kind of hypothetical consent they involve captures whatever it is that matters in real-consent accounts—for example, that it represents the true will of the agent. To that extent they suffer from some of the limitations of real-consent accounts—that is, those which affect not only the form of consent, but its underlying rationale. An important aspect of consent,

---

[10] This is not to deny that arguments which are not consent-based cannot be presented as relating to hypothetical consent: Suppose you have an obligation deriving from whatever source to recognize the authority of certain governments. It follows trivially that if you know your obligations you would consent that you have an obligation to recognize the authority of such governments.

as of all human action, is that it is given for a reason—that is, a reason the agent regards as a good reason, in light of all the considerations, moral considerations included, that apply to the case. The reasons agents believe in may not be good reasons, or not adequate to the task, and the agents may even know this and give their consent out of weakness of the will. However, I know of no consent-based account of authority that does not assume that the reasons for the consent are cogent and adequate. Indeed, it would be impossible to base authority on consent that is misguided and ill-founded—again, I am afraid, not a point that can be established here. But if so, then the consent is given in the true belief that there is adequate reason to recognize the authority of the institutions, or principles, in question. The question arises whether these considerations are not enough to establish the authority of those bodies or principles, independently of the consent.

Obviously, in many cases consent is required for one to have an obligation. But typically these are cases in which the wisdom of the consent is not in question (for example, with few exceptions, a promise is binding whether or not one's reasons for making it are good reasons). It is equally clear that not all obligations arise out of consent or undertakings (for example, the obligation to keep one's promises does not depend on consenting to do so). Nor do all our obligations to accede to the will of others arise out of consent (for example, we have an obligation to accede, within bounds, to the will of our parents, which—at least in the conditions prevailing in some societies—extends beyond childhood and applies to the relations between adults and their parents as well). So the question arises: If consent to authority is effective only when based on adequate reasons to recognize the authority, why are these reasons not enough in themselves to establish that authority?

This is a serious question, not a rhetorical one. We can well imagine answers which would show that in certain matters no one can have authority over another except with that person's consent. Such may be the case in matters that relate to what we call 'private' areas of life. What is much more difficult to imagine is that no political authority can be legitimate without consent—that is, that there is no area over which an authority may have legitimate power independently of consent. Many areas of governmental action (for example, determining the relative contribution of individuals to the maintenance of essential common services or securing that those who injure others compensate them for the harm caused, when fairness or justice require that they do so) are matters of setting up schemes to facilitate conformity with precepts of justice and morality, and these are typical of matters where obligations that are not voluntary abound.

Assuming that in many areas authority need not depend on consent makes it more likely that in these matters at least consent is not a way of establishing authority at all.[11] For it seems reasonable to suppose that, regarding such matters, the only reasons which justify consent to authority also justify the authority without consent.

If the sketch of the argument offered here can be fleshed out to make a sound argument, then consent is not at all an important way of establishing legitimate political or legal authority. This puts an end to the consent-based argument to show that the authority of constitutions cannot derive from the authority of their authors.

4. The dead hand of the past

We should turn to the best known and most powerful argument aiming to sever the authority of constitutions from that of their authors. No one, the argument goes, can have authority over future generations. Therefore, the authority of a constitution cannot rest on the authority of its makers. Let us examine it.

First, a couple of obvious qualifications: The argument does not apply to new constitutions. But constitutions are meant to last for a long time, and it is fair to concentrate on older constitutions, as all constitutions are meant to be one day. Equally obviously, at least *prima facie*, the argument applies equally to old statutes. There may be differences between constitutions and ordinary law, arising out of the differences in their content, which affect the argument. But these remain to be argued for. Neither of these points substantially affects the force of the argument.

The way the argument works is this: We are looking for the conditions under which constitutions can be justified, can enjoy legitimate (moral) authority. Whatever they are, it cannot be the case that the authority of an old constitution can derive from the authority of its authors. For there is no reasonable way of justifying the authority of any institution that allows it to have authority stretching long into the future. How much into the future can authority stretch? Does the power of an authority die with it? And if so, what is the lifetime of an institutional authority (is it the period between elections, does the USA Congress change every two years or every six years, or is it a continuous body that will die only with a fundamental change in its constitution)? Or should we think of the

---

[11] Or that it plays only a secondary role in establishing authority over such areas.

lifetime of an individual authoritative decree, the lifetime of each individual statute or regulation, or that of every constitutional provision? The second seems the more reasonable approach.

The authority of institutions to issue binding decrees is limited in various ways: Some institutions have authority to lay down binding rules about the way banks should be run; others may have authority to direct the running of schools. Possibly, no institution can have unlimited authority regarding all subject matters. Similarly, the authority of any institution is limited by the range of people subject to it. Some have authority over people in Kansas, others over people in France, and so on. The considerations that limit the authority of others over us are, roughly speaking, of the same order as those that establish the immorality of slavery. They set limits to subjugation, to the subordination of one person to the will of another. Just as they do that by setting limits to the subject matter regarding which different authorities can have power and to the range of people over whom their power extends, so those very same considerations limit the temporal validity of their directives. Just as the range of subject matter and people will vary from case to case, so the temporal duration of an authoritative directive will vary depending on the circumstances. But it is reasonable to think, say, that none will be valid one hundred years after its passing. That is, if it were still valid at that time, that would not be due to the authority of its original author.

It is tedious to spell out the argument to this conclusion in full detail. But it may be helpful to provide some pointers to the sort of considerations involved. They come at two levels: (1) the types of factors that determine whether laws are good or bad and (2) the factors that determine the competence of political authorities to achieve worthwhile goals, which thereby both establish and limit the scope of their legitimate powers. Considerations of both levels must be combined to establish the boundaries of political authorities.

I will illustrate the first level by mentioning two categories (simplified for the purpose of the present discussion):

(i) Some law, if it is good law, directly[12] implements unconditional moral imperatives. Here one may mention the basic legal protection of personal safety in the criminal law and (to a certain degree)

---

[12] The directness is important here. Ultimately all moral principles either are or derive from universal principles. The laws belonging to this category are justified by direct reference to universal principles of conduct, without the mediation of complex arguments regarding the way these apply to social and economic conditions.

tort law. Some civil rights, like freedom of religion or of thought, are often thought to belong to this category.

(ii) Much law, if it is good law, reflects a fair distribution of opportunities, resources, and amenities among members of the population, given their actual or likely needs, goals, and aspirations, the existing technological and economic resources, and the existing social organization. Laws whose value is to be judged by these criteria should be subject to continuous review, as the factors that make them satisfactory at any time are subject to frequent and significant changes. These include all welfare law, planning and zoning laws, consumer protection legislation, safety regulations, health provisions, education law, and much else.

It may be thought that laws belonging to the first category do not require frequent adjustment. They incorporate into law immutable moral principles. Therefore, it may be argued, the authority of law-makers to make these kinds of law is long-lasting. But the argument fails on both counts. First, while arguably the moral precepts that these laws are there to enforce are immutable, it does not follow that so are the laws that protect and enforce them. Take a simple example: The moral wrong committed by rape may involve the violation of a universal moral principle. But the legal regulation of rape may rightly vary from place to place and from time to time. To go no further, it is far from a universal principle that rape should constitute a separate offence rather than be assimilated to serious assault. There is no generally cogent reason for there being a one-to-one correlation between type of moral wrong and type of offence. Whether and when a sexual motive should determine the character of the offence, rather than be relevant to the sentence only, whether or when penetration should single out some sex offences from others, whether or when violence matters or not (it is not a necessary ingredient of rape, according to most jurisdictions)—all these are questions sensitive to social conditions, to perceived social meanings, to the informal consequences of criminal convictions, and to many other factors that are as variable as any. Hence, the first step in the argument for a long-lasting authority regarding laws directly implementing universal moral principles of conduct is unsound.

The second leg of the argument is no more sound. To see that, let us waive the objection I raised in the preceding paragraph. Let us assume that there is a category of laws whose validity is as timeless as that of the universal moral principles from which they derive. Would that show that long after their enactment the authority of these laws rests on the authority of their makers? Far from it. This may be the case should the authority of the laws derive from the authority of their makers. But the very fact that they have, as we suppose, timeless authority militates against that view. The timeless authority of these supposed laws depends on their content. If they are timelessly valid, that is because they express universal moral principles. They are not timelessly valid because they were enacted by a fallible social institution or approved by a referendum. For an authority to be able to pass timelessly valid laws of this kind it must be counted as an expert on morality—that is, as having a significantly superior grasp of abstract moral principles than do the people who are bound by its laws. While there seem to be people who acquire moral expertise in some specialized problems of applied morality (eg the knotted issue of consent to medical experimentation), there is no reason to think that anyone or any institution can claim expertise in the very abstract basic principles of morality. Therefore, the authority of laws that express such principles cannot derive from that of their authors at all. As I indicated in my comment on the first step of the argument, in fact the authority of the law can be said to derive from that of its author at least inasmuch as the laws determine the temporary, and socially sensitive, way in which moral principles are to be enshrined into law. But that does not help show that anyone can have law-making authority to make laws that last for very long.

On the whole the case for the temporally limited authority of institutions regarding laws of the second kind—those that allocate resources, burdens, and opportunities fairly among people—is easier to establish. It seems impossible to formulate these laws in ways that do not necessitate frequent revision. Given that law-makers cannot make laws that remain good for long, their authority cannot be the reason for the authority of old laws that they made.

To see this point more clearly we need to turn to the second level of considerations, to the factors that determine the competence of institutions to function well and, therefore, to be legitimate authorities. These have been touched upon in the preceding few paragraphs but deserve separate consideration, however brief.

Broadly speaking, political authority can be based on one or more of three types of considerations: expertise, coordination, and symbolic value. Considerations of expertise underlie, for example, much consumer protection law, safety at work law, and most other safety regulations. They are also relevant to many laws that implement direct moral imperatives. Medical expertise is relevant to the definition of death, as well as health, illness, injury, and the like. Psychological expertise is relevant to many aspects of family law, and so on. To assume that expertise gives law-makers timeless authority is to assume that either no advance in knowledge in the relevant area or no advance in its spread is likely, or both. Such advances would negate the expertise of the old law-makers relative to new experts (new advances in knowledge) or relative to the population at large (the spread of knowledge). Either would denude them of legitimate authority insofar as it is based on expertise.

Much law is a matter of securing social coordination. Securing coordination predominates when the law aims to secure social conditions whose achievement depends on the conduct of a number of people, and when, should enough of them not behave in a way conducive to the achievement of the desired conditions, there is no reason (or no sufficient reason) for others to behave in that way either.[13] The law can help to secure coordination, and in fulfilling these functions it can achieve a variety of goals, including all those that fall into the second category listed earlier. In as much as forms of coordination have to be adjusted or replaced by others in changing circumstances, and in as much as there is a limit to anyone's ability to provide for such changes in advance, there is a limit, a temporal limit, on the laws they have power to make.

The third factor that can endow institutions with authority is the symbolic value of their position as legal authorities. Here we have to distinguish between the value of an office and the value of having a certain person, or group of people, holding the office. Some people qualify for positions of high authority in having become symbols of their nations in periods of transition or struggle. The position of Václav Havel in the years immediately following the democratization of Czechoslovakia (and later in the Czech Republic) is an instance of that, and there are many others. Our concern, however, lies in the less common, or at least less easy to document, case in which an institution has acquired symbolic value. Arguably, the Crown has such a position in the United Kingdom. It expresses and symbolizes the unity of the country (which is not a nation-state). The symbolic meaning of an institution is itself reason to recognize it as enjoying morally legitimate standing. While the symbolic value of giving office to certain people

---

[13] This notion of coordination captures, I believe, the natural meaning of the term as used in political discourse. I have used it in this sense in writing about the justification of authority. Consequently it varies from the artificial sense given the term in game theory.

does not affect the theory of authority, the fact that an institution has symbolic value may feature in an argument establishing its legitimate authority. But it is unlikely to affect it in a timeless way. After all, there is *prima facie* reason for not accepting laws as valid unless they are the sorts of laws one should have. That the institution making them is of value does not show that the laws it has enacted are good. Even if the value of the institution may nevertheless provide an argument for recognizing its authority, it is not likely to extend to endowing it with timeless authority.

I have rehearsed these familiar considerations because they are of the kind that tends to establish that no human institution has authority to make laws which last forever, or for a very long time. It follows that even if new constitutions may derive their authority from the authority of their makers, old constitutions, if morally valid at all, must derive their authority from other sources. While with new law the authority of the law derives from the authority of its makers, the authority of old law must rest on other grounds.

B. Principle and practice in justification

1. Difficulties about facts and norms

This conclusion is liable to appear paradoxical on a number of grounds. It may be thought to give rise to a paradox of change: The constitution that is valid in the United States today is the one that came into force in 1789 and has been amended a few times since, most importantly between 1865 and 1870. But if my conclusion is right, some may object, then some time after its adoption the constitution lapsed and a new different constitution came into place. But this is a simple misunderstanding. My argument is not that the constitution changed, but that the reasons for its validity did. The same law can be valid for a variety of reasons, and these may change without the law changing.

There may be a deeper worry in the background, which I am groping to identify. One strand in it arises out of the worry that my argument leaves unexplained the full role of the original constitution-makers and their importance in the life of some countries. It is not exhausted by their role in the early life of the constitution. There are countries where respect for the authors of the constitution is very much a living political force long after the validity of the constitution has ceased, according to the argument of the preceding section, to depend on their authority. But that need not be an obstacle to accepting the argument. The authors of a constitution, especially the authors of a country's first constitution, sometimes become political symbols, people respect for whom unites the country and appeal to whose wisdom becomes the common currency of political argument. Such political facts—justified or otherwise—need have no bearing on the narrower issue of the grounds for the legitimate authority of constitutions, where they have such authority. Nor is the fact that the wisdom of the founding fathers, and so on, is appealed to in interpreting a constitution an objection to the argument, for, as will be seen later, local interpretive practices are to a degree self-legitimating.

But these are not the only worries the argument of the preceding section gives rise to. It also raises new questions about the relations between law and morality. We recognize the dual character of the law. On the one hand it is a social rather than a moral fact that the law of one country or another is so and so, and not different. This aspect of the law derives from several features fundamental to our understanding of its nature: First, it explains how there can be not only good and bad law, but also law and governments lacking all (moral) legitimacy, as well as those that are (morally) legitimate.[14] Second, it explains why we cannot learn what the law in a certain country, or on a certain matter, is simply by finding out what it ought to be. Third, it explains how two people, one believing the law to be legitimate and the other denying its legitimacy, can nevertheless agree on what it is. What accounts for these and other simple but deep features of the law is that it is a social fact, which means that its existence and content can be established as social facts are established, without reliance on moral arguments.[15] On the other hand, the law has a different, normative aspect. It aims to guide people's conduct and it claims moral authority to do so. And while it may fail to enjoy such authority, it must be in principle capable of making its claim good. That is, the law is a social institution that claims moral authority over its subjects and is in principle, by its nature, capable of enjoying such authority.

[14] Bad laws, ie laws that should be repealed or amended, can have moral legitimacy; that is, one may have a moral obligation to apply them or to obey them.

[15] As is well known, this claim needs careful statement that may include clarifications we need not enter into here. It may, for example, be the case that only creatures having a capacity for moral knowledge, and moral life, can have the ability to identify and understand social facts.

A theory of law must explain this dual nature of the law, as fact[16] and as norm. The doctrine that the (moral) authority of all law derives from the (moral) authority of its authors provides an easy way of doing so. There are, according to the simple version of this explanation, two steps in establishing the moral validity of the law. First, one has to establish the moral authority of the law-makers to make law, and then one has to establish as a matter of social fact alone that those law-makers made this particular law—that is, a law with this particular content. The two aspects of the law are thus separated into these two stages in establishing the legitimate authority of the law. According to this explanation, the moral authority of the law, if it has any, derives in part from its factuality. That it consists in such and such social facts becomes the core of the moral argument for its authority: When these facts are of such and such a character, moral arguments endow the law with moral legitimacy, but when they have this and that character, there is no moral argument that can legitimate the law. This explains why the content of the law can be established independently of any issues regarding its moral legitimacy. Here morality follows the facts: It applies to independently established facts.

But all this presupposes that legislators, in the form of social institutions, mediate between law and morality. They provide the factual anchor of the law; they are part of its factual aspect, which is then submitted to moral scrutiny. Much in this simple picture is correct, but it unnecessarily focuses on legislation as the one feature that allows for an account combining the two aspects of the law. An adequate account of the dual nature of the law along the suggested lines[17] requires (1) that the content and existence of the law be determined by social sources and (2) that the moral argument for the authority of the law depends on the actual nature of the social sources. It does not require that the social sources take the form of legislation. They can be custom, common law, juristic opinions, and much else.[18]

It may help clarify the picture to reflect on the implications for the relations between law and morality of the dual aspect of law. The two

---

[16] For reasons of convenience I follow the convention of contrasting fact with norm, or with morality or value. I do not mean to imply that there are no moral facts.

[17] And there are possible alternatives that deviate from the simple way in which fact and norm are neatly separated into two distinct stages, and allow some mixing in certain circumstances.

[18] Not every social fact can be a source of law. It must satisfy other conditions that need not concern us here.

aspects of the law are reconciled by the fact that the application of morality to our conduct is mediated by its application to norm-making social facts. This is a special kind of mediation. It is not surprising that our moral rights and duties depend on how things are with us and with the world in which we live: 'I should not take this or that action, for there are people around who may get hurt by it.' 'I should offer assistance to this person, for he fell down and needs help.' 'I should give the car to my neighbour next week, for I promised to do so.' These are common instances of the way the implications of morality depend on facts. But none of them are norm-creating facts.

Not so in its relations to the law. Here morality applies by sanctioning (or condemning) norms generated by the social facts of legislation, custom, and so on. Why must it be mediated in this special way when it comes to law? Not because all moral considerations have to be mediated by socially generated norms. The reasons for this are, at least in part, well understood. The law can help in securing social coordination and in bringing to people the benefits of information that is not generally available. The ability to benefit from such information and to secure social coordination is often advantageous or even necessary to achieve valuable goals, and even for compliance with moral requirements. But why cannot people coordinate their actions or share information without the mediation of legal norms? If moral norms are enough to justify coordination and sharing of information, why do not people act to achieve these goals simply because they are aware of the moral reasons for doing so? Sometimes they do, and when they do legal mediation is not necessary. But sometimes they do not, and for all too familiar reasons. Among the reasons that have attracted much attention in recent writings are (1) the fact of disagreement about which goals one has good (moral) reasons to pursue; (2) collective action problems; and (3) the indeterminacy of moral reasons. These factors sometimes make it difficult to secure coordination and sharing of information, except through the intervention of social or legal authorities whose legitimacy is acknowledged and who possess enough power to enforce a reasonable degree of compliance from those who doubt their legitimacy or who might otherwise be tempted to free ride and so on.

Perhaps the last factor mentioned is the least familiar.[19] The underlying thought is simple: Barring ignorance and disagreement about

---

[19] In recent times its importance has been emphasized by J Finnis, *Natural Law and Natural Rights* (Oxford: OUP, 1979).

moral goals or the best ways of implementing them, and barring backsliding, free riding and their like, were moral considerations to indicate how things should be arranged in society in a univocal way then people would follow these considerations. But when moral considerations underdetermine the goals to be pursued or the ways to pursue them, there may be additional difficulties in securing coordination, and to overcome them the mediation of the law is sometimes helpful, and in some cases necessary. Think of a hypothetical example: Assume that the theory of democracy yields only a general principle—for example, that a democratic government is one where there are formal legal mechanisms making the content of policies and the identity of those in charge of implementing them sensitive to the wishes of the governed, in a way that as far as possible does not give any individual greater political power than that enjoyed by any other. It follows that there can be in principle many morally legitimate ways of organizing democratic governments: federal republics and unitary constitutional monarchies, single-member constituencies, and proportional representation systems, parliamentary government and elected presidential systems, and so on. All these radically different systems would be adequate democratic systems of government. Possibly, the circumstances of one country or another will make one or more of them inadequate for that country. But—that is the assumption underlying the example—such considerations will not reduce the number of acceptable systems to one.

In such circumstances mediation through law serves the role of concretizing moral principles—that is, of giving them the concrete content they must have in order for people to be able to follow them. In our example a country must have one or another system of democratic government. So the law determines which one it has. Of course, to do so the law itself must be a matter of social, not moral, fact. Its point and purpose, as far as this example goes, is to supplement morality. To do that, its content cannot be determined by moral considerations. It must reflect social practices or traditions or some other social facts.

These considerations show how the fact that the content of the law is determined by facts and not by norms not only explains the fundamental truisms about the law that I stated earlier, and others like them, but also contributes to an account of how the law is capable of discharging some of its basic functions (such as tackling disagreements about morality and concretizing moral principles). The very same considerations explain how sometimes it is advantageous, morally speaking, for the mediation to be through legislation, whereas in other circumstances it is better for it to be through other means. Legislation would be the preferred method of mediation when changes in the law become desirable frequently, or suddenly, and when the adjustments to the law that become desirable can be worked out through deliberation or negotiation. But other forms of mediation are preferable when the adjustments to the changes can be slow and gradual, when neither deliberation nor negotiation is of much help, and especially when it is important to secure continuity, to discourage premature or hasty change, to deny interest groups the possibility of blackmailing (or twisting the arms of) the rest of the community into agreeing to change, and so on. In brief, mediation should not be carried out exclusively through legislation when the matter is of constitutional importance, that is when it should form part of an entrenched constitution.

2. Legitimacy through practice

The discussion of the relations between norm and fact is instructive. But the conclusion it points to may seem problematic. Let me put it in the most paradoxical form: Constitutions, at least old ones, do not derive their authority from the authority of their authors. But there is no need to worry as to the source of their authority. They are self-validating. They are valid just because they are there, enshrined in the practices of their countries.

Obviously to put it thus is to misrepresent the conclusions that the preceding discussion yields. A most important qualification should be added to them: *As long as they remain within the boundaries set by moral principles*, constitutions are self-validating in that their validity derives from nothing more than the fact that they are there. It should be added that this conclusion follows *if morality underdetermines* the principles concerning the form of government and the content of individual rights enshrined in constitutions. I have said nothing in support of the underdetermination thesis, nor will I do so in this chapter. However, since I believe this to be the case,[20] I will explore here some implications of this position.

The main implication is that within the broad bounds set by moral principles, practice-based law is self-vindicating. The constitution of

---

[20] The fact that morality underdetermines the content of the constitution seems to follow from the thesis that moral values are extensively and significantly incommensurable. I have explored this view in several publications, especially in *The Morality of Freedom* chapter 13 and chapter 3 of *Engaging Reason* (Oxford: OUP, 1999).

a country is a legitimate constitution because it is the constitution it has. This conclusion has to be explained and elaborated before we can accept it.

First, the fact that moral principles underdetermine the content of the constitution does not mean that the people or institutions who adopt constitutions or amend them do not do so for reasons, or that they cannot have adequate reasons for their decisions. It only follows that their reasons are not ones of moral principles (ie not the moral principles that determine which constitution is legitimate and which is not). For example, a government may support a change in the constitution that is not required by principled moral grounds for the reason that it is popular with the electorate or for the reason that it will offer some advantage to a group that is currently resentful and alienated and will thus help reconcile it to the state, or to the larger society. Alternatively, such a change may recommend itself simply because it is a change, and a change will infuse a new spirit in a society that has grown moribund and stagnant, or because every change leads to some people losing power and others gaining power, and it is good to reduce the power of the people or groups who currently hold power in the country.

Such reasons and many others are in a sense moral reasons, and they can be perfectly adequate reasons for adopting changes in a constitution. The point is that none of them is what I will call a 'merit reason'; none derives from the moral desirability of any constitutional provision. I will call reasons that bear on the merit of being subject to a particular constitutional provision 'merit reasons', to distinguish them from reasons for adopting a constitutional provision or for amending it that do not derive from the good of being subject to it. On the contrary, they are all examples of how constitutional amendment may be justified by reasons that do not bear on the merit of the constitutional change they justify. In that, they are also examples of how ordinary political concerns, even relatively short-term political concerns, can have a legitimate role in the politics of the constitution.

The self-legitimating aspect of practice is not negated by the fact that action for and against constitutional reform may be taken for good reasons. Because reasons of the kind just illustrated are not merit reasons and do not bear on the merit of the content of the constitution, they do not bear on its legitimacy. That is determined primarily by merit reasons that show the content of the constitution to be morally acceptable, and nothing in the examples undercuts the claim that merit reasons typically greatly underdetermine the content of the constitution, leading to the conclusion that within the boundaries they set, constitutions are legitimated by their existence.[21]

3. Stability and continuity

I introduced the idea of self-legitimation, of the legitimating effect of practice through reflection on the fact that moral principles under-determine the content of constitutions, and practice takes on the slack. But as is well known, the self-legitimating power of practice is not confined to this. Conventions are, perhaps, the most familiar example. Conventions illustrate a larger category in which behaviour is justified if, and normally only if, a general practice exists: One should not cross the lawn if there is a general practice not to do so. That things happen in a certain way makes it right, or good, that they should continue to happen in that way.

An important concern of a similar nature is the concern for stability. The need to secure stability is in itself indifferent to the content of the constitutional practices prevailing in any time or place. Whatever they are, the concern for stability indicates that they should be perpetuated. Stability is not always an advantage. In the preceding subsection I noted that shaking things up can be desirable when it can change a moribund or corrupt power structure, infuse a country with a sense of energy and hope, and so on. However, stability is often desirable, and for many reasons. Remember that here as before the reference to the 'self-legitimating' character of the 'constitution' is not to the formal legal existence of the constitution but to the constitution as it exists in the practices and traditions of the country concerned. Constitutions are meant to provide a framework for the public life of a country, giving it direction and shape. For this to be achieved, widespread knowledge of the constitution has to be secured. This requires knowledge not only of the text but of its significance—that is, knowledge of the constitutional practices in the country. Until people absorb and adjust to it, a radical constitutional change upsets these practices. It has ramifications regarding different aspects of public life, and there is bound to be a temporary uncertainty regarding the way the reform or change will affect various aspects of constitutional practice. The uncertainty affects people's ability

---

[21] This conclusion can be strengthened. Even when an alternative constitution is somewhat better than the one we have, the fact that this is the one we have makes it legitimate. The considerations that support this conclusion and give it more precise meaning arise out of the cost of change and the conservative presumption. These are discussed later.

to function. It is made worse if it generates fear of continuous change, leading to a sense of dislocation and loss of orientation.

These are some of the many, mostly familiar reasons for preferring stability to instability. They do not amount to a rejection of change, but they create a reason to prefer continuity to change, unless there are really good reasons for the change. They add to the main and powerful conservative argument: While it is possible to predict the direct consequences of small changes in legal and social practices, changes that take place within existing frameworks and do not upset them, it is impossible to predict the effect of radical, large-scale changes. They are liable to affect the legal and social framework, which constitutes the background conditions that make predictions of social events possible. Hence, while radical reform may be inspired by cogent reasons to bring about different social conditions, there is no adequate advance reason to believe that it will bring about the hoped-for consequences. In itself this is no argument against radical reform and change. It does not show that radical change is likely to be for the worse. But it does undercut many reasons that people often advocate in pressing for radical change. Taken together with the advantages of stability, it adds to a certain conservative attitude sometimes expressed by saying that in relatively stable and decent societies there is a presumption in favour of continuity against which all proposals for change should be judged.

Broadly speaking, the argument for stability and the underdetermination of constitutional principles by morality combine to establish the self-legitimating aspect of constitutional practices and traditions.[22] Yet lumping them together like this runs the risk of obscuring the two fundamental differences between them.

In the first place the underdetermination argument means that within broad boundaries set by moral principles the very existence of a constitution establishes that it is a good constitution for the country in question. Others would have done, but given that they were not adopted, not they but the one enshrined in the practices of that country is its legitimate constitution. The desirability of stability does not establish that the constitution is legitimate. It applies even to illegitimate constitutions. The drawbacks of instability apply there too, though they are overcome by other considerations.

---

[22] One should always remember, but I will not repeat the point again, that the self-legitimating aspect of constitutional practices is subject to their falling within what is morally acceptable.

Second, while the argument from underdetermination allows that, within bounds, existing constitutions are self-legitimating, it does not constitute a reason for not changing the constitution. The constitution is legitimate, but so would be many alternatives we might have in its place. The arguments for stability, on the other hand, while they do not establish the legitimacy of the existing constitution, establish the existence of reasons for not changing an existing constitution.

Things are different if the constitution is morally legitimate—that is, if it instantiates one of the permissible forms of government, if it lies within the permissible as determined by moral considerations. When this is so, the arguments from underdeterminacy and from stability combine to legitimate the constitution and provide a reason for keeping the constitutional tradition going as it is.

What role if any do the authors of the constitution play in providing it with legitimacy? Their role can be of enormous practical importance, though it is a secondary role, from a theoretical point of view. Basically they help launch the constitutional tradition, and sometimes their reputation helps to keep it going. They may endow it with authority in its early years, and the respect in which they are held may be of great importance in determining the willingness of the population, and its politically active groups, to abide by it. This willingness is crucial both to the survival and to the legitimacy of the constitution. But it is so to the extent that it helps to bring the constitution within the bounds of the morally permissible.

III. Interpreting Constitutions

A. Interpreting the constitution: on the nature of interpretive doctrines

We can take constitutional interpretation as an established practice and confine ourselves to studying how it is conducted in different countries. Such a study would not be without interest, but from a theoretical point of view its benefits would be limited. A study based on this kind of survey and classification of interpretive techniques would yield an unwieldy plethora of interpretive styles and techniques, varying within countries as well as between countries and changing over time. It would also reveal large disagreements among judges about the proper methods and techniques of constitutional interpretation.

Finally, it would show that not infrequently what judges say is one thing and what they do is another. The practice of some judges does not accord with their more general statements about the nature of constitutional interpretation.

Perhaps in part for these reasons, many legal philosophers have either shied away from writing about interpretation or offered normative accounts of interpretation generally and of constitutional interpretation in particular. Does this betray the task of explaining the law as it is rather than as it ought to be? Not necessarily. First, legal interpretation is much more than a method of establishing what the law is. When used by courts and by lawyers, or commentators and academics who focus on the interpretations that courts should adopt, legal interpretation is also a tool for developing the law, changing and reforming it. Second, while it is generally accepted (for reasons that will emerge in the sequel) that there is a point in following established interpretive methods, to the extent that they exist, it is also generally accepted that interpretations are subject to objective assessment, that some are defensible and others are not.[23] Moreover, it is part of the practice of legal interpretation as it is in many countries that courts are not bound to follow past interpretive techniques if they can be shown to be mistaken or less desirable than some alternatives. They can modify them or replace them with better ones. This is the case, for example, in all common-law jurisdictions. In such countries the study of sound interpretation is also part of the study of the law as it is. But it is a study of a very special aspect of the law, one that demarcates some of the law-making powers of the courts and the circumstances for their legitimate use.

Therefore, when reflecting on constitutional interpretation, we should start not from the fact that certain methods of interpretation are used, and others not, but from the question: Why is interpretation so central to constitutional adjudication? The answer, as always when there is reason to resort to interpretation, turns on a combination of reasons for respecting the constitution as it exists and reasons for remaining open to the possibility that it is in need of reform, adjustment, or development in order to remove shortcomings it always had or shortcomings that emerged as the government or the society that it governs changed over time.

---

[23] As is clear, this does not imply accepting that for any question about the interpretation of the law there is only one acceptable answer.

It may be worth emphasizing that this Janus-like aspect of interpretation (that it faces both backward, aiming to elucidate the law as it is, and forward, aiming to develop and improve it) is not special to legal interpretation. It is the mark of interpretation in general that it aims to be true to an original that is being interpreted and to be open to innovation. In the performing arts such as the theatre, for example, good performances interpret the text and in doing so they often express the views of the performers at the same time. This does not mean that all good interpretations are innovative, merely that interpretations can be innovative and therefore are ever open to this possibility. This is not the place to consider the nature of interpretation in general.[24] But we should reflect on the reasons why constitutional interpretation should be double-sided.

The reason for the backward-looking aspect of constitutional interpretation takes us back to the principle with which we started. The doctrines of constitutional interpretation, it was our assumption from the beginning, are based, at least in part, on the doctrine of sources of the authority of constitutions. Since the authority of a long-established constitution rests primarily on the desirability of securing continuity, the same desirability should inform constitutional interpretation as well. To secure continuity the interpretation should be backward-looking. It should be faithful to the constitution as it exists at that time. If so, should not this consideration dominate constitutional interpretation to the exclusion of all else? The moral importance of the issues decided upon in constitutional cases would not allow this to happen. Courts whose decisions determine the fortunes of many people must base them on morally sound considerations. Nothing else could justify their actions. If we admit that, does it not follow from the preceding argument that the morally correct decision is the one which is purely backward-looking—that is, which does nothing more than set out the content of (the relevant parts of) the constitution as it is at the time? This may be the right course for them to take, but only when it would be morally required, or at least morally reasonable, to rely on considerations of continuity above all else.

---

[24] For the reasons for denying that every time we understand something we interpret it see A Marmor's application of Wittgenstein's position in *Interpretation and Legal Theory* (Oxford: OUP, 1994). For my own stab at a general account of interpretation see chapter 10 of the present volume.

In other words, given the impact that constitutional decisions, like many other legal decisions, have on people's lives, they are justified only if they are morally justified. As we saw, considerations of continuity are of great moral importance, and they are the primary considerations determining the continuous legitimacy of the constitution. But they are hardly ever the only moral considerations affecting an issue. When they are not, courts should try to reach decisions that satisfy as much as possible all the relevant considerations, and when it is impossible to satisfy all completely, they should strive to satisfy them as much as possible, given their relative importance. Hence, while on occasion the desirability of continuity in the matter concerned will prevail over all else, often this will not be the case, though even when continuity does not override all else, it should still be taken into account as much as possible. Hence, in such cases, while the courts should still interpret the constitution, for they are still rightly moved by considerations of continuity, they should also give weight to other moral considerations. That is, their interpretation should also be forward-looking. None of this should be taken to imply that all defects in a constitution can be put right through ingenious interpretation. All I am saying is that sometimes this is possible.

Yet again, an objection that this view is misconceived for it overlooks the fact that the doctrine of constitutional interpretation is a *legal*, not a moral, doctrine is bound to occur to some. Whatever the moral merit of my observations, the objection goes, it is irrelevant to an understanding of constitutional interpretation. That doctrine is a legal doctrine and there is nothing judges may do other than follow the doctrines of interpretation that are binding on them according to the law of their own country. Let me concede right away that there is something to the objection. Judges who follow the views on interpretation developed here may find themselves morally obliged to disobey the law of their country. That is the result of the fact that I am developing an approach to constitutional interpretation that, for lack of a better word, we may call a moral approach. The law of any country may be at odds with morality in a variety of ways. One of them is the existence of locally binding rules that prohibit the courts from following any morally acceptable interpretation.

I am not proposing the observations in this chapter as a substitute for an examination of the rules and doctrines of interpretation prevailing in this country or that. That is clearly an important task for those interested in the law of the countries concerned. Nevertheless, it would be false modesty to say no more than that the topic of my discussion is different. I am also making claims for its importance. Let me first recapitulate: First, while there is every reason for people interested in this or that legal system to study the rules of interpretation binding in it, there is no universal theory of interpretation that applies to all law, except as a normative theory—that is, of what interpretation should be like. Second, whether they like it or not, courts face moral problems and should behave in a way sanctioned by morality. This may bring them into conflict with the law. Third, quite often the proper ways of interpreting constitutions are controversial. Fourth, typically courts have power to adopt new ways of interpreting the law and to revise established ones when they have good reason to do so.

The last two points are interconnected, and both stem from a fact not yet mentioned: At the most basic level there are not, nor can there be, specifically legal ways of interpretation. Of course, most legal systems have rules of interpretation laid down in legislation or precedent that are special to them. But most interpretation does not, cannot, depend on them. This is not only, not primarily, because rules of interpretation themselves often require to be interpreted. It is primarily because problems of interpretation are rarely problems of the meaning of one term or phrase. They are more often than not questions of the interpretation of sentences, or of articles in statutes or in constitutions, or of moral and political doctrines. And they can arise in unexpected places. No set of explicitly articulated rules of interpretation can deal with all of them. The same is true of rules of interpretation implied in a legal culture, rather than explicitly articulated in its laws. Such rules cannot settle all possible issues of interpretation. All too often interpretation is just a matter of reasoning to a reasonable view on the basis of a variety of considerations, some reinforcing each other, some clashing. There is no way of reducing such reasoning to the application of rules, or other norms, nor is there any way of eliminating the need and the desirability of interpretation that consists in and results from such reasoning.

This explains why the law of interpretation, meaning the rules and doctrines of interpretation in force in any given country, useful as they may be, cannot contain all that can and need be said in an account of legal or constitutional interpretation. Ultimately an account of constitutional interpretation has more to do with understanding legal or constitutional reasoning than with understanding any legal doctrine specific to this or that country. Reasoning that aims to establish the meaning of a law, a work of art, literature, religion, or anything else and that combines respect for its original expression or its traditional or current meaning with openness to innovation is interpretive. For the reasons already given, constitutional reasoning is to a considerable degree interpretive reasoning. But accounts of reasoning are accounts of rationality in belief, and they are universal normative accounts, specific to any locality or subject matter only in the details of their application.

All this was said to explain the importance of a normative account of constitutional interpretation, an account that goes over and above the study of the rules and doctrines of interpretation established in one country or another. But the drift of these remarks raises a different objection to the thought that there can be a general study of constitutional interpretation. If the study of interpretation is just the study of reasoning that is constrained by the condition specified earlier, and if the study of constitutional interpretation is just the study of such reasoning when applied to constitutions, can anything specific be said about it beyond the unhelpful but sound advice that in interpreting constitutions one should reason well? There may be a general account of reasoning, and perhaps even a general account of interpretive reasoning. But once one has mastered those is there anything more that is special to constitutional interpretation and that is not merely an application of the general account of interpretive reasoning to the content of the constitutions of specific countries?

This revives the doubt about the possibility of a general theory of constitutional law raised at the outset, but this time addressed specifically to issues of interpretation. As I explained there, I believe that there is much truth in the doubt. There is no general theory of constitutional interpretation if that is meant to be a general recipe for the way such interpretation should be conducted that is set out in some detail in order to guide the interpreter every step of the way with practical advice. There is little more that one can say other than 'reason well' or 'interpret reasonably'. What little there is to say consists mainly of pointing out mistakes that have been made attractive by the popularity they enjoy among judges, lawyers, or academic writers.

B. Fidelity and innovation

Interpretation, it was suggested, lives in spaces where fidelity to an original and openness to novelty mix. It exists in a dialectical tension, as some might say. The reason we find this tension in reasoning about constitutional law, I claimed, is that constitutional decisions are moral decisions that have to be morally justified, and the moral considerations that apply include both fidelity to the law of the constitution as it is, arising out of concern for continuity, and openness to its shortcomings and to injustices its application may yield in certain cases, which leads to openness to the need to develop and modify it.

Two opposing mistakes are invited by this fact. The first is to think that because a good interpretation may combine both elements, the distinction between the constitution, and more generally the law, as it is and as it ought to be is illusory. Constitutional interpretation, one argument runs, establishes the meaning of the constitution. That is, there is no sense in talking of the content of the constitution except as it is determined by a process of interpretation. Since interpretation mixes fidelity and innovation, it undermines both notions. It breaks down the distinction between them, for fidelity assumes that the content of the constitution, to which one is supposed to be faithful, can be established independently of interpretation and, by the same token, so does innovation, since it is identified as deviation from pure fidelity. Without an interpretation-independent identification of the content of the constitution, we cannot tell fidelity from innovation, and since the content cannot be identified independently of interpretation, it follows that there is no coherent meaning to the notion of fidelity to the constitution and none to constitutional innovation either.

This argument fails. I intimated earlier that not all explanations of meaning are interpretations. But we need not rely on this in refuting the argument. It overlooks the fact that the reason fidelity and innovation are often mixed is that we often have reasons to interpret in ways that mix them. But this is not always the case. Sometimes we have reason to interpret the constitution in ways that simply elucidate its content at the moment, warts and all. Such an interpretation, I call it 'a conserving interpretation', will be successful if it is true to the existing meaning of the constitution. It will include no mixing of conflicting elements. It will display no dialectical tension, and it will establish the benchmark by which we can measure other interpretations to see whether they are more or less innovatory.

The failure of the preceding argument does not mean, of course, that there are no other better ones. But I do not know of any successful argument to the same conclusion. It does not follow that in every case we can establish what the law is. The evidence may be incomplete. Moreover, it is not the case that we can establish the legal answer regarding any legal question, since the law is often indeterminate on various issues. As a result, when the constitution is interpreted with the goal of establishing just what it is at a given moment in time the interpretation will show it to be vague and indeterminate. Granted all these points, it is still the case that when the evidence is available it is possible to establish what the law is, and therefore to distinguish between innovatory and conserving interpretations. I suspect that one reason which encourages people to assume that it is impossible to interpret the law, to establish its meaning at any given time without changing it at the same time, is the following sort of argument: (1) Courts can always change the law that is relevant to the case in front of them. (2) Courts can change the law only when it is indeterminate. (3) It follows that the law is indeterminate on all issues. (4) Therefore, no interpretation can simply establish what it is without changing it. The argument is invalid, for from the claim that the law is indeterminate on all issues it does not follow that an interpretation cannot merely describe it without changing it. All that follows is that such an interpretation will describe it as indeterminate. More important, the second premise is simply false. Courts can develop the law even when it is determinate. They can and often do simply change it.

This brings us to the second mistake one should avoid, which in some ways is the opposite of the first. Some may think that if there is a distinction between a conserving interpretation that merely states the law as it is and an innovatory one that develops and changes it, then it must be possible to take any interpretation and point to where it stops merely stating the law as it is and starts developing and changing it. It must, in other words, be possible to separate the descriptive and the innovative elements in every interpretive statement. The thought that this is so is encouraged by the fact that sometimes such a separation is indeed possible. But these occasions are relatively rare, and it certainly does not follow from the previous observations that it is ever, let alone always, possible. In clearing the first mistake, I argued for the possibility of comparing different interpretations by their degree of novelty and of distinguishing innovative interpretations from conserving ones. (There could be several of them, since one can provide interpretations that restate the law as it was at different points in time.) That thought is very different from the suggestion that within each interpretation one can separate the elements that are true to the law as it is from those that are innovative. All that my position implies is that when thinking of the reasons that justify an interpretation one can distinguish those which suggest that the interpretation should be faithful to existing law from those which suggest that it should develop or even change the law.

Having cleared these two theoretical mistakes out of the way, we can face one of the main mistakes to which theories of constitutional interpretation are liable. Having established in the preceding section that constitutional interpretation has to answer to a variety of reasons, some urging fidelity to existing law, others urging its development, change, and adaptation, it is natural to expect that the central task of a theory of constitutional interpretation is to spell out the right proportions of innovation and conservation in constitutional interpretations, or to tell one how to determine how much of each to allow in each case. But this is a misconception, which if not checked is bound to breed many false theories. It overlooks the fact that there is no one reason to develop and change constitutional law. When it is adequate to its tasks and to the situation in the country, there is no need to change or to develop it. Modification of the law is called for either when it is undetermined on the issue the court has to decide or when it is less than adequate. In those cases the court should take notice of the reasons for having the law take one shape or another. But those are enormously varied both in nature and in importance. Any moral reason whatsoever can figure in the considerations of a constitutional court on these occasions. There cannot be a general answer to the question of how much importance reasons for change should have in their conflict with reasons for continuity.

Of course, there are certain generalizations one can safely put forward. For example, it is generally (but not universally) the case that the greater are the defects in the constitutional law concerned, the less important is it to preserve continuity and the more important is it to change it. We can also emphasize that sometimes it is possible to reconcile continuity with change, by introducing changes in the law that deviate little from it, especially in matters where established expectations led people to make plans on the basis of existing law. This is particularly true of cases in which the need to resolve legal indeterminacy on this issue or that is the only reason for deviation from existing law. In such cases, it may be that no expectations have been generated, and resolution of the case need not affect stability. One can continue in this vein to offer more helpful generalizations. But they will not amount to a general answer to the question of what is the right mix of innovation and preservation in constitutional decisions.

C. Considerations of the moral merit of the constitution and of its institutional role

So far I have argued for four main conclusions: First, there is no real theory of constitutional interpretation, in the sense of a set of principles that when applied to an interpretive question yield the correct interpretation of the constitutional provision concerned. All a philosophical discussion of interpretation can do is explain the nature of the activity and its main parameters, and help one to avoid some mistakes. Second, there is a cogent way of distinguishing between innovative and conserving interpretations, and often between more or less innovative (less or more conserving) interpretations. Third, interpretation is central to legal reasoning because in legal reasoning fidelity to an original competes with, and has to be combined with, reasons for innovation. Constitutional interpretation is central to constitutional adjudication because courts are faced with conflicting moral considerations, some militating for continuity, and therefore for giving effect to the constitution as it is at that moment, and some pointing to the need to develop and improve it. Fourth, it makes no sense to ask in general what is the right mix of conservation and innovation in constitutional interpretation.

To help us make further progress with the argument, we need to retreat and consider an objection to the third conclusion—that whatever the merit of innovative interpretations in literature, history, and elsewhere, judicial interpretations of the constitution should be purely conserving. Earlier I argued against this view on the ground that (1) courts are faced with moral issues and should make morally justified decisions, and (2) the moral considerations they face often point not only to the advantages of continuity, but also to the desirability of modifying and improving the constitutional provisions concerned. My imaginary objector agrees to both premises but denies that the conclusion follows. It seems to follow, he points out, only because I disregarded altogether the importance of institutional considerations to legal decisions. Over and above the moral considerations I gestured toward stands the doctrine of the role of the courts, which says that their job is exclusively to apply the law as it is.[25] Others have the responsibility

---

[25] We can imagine a more moderate objector who allows the courts creative functions in special circumstances. I am using the extreme position as a way to explain my argument.

to improve it. Therefore, the fact that there are good reasons for dissatisfaction with the law as it stands is no justification at all for judicial 'activism'. It is not the courts' business. They have a job to do and they should confine themselves to doing it and no more.

The value of this objection is that it reminds us of the importance of institutional considerations in justifying political and legal actions. The objection relies on a doctrine of division of labour among various organs of government. But behind it are additional complex considerations of institutional design, relative advantage in performing one task or another, and others necessary for its justification. Philosophers are sometimes prone to let institutional considerations drop out of their sight. I suspect that contributing to this is the fact that institutional considerations do not mark one outcome as better than others. They merely indicate that the court is or is not an appropriate body to adopt one interpretation or another, not that it is better for the law to be this way or that. In other words, institutional considerations do not contribute to showing which result is best. They do, however, show which decision is justified. They act something like side constraints, though they are not necessarily exceptionless.[26]

The objection is that my argument overlooks the effect of institutional constraints and that once the omission is repaired we can see that the courts may not modify the law. Is this really the sole role of the courts? My earlier argument that since the courts have to take a moral decision they have to reach the best moral result was too simple-minded. It took too simple a view of who the agent is. The courts do not act in their own name. They act as organs of the political society, that is—to simplify—of the state. It is the state that has the responsibility to reach the right result. It does not automatically follow, and that is what the institutional objection points to, that it should do so through its courts. The state has other organs, and possibly the courts should always simply apply existing law, and if that is not the right result, that is, if the law should be modified, then it falls to other state organs to modify it.

How, then, are we to determine the responsibility of different organs of state? In the first instance by examining the structure of state organs and the division of powers enshrined in the constitution. But beyond that, we need to examine the moral soundness of that structure. It is not

---

[26] A notion introduced by Robert Nozick in *Anarchy, State and Utopia* (New York: Basic Books, 1974). His notion is of exceptionless side constraints, except *in extremis*; see 28ff.

morally sound if following it is not a good way to make sure, inasmuch as that is possible, that the state reaches the right outcome in each case. In that case it falls to each state organ to consider whether it would not be morally right for it to deviate from existing law in order to secure the best outcome. It ought, of course, to weigh the reasons, of continuity, separation of powers, and others, against doing so. But it cannot avoid taking the question of the desirability of change seriously. There is no need here to explore the structure of that kind of reasoning. The important lesson is that the issue of the relative role of institutions is itself, like all the other issues we have encountered, a moral issue, and the courts have to act on moral considerations that apply to division-of-labor questions.

The salient fact for our concern is that whether or not in this state or that the role of the courts includes responsibility for improving the constitution is a question of the doctrine of constitutional interpretation in force in it. As I observed earlier, in most countries issues of interpretation at this level of generality tend to be subject to dispute and disagreement. Since in such countries there is no established practice on the issue, there is in them no settled law about it, and there is nothing to stop the courts from giving effect to the view of their own role that is morally compelling.

Is that the view which confines the courts to merely applying existing law?[27] That would be their role if and only if there were other state organs fully able to engage in improving the law when necessary. The more entrenched the constitution is, the less likely is it that there are such alternatives.

But does not the fact that constitutions are entrenched show not that there are inadequate means of amending them but rather that it is undesirable that they be amended in ways other than the procedures provided? It may mean that this is what their authors intended, but it does not follow that their view is sound. This is yet another debate that can only be touched upon here. There is a strong case for separating constitutional development and adjustment from the course of ordinary politics. In most circumstances it is advantageous to secure the stability and durability of the framework of governmental institutions and the

---

[27] I am overlooking here the objection to this position that challenges its intelligibility and claims that whatever the courts' intentions they cannot but engage in developing and modifying the law, at least on occasion. The argument in the text goes a long way beyond that conclusion and establishes that there are occasions when courts should engage in innovative interpretation even when they can avoid doing so.

fundamental principles of their operation from short-term political pressures. But the case for separation is not a case for making it difficult to change constitutional provisions. It is merely a case for a special process controlling their change. The argument against easy changes is the case for stability and continuity in constitutional law. But that case has complex conclusions. It establishes that radical changes in the structure of the constitution should not be easy to effect. Their adoption should require extensive publicity, wide-ranging public debate, and substantial and durable consensus. There is no objection to regular development of the law within existing frameworks. Such modifications do not undermine continuity. By and large they tend to enhance it. So far I have not distinguished between stability in the law—that is, the absence of change in the law—and stability in the social or economic effects of the law. Since the two often go hand in hand, there was no need to distinguish between them. But they go hand in hand only as long as the underlying social, political, or economic conditions do not change. When they do, the law may have to change if it is to continue to have the same social or economic effects. In such a case innovative interpretations that modify the law prevent it from ossifying and getting progressively less and less adequate to its task and requiring major reform. Of course, the cumulative effect of small-change reform may well amount to a radical change in constitutional law over the years. But stability is consistent with slow change, whatever its cumulative effect. Therefore, entrenching the constitution may be justified in that it secures extensive debate and solid consensus behind radical constitutional changes. But it also means that it falls to the courts to take charge of continuous improvements and adjustments within existing structures. The institutional argument against innovative constitutional interpretations by the courts fails.

D. Moral and legal considerations: where the law is autonomous

In the preceding discussion it was assumed that there are two anchors to constitutional interpretation. On the one hand, reasons for continuity militate in favour of conserving interpretation.[28] On the other hand,

---

[28] But remember the distinction between continuity in the law and continuity in its effects introduced earlier. The first is needed typically only when it is necessary for the second.

imperfections in the law militate in favour of innovative interpretation that will develop and modify the constitution. Conserving interpretations articulate or restate the current meaning of the constitutional provisions in question. That means that they aim to capture the meaning these provisions have in current constitutional practice. In the early days of a constitution this will be the meaning intended by its authors, inasmuch as it was expressed in its text as understood given the conventions of meaning and interpretation of the time.[29] In later years this meaning will be gradually overlaid by layers of interpretive decisions and by the way the relevant provisions have come to be understood in the practices of the legal institutions of that country and by its population. Naturally, quite often the constitution so understood will be vague and indeterminate on many issues. How does moral and legal underdetermination affect interpretation?

Indeterminacy in constitutional provisions will favour innovative interpretations. As long as they merely make determined what was underdetermined, they cannot offend against stability. Whatever moral reasons apply to improve the constitutional provisions involved can be given effect. Sometimes, however, there will be indeterminacy both in law and in morality. Nevertheless, the matter must be decided, and the constitutional position has to be settled. How is the court to proceed then?

A distinction introduced in section II.B is relevant here. I distinguished there between merit reasons, which bear on the merit of a constitution and its provisions, and reasons for amending a constitution, or some of its provisions, which have no bearing on the merit of those provisions. The need for a change to infuse a spirit of optimism in a new future, or in order to win the support or allegiance of some segment of the population, were examples of the second type of reason. When addressing the consequences of the incommensurability of reasons, we need to distinguish between incommensurability of all the reasons bearing on a decision and incommensurability in some class of reasons.

Merit reasons which show that one interpretation, innovative or not, makes the constitution better than its alternatives take pride of place in constitutional interpretation. This is not because the balance of these merit reasons always defeats all other reasons with which they may conflict. This is not so. Other reasons may rightly defeat merit reasons on

---

[29] This formula is meant to capture the conclusions of chapter 11, 'Intention in Interpretation'.

various occasions. The court may, to mention but one familiar consideration, adopt an interpretation that renders the constitution inferior to what it would be on one or more alternative interpretations in order to placate a hostile legislature or executive, which may otherwise take action to limit the power of the courts or to compromise their independence. Merit reasons are the primary reasons because they define the task of the courts in constitutional interpretation: Their task is to apply the constitution when it is adequate to its task and to improve it when it is wanting. Their success, and therefore the merit of maintaining the existing system of constitutional courts, depends on their being good at this task. If in the long run the constitutional courts are not good at performing their task (ie not as good as some alternative might be), then one should reform them or assign some of their functions to another institution. But, to repeat, the fact that merit reasons are primary does not mean that they are the only reasons constitutional courts can take account of, nor that they are always decisive.

In section II.B it was argued that when we consider the legitimacy of a constitution as a whole, merit reasons often underdetermine the verdict. Often the constitution we have is legitimate not because it is superior to any alternative we may have, but because we have it, and there is nothing fundamentally wrong with it; that is it lies within the bounds of the morally permissible. It would be a mistake, however, to think that it *follows* that if the constitution is legitimate then considerations of merit play no role in constitutional interpretation. Given that a country has a legitimate constitution and that it developed institutions and practices to fit its constitution, many considerations of merit apply that would not have applied otherwise. For example, given that in democracies a major consideration in defining the reach of the doctrine of freedom of expression is the importance of the freedom for democratic politics, the boundaries of the right to free expression will inevitably depend in part on the powers of government, in all its branches. Roughly speaking, the more wide-ranging are the powers of the government, the more extensive is the right to free expression.

Merit reasons also depend on other aspects of the economic, social, and legal life of a country. Compare two examples, both relating to the proper balance between freedom of expression and the protection of the administration of justice from undue influence by the media. First, this balance depends on the conduct of the media in the country. When good sense prevails in practice, freedom of the press can and should be wider than when the conduct of the media is careless of the need to protect the administration of justice from its influence. Second, the balance also depends on whether trials and other legal proceedings take place before juries or before professional judges sitting without lay jurors. In the second example the doctrine of freedom of expression is affected by merit reasons that depend on another aspect of the constitution; in the first example it is affected by social practices that are not enshrined in law. In both cases merit reasons have considerable weight even though the constitution the provisions of which are litigated is not the only morally good one, but merely a morally permissible constitution legitimated by practice.

Having said that, I should add that while merit reasons are central to constitutional adjudication they will often be incommensurate. They will fail to determine which constitutional provision is better. As was anticipated earlier, this does not mean that there will be no sound reasons for establishing that the courts should prefer one interpretation over others. For the most part, however, these reasons are particularly time-bound and agent-bound. That is, they may be reasons that apply at a particular point in time but lapse fairly quickly, and they may be reasons for the courts to interpret the constitution one way or another, without being reasons for other agents to do so. My example of the way the scope of freedom of expression depends on how mindful the media are of the need to protect the administration of justice illustrates the familiar point that the temporal relativity of reasons for a constitutional interpretation affects merit reasons as well as others. The way non-merit reasons may be relative to the interpreting agent is illustrated by the example of a preference for an interpretation that will not trigger action by the legislature against the courts. Suppose an individual relies in her dealings with an agency belonging to the executive branch of government on an interpretation that, were it adopted by the courts, would offend the legislature. The executive and its agencies cannot legitimately refrain from accepting the validity of the interpretation because of these considerations. The supposition is that only the courts are in disfavour with the legislature. Organs of the executive should, therefore, adopt the interpretation supported by merit considerations. Unfortunately, if they refuse, the individual may not find relief in the courts, which may be rightly inhibited from adopting the 'best' interpretation.

Much more can be said about the relative role of merit and other considerations. But we have to turn back to the issue of incommensurability. Let me summarize the points made so far: (1) Moral reasons motivate all interpretive decisions, both conserving ones and innovative ones, (2) Merit considerations may justify an innovative interpretation even when a conserving interpretation is possible, that is even when the issue is settled by the constitution as it is. That would be the case when the need to improve the law is greater than the need for continuity on the point, and when there is an interpretation that improves the law. (3) When the constitution is underdetermined on the issue in question, the need for improvement exists and meets no direct opposition from considerations of continuity. (4) The fact that the constitutional scheme as a whole is legitimated by practice, and is merely permissible, does not mean that merit considerations are exhausted. (5) While merit reasons are the primary reasons for innovative interpretations, they are not the only relevant ones. There are sound interpretive reasons that are not merit reasons and that compete with them. (6) Those other reasons can determine the right interpretation to adopt even when both the constitution as it is at the time and the merit reasons fail to resolve the issue at hand. The question is: How are courts to decide cases in which these reasons also fail to resolve the issue and determine the outcome of the case?

Why is this a problem? Rational action is action for a reason that is reasonably thought to be undefeated. It is not action for a reason that defeats all those which conflict with it.[30] We have no difficulty in choosing which orange to pick from a bowl of oranges just because there is nothing to choose between them. Of course, incommensurable reasons are not reasons of equal strength. But the fact that no one incommensurable reason defeats the others should not present a mystery about how we manage to choose what to do when facing incommensurable reasons.

Incommensurability of reasons is pervasive, and while we are far from having a satisfactory philosophical explanation of all its aspects, it does not pose a difficulty in explaining how we can act without belief that the act we perform is supported by stronger reasons than all its alternatives. Yet there is a problem here. It is a problem specific to law and to other public actions. It arises not from a difficulty of squaring incommensurability of reasons with a theory of rational action or rational choice, but from a principle of political morality, namely the principle of the public accountability of public actions. This principle directs not only that courts should take their decisions for cogent reasons and that they should avoid irrelevant reasons, but also that as far as possible the

---

[30] I am relying here on my analysis in chapter 3 of *Engaging Reason*.

fact that no irrelevant considerations affected the decision should be publicly visible. This principle makes it inappropriate for the courts to act as people do when confronted by incommensurability of reasons for the options facing them. People's choices are in part not dictated by any reason. They reveal dispositions and tastes they have that may or may not be important in their lives, but are non-rational in nature. It is important for institutions acting for the public not to take decisions the explanations for which are the non-rational dispositions or tastes of the people who hold office in them. Public institutions should develop or adopt distancing devices—devices they can rely on to settle such issues in a way that is independent of the personal tastes of the judges or other officials involved.

The need for this distancing is one of the reasons why many judges persist in arguing that at no point did they rely in their decisions on anything other than a conserving interpretation of the law and that there is only one such true interpretation. But the law can and should provide them with genuine distancing devices. Elsewhere I have suggested that legal doctrine can and does play such a role.[31] Legal doctrine can be, of course, no more than what morality dictates. But notoriously doctrine can take a life of its own, detached from moral considerations. This tendency in legal thought is often decried as formalism, conceptualism, or essentialism, and often it deserves the criticism. But criticism is deserved—in constitutional law—only in cases where relying on formal legal reasoning prevents a court from adopting an innovative interpretation that could improve the constitution. In cases where reasons for the two or more best interpretations are incommensurate, reliance on formal legal reasoning is justified; it serves as a distancing device.

I am not arguing, of course, that such distancing devices are always available in the law. On the contrary, I asserted earlier that often they are unavailable and the law is indeterminate. I am simply pointing out the desirability of having them available. We can now return for the last time to the argument expounded earlier in this part that it is frequently appropriate for courts to adopt an innovative interpretation even when there is a conserving interpretation they could adopt instead. Some legal doctrines and methods of interpretation fall into my category of formal doctrines—ones that are not justified by moral value or whose application to the case at hand cannot be so justified. Formal legal doctrines, I have

---

[31] J Raz, 'On the Autonomy of Legal Reasoning', in *Ethics in the Public Domain* 326.

been arguing, are valuable. But they should not be used to stop the courts from resorting to moral considerations to develop and improve the law.

They should be brought into play only once moral resources have been exhausted, when the courts need to resort to distancing devices to justify their choice between otherwise incommensurate interpretations.

E. Coda: but is it the same constitution?

Possibly this doubt is not yet laid to rest. If the courts make the constitution, does it not follow that many people who believe that, let us say, they are living under a constitution adopted two hundred years ago are mistaken? Is it not the case that if people like me are right then the constitution has been made and remade many times since, and we are not now living under the constitution then adopted? It has to be admitted that people who do not realize that the law of the constitution lies as much in the interpretive decisions of the courts as in the original document that they interpret, and who deny that courts are entitled to adopt innovative interpretations, are making a mistake. But it is not the mistake of thinking that it is the same constitution. It is still the constitution adopted two hundred years ago, just as a person who lives in an eighteenth-century house lives in a house built two hundred years ago. His house had been repaired, added to, and changed many times since. But it is still the same house and so is the constitution.

A person may, of course, object to redecorating the house or to changing its windows, saying that it would not be the same. In that sense it is true that an old constitution is not the same as a new constitution, just as an old person is not the same as the same person when young. Sameness in that sense is not the sameness of identity (the old person is identical with the young person she once was). It is the sameness of all the intrinsic properties of the object. Sometimes there are good reasons to preserve not only the same object but the same object with all its intrinsic properties intact. In the case of constitutions, such reasons are moral reasons. When they prevail, only a conserving interpretation is appropriate. Like many others, I have pointed out a range of reasons for thinking that they do not always prevail. The point of my coda is to warn against confusing change with loss of identity and against the spurious arguments it breeds. Dispelling errors is all that a general theory of the constitution can aspire to achieve.

APPENDIX

14

Postema on Law's Autonomy and Public Practical Reasons: A Critical Comment[1]

Postema's article discusses, lucidly and probingly, a central jurisprudential idea, which he calls the *autonomy thesis*. In its general form it is shared by many writers who otherwise support divergent accounts of the nature of law. It is, according to Postema, a thesis that is meant to account for a core idea, that the law's 'defining aim is to...unify public political judgment and coordinate social interaction'.[2] In some form or another this core idea is probably supported by Postema himself. However, in this article his concern is to criticize what he takes to be the widespread belief that it is explained by the autonomy thesis. The autonomy thesis is flawed and must be rejected. In arguing to that conclusion he succumbs to one of the unattractive tendencies of contemporary legal and political philosophy, namely he does not discuss anyone's view, but a family of views. This allows one to construct one's target by selecting features from a variety of authors so that the combined picture is in fact no one's view, and all those cited as adhering to it would disagree with it.

I will not examine the extent to which the article suffers from such problems. I am merely concerned with the methodological difficulty this method presents for the reader. In this comment I will not try to establish whether there is anyone who subscribes to the views criticized by Postema. My purpose is to examine whether his criticism reveals weaknesses in my own account of the nature of law.

---

[1] I am grateful to Scott Shapiro for thoughtful and helpful comments on an earlier version of the chapter.

[2] In R George (ed), *The Autonomy of Law* (Oxford: Clarendon Press, 1996) 80.

I. The Autonomy Thesis

A. The core idea

The core idea is that

while law's ultimate aspiration may be justice, its proximate aim and defining task is to supply a framework of practical reasoning designed to unify public political judgment and coordinate social interaction.[3]

This leads to the autonomy thesis that legal reasoning

is able to serve the task assigned to it because of its autonomy from moral and political reasoning. This autonomy consists in the fact that the existence, content and practical force of the norms from which legal reasoning proceeds are determined by criteria that make no essential reference to considerations of political morality.[4]

As there is much here that is not my view, and as my interest is in the relations between Postema's views and mine I will start by trying to identify which of the views expressed in these quotations I share.

1. The law's ultimate aspiration

Justice, I believe, is not the law's ultimate aspiration, for there is no one moral virtue that all law by its nature aspires to, other than to be good: that is to be as it should be. This means that it should be just, and generous, and compassionate and many other things. It is important to remember that the law has no specific function (though it, or parts of it, have many such functions). Being good is but a formal function: everything should be good, ie should be as it ought to be. That does not tell us anything of substance about how it should be. It merely says that that thing is subject to normative evaluation.

2. The law's defining task

Is the law's defining task the law's task—that is, the task of which all other tasks the law has are instances? I will call such a task an umbrella task. Does the law have an umbrella task? A good law fulfils many tasks. Not all good laws fulfil the same tasks. The tasks that good legal systems fulfil depend on the circumstances of their countries. Obviously the

---

[3] Ibid at 80.   [4] Ibid.

more abstract our description the more generally it applies. Not many legal systems have (if they are to be good legal systems) to regulate air traffic safety. There are more legal systems that have to regulate traffic safety in general. But I know of no reason to think that there is any abstract description of their function which applies to all of them and of which all other functions are instances, no reason to think that the law has an umbrella task.[5]

Quite likely Postema does not mean to contradict this. Perhaps what he means is not that supplying 'a framework of practical reasoning designed to unify public political judgment and coordinate social interaction' is the law's umbrella task, but that it is a necessary condition for the law's achieving any useful purpose, or at least that it is a necessary condition for the law's legitimacy.

But that too is a mistake. The law can achieve many important goods, which cannot otherwise be achieved, by measures that do not unify public political judgement. Unless taking such measures will have other bad effects, and it need not, that is enough to legitimate the law's use for such purposes.[6] The thought that political legitimacy depends on unifying public political judgement was debated and defended at great length by Rawls and some of the theorists influenced by him. Rawls moves from the correct observation that law is not legitimate if it rests on coercion alone, if it is not accepted in some way or another by the population it governs, to the invalid and false view that that acceptance must rest on agreement to the principles that govern the basic structure of the state. In fact, a government can be legitimate even if many among the population do not accept the moral credentials of important aspects of the basic structure, as long as they accept it in the less demanding sense of being willing to live under it. One need not deny the advantages of having a constitution which enjoys principled moral approval to deny that having this kind of approval is a condition of legitimacy.

It is possible that Postema understands the phrase 'the defining task of the law' to signify neither the law's umbrella task nor a task which is the means for the law to achieve anything of value, nor a task the discharge of which is a condition for the legitimacy of the law. Possibly he means simply that it is one of the law's tasks, but unlike all the others

---

[5] It is no doubt possible to devise an artificial formal category to serve as an umbrella task for the law. My doubt applies only to the existence of a natural and informative concept that designates the law's umbrella task.

[6] See on this J Raz, *The Morality of Freedom* (Oxford: Clarendon Press, 1986) chs 3 and 4.

which vary from country to country and from time to time, this task is universal. It is the only one of the law's tasks which it is part of its nature to have, that by necessity all laws have. This is an intriguing thought, which I will not be able to pursue to its conclusion here, as it would take us far and long. But let me make a few points.

First, it is true that by its very nature the law has certain 'tasks.' For example, I believe it to be of the nature of law that it claims authority. It follows that to be valid, and for its directives to have normative force, it must meet the conditions of legitimacy for authorities of its kind. Second, because the task Postema mentions is not necessary for legitimacy, if it is a task that all law has by its nature, it is not the only one. Third, even if we assume that it is a good thing for a society to enjoy unity in its political judgement, it is not obviously the law's task to secure it, or even to contribute to that goal. This matter requires further consideration. Fourth, unity in judgement is a by-product of true judgement. If we all have (all the) true beliefs on certain matters then we are all united in judgement on these matters. It does not follow that unity in judgement is good in itself. To be that, it would have to be a good for the sake of which it is sometimes better to have false beliefs, or at any rate dubious ones. That is far from clear.

3. *The autonomy of legal reasoning*

We need to distinguish (at least) two autonomy theses: the autonomy of law and of legal reasoning. I can be said to have embraced a thesis about the autonomy of law, ie that it is possible to identify the content of the law without recourse to moral reasoning. This is an aspect of my sources thesis. But I reject any thesis of the autonomy of legal reasoning, at least if that includes anything more than reasoning *to the conclusion that the content of the law is such and such.* 'Legal reasoning' is normally used to include any reasoning to conclusions which entail that, according to law, if a matter were before a court the court should decide thus and so (or that since it is before the court this is how it should be decided).[7] Legal reasoning is not autonomous. For example, much legal reasoning is interpretive reasoning, and interpretive reasoning is not, in general, autonomous.[8]

---

[7] Though not every argument that can appear as part of legal reasoning is normally referred to as legal reasoning when thought of on its own.

[8] The exception being what I termed 'conserving' interpretations whose sole purpose is to establish the meaning the original had at some past point in time.

Does Postema disagree with the substance of this point? He distinguishes legal reasoning from judicial reasoning.[9] Judicial reasoning is reasoning by judges to decide cases, and he explicitly denies that the autonomy thesis is meant by all its supporters to apply to it. What he means by legal reasoning is less clear. It is understood by Postema to be reasoning from legal premises. If this means reasoning whose *sole* premises are that the law is such and such, then its conclusions merely state the content of existing law. That would make 'Postema's legal reasoning' a special case of reasoning to the conclusion that the law at one time or another has this or that content. Understood in that sense the thesis is an aspect of the thesis of the autonomy of law. However, no such reasoning can by itself support any judicial decision in common-law countries. In common-law countries, courts can distinguish common-law rules, apply doctrines of equity, and use other devices to ensure that the law as applied to the case is not unjust. Therefore, in such countries all judicial decisions rely on at least one additional premise—ie that there is nothing in the situation that would justify modifying the law, or its application to the case, by this court on this occasion.

This would suggest that when talking of 'legal reasoning' Postema may have in mind reasoning whose premises are such that those of them which do not state (an aspect of) the law are relied upon in virtue of others which do state some aspect of the law. Taken in this sense Postema's 'legal reasoning' refers to the same instances of reasoning as does the notion in its ordinary sense. If Postema's autonomy thesis refers to legal reasoning in that sense, then it is a thesis I reject, and Postema's language raises doubts whether that is what he has in mind.

The uncertainty regarding Postema's intentions results from a substantial misunderstanding, on Postema's part, of the role of law in legal reasoning (in the usual sense of the phrase). The gist of it is revealed in Postema's observation that, according to supporters of the autonomy thesis, judicial reasoning is not reasoning according to law.[10] This is not my view.[11] Postema appears[12] to think that the autonomy thesis regards legal reasoning as strictly bifurcated. It is either reasoning from premises about the existence of legal norms of a certain content, or it is entirely

---

[9] George, above n 2 at 87–88.   [10] Ibid at 94.

[11] I am not confident that I always used the terms we discuss here in the same way. But here is what I said about them: 'Legal reasoning is reasoning either about what the law is or about how legal disputes should be settled according to law,' J Raz, *Ethics in the Public Domain* (rev edn, Oxford: Clarendon Press, 1995) 327.

[12] The inference is supported by other observations of his as well.

unrelated to law (except in the conclusion). He writes as if the autonomy thesis embraces MacCormick's observation that

The autonomy thesis regards legal and moral reasoning as belonging to two species of the same genus.[13]

If that is so, then this is reason enough to reject the autonomy thesis. Clearly, law and morality are not two species of the same genus. Cats and dogs are two species of the genus mammals. That entails among other things that no cat is a dog, nor is any dog a cat. But it is not the case that no law is moral, or that no legal reason is a moral reason, or that no moral reason is a legal one. Quite possibly all legal reasons are moral reasons, in the sense that they have the normative force of valid reasons only if they are morally binding. Many of them are moral in other senses as well: for example, in the sense that they embody or constitute moral considerations that are binding even if not incorporated in law.

The view that I have suggested[14] is very different from MacCormick's. Reasoning to establish the content of the law as it is at any given moment can proceed without resort to evaluative considerations—ie it is, in Postema's terms, autonomous. Such reasoning relies on the fact that certain actions took place, that they were undertaken with certain intentions, that the rest of the law is thus and so, etc. It includes assumptions regarding the moral or other evaluative views of law-makers, courts, or others. The rest of legal reasoning is (in shape and form) ordinary evaluative reasoning, which is undertaken according to law, for the law requires courts to reach decisions through such reasoning. In legal reasoning, legal rules and standards appear among the reasons inclining the argument toward one conclusion or another.[15] But they compete with other reasons. Reasoning about the content of law as it exists is not a separate species of reasoning. Though it can be undertaken in its own right, it is often but one aspect of legal reasoning.

I expect that it is now clear why we need to distinguish reasoning *to* the conclusion that the law as it exists at a certain time has a certain content, from reasoning *from* premises that the law, as it exists at

---

[13] Ibid at 83. Citing 'Natural Law and the Separation of Law and Morals' in R George (ed), *Natural Law Theory* (Oxford: Clarendon Press, 1992) 130.

[14] In various publications. See, eg, the chapter on 'The Autonomy of Legal Reasoning', in Raz, *Ethics in the Public Domain*, above n 11, from which the preceding definition is quoted.

[15] This simplifies the role of legal rules and standards in legal reasoning. Reasoning is structured, with some reasons determining the relevance of others. Legal norms function in legal reasoning not only as stand-alone considerations for one conclusion or another, but also in a structuring role, helping to determine the relevance of various considerations.

a certain time, has a certain content. The first kind of reasoning, is—I suspect—autonomous, to use Postema's term. The second includes what is normally called legal reasoning, which is simply evaluative reasoning according to law. It is not autonomous in my view, nor do I know of any serious theorist who thinks that it is.

Once Postema's misunderstanding of the nature of legal reasoning has been cleared out of the way we can see that, by and large, all judicial reasoning is legal reasoning—i.e. reasoning according to law, reasoning that imports moral and other premises in accordance with the role they have by law, or at any rate consistently with the law. The exceptions are those cases where judges feel that the law does not allow enough scope for moral reasoning, that following it compels them to endorse immoral results, and that in the circumstances it would be right to flout the law and do the morally right thing. Even such reasoning is likely to be legal reasoning in Postema's sense, given its broad meaning, since it may well proceed from legal premises, though not from them alone. But it is not reasoning according to law as I explained the phrase.

In the rest of this chapter I will use legal reasoning to refer only to reasoning according to law. Postema's sense of the term, as reasoning from premises about the law's content, is unclear, but can be understood (perhaps only by stretching his words) as roughly identical with the common meaning. As I indicated there is no serious theorist I know of who maintains that legal reasoning is autonomous. The only autonomy thesis I know of is that of reasoning *to* the conclusion that the law has a certain content. The result of these reflections is that when in the discussion that follows I defend certain views, I will not be defending the autonomy thesis that Postema attacks. Similarly, as I am inclined to reject the core idea, I will not be concerned with the way the views I defend relate to it.

Nevertheless, there is much in the rest of Postema's article which bears on views I believe to be plausible, and it is therefore relevant to my purpose to examine it.

B. The three theses

The autonomy thesis entails three theses that spell out its meaning:

Limited domain thesis: law defines a limited domain of practical reasons or norms...

Pre-emption thesis: reasons in law's limited domain operate in practical reasoning as pre-emptive reasons...that is, reasons which preclude acting for certain other reasons (falling outside the domain).

Sources thesis: membership in law's limited domain is determined by criteria which are defined exclusively in terms of non-evaluative matters of social fact (about their sources), such that the existence and content of member norms can be determined entirely without appeal to moral or evaluative arguments.[16]

As formulated, the limited domain thesis means that the law (e.g. the sum total of legal norms) is a limited domain. That can be quickly established: the fact that the expected return on the purchase of a lottery ticket is smaller than the price of the ticket is a reason against buying lottery tickets, but not a legal reason against doing so. However, if that is what the thesis means then it is unrelated to the autonomy thesis, which is not about laws, or legal reasons, in the sense explained here, but about the reasoning which takes legal norms as its premises.

To be a thesis about legal reasoning the limited domain thesis must mean that there are cases of practical reasoning which are not cases of legal reasoning. This is obviously so. For example, when in the course of an ordinary chess game a player reasons about which move would be best, his is an instance of practical reasoning, but it is not a case of legal reasoning. The same example establishes the truth of a third possible limited domain thesis, ie that not all reasoning is reasoning to the conclusion that the law at a given time has a certain content.

The limited domain theses—all of them[17]—are trivially true. The interesting theses are the pre-emption and sources theses. In my view they may be correct theses regarding the identification and force of legal norms, or legal standards.

Postema raises the question of what the relation is between the force of legal reasons and that of moral reasons: the pre-emption thesis, he thinks, answers this question. But that is a mistake. The answer to the question may be: no legal reason has any normative force unless it is morally justified, ie unless it is morally binding.

That is not a trivial answer and it is not true of every reason: the reasons for making a move in chess do not depend on being validated by morality.[18] Perhaps reasons of chess and moral reasons are more like two species of the same genus than are legal and moral reasons.

---

[16] George, above n 2, at 82.

[17] Postema may be particularly interested in one that states that not all moral reasons are legal reasons. This is also trivially true. My debt of gratitude to my neighbour is for me a moral reason, which is not, special circumstances apart, also a legal reason.

[18] Possibly one should not make the move the chess reasons suggest if it is immoral to do so. But that is a case of conflicting reasons. The thesis about the law I cited above is

In any case the pre-emption thesis is not an answer to the question about the relations between legal and moral reasons: if, as I suggested, legal reasons have normative force only if they are morally binding,[19] the relation between legal reasons and moral reasons is that of one type of moral reasons and moral reasons of other types.

It is worth noting that Postema goes on to misinterpret Hart. He alleges that Hart regarded the validity of rules of recognition as resting solely on their social acceptance. But as you will know Hart denied that it is right to talk of the validity of rules of recognition. They merely exist, and to say that they do is no more than to say that they are accepted. In *The Concept of Law* he never said that the fact that they were accepted gives anyone reason to follow them.[20] That they are accepted entails, of course, that those who accept them think that they are binding, and take themselves to have reason to follow them. But it does not follow that that reason is the fact of their acceptance. That—the fact of their accept- ance—makes them into legal rules, but it does not necessarily constitute a valid reason for following them.

Let me try to make my way back to the three theses. What have they to do with the autonomy thesis, whose content they were meant to spell out? The limited domain thesis is—as we saw—trivial, but its truth is a necessary condition for the truth of the autonomy thesis. The sources thesis is not a necessary condition of autonomy. But it is a suf- ficient condition for its truth. If true, the autonomy thesis renders the sources thesis plausible: if law is autonomous then there must be a way of establishing its content independently of morality. If legal reasoning is autonomous, the same conclusion is plausible. And it is plausible to assume that that way is through its social sources.

The pre-emption thesis is, however, irrelevant to the autonomy thesis.[21] Think of chess again: the reasons for one move or another are

different: it says that legal standards have no normative force at all; they are no reasons at all, unless they are morally valid.

[19] Remember that they can be morally binding even if they are morally defective and in need of reform. They may still be morally binding, in the sense that until changed they ought to be obeyed.

[20] Unfortunately, Hart changed his mind about the conventional character of the rule of recognition when he wrote the Postscript to the book (see 2nd edn at 255). As this makes his theory more vulnerable, and is inconsistent with some of the insights of the original, it is important to remember that this view was not part of the theory expounded in *The Concept of Law*.

[21] I do not mean to deny that, given additional premises not considered by Postema, one may construct an argument for the sources thesis from the pre-emption thesis. I have suggested such an argument in *Ethics in the Public Domain*, above n 11, ch 10. What

not pre-emptive. They are strategic reasons, rather than rule-based reasons. Yet chess reasoning is autonomous. It is autonomous because lots of good reasons, including all moral reasons, are irrelevant for it. It is autonomous because chess is an insulated activity. Other types of reasons are also autonomous without involving pre-emption: the reasons which guide architects in designing buildings, or painters in creating pictures, are autonomous in some sense. On the other hand, pre-emption is present in moral reasoning. It is a feature of rules, and there are moral rules.

C. Interim conclusions

So far I have been concerned to clarify the relations between various views and ideas. They are mostly views and ideas that Postema rejects. Therefore, if there are serious legal theorists who have espoused them, my criticisms were directed at them and not at Postema. If no serious theorist has advanced these views, then Postema may be blamed for having set up a straw man. Which one it is may not matter much. The important point is to keep in mind the difference between the autonomy of law and the autonomy of legal reasoning. I will further explore what Postema has to say about pre-emption, but we will not expect to learn anything about autonomy from that. The fate of autonomy is bound up with the fate of the sources thesis.

II. The Argument from Cooperation (The 'Generic Argument')[22]

A. The argument

Postema then proceeds[23] to offer what he takes to be a common and important (though ultimately flawed) argument for the autonomy thesis. Later in the article he upgrades the argument and calls it the canonical argument,[24] and as he does not mention the possibility of any other arguments for the thesis, he implies that it stands and falls with this master argument.

---

is denied above is the direct relation between the autonomy of legal reasoning and the pre-emption thesis asserted by Postema.

[22] This is Postema's name for it.
[23] George, above n 2, at 89–94.   [24] Ibid at 94.

Abbreviated, the argument is this: The function of law is to facilitate social cooperation.[25] The law fulfils its function through its conformity to the autonomy thesis. There are two obstacles on the road to cooperation. The problem of identification of what one should do as one's share in cooperation. And the problem of motivating people to do their share. The sources thesis enables people to establish how to cooperate; the pre-emption thesis solves the problem of motivation.

Postema is right to say that I do not support this argument.[26] I have to admit that I find no argument there at all. I think it fairly obvious that the law plays an important role in securing some forms of social cooperation in well-ordered societies. That is not the problem. The problem is how this can be an argument for the correctness of the autonomy thesis. If the autonomy thesis is correct then it is possible that it brings benefits in helping secure cooperation. But how could the fact that if it is correct it would solve the problem of social cooperation be a reason for its correctness?

You may wish to reprove me: you should not object to the argument because it is a moral argument. The essence of the law may be that it has a moral task. This is true, but I am not objecting to it on that ground. I have already conceded that the law, by its nature, has a moral task and I gave an example of one. But we learn of the moral and other tasks of the law in part from its nature. If we can show (1) that securing coordination is good, and (2) that the law is better at securing coordination than alternative methods, and (3) that its doing so has no adverse effects (or none serious enough to outweigh the advantage of its doing so) then we can conclude that it has the task of securing coordination. But to do this we need first to establish the second premise. According to Postema if the sources and the pre-emption theses are correct, then the second premise is secure. That may be so. But that is not an argument *for* the sources and pre-emption theses. It is an argument *from* them.

It is true, of course, that *if* the law's essential function is to solve the problem of social cooperation then that would be an important aspect of the law and worth pointing out. That would be a justification for including the autonomy thesis, or rather the sources thesis, in an account of the nature of the law. It would show that the thesis singles

---

[25] I will use 'cooperation' and 'coordination' interchangeably, as it seems that Postema does. 'Coordination' is the more general, and the more appropriate term. But nothing in the argument depends on the distinction.

[26] George, above n 2, at 92.

out important aspects of the law. But before we get there we have to have some reason to believe that the thesis (or the theses) is (are) correct.[27]

B. Back to methodology

There are other reasons to think that Postema is not handling arguments for jurisprudential theses in an assured way. He correctly observes that one important way in which a theory is to be assessed is by its ability to deepen our understanding of the law. Postema implies that the argument he presented does just that. But to do that it must be an argument about the law—that is, it must give us reasons to believe that it is an understanding of the law, rather than of something else, or of nothing else, which we gain. Oddly, in his methodological introduction to the argument, Postema equates deepening our understanding of the law with showing why it is important to have law.

it should not only describe *how law works,* but also, and more importantly, explain *why it is important* to have it [author's emphasis].[28]

But while no one would doubt the importance of knowing why we should have law, if indeed we should have law, this cannot be an argument for the thesis that the law *is* one way or another. Again, let me repeat that that is not because how the law is cannot be a matter of morality. It is possible that the essential properties of the law are moral. In which case *once we have shown* that it has those properties we have explained (at least in part) why it is important to have it; though even if the law has certain moral attributes it does not follow that it is better to have it than not to have it. Its disadvantages may outweigh its advantages, both those due to its nature and those it may have from time to time. However, it cannot be an argument to the effect that the law has those properties that if it has them then it would be important to have it.

---

[27] Because I find the whole approach encapsulated in the generic argument misguided, I will avoid commenting on the last section of Postema's essay. If its arguments are sound, and I am not convinced that they are, then it would show not that there is anything wrong with the autonomy thesis, but that the law is less often binding than many people think. That is my own view, as I explained in *The Morality of Freedom,* among other places. But the argument of Postema's essay and of my reply concerns aspects of the explanation of the nature of law, and not the morality of various attitudes towards it.

[28] George, above n 2, at 88.

C. The argument in detail

1. Pre-emption and motivation

Assume for the sake of argument that the pre-emption thesis and the sources thesis are correct. Do they help with coordination in the way the argument claims they do? Postema doubts that the theses are correct, but he does not challenge the argument that they would be useful for coordination in the way that the argument alleges were they correct. I believe, however, that there is little to support the generic argument on these points. Half the problem of coordination, as Postema sees it, is of motivation. The fact that the law is pre-emptive solves this problem.[29] It leads Postema to the heights of rhetoric:

The Sources Thesis without the Pre-emption Thesis is inert; the Pre-emption Thesis without the Sources Thesis is blind.[30]

First notice that the pre-emption thesis as I understand it does not say that there are pre-emptive reasons for complying with the law. It merely says that if the law is morally binding then its subjects have pre-emptive reasons to comply with it. But let's waive this point.

How does the pre-emption thesis solve the problem of motivation? People can have reason to do what they are not motivated to do, and they may be motivated to do what they have no reason to do. So even if the law's subjects have a pre-emptive reason to comply with the law, it is not clear how that can contribute to the solution of the problem of motivation.

Postema may have in mind people who are motivated to act as they are morally required, and who believe that they are morally required to comply with the law. But if they are so motivated, then they would obey the law (assuming that they know what it is) whether or not the law has pre-emptive force. Of course, if it has pre-emptive force then they will recognize its pre-emptive force. But that does not solve the problem of motivation. The problem of motivation has been solved by the original stipulation that people are motivated to obey the law.

On the other hand, if people are not motivated to obey the law then the fact that the law has pre-emptive force will do little to motivate them; at least it will do nothing more to spur their motivation than would be done by any other normative force the law may have, or may have had.

---

[29] Ibid at 92.   [30] Ibid.

Perhaps Postema has a completely different point in mind. Perhaps his point is not about motivation at all, but about the type of reasons that the need to coordinate constitutes, or the type of reasons that schemes of coordination are. He may be saying that (according to some) reasons of coordination have a special kind of normative force, and that the pre-emption thesis purports to explain what that normative force is. That would not be a solution of a problem of motivation, but an explanation of the normativity of coordination-based reasons. I am not aware that anyone ever made either of those claims. Some have argued that pre-emption is not required for coordination. I tried to reason that authority can be useful in securing coordination in some circumstances, and since authoritative reasons have pre-emptive force, pre-emptive reasons can be useful in securing coordination. But the many examples of coordination without either the law or any other norms with pre-emptive force would give the lie to any suggestion that pre-emption explains the normative force of coordination schemes.

I conclude that the pre-emption thesis is as irrelevant to the solution of the problem of social coordination as it is to the autonomy thesis.

2. Sources and identification

What of the sources thesis? Does it not solve the problem of identification which is half the problem of social cooperation? I think that the sources thesis is true of the law, and that the law can contribute to achieving cooperation. Nor would I deny that the sources thesis is relevant to the way the law helps with cooperation. But all this is a long way from even claiming that there is a problem of social cooperation and that the law's function is to solve it. Two facts to start with: Social cooperation is regularly achieved without law: speaking the same language, and following rules of polite conduct are but two examples of complex social cooperation without which there can be no social life—indeed, no law—and to which the law usually contributes not at all.

It is true that there are circumstances and forms of cooperation where the law offers the most efficient (sometimes the only) way of securing cooperation. But what does that show? It does not show that there is a problem of social cooperation as such. After all, not all cooperation is good. Think of the cooperation that went into the creation of the nuclear arsenal in various countries. It is wrong to say that the task of the law is to secure cooperation. It may be that sometimes it is good for the law to secure some kinds of cooperation. But that is because they are good in themselves or in their consequences, not because they are forms of cooperation. And there are various other goods it is right or even required that the law secure.

The right conclusion is that if the sources thesis is true, then the law is morally binding if, and by and large only if, it secures valuable cooperation, as well as other goods, better than they can be secured without it.

Has the sources thesis much to do with certainty? I do not think so. I do not think, for example, that there are fewer, or less serious controversies among economists about the likely course of the economy under various circumstances than controversies among people regarding moral issues. In other words, I know of no general reason to think that so-called factual issues are easier to resolve than moral ones, or that there are fewer controversies regarding them. But the sources thesis distinguishes not between ways of establishing the law with certainty and those open to doubt, but between non-evaluative and evaluative criteria.

Moreover, uncertainty in the law is not always undesirable. It has effects on the conduct and powers of individuals and legal institutions that are sometimes welcome. It may be a way of transferring power to institutions that do not judge by rules, but by a sense of what is just in the circumstances of each case, for example. I would not deny that often a large degree of certainty is welcome, but it is wrong to elevate it to a matter of unique and central importance for the law. The sources thesis is a general thesis, which applies when certainty is desirable as well as when it is not.

Those who think of law as 'solving the problem of uncertainty' normally have in mind legislation, the one area where most legal systems take special measures to minimize doubt about the occurrence of acts of legislation and about the text endorsed in them as law. The argument does not even begin to be plausible regarding customary law, and is hardly more convincing regarding the common law. But both customary and common law are sources of law, recognized by the sources thesis.

The pursuit of certainty is no part of the sources thesis. Finality is.[31] It is in the nature of the law that it claims authority, ie, that it claims to be authoritative, and that means that it claims to have settled moral and other social issues (and not necessarily because they were controversial; sometimes there is simply a need for someone to decide, even when the matter is not controversial).

---

[31] Which in the present context does not mean non-revisability.

III. Postema on the Sources Thesis

Postema proceeds to reject the sources thesis on the basis of one argument. The argument, he says, does not refute the thesis. It can be defended against it, but only at the cost of giving up 'the generic argument' from social cooperation. As I am not wedded to the 'generic argument' this is no cost to me. In fact, it is no cost to anyone, for the problem Postema sees for the sources thesis is not there.

The alleged difficulty arises out of the fact that to discover the content of a rule established as precedent in a court's decision one sometimes has to reconstruct that court's reasoning, or parts of it. The rule the court has established is the rule which it took to justify its decision, as that rule was expressed by the court in its judgement.

It is important to remember that only the *given* reasons constitute the court's ruling. The judges usually have further reasons in mind, especially reasons justifying the reasons they gave in their judgement. But those are not the ruling of the court. But while the ruling is expressed in the judgement there is no canonical formulation of it, and some aspects of it are implied, rather than explicitly stated. That is why not infrequently in order to establish what the ruling was, one has to reconstruct aspects of the court's reasoning. On my view that is consistent with the sources thesis. It is true that the reasoning of the court may well have been moral reasoning. But in reconstructing it we do not engage in moral reasoning ourselves. We are merely recreating the court's moral reasoning. Here Postema finds a difficulty for the sources thesis:

[O]f course, one can reason in a 'detached' way (that is, without endorsement) . . . to a practical decision or judgment—consider the rabbi who advises a Catholic about her moral duties as a Catholic regarding abortion—but this does not make the practical reasoning involved non-evaluative.[32]

Postema is right that the same difficulties which engaged moral reasoning leads to are equally encountered in the parallel detached reasoning. But reconstructive reasoning is not detached reasoning. Detached reasoning is reasoning that proceeds through making detached statements and drawing conclusions from them. It is like saying 'I do not accept any of what follows, but let us suppose it for the sake of

---

[32] George, above n 2, at 97.

the argument' and then proceeding to make statements and draw conclusions. So both committed and (its parallel) detached reasoning proceed from the same assumptions, and they both encounter the same problems.

Reconstructive reasoning, on the other hand, does not suppose anything. It says (to give but one example of the type): Judge A is known to believe in (let us say) tough punitive policy, and he wrote in his judgment that.... Those who have his views on penal policy often use the same words to express the view that.... We can therefore assume that in writing what he wrote, Judge A made the statement that.... For the purpose of the present argument the crucial difference between reconstructive reasoning and detached reasoning of the kind Postema gives in his example is that the latter deals with the implications of a moral or religious system of belief, with all its complexity, whereas the reconstructive reasoning involved in working out the ruling in a case deals with the views of a few people at a specific point in time, *insofar as they were expressed* in a particular document, *or are relevant to establishing what was expressed in it*. It is an attempt to reconstruct the actual reasoning engaged in by actual people.[33]

Postema suggests that inevitably in reconstructing the evaluative reasoning of another we do, and must, use our own ideas of what makes for a good argument in order to help us decide what the judge must have meant. In a sense this is right. Only someone who knows how to reason can reconstruct the reasoning of another. And only someone capable of evaluative thought can reconstruct the evaluative thought of another. Such very general capacities, capacities which are among those that define personhood, are not to be confused with the deployment of evaluative premises of the kind relevant to the justification of legal standards,[34] which are excluded by the sources thesis.

Postema, we may assume, is not content with asserting that reconstructive reasoning involves these general capacities for reasoning and evaluative thought. His suggestion is that we resort to ideas about what is a plausible *moral* or *evaluative* argument. That seems to me to be a

---

[33] Perhaps one can engage in detached reasoning in discharging aspects of this task. That would be to surmise what the judge in the case said by simulating his thought processes. But such simulation is controlled by concrete factual checks: 'True,' the simulator will say on occasion, 'that reasoning from these premises requires the conclusion that.... But the judge is on record as rejecting it; therefore, we can assume that he did not draw that conclusion. It is likely that he committed the fallacy...,' etc.

[34] The sources thesis does not exclude reliance on logical norms.

mistake. There is no reason to believe there is a form of reasoning special to evaluative thought.

Granted that there is no special general form for evaluative arguments, do we not rely on our views as to whether an argument from specific given premises to a specific given conclusion is sound? I agree, of course, that in fact we often rely on our ideas of what is reasonable in reconstructing other people's thought. But if we are any good at the task, we do so only when we have reason to think those others share our view of what is a reasonable opinion, or a plausible argument. Generally we are no less able to surmise how someone with views we totally reject has reasoned, provided we are familiar with the beliefs of that person and of others like him, and with typical logical fallacies they are liable to.

When assessing Postema's objection, the crucial test is not how we reason, but how we should reason, what we do when we reason correctly. The crucial test is what shows that we succeeded in our reasoning. When we engage in moral reasoning we succeed when our conclusions are morally justified. But in establishing the ruling set in a previous case we succeed when our reasoning leads to the rule the court in that case really expressed in its judgment. It may not have been morally justified, and the reasoning we reconstruct, while being evaluative in the content of the considerations it rehearses, as Postema rightly says, is a good reconstructive argument even though it is a bad evaluative argument. It is a good argument because it is a successful reconstructive argument, and the fact that it is a bad evaluative argument does not matter, as it is not an evaluative argument at all.

Postema does not see this point because he is still mesmerized by the generic argument from social cooperation. His argument, he writes—continuing from where we left off in the previous quotation—constitutes an objection to the sources thesis

> At least if we keep in mind the social purposes to be served by law modeled on the sources thesis. . . . The problem [to which the sources thesis is addressed] is *uncertainty* of mutual identification of the practical rules that are supposed to govern our social interaction.[35]

But the sources thesis is not addressed to this problem, nor to any other problem. It is true—if at all—because it captures an essential property of the law, not because it is a property which it would be useful for the law to possess.[36]

---

[35] George, above n 2, at 97.

[36] There is no need to repeat the point made earlier that I do not share Postema's assumption that evaluative reasoning is more likely to be controversial than non-evaluative reasoning. I do, however, believe that were this the case then evaluative

IV. Postema on the Pre-emption Thesis

A. Locating the objection

As I explained, Postema's discussion of the pre-emption thesis has no bearing on the autonomy thesis. However, as I believe that the pre-emption thesis may well be correct, it is interesting, at least to me, to examine Postema's criticism of the thesis. He begins by correctly noting that it is not uncommon for courts to appeal to non-source-based principles to justify interpretations which set aside the settled or plain meaning of statutes, and to justify distinguishing (modifying by narrowing) or even overruling established precedent.[37]

He notes that this fact can be made consistent with the pre-emption thesis if that thesis is not meant to apply to courts. 'But this rescue strategy,' he says, 'faces two serious problems.' I will examine them one by one.

B. The first objection

First, the restriction of the subject scope of the law's pre-emptive force appears entirely ad hoc motivated by the need to fit legal practice, but not rooted in any normative argument for the restriction.[38]

The first point to note is that Postema recommends replacing what is admittedly an imperfect but good argument with a bad one. Whether or not it is good for the law to have pre-emptive force is irrelevant to the question of whether it has such force. It is true that there is something suspect about ad hoc elements in a theory. If they are ad hoc they may be false: they may fit one aspect of one legal system, but not be true of law in general. They may fail to capture an essential aspect of the law. I suspect that the 'restriction' of the law's pre-emptive force contemplated here by Postema is indeed flawed. But it is unnecessary. No desperate 'rescue' of the original thesis about the pre-emptive force of law (at least as I advanced it) is necessary.

reasoning would be more likely to be controversial than the reconstruction of the reasoning of others. It may not be easier to engage in detached reasoning about Catholic morality than in engaged reasoning about Catholic morality, but it would be easier to engage in reasoning about how Bishop X interpreted Catholic morality than to engage in reasoning about Catholic morality.

[37] George, above n 2, at 99.   [38] Ibid.

The pre-emption thesis says, roughly, that if the law is valid and therefore binding then the fact that it requires a certain action is a reason for performing that action, and a reason for not acting for certain conflicting reasons. A legal requirement constitutes two reasons. The first is a reason for performing the required action; the second is a (second-order) reason for not acting on some other reasons.[39] As Postema notes, this leaves open the question of which reasons are excluded.[40] He also says that it leaves open the question of the personal scope of the exclusion, ie of who is bound by it. This is not so. Postema seems to have overlooked the simple answer. Those to whom the legal requirement is addressed are those who are bound by it; it is for them that the requirement is a dual reason, a reason to perform the required action, and not to act for the excluded considerations. Who else can be bound by it?

Does the pre-emptive force of the law apply to the courts? Of course it does. But equally, just as I am only bound by the laws that apply to me, so the courts are only bound by the laws that apply to them. For the problem at hand the relevant question is: What does the law require the courts to do regarding laws which apply not to them but to the litigants in front of them? This again is a question to which different legal systems give different answers, and the answers in each legal system differ from court to court. Roughly speaking, the answer is that courts must (and this is a requirement enjoying a pre-emptive force) apply the law to the litigants unless (1) they have power to change it, and (2) it would be right to do so. If they do not have the power to change the law they are subject to a duty (with pre-emptive force) to apply it. If they have power to change the law they may still have conclusive reason not to change it: It may be better than the alternatives, or changing the law may cause more upset and harm than the improvement in it will warrant. But such reasons for not changing the law are not pre-emptive.

---

[39] This is roughly the form in which I advanced the thesis in *Practical Reason and Norms* (2nd edn, Oxford: OUP, 1990) and *The Authority of Law* (Oxford: OUP, 1979).

[40] Up to a point this question has no general answer. The law itself can indicate which reasons are to be excluded. But as I indicated in later writings there is a default exclusion which the law has unless it indicates otherwise. The default exclusion is of the normative considerations that underlie the requirement, ie those considerations against the required action which, should they prevail, would lead to rejecting the requirement. I will not expand on the reasons for this default understanding of the exclusion here. They are not in question.

The hard question is: When do the courts have power to change the law? In many common law jurisdictions there are two kinds of such powers vested in (some) courts: the power to distinguish and the power to overrule. Many years ago I had a stab at describing their scope as it then was in the English courts.[41] The precise definition does not matter here. What does matter is that Postema is clearly considering the very same powers of the courts to change the law. The quotation given above is explicit on this point. Consequently, he is right in thinking that those who believe in the pre-emptive force of the law do not believe it applies to the courts when they have power to change the law.[42] To think otherwise makes as much sense as to believe the legislature cannot change the law, because once it made it it is binding and if it is binding it cannot be changed. What is surprising is that Postema should think this to be an '*ad hoc*' 'rescue' attempt, rather than a statement of the core idea of the thesis of the pre-emptive force of the law.

C. The second objection

Postema's second objection is that the law cannot have pre-emptive force for its subjects if it does not have pre-emptive force for the courts:

Legal norms have pre-emptive force only insofar as agents to whom they are addressed accord the norms pre-emptive force in their practical reasoning.

However, I shall argue that agents will have reason to accord them that force only to the extent that they believe the *courts* reliably do so.[43]

To make sense, we should read Postema as saying that legal requirements have pre-emptive force for the people they apply to only if the courts are required to apply those laws to litigants before them, and only if that requirement has pre-emptive force for the courts.

The objection points to a serious question. I have discussed a closely related problem before. 'My' problem arises out of the fact that the law is an institutionalized normative system. In particular, it is a system of norms coupled with a system of adjudication. The norms that belong

---

[41] J Raz, *The Authority of Law* (Oxford: OUP, 1979) essay 10.
[42] You may say that the pre-emptive force of two kinds of laws cannot apply to the courts in such cases: They may not be bound by the law which applies to the litigants, for it does not (normally) apply to courts. And they are not bound by the law which requires courts to apply the law which applies to the litigants, for in the circumstances of the case, the law allows them to change the law which applies to the litigants.
[43] George, above n 2, at 100.

to the system are those that the courts or other law-applying institutions have a special institutional duty to apply. So a legal standard does not bind its subjects unless the courts are bound to apply it. But if the courts can change the norm any time it comes up for adjudication, does it make sense to regard it as binding on its subjects?

Postema's related problem arises out of the statement that 'legal norms have pre-emptive force only insofar as agents to whom they are addressed accord the norms pre-emptive force in their practical reasoning'. Although I tend to think that something like this thesis is plausible I am not sure that my reasons are the same as his. Postema's reasons may have to do with the problem of social cooperation, which as I explained I do not see in the same way. So here is my reason for thinking that a version of Postema's premise here is plausible: The legitimacy of many aspects of the law depends on its acceptance by the population which it purports to govern. This means that while Postema's premise cannot stand as formulated, for whether or not norms have pre-emptive force does not depend on people's beliefs or attitudes, there is another thesis that can take its place: The legitimacy of norms as binding legal norms depends on their acceptance by the population to whom the legal system as a whole is addressed. Given that premise we can see how the problem I stated above arises in yet another guise.

Assuming that the legitimacy of much of the law depends on its general acceptance by the population, the question arises whether anyone can accept the law as binding[44] knowing that whenever a question relating to it arises before the courts, the courts may change it. This is the gist of Postema's version of my problem, as I understand it.

I believe that the answer I gave to my version of the problem holds good of Postema's version of it as well. The limits on the intelligibility of the claim that a norm exists are transgressed when every occasion for its application is also an occasion for its modification or repeal. But when this is not so, when there are occasions of its application which are not occasions for its modification, there is no such problem. The case of being subject to revision by the courts is a long way from getting near the borderline of intelligibility. In the nature of things only an infinitesimally small proportion of the circumstances to which the law applies *can* ever be subject to litigation in the courts. When the application of the law to a situation is challenged in the courts, the matter is decided

---

[44] Note that since, as I argued on independent grounds, the law claims to have pre-emptive force, to accept it as binding includes accepting its pre-emptive force as binding.

after a significant time lag, and in deciding to take matters to court most people incur risks of considerable costs (not only financial).

In such circumstances no problem regarding the binding force of the law arises out of the fact that it is revisable by the courts. As for Postema's version of the problem, it is true that the easier it is for a person to get the law changed, the less motivated he is to comply with it. This is a reason, well appreciated by the courts, not to make it too easy for litigants to get the law changed. A variety of strategies are employed to that effect. The matter is of considerable practical significance. But it has no theoretical significance at all. The fact that various people will be variously motivated to take the law seriously does not cast doubt about its normative character, or about its legitimacy. It is true that law's legitimacy depends on it being complied with by the bulk of the population, but nothing in the facts to which Postema draws attention would suggest that people would be irrational to comply with the law, once we—and they—pay attention to the facts to which I just drew attention.

My conclusion is that Postema's critique of the sources and preemption theses fails. He is right, however, to reject the thesis of the autonomy of legal reasoning. Moreover, there may be no need to look for an alternative to it, at least no need to look for an alternative that will capture the core idea that the autonomy thesis was meant to encapsulate and explain. For it is far from clear that the core idea is sound.

Index